*Frank Porter Graham
and the 1950 Senate Race
in North Carolina*

The Fred W. Morrison
Series in Southern Studies

Frank Porter Graham
and the 1950 Senate Race
in North Carolina

Julian M. Pleasants • Augustus M. Burns III

The University of North Carolina Press

Chapel Hill • London

© 1990 The University of North Carolina Press

All rights reserved

Library of Congress Cataloging-in-Publication Data

Pleasants, Julian M.
Frank Porter Graham and the 1950 Senate race in North Carolina /
by Julian M. Pleasants and Augustus M. Burns III.
p.   cm.—(The Fred W. Morrison series in Southern studies)
Includes bibliographical references.
ISBN 0-8078-1933-6 (alk. paper)
1. North Carolina—Politics and government—1865–1950.
2. Elections—North Carolina—History—20th century.   3. Graham,
Frank Porter, 1886–   .   4. United States. Congress. Senate—
Elections, 1940.   5. North Carolina—Race relations.   I. Burns,
Augustus Merrimon, 1939–   .   II. Title.   III. Series.
F259.P64   1990   90-50011
324.9756'043—dc20   CIP

The paper in this book meets the guidelines for permanence and durability
of the Committee on Production Guidelines for Book Longevity of the
Council on Library Resources.

Design by April Leidig-Higgins

Manufactured in the United States of America

94 93 92 91 90   5 4 3 2 1

For

Donna Marie Bishop
and Katherine Mills Burns
whose support, patience, and unstinting
affection have enabled us to see
this book to completion.

Contents

Illustrations

Preface

The Senate primaries between Frank Porter Graham and Willis Smith—a political fight that stirred the state of North Carolina in 1950—first came to our scholarly attention when we were graduate students at the University of North Carolina at Chapel Hill. We were each pursuing research topics tangentially related to the Smith-Graham race, and independently we noted the interest and appeal of this contest as a possible research project. Our scholarly interest in the campaign was no doubt spurred by our own boyhood memories of it, shadowed though they were by the far more critical exploits of Charlie Justice and his teammates on the gridirons of Kenan Stadium and fields beyond.

When we began our study in earnest in the mid-1980s, we were confident that we could complete the project in three years. Early on we were disabused of that folly. As we researched, we found a corpus of primary materials far more extensive than we had envisioned. Many of the manuscripts we located had never been examined by researchers, some becoming accessible only as we were working. Others, including the mountain of materials in the Frank Porter Graham collection in the Southern Historical Collection at the University of North Carolina at Chapel Hill, had never been combed for Graham's 1950 Senate campaign. To mention three of the many collections we examined, we were the first scholars to utilize the papers of Allard K. Lowenstein, Daniel A. Powell, and Charles W. and Gladys A. Tillett, also in the Southern Historical Collection, as they related to the 1950 Senate race. We located other manuscripts, as our bibliography indicates, and were able to compose the bulk of our study from these primary sources.

We also found our conversations with campaign participants and their associates to be of immeasurable value. Especially useful were our interviews with Smith partisans, a number of whom were both cooperative and forthright in their discussions with us. To observe firsthand the hold that this race continues to exert on its surviving participants—Smith and Graham supporters alike—is to be reminded of the depth of emotions and beliefs that this contest aroused.

The interviews with Smith supporters were critical to our research because, despite our persistent efforts, we could not persuade members of the Smith family to lift the seal on their father's papers, which are housed at Duke University. On three separate occasions we sought access to the papers of Willis Smith. First, we wrote a formal letter of request to the late Dr. Mattie Russell, then director of manuscript collections at Duke. Dr. Russell added her strong support to our request when she submitted it to the Smith family, but to no avail. We next contacted Willis Smith's son Lee, who again denied us access to the papers. After a time, we appealed to the Smith family through James K. Dorsett, Jr., Smith's former law partner and the husband of Smith's daughter Anna Lee. Mr. Dorsett explained our need to examine the papers but conveyed our intention to proceed with our study even without them. The family turned us down yet again, and at this point, we yielded. Upon completion of the manuscript, however, we offered family members, through Mr. Dorsett, an opportunity to review our work for factual accuracy, which they declined. In the summer of 1990, we were finally allowed to read the papers, but the materials on the 1950 campaign proved to be insubstantial.

The refusal of the Smith family to cooperate with us was our major research disappointment, although some campaign participants would not discuss the race with us. Neither Smith workers John Anderson and Tom Ellis nor Lee Smith would talk to us. On the Graham side, only former Graham Senate aide John D. McConnell refused our request for an interview. Other participants we approached were cooperative, including many Smith partisans. James K. Dorsett, Jr., J. C. B. Ehringhaus, Jr., Jesse A. Helms, William T. Joyner, Jr., Richard Thigpen, and others shared their reminiscences with us to our great benefit.

Graham supporters whose remembrances were especially helpful included R. Mayne Albright, J. Melville Broughton, Jr., Kathryn N. Folger, William C. Friday, Kate Humphries, David M. McConnell, Terry Sanford, and the indomitable Roy Wilder, Jr. Our bibliography includes the names of many others whose assistance we value, but who are too numerous to mention here. The opportunity to meet and talk with these North Carolinians was itself a rewarding personal and historical experience.

We also found rich newspaper coverage of the campaign. North Carolina dailies and weeklies alike followed the primaries unrelentingly, as did national papers and syndicated columnists, many of whom came to North Carolina to observe the race firsthand. At times it seemed as if North Carolina papers were covering little else. These newspapers were important not only because they followed the race day-to-day, but also because a number of journalists and editors were fierce partisans and participants. D. Hiden Ramsey of the Asheville *Citizen*, Jonathan Worth Daniels of the Raleigh *News and Observer*, Louis Graves of the Chapel Hill

Weekly, and H. Galt Braxton of the Kinston *Daily Free Press* were four

editors who were ardent Graham backers and confidants. Indeed, Jonathan Daniels's support of both Graham and Governor William Kerr Scott,
while he was a member of the Democratic National Committee, made
Daniels himself a campaign issue, as did the partisan coverage by his
family's newspaper. In the Smith inner circle were Robert L. Thompson
of the High Point *Enterprise*, John Park of the Raleigh *Times*, and Lynn
Nisbet, a Raleigh political columnist syndicated in many of the state's
afternoon dailies.

In their editorials and commentary, these newspapers often offered
insights into campaign strategy that no other source revealed, a point of
special significance for information about the Smith campaign. For despite the abundance of manuscript sources relating to other aspects of
this race, a paucity of Smith materials confronts the researcher. In addition, newspapers were the forums in which the rival campaigns lodged
their major charges and responses in political advertisements. Half-page
ads were ordinary in this race, and full-page statements in papers
throughout the state were not unusual. Newspaper advertising in this
contest was far more important than radio spots (some recordings of
which survive), handbills, or any other type of formal political exchange.
(Candidate debates were not a part of this race.) The heavy reliance on
advertising further heightened the pivotal role of newspapers in this
Senate primary.

From the distance afforded by four decades, we have endeavored to
write a dispassionate and measured account of a tumultuous and sometimes frenzied political contest. It was not our purpose to write a brief for
any of the participants. We began our inquiry convinced that the Smith-
Graham election was the most intense in North Carolina's modern history, and our examination has only strengthened that belief. We are
further convinced of the campaign's enduring importance. We believe
that the race resulted in long-term consequences for the state, and that
the contest had meaning for the larger history of North Carolina and the
South—a meaning that extended far beyond the immediate result.

Writing this book has brought numerous interpretive challenges. Our
most consistent objective throughout has been to present a full portrait
of the campaign, with all its perplexities and incongruities. We confess to
a sense of wonder that no full-length treatment of this race has appeared
previously, and we are now even more aware of the major gaps that exist
in the political historiography of twentieth-century North Carolina. We
hope that this study will encourage additional scholarship.

As we labored on this book, many people gave us assistance, often far exceeding their professional responsibilities to us. Most memorable was the interest and support we found at the Southern Historical Collection and North Carolina Collection at the University of North Carolina (UNC) at Chapel Hill. Dr. Carolyn Wallace (now director emerita at the Southern Historical Collection), Dr. Richard Shrader, and Dr. H. G. Jones pointed us toward sources we might have missed and met our every research request. Their staffs cheerfully assisted us in the copying of documents and were unfailingly cooperative as we worked. The late Dr. Mattie Russell was likewise a congenial and informed guide to the collections at the Perkins Library at Duke University. We found similar assistance elsewhere, notably at UNC-Greensboro, UNC-Charlotte, the Library of Congress, and East Carolina University. The North Carolina Department of Archives and History in Raleigh convinced us that its reputation as perhaps the best-run state archives in the country is well deserved. We thank especially Dick Langford and Roger Jones of that agency.

Our editor at the University of North Carolina Press, David Perry, has provided encouragement and an acutely critical eye. We are grateful for his continuing support. We owe an equal debt to Sandra Eisdorfer, the press's managing editor, who skillfully guided the manuscript to publication. Paula Wald, our copy editor, improved the book in countless ways, and for her effort we are thankful. We also express our appreciation to Matthew Hodgson for his help. Without the effort of these people, this book would simply not have been completed.

At our study's inception, George Tindall urged us on. His encouragement has sustained us, as has the continuing support of Frank Klingberg, Alexander Smith, and Dan Singal. Our colleague Harold Wilson has kept us honest, which was no small feat. James C. Parham, Jr., of Greenville, S.C., generously shared with us both his knowledge of this campaign and his superb senior thesis on the subject, written at Princeton University. Frank Graham's biographer, Professor Warren Ashby, was equally helpful, both in his counsel and in making materials available to us. R. Mayne Albright was a knowledgeable guide to the campaign and was continually supportive, as was emeritus UNC President William C. Friday, who viewed the campaign from very close range. We owe a special debt to John Sanders of the Institute of Government, whose unrivaled knowledge of this era in North Carolina politics saved us from numerous mistakes. Mr. Sanders talked to us at length about the campaign and gave our work a thorough screening. James K. Dorsett, Jr., is another interview subject whose assistance went beyond his willingness to talk with us about Willis Smith, his father-in-law and former law partner.

Our colleague Kermit Hall somehow found the time to give an early draft of our study a thorough reading, and his suggestions for improvement have significantly sharpened the manuscript. We have been continually grateful for the interest and counsel Professor Hall has given us. He has supported our efforts in every circumstance. Another early reader was John S. Otto, who also gave us important advice. We are much indebted to our anonymous critics at the University of North Carolina Press. Their careful reading immeasurably improved this study. We also thank Mern Johnston-Loehner and especially Joyce Phillips for their assistance in manuscript preparation.

None of these people told us how to write the book or how to interpret the campaign and its principal participants. In matters of interpretation and factual accuracy, we are solely responsible.

Finally, we acknowledge the support our families have extended. In the course of this study, we have thought often of our parents, Mr. and Mrs. James Pleasants and A. M. Burns, Jr., all now deceased, and of Jane Cobb Burns. They all experienced the campaign and encouraged us in our academic pursuits. For Jane Katherine Burns, age 5, we hope this book will someday provide a partial explanation of what her "uncle" and her father have been up to these last several years.

Frank Porter Graham

and the 1950 Senate Race

in North Carolina

Introduction

Crucible of Southern Liberalism

Of North Carolina politics in the first half of the twentieth century, the central facts are four. First, the white supremacy campaigns of 1898 and 1900—by hook and by crook—brought the Democratic party into dominance of the state's politics, a dominance the party would sustain through mid-century.[1] Second, within the Democratic party, a faction under the control of Senator Furnifold M. Simmons held sway until 1930, when Josiah William Bailey dethroned Simmons and ended Simmons's thirty-year Senate career (a defeat caused by Simmons's 1928 defection from the support of the candidacy of Democratic presidential nominee Al Smith and the resultant victory of Republican Herbert C. Hoover in North Carolina). Third, the replacement of the Simmons group by a "Shelby Dynasty" created by Governor O. Max Gardner (1929–33), and the simultaneous state centralization of many services and functions previously controlled by counties.[2] Finally, the unraveling of the Shelby faction, largely accomplished by 1948 and capped by the election of a liberal insurgent governor, W. Kerr Scott (1949–53), who worked diligently to create his own statewide organization.

These factional struggles distinguished Democratic politics in North Carolina from the politics of other southern states, as V. O. Key, Jr., noted in 1949. Intraparty rivalry, Key observed, was proof that Tar Heel Democrats constituted an authentic political organization and that their struggle for power and office was not simply an individualistic free-for-all.[3] In North Carolina, Key pointed out, Republicans maintained a semblance of genuine political competitiveness, as the 1928 general elections had made clear.[4] The white supremacy campaigns of 1898 and 1900, in other words, had scotched the Republican snake but had not killed it. Hence, Democrats were required to maintain a minimal level of party discipline—and candidate decorum—or face the risk of a serious Republican challenge.

The Democratic senatorial race between Frank Porter Graham and Willis Smith in a sense drew this era of North Carolina politics to a close. In the years immediately following the 1950 race, television changed the method of campaigning, transportation improvements diminished sectional divisions, and political amateurs—people who did not derive their sustenance from full-time electioneering—no longer dominated campaigns. The age of the media specialist, the pollster, and the professional consultant was at hand. They all were absent in 1950. Even more important, the era of Democratic dominance began the process of erosion from which North Carolina emerged as a legitimate two-party state.

In another sense, the Smith-Graham contest revived the fierce political debate that dominated at the turn of the century. The question of race relations moved to the center of the political stage after fifty years of unsettled quiescence. The 1950 campaign was not, however, a repetition of an earlier day. History is hardly so tidy. In 1950, the Democratic insurgents—the Scott faction—literally, in several instances, the sons of turn-of-the-century white supremacists, were striving to nudge the state away from an all-white polity rather than toward it. They sought to create in North Carolina an organization more supportive of the policies of the national Democratic party and its leaders, notably President Harry S Truman. They intended, in short, to move North Carolina Democrats more nearly into alignment with the party's urban, labor, and ethnic base, itself the creation of the dominant Democratic personality of the twentieth century, Franklin Delano Roosevelt.

The Democratic Senate fight of 1950 provided the forum for this effort, and the ensuing struggle took on the trappings of a factional brawl, made all the more confusing—and intense—because the contest occurred as the Gardner faction's influence was receding. In this Senate race, therefore, the lines of loyalty were smudged, although a general pattern of Scott-Graham liberal insurgency challenging a faction of conservative traditionalists, as represented by Willis Smith, was discernible—at least through the first primary. This pattern conformed to the traditional factional split in North Carolina politics between the Gardner stronghold in the western piedmont and its rival wing, the heart of which was in northeastern North Carolina. In the second primary, however, a different configuration developed in which both sections agreed on a Senate candidate. For the first time in modern memory, there was an alliance between these two sections. It was not clear in 1950 whether this alliance would have a future or what form it would take in subsequent elections.

The 1950 Senate campaign was, however, more than simply a factional battle. It was a family fight. Democratic party politics in North Carolina in the years 1900–1950 were both provincial and clannish, replete with incestuous shadings. Woe to the aspirant for statewide office not born, bred, and educated in the Tar Heel state, as gubernatorial candidate Ralph McDonald learned the hard way in 1936 and again in 1944. Further, the stronger the personalities of rival candidates, the fiercer the fight. Even the casual student understands that North Carolina politics in the first half of the twentieth century were almost entirely inbred—a closed culture. There were few strangers in the political arena—whether in the press gallery or on the House floor—and this familiarity engendered rivalry and competition that spanned generations and sometimes divided families.

Finally, and most important for this study, the focus of these issues and circumstances found personal expression in the unique candidacy of Frank Porter Graham. President of the Consolidated University of North Carolina from 1933 until his surprise appointment to the Senate in 1949, Graham was first of all a Tar Heel nonpareil. He met every test of blood, background, and provincialism required of Tar Heel politicians in his generation, even though he was a newcomer to political office. He was arguably the most widely acquainted person in the entire state. But Graham was not a typical state politician, either by instinct or by experience. He brought to the 1950 campaign a record of political liberalism and racial enlightenment unique in North Carolina politics. Graham's résumé displayed three decades of high profile activity as a nationally prominent educator and social activist, the price of which was a portfolio bulging with controversy. He was, in addition, as unlettered in the ways of campaign politics as were his University of North Carolina freshmen in the dialogues of Plato. He not only lacked election experience, he had never, prior to his Senate appointment, even contemplated running for an elective office.

His Senate campaign, as an historical episode, assumes a dual significance. It has value first as the climactic event in a unique personal odyssey—the life of Frank Porter Graham. Graham's run for the Senate became his crucible—a trial of both his political beliefs and his life's work. In a broader context, the campaign compelled statewide examination of major domestic questions that the United States—and North Carolina—would debate for the balance of the century: questions concerning race relations, civil rights, and the social and economic role of the federal government. As the campaign revealed, North Carolinians could not debate these matters without raising their voices. Indeed, they found it impossible to talk of racial change and remain rational—at least during the six-month election campaign.

Over the years, a settled interpretation of this episode in North Carolina politics has been told and retold. The retelling, however, has rarely involved additional investigation into the election. Readers will discover in these pages a treatment that in some ways affirms the interpretation embraced by nearly every writer who has discussed the Smith-Graham campaign. In other ways, however, our narrative represents a substantial departure, shaped by the voluminous source materials on which the book is built.

This contest is best understood within the context and patterns of North Carolina politics viewed over time. National issues, most importantly the incendiary question of race relations, were the political substance on which the campaign was based. But this election also must be understood as a chapter in the state's political history, both in terms of party infighting and sectional divisions. Out of this history, the race unfolds and the issues emerge. The point may be obvious, but it has often been ignored.

This election campaign was a difficult experience for North Carolinians—white and black. Among its legacies were a residue of ill will and a legion of sullied reputations. The state's long-remarked claim as a national model of race relations was likewise permanently compromised, and the principal protagonists—Frank Porter Graham and Willis Smith—were forever marked by their roles in this political drama. It is safe to say that those who witnessed this campaign never forgot it.

There was, indeed, much to remember. The campaign produced a political intensity rarely matched in the state's history. Graham's opponents pummeled him for his left-wing past, and ridiculed his ties to Governor Scott, Raleigh *News and Observer* editor Jonathan Daniels, and the Truman administration. They claimed that Graham's racial views were at odds with the state's white voters and invoked the vision of a race-mingled future, with all its attendant horrors. Graham's powerful allies countered that Smith was a tool of moneyed interests and a betrayer of the Democratic tradition. He was a corporate lawyer indifferent to the struggles of common folk, hostile to both labor and social welfare. In his heart, he was probably a Republican, they claimed.

Between the trading of these charges and the perfervid emotion of the moment, Robert Rice Reynolds, North Carolina's foremost political buffoon, and Olla Ray Boyd, a publicity-seeking pig farmer, provided occasional comic relief. They vanished after the first primary, however, and the guffaws they had elicited went with them. Nobody laughed during the second primary.

It is a truism that in the one-party South of the first half of the twentieth century political campaigns rarely involved disagreements on substantial policy matters. This truism does not hold for the Smith-Graham primaries in 1950. The differences among the rival Democrats were so fundamental and so deep that they should have provoked a little-asked question: How long could Democrats so divided on policy matters continue to share the same political party?

1 · *Appointment*

Scott's Surprise

On a cool March evening in 1949, North Carolina Governor William Kerr Scott, less than three months into his four-year term, got into his state limousine for a short trip to the nearby university town of Chapel Hill. He went on a ceremonial mission—or so it seemed—to present the first annual O. Max Gardner Award. The award, a new honor in memory of North Carolina's distinguished late governor (1929–33), was to be given each year to a Consolidated University of North Carolina faculty member who had made a significant contribution to human welfare.[1]

The awards dinner itself was of relatively little concern to the hard-pressed governor. A surprise winner in the 1948 Democratic primary, Scott had busied himself with the most active shake-up of state government in fifty years. In addition, he had embarked upon a broad range of new state programs, under the slogan "Go Forward." To add to Scott's problems, on March 6, 1949, just seventeen days before the Gardner dinner, North Carolina's junior senator, former Governor Joseph Melville Broughton (elected to the Senate in the same election that sent Scott to the governor's mansion), had dropped dead in his Washington office. As Scott motored to Chapel Hill on March 22, the vacancy remained unfilled.[2]

Senator Broughton's death had stunned North Carolinians. Seemingly in vigorous health, he had won a tough primary victory in 1948 over Durham attorney William B. Umstead, a 1946 Senate appointee to fill the unexpired term of the late Josiah William Bailey. The state's citizens had anticipated a long and distinguished Senate career for the popular ex-governor; now he was dead. As the immediate shock of his death—and the accompanying tributes from across the state and nation—subsided following Broughton's funeral on March 9, political speculation regarding Broughton's successor intensified. Indeed, among the state's political leaders and press observers, maneuverings and discussion regarding the Senate vacancy did not wait upon Broughton's interment. The dean of North Carolina political writers, "Boswell to the state government," W. T. "Tom" Bost, remarked in the Greensboro *Daily News*: "There was no way to contain a commonwealth willing enough to mourn the loss of one of the most illustrious of its modern figures, but too impatient to await the orderly selection of his successor. This isn't seemly, but it is inevitable."[3]

The political scurrying would have been expected in any similar circumstances, but it had been heightened by Scott's unexpected ascension to the governor's mansion in 1948. Scott, a plainspoken, cigar-chewing dairy farmer from the textile and mercantile town of Haw River (or, more accurately, the Hawfields community near Haw River) in piedmont Alamance County, had brought off a huge political upset in 1948. The former state agriculture commissioner had beaten State Treasurer Charles M. Johnson, the designated candidate of O. Max Gardner's "Shelby Dynasty," which had successfully elected every North Carolina governor since Gardner's own term.

In engineering this political upset, Scott had fashioned a coalition very different from the "progressive plutocracy" of banking, tobacco, and textile interests identified by V. O. Key, Jr., as the state's dominant political forces. Scott had won by getting the support of the "branch head boys"—farmers isolated by unpaved roads and a lack of telephone service. He had combined this farm support with the backing of organized labor and a subtle appeal to the state's growing number of black voters and had promised in his "Go Forward" program to raise teacher salaries, improve public education, and get farmers out of the mud. Scott was, in addition, closely aligned with the Democratic administration of Harry S Truman and the New Deal wing of the North Carolina Democratic party, led by the Raleigh *News and Observer*'s Jonathan Worth Daniels and others favorable to Truman. Consequently, Scott saw in Broughton's death an opportunity to strengthen his political grip. He would appoint to the Senate someone more favorable to his own views than members of the conservative wing of the party. Playing the drama for all it was worth, Scott promised no quick decision on Broughton's replacement.[4]

In short order, however, the focus on possible successors narrowed to three: High Point newspaperman Capus Miller Waynick, a former chairman of the State Highway Commission, Scott's 1948 campaign manager, and currently chairman of the State Democratic Executive Committee;[5] Greensboro attorney Major Lennox Polk McLendon, son-in-law of Charles Brantley Aycock and an avid Scott supporter; and former Senator William B. Umstead, the Durham attorney whom Broughton had defeated in 1948.[6]

Of the three, Waynick was the early favorite, his candidacy marred by only one obstacle: he was from the "west." In a state where east-west conflict had been a shaping force antedating the American Revolution, political tradition required North Carolina to maintain a geographical balance: one Senate seat for the "east," one for the "west." Unfortunately for Waynick, the westerner from High Point, Broughton's death

Governor W. Kerr Scott, ever-present cigar in hand, during his gubernatorial term. Scott's appointment of Graham astonished the state in 1949. (North Carolina Collection, University of North Carolina at Chapel Hill)

had vacated the eastern seat. Clyde Roark Hoey, former governor and brother-in-law of O. Max Gardner and a Shelby resident, was the current westerner. It made no difference that Waynick was a recent Raleigh resident; his High Point newspaper career made him a western candidate. And his geographical affiliation would prove to be an insuperable obstacle to his Senate aspirations,[7] even though Scott's own election had violated the east-west tradition.

North Carolina newspapers, of course, filled their political columns and news stories with endless speculation and analysis, much of it designed to influence Scott's choice. Jonathan Daniels's *News and Observer*, a pro-Scott oracle, on March 8 pinned its hopes on Waynick, with McLendon the likely compromise choice.[8] The anti-Scott Charlotte *Observer*, on the other hand, favored former Senator Umstead because he was an easterner, and had important Washington experience. That Scott and Umstead had unbridgeable political differences went unremarked, but the paper did point out that an Umstead appointment might ease Scott's path in negotiating his "Go Forward" program through a skeptical state legislature in which Umstead had many friends.[9]

Scott's initial public statement about the Senate vacancy came on March 8 at a Raleigh press conference. He said that he planned to appoint a Senate successor only after "due deliberation," a process that could last a week or more. Further, he told reporters, he would not rule out the possibility of appointing a westerner, which fueled speculation that Scott might appoint Waynick or McLendon. In vigorous language, he scotched rumors that he might resign as governor to be succeeded by Lieutenant Governor H. Patrick Taylor, Sr., in order that Taylor could then send Scott himself to Washington as Broughton's successor. "The people of North Carolina have given me a definite assignment," Scott remarked. "I would not take advantage of a State and national tragedy to further any personal ambition."[10]

Scott, who throughout the appointive process played a very close hand, did admit to reporters that he was overrun with political advice. Already more than a thousand telegrams had arrived, the telephone was ringing incessantly, and people were even stopping the governor's counselors on the street to discuss the vacancy. "Evidently," Scott observed, "there is some sort of campaign going on."[11]

In fact, several campaigns were underway, and only an actual appointment could still them. The longer Scott hesitated, the more feverish the posturing to influence his choice. Thousands of letters, telegrams, and phone messages rolled into Raleigh, suggesting more than seventy nominees. The principal beneficiary of the mail campaign proved to be former Senator Umstead, although the messages reflected the early analysis that Waynick, McLendon, and Umstead were the leading candidates.[12] Perhaps the only political figure who remained mute was North Carolina's surviving U.S. senator, Clyde Roark Hoey. Concerned with his own reelection bid in 1950, Hoey throughout maintained a splendid neutrality.[13]

The press of advice only compounded the difficulty of Scott's choice. Clearly astounded—and perplexed—at the mountain of conflicting counsel, Scott delayed his choice, in part owing to the mixed messages raining in upon him. More importantly, Scott became convinced that his appointment of one of the three principal candidates—Waynick,

McLendon, or Umstead—would so incense the disappointed advocates of the rejected candidates that the choice could well imperil Scott's own administration. For example, Congressman Thurmond Chatham urged the selection of Umstead; he had the experience to step into the job, and the appointment would obligate many people to Scott who were otherwise cool toward him.[14] Conversely, the North Carolina State Federation of Labor strongly opposed Umstead as antilabor and favored Waynick, a liberal and a friend of labor.[15]

The prospect of harm to his governorship, therefore, led Scott to consider the possibility of an alternative choice. Oregon Senator Richard Neuberger wrote Jonathan Daniels, offering to help Daniels enter the nomination sweepstakes.[16] Daniels, son of the Raleigh *News and Observer's* storied founder and editor Josephus Daniels, was a figure of high visibility in North Carolina and the nation. A best-selling author (*A Southerner Discovers the South*, 1938; *Tar Heels: A Portrait of North Carolina*, 1941), administrative assistant to President Franklin D. Roosevelt, press secretary to President Harry S Truman in 1945, and at the time of Broughton's death, a putative Truman biographer, Daniels's vast experience made him a formidable figure. He was, in addition, a major booster of the governor and one of Scott's closest counselors. But Daniels had no thirst for the rigors of candidacy, and his close association with the Truman administration did not sit well with many conservative North Carolina Democrats.[17] Nor did state politicians, sometimes stung by the *News and Observer's* acerbic editorials, look upon Daniels with warmth; some of them loathed him. Governor Scott understood that Daniels's close ties with the Raleigh paper, his association with the Truman administration, and his somewhat imperious mien made him a divisive figure in North Carolina politics.

The least controversial choice suggested to Scott was the appointment of Broughton's widow to fill the Senate seat until voters in 1950 could elect someone to serve the remainder of Broughton's term. Scott could thereby distance himself from the political free-for-all that surely would erupt in 1950.[18] But Mrs. Broughton had no interest in the Senate, and Scott never contacted her. Obviously, had he made such a choice, Scott would have given up the opportunity to shape the views of the North Carolina Senate delegation, at least until his own term as governor was up and he could stand for the Senate himself. Such indirect maneuvering to further his own career would have been uncharacteristic of Scott's direct manner. The appointment of Mrs. Broughton in Scott's view would have amounted to an abdication of responsibility.[19]

Many of the letters sent to Scott did not promote a particular candidate but urged Scott to make an immediate appointment for the good of the state.[20] Some urged the choice of a Christian leader and statesman rather than a shrewd politician;[21] others wanted someone friendly to labor and sensitive to the needs of minorities and education.[22] One writer merely asked that Scott seek guidance from the Heavenly Father,[23] to which Scott replied that he was naturally "seeking divine guidance as I approach the hour of decision."[24]

Several of Scott's mail counselors suggested even more unorthodox choices. One citizen observed that the list of nominees included everyone except himself and his next-door neighbor, and they hereby endorsed each other for the post.[25] Writing from the Veterans Hospital in Swannanoa, Robert Mullikin explained his position: "I'm the last applicant in line. Don't appoint anybody until you see me. I want to unstall the 81st Congress. I want to give 'em a lecture in filibustering."[26]

Norwood Lane wrote that "North Carolina needs a live man in the Senate," and since his own record was "clean, just and hard," he was willing to accept the appointment.[27] Fred Bonitz, an old friend of Scott's, sympathized with Scott's problem and reminded him that "no matter who you name you will make the others peevish to say the least and you will have to hunt up jobs for all of them." Bonitz's own choice was Waynick, who could make a better speech than long-haired Hoey "and thank God he dont wear a jim swinger coat or come from Cleveland County."[28]

A classic of its genre was the note written by Ormond Fooshee of Sanford: "I would like to get the job as Senator for N.C. for the next two years." Fooshee was not sure he could fill Broughton's shoes but thought he could handle the job. "I am not a member of nothing but the church an the Farm Bureau so I don't owe any one any thing. I don't think people would through you out of office if you gave me the job." Fooshee, a thirty-four-year-old unmarried farmer who did not drink, thought he had "as good horse sense as the next man" and, on world problems, "could do better than some of the birds up at Washington." Fooshee implored Scott to make certain that whoever was appointed had "back bone enough to say no. An another thing the world isn't going to hell who every gets the job. The most of the people we have sent to Washington you wouldn't know they were up there if they didn't come up for election once in a while. I would like for you to think it over for I still want the job."[29]

While Scott deliberated—communicating his thoughts only to a very tight circle—the state's press imagined itself at Churchill Downs on Derby Day. "A field of more than twenty entries," as the Charlotte *Ob-*

server called it, "rounded the turn in the senatorial sweepstakes, with L. P. McLendon . . . and Fred Royster considered slightly in the lead."[30] Royster, a Henderson tobacconist who was the unanimous choice of the state Farm Bureau and the tobacco interests, unfortunately had opposed Scott in 1948, as had the Farm Bureau. He was a late entry into the field and a long shot. Both Umstead and Waynick were expressing interest in the post, although both disavowed any participation in campaigns to pressure the governor. Whatever the outcome, it seemed a certainty that Umstead planned to be in the Senate race in 1950.[31]

Undoubtedly, Waynick was the most likely candidate. As Scott's 1948 campaign manager, custom dictated his selection. Moreover, he had refused any state appointment after Scott became governor, implying a desire for the western Senate seat should the fates intervene. Senator Hoey, however, seemed in excellent health, likely, as Waynick told Scott, "to outlive us both." To which Scott replied, "Well, we can hope for the best." And in a telephone conversation recalled by Waynick, he and Scott, speaking of Waynick in the third person, contemplated the choice:

> Scott: People are saying this fellow Waynick would make a good senator.
>
> Waynick: Governor, he'd make a great Senator. But if there's any embarrassment to you whatsoever, don't you name him. I won't lift my hand to get you to do it.[32]

Scott then sent Waynick's candidacy through the escape hatch Waynick had opened, citing respect for the east-west tradition. In actuality, that custom would not have restrained a political maverick like Scott unless he had also been concerned that Waynick would have difficulty holding the seat in 1950. Exit Waynick.[33]

At the same time, the governor decided to eliminate McLendon, Umstead, and recent arrival Fred Royster as well. Like Waynick, all three had vigorous sponsorship within different groups of North Carolina Democrats. The appointment of any of them might alienate the others' supporters, imperiling Scott's already delicate legislative relations. More importantly, neither Royster nor Umstead was a Scott ally—indeed, Umstead was an adversary—and McLendon seemed almost indifferent to the post. Thus, as partial recompense for canceling Waynick, Scott dispatched all the favorites and launched his search anew.[34]

Scott now had a clearer idea of the candidate he sought. According to the Greensboro *Daily News*, Scott needed a solid supporter of his administration, whose appointment would bolster his growing political strength. He wanted someone acceptable to Broughton supporters, who had broad experience and could win reelection in 1950. Upon reflection, none of the four front-runners had measured up. Waynick, as stated, would likely lose the race in 1950, Umstead could hold the seat but would not strengthen Scott's hand in doing so, Royster was inexperienced, and McLendon did not want to serve past 1950.[35]

Hence, five days after Broughton's death, the governor publicly interred the Senate hopes of the four favorites. In a March 11 news conference, Scott described the position as still "wide-open." Asked if there were any dark horses, Scott replied, "One comes through my door every hour or so," indirectly confirming reporters' impressions that the leading candidates had been cashiered.[36] The Charlotte *Observer*'s Wade Lucas now wrote that Scott might do his usual act of pulling the unexpected, appointing someone like Dr. Clarence Poe, editor of the *Progressive Farmer*, as a caretaker candidate who would leave the seat for Scott in 1950.[37] Jonathan Daniels wrote Lindsay Warren that there was "a terrific scramble going on down here in connection with the senatorial vacancy, but nobody seems to know exactly what the outcome will be."[38]

The longer Scott delayed, the more likely a surprise appointment became. But Dr. Clarence Poe was not in the running, and Scott was not looking for a caretaker. When asked on March 15—nine days after Broughton's death—whom he would name to the Senate, Scott merely distributed a list of forty-eight names submitted to him with one or more endorsements. Asked when he would appoint someone, Scott replied blandly that he needed time to read the thousands of telegrams and letters he had received before he could make his selection. "Just appoint whoever you damn well please," counseled Scott's favorite telegram, which he displayed to reporters. That was precisely what Scott intended to do, he implied, even if it meant nominating someone other than one of the forty-eight candidates he had just disclosed.[39]

Undetected by the press, Scott's dissembling was a purposeful tactic. No reporter guessed that Scott's delay masked a frantic campaign to impress into service the most improbable of all serious candidates. For by March 12, Scott had made up his mind to offer the Senate seat to Consolidated University of North Carolina President Frank Porter Graham, the most renowned southern liberal of his time.

The path to Graham's selection—and his tortured acceptance—was both circuitous and difficult. It began when Governor Scott's wife, known to all including the governor as "Miss Mary," came across the list of forty-eight names in Scott's suit pocket. She asked Scott to read the list to her. At first he would not do it, "but like a lot of wives, I nagged until he did." Scott began reading the names, and when he came to Frank Graham, Mrs. Scott remarked, "Well, you can stop right there. So far as I'm concerned, that's it."[40] Scott paused. For probably the first time, he thought about Graham as a serious candidate.

Later that day, March 12, Scott and Jonathan Daniels conferred about the Senate vacancy, and Daniels also suggested Graham. Scott responded, "I think that would be wonderful if you could persuade him to take the job." Daniels agreed to go to Chapel Hill at once and approach Graham.[41] Thus began a bizarre period of eleven days in which Scott and Daniels repeatedly tried to convince Graham to enter elective politics—a role Graham had never envisioned for himself.

Daniels's first conference with Graham and his wife Marian was inconclusive. Despite a supporting call from Governor Scott, Graham specifically declined but discovered that the manner of his refusal only spurred the ardor of his pursuers.[42] Daniels, at the behest of Scott, returned the next day. He stressed the critical need for Graham's acceptance, at which point Graham capitulated. Hours later, recalled Scott, Graham called on the governor and reneged. "He apparently became so overwhelmed with the thought of taking on such a task and leaving the university that he came to me and said he positively would have to withdraw his decision."[43] Scott responded by continuing to pressure Graham, who eventually agreed to consider the offer conditional upon passing a physical examination. Graham passed but again said no.[44]

As the campaign to persuade Graham continued, public pressure on Scott to make an immediate selection reached a new level of intensity. Congressman Thurmond Chatham, speaking to a North Carolina Democratic Club dinner on March 18 in Washington, publicly urged Scott to appoint a successor forthwith. Important Senate business was pending, and North Carolina needed its two Senate votes. In the state senate, a bill was introduced giving the General Assembly the authority to pick a new senator if the governor failed to act. Journalists interpreted the action as an effort to prod Scott into filling the vacancy in order to help southern senators in their filibuster against President Truman's pending civil rights legislation.

In the face of this pressure, Scott stalled, declaring that there was no need for precipitate action. The problem of selecting a senator was difficult, he argued, and he was still undecided on his choice.[45] Nonetheless, the state press joined the chorus. Both the Gastonia *Gazette* and the Charlotte *Observer* wrote that the long delay was harmful to the state and nation. Scott, the papers argued, was putting politics ahead of the state's welfare.[46]

Spurred by public criticism, Scott turned his full power of persuasion on Graham. Jonathan Daniels returned to Chapel Hill for yet another session with the reluctant candidate. He argued forcefully that Graham could not refuse the governor. He must go to the Senate, where he could work with all his skill and talent in service to his lifelong goal: world peace. As Daniels noted the critical shape of world events in 1949, he drew for Graham—a lifelong Wilsonian—a vision of an isolationist-ridden Senate where Graham's vote and influence were potentially determinative.[47]

In addition, Daniels bluntly told Graham that his work at the university was completed. A far greater challenge awaited him as a senator, a position that demanded people who were committed to democratic ideals and who knew the faces of fascism and communism. Daniels further reminded Graham that the Senate would provide him with a forum through which he could pursue cherished domestic goals, notably federal aid for education, better agricultural programs, and more sensible labor-management relations than those outlined in the recent Taft-Hartley legislation.[48] Governor Scott later recalled that in the conversations with Graham, no one ever asked the educator's opinions on any specific issue, save one: would he become a senator?[49] Except for the assurance that he would run in 1950, Scott asked only one commitment from Graham: "to go up to Washington and then be on your own."[50]

The call to duty was the credo by which Graham had lived his life. Indeed, as Daniels knew, Graham would accept no other summons. His service as a marine in World War I, his election as president of the University of North Carolina (preconsolidation) and of the Consolidated University, his answer to calls from Presidents Roosevelt and Truman for service during and after World War II, the chairmanship of the Southern Conference for Human Welfare (SCHW), and all other leadership positions Graham had filled had been in response to this kind of appeal. In nearly every instance, moreover, he had turned away from the initial offer. In the end, of course, he almost always accepted. Now he agreed to the appointment, provided the chancellors of the three University of North Carolina campuses would consent to his leaving his post. Graham attached this condition because his absence from his presidency in 1947–48 on a United Nations mission to Indonesia had left important university decisions unresolved. The chancellors, all Graham's friends, had made known their concerns about his leave-taking. Graham now wanted the approval of the chancellors because he had promised them upon returning from Indonesia that he would not leave again.[51]

The polling of the chancellors took place in a secret meeting at the governor's mansion on Sunday, March 20. W. C. Jackson from Woman's College in Greensboro, Robert B. House from Chapel Hill, and John W. Harrelson of North Carolina State College in Raleigh assembled at Scott's residence in the company of University of North Carolina Comptroller William D. "Billy" Carmichael, Jr., Jonathan Daniels, and Scott. In response to a direct question from Scott, none of the chancellors raised an objection to the appointment. No objections had been anticipated, and the quest for a nominee was thereby concluded. All understood that Graham now had committed himself to serve until 1950, at which time he would run for reelection for the remaining four years of Broughton's term.[52]

All that remained was a public announcement. Rather than call an immediate press conference, Scott decided to defer notice for an additional two days. He determined to announce his decision at the first O. Max Gardner Award dinner in Chapel Hill, to be held the Tuesday following the Sunday Raleigh meeting. The method Scott chose for informing his audience was ambush, for the selection remained undisclosed except to half a dozen people who were pledged to secrecy. "While I'm on my feet," Scott told his Lenoir Hall audience after presenting the award, "I want to make the announcement here tonight that your next Senator . . . is Dr. Frank Graham."[53]

For a moment, those present sat stupefied, none more so than the now upstaged winner of the Gardner Award, Louise B. Alexander. A more unlikely choice to replace Senator Broughton could not be imagined. Then came cheers and a thunderous standing ovation for the beloved president of the consolidated university. To Scott's great delight, his surprise had worked to perfection.[54]

Frank Porter Graham, the diminutive sixty-two-year-old educator and liberal activist, waited until the applause subsided before arising to accept Scott's appointment. With customary self-effacement, Graham observed that he had rejected Scott's importunities two or three times, "but he is a stubborn Scotch Presbyterian. I found that I would have to say yes." Accepting the appointment had been the most difficult decision of his life, Graham confessed. It meant that he would leave "the institution and the people who have been part of my life for more than forty years." Scott, always one to have the last word, arose again to confirm Graham's story of his reluctant acceptance, assuring the crowd that Graham had indeed said no to his offer two or three times, "but I would not take 'no' for an answer."[55]

For thirty minutes thereafter, "Dr. Frank," as he was known to thousands, accepted congratulations from those present. From chancellors to dining hall waiters, his Chapel Hill friends and associates crowded around him offering their good wishes and their regrets at his leaving the university.[56]

Graham's departure from his post at the university came immediately. The governor, as chairman, called the trustees' executive committee into informal session that evening, and Graham submitted his resignation. Some trustees suggested the possibility of a leave of absence for Graham, but Scott, anxious to avoid the impression that Graham's Senate assignment was a temporary mission, carried the argument against a temporary leave.[57] The senator designate thus went home as former President Graham, and Gardner Award–winner Louise B. Alexander motored back to Greensboro all but forgotten in the Senate clamor.

For Kerr Scott, the principal force in the appointment process, the decision to appoint Graham made sense for several reasons. Recognizing Frank Graham as a great humanitarian, Scott admired his Christian stewardship and his identification with the dispossessed. As a self-styled "man of the people," Scott himself had won office by promising to be responsive to groups often overlooked in North Carolina politics: small farmers, rural inhabitants, organized labor, and minorities. Scott knew of Graham's work for a broadened medical program in North Carolina. He was aware that Graham had endorsed the road program, school construction, and the plan for expanded rural telephone and electric service—in essence, Scott's "Go Forward" program. Seemingly, Scott and Graham were in general agreement on every major state issue.

Scott believed as well that his appointment was good politics. Graham's Senate career would enable Scott to expand his support among the groups that had elected him in 1948. He liked Graham also because Graham, although a member of the North Carolina bar, had never been a practicing attorney, the profession from which North Carolina senators customarily came. Scott believed it would be "wholesome for North Carolina to have a layman as Senator whose background particularly has been one of constantly working for the masses of people."[58] Scott possessed an innate distrust of lawyers, and he saw in Graham a visible public figure who was not in politics and who would represent a liberal point of view very different from his conservative future colleague, Clyde Hoey.[59] That Graham had no experience in elective politics did not concern Scott. He calculated that Graham's popularity and national prestige would make him a powerful and successful candidate in 1950, perhaps scaring off all rivals.[60] The Goldsboro *News-Argus* concluded that, as expected, Scott had done the unexpected. He had neatly sidestepped "any personal complications which might result from his having named a man who seriously sought the place."[61]

On national issues, Scott knew that Graham was a "Truman man." He agreed generally with the Fair Deal programs and would be a valuable asset to the national administration, especially in civil rights, foreign policy, and labor issues. In fact, shortly after Graham had consented to the appointment, Scott telephoned John R. Steelman, a Truman aide, to notify the White House of his choice. In reply, Steelman observed that Truman knew Graham personally and was pleased with his selection.[62] The New York *Times* even claimed that Scott had consulted National Democratic Chairman J. Howard McGrath before choosing Graham.[63] Such national contacts later fed the speculation of critics that Scott had followed the dictates of President Truman and his former Press Secretary Jonathan Daniels in appointing Graham.[64] No surviving evidence supports the charge, which is further rebutted by Scott's well-earned reputation for political independence—some would say stubbornness. His courtesy calls to McGrath and Steelman were strictly advisory.

The Truman administration did assist Scott in cushioning Capus Waynick's disappointment at having been passed over in the selection process. The administration granted Scott and Daniels's request of a diplomatic post for Waynick. In response to Waynick's stated preference, he was posted to Managua as ambassador to Nicaragua.[65] The appointment would subsequently be read by at least one press observer as proof of a Truman payoff to Scott for sending a liberal to the Senate, although this interpretation is not convincing. Convincing or not, of course, it lent controversy to the entire appointment process.[66]

Graham's appointment confirmed Jonathan Daniels's intention to play an active role under Scott in North Carolina politics, not merely as a journalist and critic, but as a mover and shaker—a politico. In this effort, Daniels intended to strengthen his position as a principal Scott ally and confidant, roles he had already played in convincing Graham that he was indispensable and must go to the Senate. In fact, Daniels had been the essential agent in the appointment process. He understood both politics and Frank Graham and was probably the only Scott intimate who could have persuaded Graham to leave Chapel Hill. Graham's success in the Senate would now become, in some degree, Daniels's success. On policy matters and in their views of North Carolina's political future, Daniels and Graham were in general agreement, although Daniels's career throughout had been marked by a caution Graham had never heeded.

Frank Graham's reasoning in accepting Scott's offer is at once more understandable and yet more unknowable than the actions of either Scott or Daniels. By his own admission, the acceptance of Scott's call was the most difficult decision of his life.[67] He found Daniels's logic convincing:

the university would survive without him; his work there, seventeen years of it as president of the consolidated university, was done; and he would have unlimited opportunity for service—a higher calling—in the Senate. Graham could not shirk this duty—the state and nation needed him. Graham also desired a chance to address international concerns, especially the Wilsonian objectives of the United Nations. As an internationalist and a world federalist, Graham was drawn to the Senate where he could be more than a spokesman, he would be a voting member in the most important legislative body in the world.[68] The idea of new surroundings likewise drew him. The battle scars from promoting and defending the university could at last be salved: "It's just as well to move on and let some younger person come in and carry on. I think it . . . better really, for the University for me to . . . not pass away, but to pass on."[69]

Finally, ambition must have played some part in Graham's acceptance of the Senate seat, but if it did, Graham certainly could not admit it. His code was selflessness, and service to others was his only admitted motivation. It was a heartfelt position from which he had never budged. It was, in addition, a trait of character that had brought him great success and even greater recognition, including, among other honors, twelve honorary degrees. Graham had sought neither the presidency of the university, the Senate appointment, nor any other duty he had ever undertaken, but in each instance, he accepted responsibility thrust upon him because he believed in his ability and his qualifications. His self-effacement did not mean that Graham questioned his ability; he had great self-confidence.[70] Despite his avowed modesty, whenever Graham was offered a chance to advance his career, he took it. The Senate offer was no exception.

Throughout the appointment process, Graham's decision was complicated by his wife's continued opposition to his acceptance. Marian Graham held that her husband's move to the Senate was a mistake, and she could not be budged from that belief. Politics would take Graham out of his element. Having never held a public office or been involved in electioneering, Graham had been concerned for all of his life with issues and causes exclusively. Marian Graham feared that politics would subject Graham to pressures and forces that might well destroy him. It was a world he did not know and for which his idealism had not prepared him. Nonetheless, Frank Graham finally succumbed to the blandishments of Daniels and Scott and overruled the counsel of his wife. From now on, he would be Senator Graham.[71]

Frank Porter Graham, now the junior senator designate from North Carolina, could rightly claim kinship with a sturdy line of Tar Heels. As with nearly every state political figure in the first half of the twentieth century, he was a lifelong resident of North Carolina. His father, Alexander Graham, was a Confederate veteran who had studied at the state university after the war, leaving in 1868 prior to graduating. Although lacking a degree, Alexander Graham began his lifework as a "school man" in Bladen County, where he was a public school principal. In 1871, upon recommendation of a university friend, Frank Porter, Alexander Graham left Bladen County for New York, where he taught grammar school. Simultaneously, he enrolled in Columbia Law School, receiving his Bachelor of Laws degree in 1873. Meanwhile, Graham's friend Frank Porter, newly graduated from Yale Law School, had opened a law practice in Fayetteville. Porter was also assisting in the organization of a graded school system in Fayetteville and in 1878 recommended his friend Alexander Graham as the system's first superintendent.[72]

In 1875 Alexander Graham had married Katherine Sloan, like her husband a North Carolina Scotch Presbyterian. From this union came nine children, the sixth of whom was a boy named in honor of Alexander Graham's friend, Frank Porter. Frank Porter Graham was born on October 14, 1886, in Fayetteville. In 1890 his family moved to Charlotte, where his father had been named superintendent of schools. Here Graham grew up, in a home where books were plentiful and reading the most important pastime. His parents were faithful to their Presbyterian roots, nurturing Frank Graham's sense of moral values.[73]

From the beginning, Graham was an able student. Graduating from high school in 1903 at age sixteen, his college matriculation was postponed by a measles attack in his senior year of high school, which weakened his eyesight. In 1904 his parents decided to send him to the Warrenton Academy, which was under the direction of Alexander Graham's younger brother John. From Warrenton Graham went to Chapel Hill and the state university in the fall of 1905.

From his years as a University of North Carolina undergraduate, Graham's life and the life of the university intertwined, until, for a time, they seemed almost to merge. It is impossible to say which effect was greater, the university's on Graham, or, eventually, Graham's on the university. In either case, it is hard now to overstate the impact of each on the other.

As an undergraduate, Graham met fellow students who would be his lifelong friends, confidants, and advocates: Charles Tillett, Francis Winslow, John Wesley Umstead, John J. Parker, and Kemp Davis Battle, among many others.[74] He was both an accomplished student and a student leader. Ranked second in his class academically after three years, he was elected to Phi Beta Kappa as a junior. In his senior year, he edited the student newspaper. During his undergraduate summers, he attended Young Men's Christian Association (YMCA) Southern College conferences in western North Carolina, near Asheville. There, speakers challenged the students to devote their lives to the advancement of Christian democracy in the South.[75] In the words of the *Yackety-Yack,* the university's yearbook, Graham left the university as a man characterized by idealism, fair play, integrity, and the belief that others were trustworthy.[76]

For all his absorption in college activities, however, Graham's life beyond his student years remained unfocused. Upon graduation in 1909, he had no immediate plans. Following his friends Battle, Tillett, and Winslow, Graham wandered into law school, even though he had never envisioned a legal career. Law school deepened his friendships with his undergraduate chums, but it neither excited his intellect nor launched him into a profession. When an offer came from Raleigh at the end of 1910 to teach high school English, the twenty-four-year-old Graham accepted forthwith.[77]

He spent two years in Raleigh and while there declined an offer to journey to China to teach at Hangchow College.[78] Instead, he returned to Chapel Hill in 1912 to resume his law studies, having been present that summer at the Democratic National Convention that nominated Woodrow Wilson for the presidency. Wilson had been an inspirational force for Graham since a 1909 Chapel Hill visit in which the Princeton president delivered an eloquent address extolling the virtues of life in the service and advancement of Christian democracy.[79]

After his second year of law school, Graham was admitted to the North Carolina bar, although he would never practice law. He then accepted a position as secretary of the university YMCA, and in the fall of 1914, he was asked to teach a course in the understaffed history department. He found the experience exhilarating, and as a consequence, he determined to begin graduate work in history, intending to return to Chapel Hill to join the permanent faculty. He thus enrolled in Columbia University in the fall of 1915 and completed work for his master's degree in June 1916.[80]

In early 1917, as U.S. diplomatic relations with Germany worsened, Graham tried mightily to enlist in the army but with no success. He then tried the navy and the marines with the same result. His small stature (5'5"), slight physique, and poor eyesight barred his acceptance into service. Following President Wilson's ringing call to arms on April 2, 1917, he tried again, and this time the marines took him. He remained in uniform until the war was over, although he got no nearer to European

combat than Philadelphia, where he was stationed for part of his time in service.[81]

Mustered out of the marines, he returned to Chapel Hill, having been asked by University of North Carolina President Harry Woodburn Chase to become the university's first dean of students. Graham served one year as dean and assistant professor of history, then resigned the deanship and returned full-time to the history department. During the 1920–21 academic year, Graham was summoned by Chase and university librarian Louis Round Wilson to be the field leader in an unprecedented effort to convince the state legislature and Governor Cameron Morrison to make a $25 million bond issue investment in state-supported higher education in North Carolina. Graham traveled throughout the state for six months, by bus and train, rallying alumni and public support for the campaign. His effort succeeded, and with the fund his effort had generated, his university began its modern history. Graham was now a rising star at Chapel Hill.[82]

He was, in addition, now fully committed to an academic career. That commitment led him, in the fall of 1922, to the University of Chicago to begin work on a Ph.D. degree. He would study with Professor William E. Dodd, specializing in the history of his native South. But he remained at Chicago for only one year. The arid demands of academic inquiry simply held no fascination for Graham. Once he left his work at Chicago, he would never again pursue formal academic study. In the spring of 1923, however, he learned that Professor Dodd had nominated him for an Amherst Memorial Fellowship in the Study of Social, Economic, and Political Institutions in preparation for a career in either the ministry or teaching. The grant was for two years, the first of which Graham spent at the Brookings Institution in Washington, studying economics. The second year, he went to the London School of Economics. He took no formal courses at either institution, but his stay at the London School of Economics brought him into contact with both R. H. Tawney, the historian and Fabian socialist, and Harold Laski, the political scientist and British Labourite.[83]

Graham was now convinced of the necessity to work for "social betterment," to find a true balance between material and humane values. He hoped to help his native South achieve greater economic wealth and broader social and political equality. Determined to live his life in service to others, Graham believed that the Sermon on the Mount was sound social and economic doctrine and that he should strive to help implement its principles. From this conviction he never wavered.[84]

His academic training now concluded, he returned to Chapel Hill in 1925 as associate professor of history. He taught his classes and busied himself with public concerns, among them the Citizens Library Movement and the North Carolina Conference for Social Service, which he served as president in 1928 and 1929. In addition, he involved himself in more controversial public issues. He appealed publicly for fair treatment for the mill workers accused of killing Police Chief D. A. Aderholt in the 1929 Loray Mills strike in Gastonia. Shortly thereafter, he drafted an Industrial Bill of Rights designed to protect workers' rights. His statement earned him the respect of many fellow Tar Heels, but it upset some textile owners and engendered the permanent enmity of David Clark of Charlotte, editor of the *Southern Textile Bulletin* and a University of North Carolina trustee.[85]

In early 1930, President Chase resigned his post, and Graham found himself brought forward as a candidate to succeed Chase. Despite sincere protestations that he did not want the job, Graham's friends—among them Kemp Battle, John Parker, Charles Tillett, Raleigh *News and Observer* editor Josephus Daniels, and Governor O. Max Gardner himself—wore him down over a period of months and voted him in without his consent. When presented with the fait accompli, he relented and accepted. He was forty-four years old.[86]

The Great Depression presented state-supported higher education in general, and the University of North Carolina in particular, with the gravest crisis since the Civil War. In an effort to make state services more efficient (and, not incidentally, to expand his own power), Governor Gardner undertook several ventures in state centralization, among them complete state responsibility for public roads, a state-funded six-month public school term, and the consolidation of the three major institutions of higher education, the University of North Carolina, Woman's College in Greensboro, and North Carolina State College in Raleigh. As a consequence, two years after he had been impressed into the presidency of the University of North Carolina, Frank Graham became the first president of the Consolidated University of North Carolina, again over his protestation. He would continue in that post until his Senate appointment.[87]

As president, Graham proved to be an inspirational leader, and his work for the university made him a nationally renowned educator. His initial struggle during the depression, of course, was simply to keep the university afloat and to find ways to enable students to remain in school in the face of failing family finances. He proved to be a persuasive advocate for his university in legislative halls and a compassionate and tireless advocate of its students' economic needs. He often committed his own money to students and repeatedly cosigned loans to help students stay in school. Further, he used the spacious president's home as a boardinghouse for needy University of North Carolina students, a practice that was not halted when he married Marian Drane,[88] daughter of an Edenton, North Carolina, Episcopalian minister, in July 1932. They would live in devotion to each other for the remainder of their lives.

Financial crises were not the only threat to the university in the 1930s. Repeated challenges arose that attempted to compromise the university's commitment to open academic inquiry. In each instance, whether the controversy concerned the campus visit of black poet Langston Hughes or of British philosopher Bertrand Russell, Graham stoutly defended the university from attacks that challenged the propriety of such activities. He tirelessly championed the University of North Carolina Press and its director, William Terry Couch, as the press brought out a seemingly endless succession of titles during the 1930s dissecting and analyzing the social, economic, and political dilemmas of southern society. Many of these works were the products of University of North Carolina sociologist Howard W. Odum's social science research institute, itself a dismaying feature of the university in the eyes of some critics. The press's books examined subjects southerners "had not been accustomed to discussing," especially race relations, and while they enhanced the university's academic prestige, they also fueled criticism within the state that questioned the wisdom of such investigations. In these and other incidents, Graham repeatedly shielded his faculty from protest and occasional demands for peremptory dismissal.[89]

Almost as nettlesome were the territorial struggles that accompanied the administrative consolidation of the University of North Carolina, Woman's College, and North Carolina State College. The most controversial issue in that reorganization was the decision Graham reached in 1935 to close the prestigious school of engineering at Chapel Hill and move all engineering programs to North Carolina State. Predictably, the decision was soundly denounced in Chapel Hill but cheered by alumni of the Raleigh school, who had feared that consolidation might gut their institution. Other fights accompanied the reorganization, but as the changes took hold, dissension subsided.[90]

University concerns were by no means the only focus of Graham's energy in the depression decade. As international events—the Japanese invasion of Manchuria, Hitler's rise to power, the Spanish Civil War, the Munich conference, the Molotov-Ribbentrop pact, and finally World War II—commanded attention, as American politics moved leftward in the flush of New Deal enthusiasms, and as many social activists moved well beyond the New Deal, Graham became deeply involved in a profusion of social and political causes and concerns. As he said himself in an Atomic Energy Commission "Personal Security Questionnaire" in 1947: "During the past fifteen years, I have belonged to hundreds of committees," organized to promote a bewildering array of activities: rallies, protests, statements of conscience, and policy appeals.[91] An examination of his papers suggests that Graham, using his title as university president, signed almost every petition and plea for support that moved across his desk, to the not infrequent consternation of his friends and the consistent concern of his critics. Inevitably, this activity took him far afield from his responsibilities as consolidated university president and immersed him in controversy.

His response to an episode that grew out of the nationwide textile strike in 1934 was one of his more widely publicized acts. On September 1, 1934, a general strike idled over half the roughly 700,000 textile workers across the United States, including two-thirds of the 111,000 textile workers in North Carolina. In High Point, police arrested a young man, Alton Lawrence, a former University of North Carolina student then secretary of the state Socialist party, charging him with forcible trespass in strike-related activity. When Graham heard of Lawrence's arrest, he was vacationing at Pawley's Island, South Carolina. Immediately, Graham wired Lawrence, whom he remembered well from Lawrence's student days, and offered to put up Lawrence's bond. Graham added that he was confident Lawrence had committed no crime. The story, complete with full quotation of the telegram, was featured in newspapers statewide and created a sensation. Graham's actions provoked the wrath of a number of influential North Carolinians, confirming their suspicion that he was a reckless radical, but they endeared Graham to Lawrence and many other young people. The telegram also earned Graham the private rebuke of sociologist Howard W. Odum, who remarked to friends: "What tactics. Now he's got a whole lot of enemies and he hasn't done a damn thing."[92]

An ardent New Dealer, Graham's career as a social activist did not signify his conversion to the role of political radical. Rather, his activism was visceral. It was an emotional response to the depression's misery and the world's turbulence. Ideologically, he never went beyond Franklin Roosevelt and the Democratic party. Nor did he ever fully grasp the bruising quality of the left's internecine struggles of the 1930s. He was, therefore, quite willing to work with people in a common cause and to assume in the common effort a generalized purity of motive. No episode better illustrates this pattern than Graham's involvement with the Southern Conference for Human Welfare.

Organized in 1938, the SCHW had its first meeting in Birmingham, Alabama, in November of that year. Its initial purpose was to create a mass southern organization to address the South's myriad economic, social, and political problems and to promote an unofficial connection with the New Deal. The speakers' list for the Birmingham meeting was replete with New Dealers, among them Eleanor Roosevelt, Aubrey Williams of the National Youth Administration, Senators Claude Pepper of Florida and John H. Bankhead and Lister Hill of Alabama, and Supreme Court Justice Hugo L. Black. Graham, who delivered the keynote address, had to leave the conference early, after stating that he did not want to be considered as SCHW's first president. He was elected anyway and when informed of his selection by telegram, agreed to serve.[93]

From the beginning, two problems dogged the SCHW. The initial problem was the issue of segregation. Delegates had been sitting in unsegregated fashion at their meetings, but a confrontation with Birmingham Police Chief Eugene "Bull" Connor required the delegates to segregate. Garbled accounts of the incident created the impression that the conference had gone on record endorsing full racial equality. This claim alone would have seriously imperiled the conference's future, since many southern moderates and political leaders simply would not align themselves with any organization that was alleged to be seeking full racial equality in the South.[94]

The second problem was even more forbidding. At the peak of its popular front posture in 1938, the Communist party insinuated itself into the SCHW, and from the beginning the conference was plagued with this taint. The suspicions of some liberals, first aroused at Birmingham, were reinforced when Joseph Gelders, a fellow traveler and/or party member, assumed control of the conference's civil rights committee in February 1939, and Howard Lee, a secret party operative, became the conference's executive secretary in mid-1939.[95]

As SCHW president, Graham was sufficiently concerned about rumors of Communist influence to initiate his own inquiries. He wrote Howard Kester, veteran southern radical and, at the time, general secretary of the Fellowship of Southern Churchmen, in December 1939, asking him to check the lists of officers and committees of the SCHW for names of party members. Such a task was not easy, Kester responded. He could only reply on the basis of observation, drawing on fifteen years of experience and association with a broad range of southern radicals. Kester named Gelders, Lee, and several others as either party members or fellow travelers and cautioned Graham that if these people got control of key committees, they could dominate an organization even if their numbers were few.[96] Others, among them American Civil Liberties Union head

Roger Baldwin and Frank McCallister of the socialist Southern Workers Defense League, volunteered information that confirmed Kester's
report.[97]

Heeding the advice of Kester and others, Graham wrote Gelders and
Lee and asked them point-blank if they were party members. "I am not
personally concerned with your politics, religion, or economic views," he
told Gelders. "I simply wish, however, to have in writing from you a
statement on which I can stand in my answers, whatever the accurate
answers may be."[98] Gelders responded two days later, assuring Graham
that he was not a party member, as Howard Lee had done in a letter to
Graham on November 4, 1939.[99] Graham took no further action, largely
because he did not oppose admitting Communists to membership.
Where disagreements developed, he believed he could defeat them in an
open and free debate, through education, rational discussion, and humane goodwill.[100]

Meanwhile, the exodus of southern liberals and moderates out of the
conference continued. From the beginning, Jonathan Daniels had declined any association with the organization, as had Howard Odum.[101]
Claude Pepper resigned from the executive committee on February 6,
1939, and requested removal of his name from any association with the
SCHW.[102] Marjorie Westgate McWhorter of Birmingham quit in October
1939, protesting Joseph Gelders's leadership of the Civil Rights Committee. Brooks Hays of Arkansas, who would be elected to Congress in 1942,
left in November. Francis Pickens Miller of Virginia had already resigned
in December 1938.[103] A number of others who had been in attendance
in Birmingham, but had not joined, had simply severed any tie with the
organization at the conclusion of the initial meeting.[104] Following an
acrimonious second conference in Chattanooga, Tennessee, in April
1940, brought on by his resolution condemning Soviet invasion of Fin-
land, University of North Carolina Press Director William Terry Couch,
one of the SCHW's organizers, likewise left the organization.[105]

Other resignations followed: executive board member J. C. Cox of
Tennessee in April 1941 and Barry Bingham and Mark Ethridge of the
Louisville *Courier-Journal*, also in 1941, after Bingham had expressed to
Graham his deep concern about Graham's continuing role in the SCHW.
"I am more concerned for your prestige and for the maintenance of your
full usefulness than I am for any other factor in this whole situation,"
Bingham wrote. "The South cannot afford to lose one whit of your
leadership."[106]

Disavowing this counsel, and much additional similar advice, Graham
did not resign from the SCHW. He did resign the presidency in 1940, to

be replaced by an Oklahoma Presbyterian minister and fellow traveler, John B. Thompson. Graham continued as honorary president, a position that kept his name on the SCHW letterhead even as his influence on SCHW policy diminished. He would continue to hold his honorary office until the conference officially disbanded in October 1948. In terms of its promise, however, the SCHW's momentum was largely dissipated by the end of 1941 due to internal conflict focused largely on World War II, the question of Communist participation, and the vicissitudes of Soviet foreign policy. Graham's role in the organization would remain a subject of controversy for years to come.[107]

Graham himself never doubted the proper response to the onset of World War II. An ardent supporter of Great Britain from the beginning of the war, he championed Roosevelt's effort to assist the British. Moreover, his ties to Roosevelt sent him to Washington in 1941 as a member of the National Defense Mediation Board. After Pearl Harbor, the board was reconstituted as the War Labor Board. It had the duty to settle all labor disputes in any industry that was related to the war effort and to prevent work stoppages that might imperil war production. He remained with the board throughout World War II, returning to Chapel Hill only on weekends. He received a salary only from the federal government while involved in this service, although he continued to govern the consolidated university as best he could. He returned to the university full-time in January 1946, amidst much grumbling at the problems caused by his prolonged absence, but in September 1947, he was off again. Secretary of State George C. Marshall asked Graham to join a three-person United Nations team to negotiate between the Netherlands and anticolonialist forces in Indonesia. Graham accepted Marshall's invitation and left Chapel Hill in October 1947, having been granted an indefinite leave by the university's board of trustees. He completed his work in February 1948 and returned to Chapel Hill. Between the War Labor Board service and his Indonesian duty, he had found time to serve on President Truman's Committee on Civil Rights, whose historic—and controversial—document, *To Secure These Rights*, had been presented to the president in October 1947.[108] Eleven months after Graham was settled yet again into his South Building office on the University of North Carolina campus, syndicated radio commentator Fulton Lewis, Jr., startled him with a series of broadcasts attacking his memberships and associations. Lewis's commentaries, spanning six five-minute programs, began on January 11, 1949. The broadcasts led to a national news story and were aired just as Graham was participating in a conference on Indonesia at Lake Success, New York.[109] Specifically, Lewis drew attention to the manner in which Graham had gained security clearance in his role as president of the Oak Ridge Institute of Nuclear Studies, a university consortium associated with the atomic energy program at Oak Ridge, Tennessee.[110]

The Atomic Energy Commission had announced Graham's clearance on December 10, 1948, but only after overruling its own security board, chaired by former Supreme Court Justice Owen Roberts. Apparently convinced that Graham's record had compromised his judgment, the board had recommended unanimously that Graham be denied security clearance. Atomic Energy Commission members, led by Chairman David E. Lilienthal, then reversed the security board and declared their full confidence in Graham. Subsequently, the security board was disbanded.[111]

The commission's press release and Lewis's subsequent broadcasts compelled Graham to reply, and he cabled Lewis a three-page statement on January 13, which Lewis read in its entirety on the air. Requiring two broadcasts to complete, it was a spirited, general defense of Graham's record, declaring his opposition to communism and "all totalitarian dictatorships" and vigorously affirming his democratic faith. Acknowledging that his advocacy was often controversial, Graham recanted nothing.[112]

Lewis was not completely placated by Graham's response (although he did acknowledge the force of his reply) and continued to ask over the radio if Graham would "publicly disavow his [current] associations with these [suspect] organizations, and publicly resign from them." Graham, however, made no further reply to the broadcaster, and Lewis moved on to other matters,[113] while the Graham story moved to the U.S. Congress. On February 3, 1949, Louisiana representative F. Edward Hebert, commenting on the Atomic Energy Commission disclosure, reproved Graham sharply. He found it "disgraceful that a man in so great a position should so conduct himself that he cannot be trusted in any situation involving his country." Graham had no right to continue as president of the University of North Carolina, Hebert maintained.[114] Other Capitol Hill colloquy ensued, but by the middle of February, the story of Graham's Atomic Energy Commission security clearance was exhausted as a news item.

The month of criticism and controversy deeply disturbed some of Graham's oldest friends. Kemp Battle wrote on February 9 that Graham's telegram to Lewis had "convincingly covered your personal beliefs, but did not explain the so-called subversive organizations, your membership in which was the point of the attack. . . . I know that from some of them you resigned and doubtless there are convincing explanations as to all of them." The bewildered Battle advised that Graham should now prepare a full statement explaining his activities: "It seems to me that you owe a statement, not to yourself, but to thousands of North Carolinians who believe in you and are troubled by what has been said."[115] President Truman, on the other hand, consoled Graham by writing that the criticism was "unjustified."[116]

Graham made no additional statement, nor did he give any outward indication that the controversy troubled him. He did take the time, however, to gather a group of letters from his files and have them notarized. On February 9, 1949, he had notary seals put on a 1940 letter to Howard Odum, asking if Odum would assume the presidency of the SCHW, provided that Will Alexander would become executive secretary, and on letters to Frank McCallister and Marjorie McWhorter discussing Communist influence in the SCHW. In his letter to McCallister, who had made specific charges about Joseph Gelders and Howard Lee, Graham explained that he had written statements from each denying that they were Communists and thanked McCallister for "your letter and deep interest in the Conference."[117]

On February 11, Graham had three additional letters notarized. Two, written in late 1941, were to academic colleagues, Harry Gideonse, president of Brooklyn College, and Ned H. Dearborn, dean of the School of Education at Columbia University. The letters discussed possible Communist influence in the American Committee for Democracy and Intellectual Freedom, a nearly all-academic group chaired by Dearborn, on which Graham served as a member of the national committee. Both letters conveyed Graham's concern about possible Communist participation in the group and requested from Gideonse and Dearborn information that would confirm or rebut the charge of strong Communist influence.[118]

The third notarized letter was from Graham to a Lincoln, Nebraska, businessman, written on May 11, 1942. L. L. Coryell had received a mailing from the Citizens Committee to Free Earl Browder—Professional and Cultural Division and had seen Graham's name associated with the effort to secure release for Browder, an American Communist then in prison. "I thought he pleaded guilty to forging a passport," Coryell wrote Graham. "Just how a man of your profession can take the position which they purport to take is more than I can understand. Professional men of your type have a large influence. Many less cultured men believe in you because you are listed among our really great men."[119]

Graham wrote back, explaining that he had signed the petition on

Browder's behalf because Browder had already served more than twice the prison term usually accorded similar cases. "I do not believe in the political views, or philosophy of Mr. Earl Browder. I have long openly opposed those views, and do not want him or his party in charge of the government of the United States. I do not believe, however, in making a political martyr of Mr. Browder. . . . In the matter of his views . . . I am as strongly opposed as you are."[120]

This controversy, triggered by the Atomic Energy Commission news release, was more public and more stinging than the verbal assaults and criticism Graham had encountered over the years. His action in notarizing letters to use in his defense, should the need arise, suggests that the attacks troubled him deeply. The clamor subsided quickly, however, although the claims made against him were duly noted by his critics. Scarcely a month later, Jonathan Daniels came calling, conveying the message that Governor Scott wanted not to investigate "Dr. Frank" but to appoint him to the U.S. Senate.

Graham thus began his political life after a career of service and disputation. Yet his lifelong friends outside the academy, beyond the province of his popular front activities, never grasped the depth of controversy that followed their friend. They cheered his appointment, but few of them knew—not even in the current surge of publicity—the details of Graham's steadfast support for left-wing causes in the 1930s; they were not similarly engaged. But they trusted Graham and had confidence in him. They dismissed all attacks upon him as spurious— the ranting of bigots and ingrates—because their faith in Graham's goodness was total. These friends could never understand why Graham's critics failed to share their view of him as a beneficent (and benign) social healer. Nor did they know that a number of Graham's university associates, all of whom wished him well, had over the years confessed doubts about Graham's perspicacity that paralleled the complaints of his scorners. His critics and associates questioned his judgment—his "sense of proportion," as Gerald W. Johnson put it in a long letter to Howard Odum in 1936. Graham, Johnson wrote, was a man "bound to play the little tin god," whose unblemished past gave him no pause in "helping God run the universe."[121] It was a concern his friends from the towns and farms of the state did not understand. Nor did the governor, who did not know exactly what he was getting when he named Graham to the U.S. Senate.

2 · *Reaction*

"Our Hearts Swell with Gladness"

Press and public response to Graham's nomination gave vivid illustration that Scott's decision had the potential for spectacular political conflict; the lines of division were visible from the very beginning. The exuberance of Graham's supporters was matched by his opponents' groans and lamentations. Nor was the appointment debate confined to the state—or the region. Scott's designee drew commentary from nearly every national newspaper and journal and even generated a momentary tiff on the floor of the U.S. Senate. Clearly, the Graham appointment was big news, a remarkable result of the routine political act of naming a replacement for a deceased senator.

The North Carolina newspapers favorable to the Scott administration, to Harry Truman, and to Graham personally hailed the new senator. The loudest hosannas, predictably, came from the Raleigh *News and Observer*. "Our hearts swell with gladness," wrote Jonathan Daniels, quoting a phrase from the official state song. Praising Scott for choosing an appointee best representative of the state's new "Go Forward" spirit, Daniels limned Graham as "the clearest living symbol of full faith in the powers of the people and the most vital advocate of full and equal opportunity for them all." Scott had "lifted the spirits and faith of North Carolina people in their destiny to go forward [toward] the fulfillment of the best that [is] in them" and had "given the nation a Senate member who would be recognized for his wisdom and worth as a devoted and devout advocate of peace and democratic ideals."[1]

The Chapel Hill *Weekly*, Graham's hometown newspaper, was equally ecstatic, stating that Scott "could not have found anyone better qualified for membership in the Senate by character, intellect and training."[2] The morning dailies in Greensboro, Asheville, Durham, and Winston-Salem added their enthusiastic approbation.

The Greensboro *Daily News* called Graham the best the South had to offer in wisdom, learning, and courage,[3] while the Asheville *Citizen* welcomed the new senator but noted that reactionaries were afraid of his humanitarianism and radicals feared him because he was utterly independent. No thinking person would impute to Graham anything "save the purest of motive, . . . the deep and unselfish instinct to serve fellow men."[4] The Durham *Morning Herald* saw Graham as one of the best-loved men in the state, held in such esteem by North Carolinians that no one could beat him in 1950, despite the fact that some politicians were unhappy with such an unconventional choice.[5]

Specifically denying Graham's radical past, the Winston-Salem *Journal* commented that the appointee was not and never had been "a reckless, irresponsible or impractical leftist." His appointment provided a convincing answer to "the traducers who had tried to twist his earnest belief in and consistent adherence to the principles of sound Jeffersonian democracy and brand him a Communist or fellow traveler of the Marxists."[6]

The chief traducer in High Point was Robert L. "Battlin' Bob" Thompson, editor of the *Enterprise* and a consistent Graham critic over the years. Thompson, writing ironically, commented that Graham would certainly perform better as a senator than he had as a university president. How could he be worse, implied Thompson. Scott had done a fine thing for the university. Now perhaps the university could get a forceful, full-time president who was not a career leftist.[7]

The Fayetteville *Observer* recognized that the choice of Graham was controversial and argued that his political tenure might be brief: "Committed to Truman's civil rights issue, he will find he had many friends who could go along with his advanced liberalism at an academic level who will not be there on a legislative level."[8] And *The State* magazine, although thinking that the appointment was satisfactory, expressed serious reservations. Any citizen, *The State* opined, would feel apprehension over Graham's liberal tendencies. Graham was no Communist, the magazine observed, but as a liberal thinker he was ten to twenty years ahead of his time: "When a man thinks in advance of the period in which he is living, he is bound to be criticized."[9]

On balance, however, a clear majority of the state's press editorially supported the appointment. Even the traditional Charlotte *Observer* approved, lauding Graham for his ability, integrity, and sincerity of purpose. Graham's experience and keen mind would enable him to render outstanding service in the Senate, even though as a liberal, he would disappoint many North Carolinians by his support of the Truman administration.[10] The *Observer*'s evening rival, the Charlotte *News*, echoed this position but noted: "No one else inspires such fierce loyalty and devotion, no one else arouses such bitter enmity." The *News* hoped Graham would temper his socialistic theories when faced with political realities, since the people of North Carolina would have the opportunity to pass on his stewardship in 1950.[11] Even longtime Graham critic John Park stated in his Raleigh *Times* that the caliber of the Senate would be enriched by Graham's vision and statesmanship.[12]

For the state's black press, Scott's appointment of Graham was almost too good to be believed. Writing from Durham in his *Carolina Times*, editor Louis Austin regretted Graham's leaving the state university but felt that his move to the Senate symbolized nothing less than the ultimate triumph of truth. Graham and Governor Scott were men of destiny who would hasten the death of the old order in the South. To Austin, the old order meant the South's pernicious racial segregation, police brutality, lynching, denial of the ballot, and associated injustices. To the proponents of segregation, Austin believed, Graham's appointment was a funeral dirge—the beginning of the end to terror and intimidation, as liberal southerners of both races marched toward the goal of real democracy.[13]

Nationally, Graham's appointment received full coverage and occasioned editorial comment from nearly every major daily. The Washington *Post* celebrated Graham's nomination, arguing that the new senator could look beyond narrow parochialism and serve his state by advancing the national interest. Unconcerned with Graham's sponsorship of questionable organizations, the *Post* expressed confidence in his loyalty, believing him to be a sounder spokesman for liberty than his detractors.[14]

The New York *Herald Tribune* reiterated the views of the Washington paper. Senator Graham would add to the number of southern representatives who thought beyond selfish sectional lines. And in a long article on April 21, reporter Henry Lesesne observed that it was predictable that an outstanding southern liberal had been sent to the Senate from North Carolina, the southern state that had been the region's pacesetter in matters of race and social justice.[15] Variations on this theme, all strongly supportive of the appointment, came from the *Christian Science Monitor*, the Philadelphia *Bulletin*, and the New York *Times*.[16] Both *The Nation* and the *New Republic* added their enthusiastic ratification.[17]

Closer to home, however, the reaction had more bite. Frank Graham, noted the Atlanta *Journal* in approving his move to the Senate, was a divisive figure revered by his supporters, detested by his detractors. While his friends saw him as a great democrat, a compassionate soul, and a disciple seeking to practice the precepts of Christ, his opponents saw him as a dreamer who was sympathetic to alien ideologies and a menace to society.[18] The dilemmas of Graham's budding political career were not lost on Douglas Southall Freeman. In the Richmond *News Leader*, Freeman observed that liberals were delighted that they now had a representative who would defy the lily-whites and the despicable reactionary elements of the Democratic party. But Graham's adversaries, "found everywhere from Currituck to Cherokee," rejoiced to have Graham gone from Chapel Hill. "To add to their excitement, they now could take a crack at him if he ran in 1950." Governor Scott, Freeman projected, may have sounded the trumpet for an unforgettable fight. And Graham, who had withstood recurring attacks with an air of martyrdom, might welcome the chance to confront his opponents.[19]

Lest Graham and his friends underestimate the opposition to his appointment, they had only to read the reaction of many out-of-state southern papers. Graham's selection was abhorrent to the Nashville (Tenn.) *Banner* because of his seldom-matched gift for affiliating with disloyal organizations. Graham's liberalism was "either blinded by zealotry to the intellectual facts of life or intellectually dumb as the iconoclast becomes when steeped in the intoxicating fumes of his own theory."[20]

The Montgomery (Ala.) *Journal* claimed that Graham was unrepresentative of the people of North Carolina. They did not like his subversive associations, his kowtowing to labor unions, or his membership on Truman's Committee on Civil Rights. Should he be brave enough to run in 1950, the paper predicted, he would be one of the most badly defeated men of his generation.[21] In the same vein, the Mobile (Ala.) *Press* assumed that the "civil strife" camp was "grinning like Cheshire cats" and riotously celebrating "Graham's anticipated support for federal measures to bring overnight changes to the South by federal fiat."[22]

Perhaps the most sober analysis came from the Danville (Va.) *Register*. The latitude Graham had enjoyed as a university president, the paper pointed out, could not be carried to the Senate where one must be a politician as well as a statesman. "By playing politics Graham will fall off the pedestal upon which North Carolinians of every political hue have placed him as a seeker of truth and justice." Acceptance of the Senate seat would diminish the idea of Frank Graham as a man whose career was uniquely characterized by the complete absence of selfish interests. Politician Graham would lose the aura that had made him such an effective force in North Carolina and the nation and that had protected him from the long knives of his opponents. Graham would have been worth more to his state, the paper concluded, had he remained an educator and exponent of Christian brotherhood.[23]

No doubt the strongest endorsement of Scott's appointment came from the massive correspondence directed to both the governor and the senator designate, the overwhelming majority (88 percent) of which was congratulatory. The letters to Graham were not only numerous, they were also from a dazzling array of people in every station of life. Farmers, schoolteachers, principals, laborers, as well as a wide cross section of professional people in North Carolina and throughout the nation signaled their enthusiasm over Graham's move into the Senate. Lennox Polk

McLendon, Raleigh attorney Willis Smith, federal judge John J. Parker,

Carolina Israelite editor Harry Golden, and countless others formed a
representative circle of approving friends. Wrote Golden: "Now is the
winter of our discontent made glorious summer by the two sons of
Carolina, Scott and Graham."[24] National and international leaders likewise sent congratulations. President Truman himself, Philippine patriot
Carlos P. Romulo, White House aides Clark Clifford and John R. Steelman, Eleanor Roosevelt—long a Graham associate—and a host of other
public figures proclaimed their approval of the appointment. General
George C. Marshall struck a refrain many were to repeat: "Really it is this
country that is to be congratulated, and I think I am the best qualified
witness to this view of the appointment."[25] Graham's longtime friend
Norman Thomas also expressed his pleasure, believing that Graham
could be the voice of the South at its best.[26]

The acclaim these letters conveyed did not, however, obscure the
reality that some people were very unhappy at the prospect of Senator
Frank Porter Graham. Graham had bitter enemies of long standing, and
some of them chose to direct their fury at Governor Scott rather than at
the appointee. One group of Scott critics complained principally on
matters of race. One state representative knew that Graham was an able
man and would be "right close to the president" but wondered about
Graham's attitude on civil rights.[27] An anonymous postcard dropped the
level of discussion a few fathoms and revealed the depth of racial animosity in North Carolina: "Sir, it looks like you and Harrys is right together
on the civil rights issue. There is Thousands of us Tar Heels that is more
than surprised as to your attitude in trying to force the nigs and whites to
mingle and mix together so we are dun with you and him also not the
friend we was."[28] Another angry voter accused Scott of selling out North
Carolina to the Negro-loving Truman administration. Walter White and
Truman now counted Scott as one of their own, and they were welcome
to him since "no self-respecting white man wants you."[29]

Other citizens found Graham's involvement with left-wing social
causes a disturbing specter. One wrote that he knew no better way to slap
the people of North Carolina in the face than to send Graham to the
Senate, as he was an advocate of civil rights and belonged to numerous
subversive organizations "playing drop the handkerchief with Joe Stalin."[30] Indeed, many letters of protest made some reference to Graham's
affiliations with various left-wing political groups and causes. "Why send
the Socialist-Communist Dr. Graham to the Senate? We already have too
many Reds and Pinks. . . . Why not send Graham and all like him to
Moscow?"[31] An unsigned letter published in the Charlotte *Observer*

argued that at a time when America was fighting against the rising tide of socialism, the Graham appointment was disastrous; he was a dangerous man "in that he is intelligent and honest in his views."[32]

Writing to "Governor Cur Scott," a Pennsylvania resident claimed that North Carolina must not have any respectable non-Communist citizens to be appointed to the Senate "or else you are merely one vile politician trying to play the same rotten game as S.O.B. Truman as his understudy."[33] Eighteen signers of a letter from Statesville, North Carolina, expressed worry that while Graham presented himself as opposed to communism, he allowed Communist groups to flourish at the university. "The only reason we didn't get ten thousand signatures," they warned Scott, "is that there is not room on the letter."[34]

Several Graham opponents cited to Governor Scott the January 1949 Fulton Lewis, Jr., radio attacks on Graham as proof of Graham's Communist affiliations. They listed the organizations alleged to be subversive and protested that a man with Graham's record should not be appointed to a position of trust.[35] Edith Dickey Moses wrote Scott that Graham's "cheek-by-jowl association with Communists for years and years and his activities in their conspiratorial 'fronts' . . . disqualified him for public office."[36] Finally, these were the blunt words of an anonymous and hostile critic: "A fine appointment you made. Comrade Graham will serve faithfully and we can depend on him for much valuable information. . . . I am recommending you for the Red Star Medal. [signed] Your Friend, Joe Stalin."[37]

Other critics claimed that Scott had deceived them, and they demanded that he resign as governor "at once, if not sooner."[38] Perhaps the most unusual response came from James R. Patton, Jr., a Durham lawyer: "Not being accustomed to fetish worship, nor believing in what seems to be the accepted dictum that a benign Providence has sent us a part of Divinity reincarnated in Frank Graham, your appointment of him leaves me apathetic and cold." Commenting on the recent comparisons of Graham to Christ, Patton wrote: "I felt that if we should have a Second Coming that no more appropriate place could be selected than Chapel Hill, but I had not anticipated that the resurrection had already taken place and I was oblivious to same."[39]

Without a doubt, the state's politicians were the group most perplexed by Scott's little surprise. The state's senior U.S. senator, Clyde Hoey, was so stunned that on first hearing the news of the appointment, he could not summon any response save "no comment." Later, fully recovered, Hoey praised Graham as an outstanding educational statesman with wide experience. Hoey predicted that Graham would make a great contribution to state and nation in the Senate.[40] Nor were the rejected senatorial aspirants any more expansive than the rarely dumbstruck Hoey. Fred Royster could muster only a "no comment,"[41] and Capus Waynick merely wished Graham well in handling a very great responsibility.[42] William B. Umstead simply congratulated Graham, acknowledging that Scott had been placed in a difficult position when Broughton died.[43]

Lieutenant Governor H. Patrick Taylor, Sr., expressed the viewpoint of many Tar Heel politicians: he was "surprised [Graham] was appointed and surprised he accepted."[44] In fact, when the news was broadcast at Raleigh's Sir Walter Hotel, the home away from home for the General Assembly (which was in session), the immediate response of the representatives and lobbyists gathered in the hotel lobby was a heavy, prolonged silence, followed by statements expressing near incredulity.[45]

State Agriculture Commissioner L. Y. "Stag" Ballentine and Attorney General Harry McMullan refused any public comment at all—not even "no comment." However, state senator Wade Barber was more responsive and more enthusiastic; he decided that Scott had named the greatest man in North Carolina to the Senate. Barber predicted Graham would have no opposition in the next primary.[46]

Nationally, liberals and Truman supporters—and the president himself—praised the wisdom of Scott's choice. Truman was delighted to welcome to the Senate an enthusiastic southern supporter, a man of highest character and integrity who possessed an enlightened viewpoint and was an earnest champion of the forgotten man.[47] The president of the Congress of Industrial Organizations (CIO), Philip Murray, wired Scott his warmest congratulations,[48] and United Automobile Workers President Walter P. Reuther told Scott he deserved the nation's thanks for his determination to act in the best interests of all citizens.[49] Jack Kroll, political action director for the CIO, added his praise.[50]

From Alaska, Governor Ernest Gruening told Scott he could not recall a better senatorial appointment.[51] Californian Helen Gahagan Douglas congratulated Scott,[52] as did Florida Senator Claude Pepper. Pepper called the naming of Graham "one of the most significant and courageous public acts within my knowledge."[53] Historian Arthur M. Schlesinger, Jr., in extolling Scott's act, noted that Graham had stood all his life for the highest principles against all forms of totalitarianism. "I think you have rebuked Fulton Lewis, Jr., in the best of all possible ways," concluded Schlesinger, referring to the radio commentator's January 1949 attacks on Graham's record.[54] And finally, Channing H. Tobias, director of the Phelps-Stokes Fund and a colleague of Graham's on the Truman

Committee on Civil Rights, explained to Scott that his selection of Graham brought joy to the hearts of fifteen million black Americans who appreciated Graham's sense of justice and fair play. Graham could be depended upon to advocate a single standard of citizenship. His move to the Senate made Tobias "more hopeful of the future of America than I have been for a very long time."[55]

Were any additional evidence necessary to confirm the controversial nature of Scott's selection, one need only look to the chamber for which Graham was bound. On the day following Scott's appointment, Ohio Senator John W. Bricker surprised his colleagues when he took the Senate floor to demand a congressional investigation into Graham's background. In a reprise of the Fulton Lewis, Jr., broadcasts, Bricker once again went through the story of Graham's Oak Ridge Institute of Nuclear Studies security clearance. Pressing his claim, Bricker read into the record the testimony of Paul Crouch, a former Communist and Federal Bureau of Investigation (FBI) undercover agent who had been active for eighteen years in the Communist party. Crouch had argued repeatedly, as a witness at various investigatory forums, that party members consistently took advantage of liberals like Graham and that Graham's record of collaboration should not be overlooked.[56]

In his effort to embarrass Graham—for his remarks could not be used for any other purpose—Bricker was joined by Indiana Republican William E. Jenner. It was common knowledge, Jenner said, that Graham was soft on communism, even though Graham had never been a party member himself. Jenner then commented: "With his weakness, I would rather see him in the United States Senate, where he can only talk, instead of the Atomic Energy Commission, because down there he could do a heck of a lot of damage."[57]

Bricker's trial balloon, kept aloft momentarily by Jenner's hot air, quickly deflated. Indeed, Bricker told reporters he did not wish to delay Graham's appointment or to question his right to serve as a senator. Complaints about Graham's Atomic Energy Commission investigation had been on his desk for some time, Bricker insisted, and now seemed an appropriate time to inform his Senate colleagues. But his claims and concerns could find no audience. The "Stop Graham" movement never got beyond this point.[58]

In fact, the remarks of Bricker and Jenner provoked a fierce rebuttal. Senator Hoey, resplendent in English walking coat and full of old-school southern courtliness, came swiftly to Graham's defense. Expressing dismay at Bricker's timing and, inferentially, his boorishness, Hoey explained that he could not remain silent while insinuations questioning

Frank Graham's loyalty were made on the Senate floor. He had known Graham all his life, Hoey told his Senate colleagues, and he considered Graham to be "as loyal as any American who walks this earth." He did acknowledge disagreement with Graham on many issues but insisted that Graham's loyalty was unquestionable. Hoey cited Graham's military service in World War I and his distinguished career as "an educational statesman" to rebut the charge of disloyalty.

Hoey did admit Graham's carelessness "in permitting his name to be associated with certain organizations before he has learned exactly what they were. When an organization which has seemed to be a good one and has seemed to be serving the interests of the country has asked permission to use his name, he has sometimes been too lax in permitting" such use. That criticism had been heard in North Carolina, Hoey remarked, but no charge of disloyalty had been made. No one who knew Graham would hesitate to trust him with any secret America might have.[59]

Hoey's remarks revealed his willingness to defend Graham vigorously, but they also showed Hoey's clear intention to hold Graham's political ideals and social causes at arm's length. Up for reelection in 1950, Hoey had his own political fences to tend, a task he had always performed flawlessly. Nonetheless, he was genuinely offended by the oafishness of Senators Bricker and Jenner. In personal correspondence, Hoey made it clear that he could never vote against the admission of Graham to the Senate. He would, in fact, welcome Graham. And he continually ridiculed the issue of Graham's potential disloyalty, although he hoped Graham would become more cautious in authorizing the use of his name in the service of social causes.[60]

Hoey's response on the Senate floor was joined by even more indignant retorts from other senators. Wayne Morse, the maverick Republican from Oregon, had served with Graham on the War Labor Board during World War II. Breathing fire, he told his Senate colleagues that Graham would rank "exceedingly high" on any list of the twenty-five greatest living Americans. Graham "was one of the most Christ-like men" he had ever met, Morse proclaimed.[61] Claude Pepper likewise stood up for Graham, complaining that Graham had no opportunity to defend himself on the Senate floor. The matter rested following Connecticut Democrat and Atomic Energy Commission member Brian McMahon's statement that he had seen Graham's file and that there was no evidence that Graham was anything but a fine, decent man. "Some organizations he belongs to—I wouldn't belong to: maybe I belong to a couple he wouldn't." Iowa Republican Bourke Hickenlooper affirmed McMahon's conclusion. Graham's file led to no suggestion of disloyalty.[62]

The issues swirling around Graham's appointment were not new, of course. Nor were all of Graham's critics animated by the same concerns. The basest charge, that he had been a Communist party member, was never raised by a serious critic. Some critics, such as the members of the Security Board of the Atomic Energy Commission, had believed Graham's judgment untrustworthy, making him a possible security risk. Others simply believed that while no security question was at issue, Graham had shown a consistent pattern of foolish associations that should disqualify him for high office. And, of course, these questions of loyalty and judgment were related to substantive public policy questions. His strongest critics were always those who opposed his positions on race, labor, foreign policy, health care, and other matters.

These attacks struck Graham as ridiculous and unbelievable. As was his custom, he offered only a general rejoinder. The primary task of defending Graham was left to his friends and supporters, who had never failed to come to his defense.[63] He did make one clear public statement in his own behalf—the only recorded response he ever gave, publicly or privately, on the specific question of working with Communists in the 1930s. He finally seemed to understand the magnitude of the problem in a rather rueful reply to a *Newsweek* reporter's blunt questioning concerning his previous associations: "I was not asking any questions about other persons' economic and political views, I guess. When the line coincided with what I regarded as the American line, I worked with them. When their line was against the American line, I opposed the line." When asked if he still had that approach in promoting liberal causes, the answer was emphatic: "No! I have learned that you can't work with Communists."[64] This was as close as Graham ever came to admitting his critics' charge that some of his former associations might have been ill-advised. And clearly he had changed his mind about people with whom he could work. He had become by 1950 an anti-Communist or Americans for Democratic Action liberal.

Now Graham readied himself for the challenges facing a new U.S. senator and prepared to depart for Washington. On March 26, the University of North Carolina trustees' executive committee had accepted Graham's resignation "with regret."[65] The following day, the Grahams had their last Sunday evening "open house" for students and residents of Chapel Hill, by then a long tradition. Fifteen hundred students, faculty and townspeople meandered through the president's home to bid the Grahams farewell. In his valedictory to them, Graham again remarked that accepting the Senate appointment had been his most difficult decision: "This

place, this institution and you people have been such a deep and happy part of my life for more than forty years. But we will be back. We can never really leave this place." The university band then played "Hark the Sound," the alma mater, and Graham joined in the singing. "We hate to see him go," commented a philosophy professor. "But then, we feel he is the best contribution that we can make to a world that needs him badly."[66] His Chapel Hill days behind him, his uncertain political future beckoning, Graham began his public career with a full and frank press interview in which he announced clear and specific positions on nearly every controversial issue of the day. "In general," Graham acknowledged his support of the Truman administration and his determination to continue that support "as specific measures come up in the light of what is most possible and effective at any given time." He did caution reporters that his support for Truman was not unequivocal; on individual proposals, he would need a period of study in order to fashion effective policies.

Nonetheless, he talked at length on various subjects. Reminding his questioners that he had been a member of the President's Committee on Civil Rights, he pointed out that he had been the author of the minority position presented in the committee's report. Graham's position opposed federal force to implement immediate change in the South's racial segregation. Only education and religion could create permanent change in race relations, Graham had argued. Describing himself as a gradualist, Graham did favor the adoption of specific proposals "as fast as the hearts and minds of the people are prepared to carry them out": full equality of suffrage, in both general elections and primaries, local, state, and federal cooperation against lynching; removal of the poll tax as a prerequisite for voting; a decent minimum wage and more job opportunities; and federal aid to education without federal control in order to provide a more uniform standard of education nationwide. "And we must also bear in mind the importance of obedience to the decisions of the Supreme Court" on such matters as suffrage, education, and interstate travel, he added.

On foreign policy matters, Graham expressed his strong support for the Marshall Plan, and, in a general way, for the North Atlantic Treaty, then under congressional discussion. And while admitting that the nation had to be economically and militarily strong, Graham felt that the country had to rely "more on democratic morale and moral idealism for leadership in this critical time" as its defense against aggression.

Asked his attitude toward the Taft-Hartley Act and proposals to repeal it, Graham temporized. "I am for preservation of the freedom and rights

of self-organization of people and their equality in our economic structure," an ambiguous reply for one identified so strongly as a prolabor
figure.[67]

Thus, in his first press conference, given before he had even sworn his
Senate oath, Graham had revealed in detail most of the policy positions
he would advance. While describing himself as a gradualist in matters of
race, he expressed views on the subject clearly at variance with a majority
of his constituency. Not only did he argue for an end to the poll tax (an
issue in much of the South in 1950 but not in North Carolina) and an
end to suffrage discrimination, he also proposed an ultimate end to
segregation, as fast as white southerners would accept it, without federal
force. Declaring himself a strong Truman man, he favored most Fair Deal
policies in education and economic matters, policy positions that had
only lukewarm Tar Heel support at best—and much active opposition.
These policy differences between Graham and his constituency, however,
could not mask the conviction that Graham, respected for his Christian
morality and service to the state, was more popular with the average
citizen than anyone else in North Carolina.[68]

With Senator Hoey at his side, Graham entered the Senate chamber on
March 29, 1950, to take his senatorial oath. Hoey and Graham were a
study in contrasts. Journalist Carroll Kilpatrick described the newest
senator as "a political evangelist with a southern accent" and a Presbyterian determination. "He is a tiny little fellow, mouse-like rather than
belligerent. His clothes never seem to fit very well. He looks more like a
weary file clerk than a university president or a United States Senator."
Kilpatrick knew the Senate would witness a marvelous spectacle when
Hoey escorted Graham to the rostrum. "Hoey is the Senate's last-remain-
ing swallow-tail coat man. He is tall . . . has long wavy hair, now snow-
white and he always wears a red carnation. He tries his best to look like a
roman."[69]

Fearing that he might slight someone inadvertently, Graham had invited only his wife and their families to the ceremony. Nonetheless, a
large group of his friends had gathered in Washington on their own
initiative, and an estimated five hundred of them nearly filled the Senate
gallery to witness the ceremony. Among those present were Governor
Scott, Jonathan Daniels, and Army Secretary Kenneth C. Royall. At 11:15
A.M., Senator Hoey accompanied Graham down the center aisle to the
rostrum where Vice President Alben W. Barkley administered the oath.
Graham's new Democratic colleagues greeted him jubilantly, especially
administration liberals Hubert H. Humphrey of Minnesota and Estes
Kefauver of Tennessee.[70]

Immediately after the ceremony, Graham announced that he would be a candidate in 1950 to serve the remaining four years of Broughton's term, whereupon Governor Scott pronounced him "a real man of the people" and unbeatable in that forthcoming contest.[71] Perhaps with an eye to the primary, Graham's friends now counseled him to resign immediately from all his directorships and associations in a long list of organizations, including some that remained on the attorney general's subversive list. Such memberships, his friends feared, continued to expose him to political attack and could complicate his upcoming campaign.[72] Graham ignored their advice; he resigned from nothing.

Following a courtesy visit with President Truman on March 31 in which the president expressed full confidence in Graham's abilities,[73] Graham received his committee assignments in early April: post office, civil service, and judiciary.[74] When asked his plans for staffing his Senate offices, Graham remarked that "Senator Broughton's staff has been most helpful and cooperative."[75] Subsequently, Graham retained Broughton's entire staff intact and made no significant staff changes for the balance of his Senate days.[76]

Graham's public statement that he would seek election in 1950 initiated a new round of political speculation in North Carolina. Most commentators now predicted flatly that the appointee would have competition and that his reelection was by no means assured. As Graham's views were more widely aired, wrote Legette Blythe in the Charlotte Observer, conservatives in the state would see to it that Graham would be given a stern test.[77] The Winston-Salem Journal and Sentinel observed that Graham's perennial enemies from his Chapel Hill days would not rest as long as he remained in public life, but the effectiveness of their position would depend on Graham's Senate performance. If he proved by his Senate votes that he was acceptable to the mainstream North Carolina voter, he should live out his years as senator from North Carolina.[78] A U.S. marshal for the Eastern District of North Carolina reenforced this view, writing that if Graham moved with care and caution, he would have no trouble in the primary.[79]

Yet potential candidates were already stirring. Robert Rice "Our Bob" Reynolds, the former U.S. senator, called a press conference to announce that the woods would be full of candidates but that he had no intention of running again,[80] and the once-spurned Fred Royster allowed that he was "seriously considering" a campaign against Graham. Friends of former Senator Umstead hinted that he was still an aspirant, provided "things work out all right," meaning Umstead's decision depended largely on what Graham did and said while in the Senate.[81]

In assessing Graham's prospects, the Greensboro *Record* identified his most serious political liability: his complete lack of elective political experience. "As a practical matter," the *Record* observed, "it usually takes more than statesmanship to win an election." Elective success would require the "know-how" of politics: patronage, fence-building and -mending, and grass roots campaigning, in and out of session—skills Graham had never needed before, and in which he was notoriously deficient. The lack of these skills could cost him dearly, concluded the Greensboro newspaper.[82]

Some observers foresaw not merely a lively election; they believed an epochal political moment was at hand. Few people, the Charlotte *Observer* pointed out, were neutral about Graham. People "are at one extreme or the other—bitter denunciation or fanatical loyalty." The editorial continued: "Maybe Dr. Graham does not realize what he is in for. Heretofore, even his severest critics have respected his position as president of a great university, and have pulled their punches. But, when he entered the political arena, the gloves [came] off . . . anything goes. It will be interesting to see how he acquits himself when he descends from the realm of pure reason and goes at it tooth and claw."[83]

The *Observer*, a constant Graham critic over the years, was not alone in commenting on Graham's changed circumstances and the difficulties they presented. His friends repeated to him similar concerns in private correspondence. Kinston newspaperman H. Galt Braxton wrote Graham that many loyal alumni "simply don't picture you in the rough and tumble of politics which the senatorial campaign will entail."[84] Others worried that the gulf between Graham's policy views and those of his constituency would imperil his political future. Nere Day, an old friend from Jacksonville, North Carolina, was certain that Graham would be denied the Senate nomination if he vigorously backed an early end to segregation and supported a federally mandated Fair Employment Practices Act. "If you can bring yourself to compromise," wrote Day, "by supporting [an end to] the Poll Tax and Anti-Lynch [a federal anti-lynching law] phases of the program, and perhaps take some active part in producing a general compromise scheme to pass those two measures and drop the other two [FEPC and compulsory desegregation], I believe our people will applaud you and return you to the Senate." Forced desegregation, concluded Day, would stir the prejudice and passions of North Carolina voters.

Graham simply could not disregard politics, Day cautioned. Day knew Graham would defend his convictions and principles without any urging, and he believed Graham could be a high-minded and clean politician as well as a successful one. "Many of your friends have the feeling that you have such a martyr-like capacity for punishment that you will joust with a stone-wall or a windmill and have nothing but chivalry for your reward."[85]

"Your [Senate] position is a dual one," counseled J. Allen Austin, another of Graham's legion of friends across the state. "It is primarily representative. It is not alone personal. I think we know North Carolina to be very conservative and strongly southern. . . . If you vote always as you think a majority of the people of the South would want you to vote you will be elected in 1950. With the issues being what they are and your personal sense of duty being what it is, I fear for my friend. Your road is going to be difficult, fraught with conflicting loyalties to your constituency and yourself."[86]

3 · Candidates

"Our Bob," "Big Willis," and the "Fightin' Half-Pint"

Governor Scott's hope that Graham's personal popularity would enable him to avoid a major rival in the 1950 primary would depend in no little measure upon Graham's political acumen: could he display political strength and organizational power early enough to discourage challengers? Within ninety days of his swearing-in, private correspondents were looking to the 1950 primary and warning Graham to make early preparations. Thomas Turner, a Greensboro attorney and Graham partisan, was one of several early exercised over the upcoming contest. On September 12, 1949, he wrote Jonathan Daniels warning that tough opposition would coalesce if Graham ignored his political duties. In a second, more urgent note to Daniels on October 19, Turner gave his fears full cry: "It seems to me that the time has arrived when Frank should awake to the political facts of life." Graham should take steps, counseled Turner, to insure the political support of those who were not yet committed to his candidacy but who, through patronage and the perquisites of office, could be enlisted in Graham's cause.[1]

Daniels was already alert to Turner's concerns. By the summer of 1949, he had created an informal statewide correspondence network seeking counsel on Graham's political future. In August he suggested a meeting to plan the campaign, which would include Charles Tillett, William D. "Billy" Carmichael, Jr., Kemp Battle, and perhaps the governor. The prospect that Graham could be elected without opposition—Daniels's original hope—was fast fading, and he wanted the opinions of informed observers. Daniels, while pleased with Graham's early Senate performance, was aware that Graham had given no thought to political organization.[2]

From Rockingham, Congressman Charles B. Deane agreed with Daniels that an effective organization could be crucial. Graham should create, as soon as possible, a group of people across the state who would champion his cause, with special attention to labor and the black vote.[3] O. Max Gardner, Jr., replied to a Daniels letter that Graham's popularity was increasing every day. He would be elected, wrote Gardner, if he exposed himself to large numbers of voters and balanced the view of many North Carolinians that he was "too leftist," a racial radical, too strongly prolabor, and careless in his support of various "front organizations."[4] In short, Graham must get out, press the flesh, and disclaim his liberal reputation.

Some of Daniels's correspondents were more optimistic. They foresaw little political difficulty for Graham. Winston-Salem *Journal* editor Santford Martin suggested to Daniels that Graham's potential opponents were in disarray, scarcely eager to undertake the strenuous effort required to unseat Graham since the possibility of success was too remote.[5] Asheville *Citizen* editor D. Hiden Ramsey, like his Winston-Salem colleague, foresaw no important challenge to Graham.[6] *The State* agreed with Ramsey and Martin in a September 1949 editorial: "With the backing of the Scott Administration, the farm people, organized labor and the Negro vote, plus the liberals and the ultra-liberals, who is there to offer effective resistance?"[7]

Further, should opposition emerge, who would lead it? R. Mayne Albright, Raleigh attorney, Graham partisan, and third-place finisher in the 1948 gubernatorial primary, identified former Senator William B. Umstead as Graham's most likely opponent. He would offer a striking contrast to Graham in political philosophy. The Graham people, cautioned Albright, should function on the assumption that Umstead would run.[8] Indeed, Umstead's candidacy seemed to many observers a certainty, as Umstead himself confirmed in late September, when he admitted publicly that he was considering a challenge to Graham.[9] It was also clear that "Our Bob" Reynolds was primed to run for something. Having "retired" from the Senate in 1944 rather than face certain defeat, Reynolds had been out of public view for five years, a situation he found intolerable. Exulting in the attention his possible candidacy was attracting, Reynolds played the role of reluctant aspirant to the hilt: "I'll tell you frankly and honestly, and every man, even a politician, ought to be honest, I'm getting a great deal of encouragement to run. And I might add," he told the Charlotte *Observer*, "that I am encouraging myself to enter the race."[10] Yet most observers expected Reynolds to oppose Hoey.[11]

Journalist Wade Lucas, writing in the Charlotte *Observer* in late September, noted that interest in the forthcoming primary rivaled the 1928 Smith-Hoover frenzy. Graham's potential opposition would be encouraged, Lucas thought, because Graham would not carry the full support of the Scott forces. His reputation as a radical might not play too well down on the farm. To offset that difficulty, Lucas believed the Scott people would run a candidate against Hoey to divide the conservative forces now fixing their attention on Graham.[12]

Meanwhile, Graham, in mid-September, set out across the state on a speaking tour that had all the earmarks of a campaign trip. The tour's highlight was to be Graham's appearance before the state's Young Democratic Club (YDC) convention in New Bern. But from the time the keynote speaker invoked Graham's name—and struck no response at all from the audience—until Graham, in his speech, depicted North Carolina as a new frontier in the South and pledged himself to continue to fight for the rights of minorities, it became increasingly clear that Graham's popularity in his own party might have been overstated. And when former Senator Umstead happened to appear later at the same meeting, the conventioneers greeted him with jubilation. To Charlotte *Observer* reporter Lucas, this scene could only mean that Umstead was poised to take on Graham,[13] a view that High Point's "Battlin' Bob" Thompson eagerly endorsed in a subsequent radio broadcast.[14]

Graham's YDC appearance troubled no one more than his friend and political ally Jonathan Daniels. Daniels wrote Graham's administrative assistant, John D. McConnell, telling him that Graham was so modest that he would have to be pushed hard to campaign. Graham needed his picture in the papers, especially on farm matters, and Daniels implored McConnell to funnel him the information he desired. "I don't know whether I am speaking now as a political friend or a newspaper editor, but we do want to have stuff on Frank as often as possible."[15] It was obvious that Daniels would do everything in his power to promote Graham's candidacy in the Raleigh *News and Observer*.

Already Graham had the assistance of organized labor. In August 1949, the Congress of Industrial Organizations' Political Action Committee had assigned David S. Burgess as a full-time political operative in North and South Carolina.[16] Burgess's task was to instruct union members on political issues, to increase voter registration among CIO members, and to promote the election of liberal candidates to public office.[17] In November 1949, Burgess met in Charlotte with Kelly M. Alexander, Jr., state head of the National Association for the Advancement of Colored People (NAACP), who agreed to work with the CIO in its campaign to elect liberals.[18] Thus, as early as October 1949, Burgess was working assiduously to get black and labor support for Graham.

In their effort to fashion an overall strategy for the spring and fall 1950 elections, CIO leaders also conferred with Governor Scott in October 1949. They wanted an opponent for Senator Hoey, whom they considered hostile to labor interests. Scott aired his several objections to fielding a candidate against the popular Hoey but was impressed by labor's argument that forces favoring Graham would suffer if Hoey ran unopposed.[19] In discussing their strategy with Scott, the CIO leaders pointed

out two possible results: retiring Hoey if possible and forcing conservatives to split their resources. Certainly Scott, Daniels, and labor had no
love for Hoey and would prefer to see him out of office.[20]

At the same time, Wade Lucas reported in the Charlotte *Observer* that
William B. Umstead had been approached with an offer not to challenge
Graham in 1950 in return for the 1952 gubernatorial nomination complete with liberal blessings.[21] In fact, one source told Lucas that the
pressure being applied to Umstead was intense,[22] even though Governor
Scott privately denied his participation in any such deal.[23] State Commissioner of Paroles T. C. Johnson confirmed that Scott had made no
such agreement to support Umstead for governor in 1952. Scott had
already expressed his preference for Capus Waynick, Johnson wrote the
Nicaraguan ambassador.[24]

Nonetheless, Jonathan Daniels and Graham's lifelong friend Charles
Tillett of Charlotte were trying hard to dissuade Umstead, even if they
were not offering a hard-and-fast deal.[25] They knew that many of William B. Umstead's closest counselors, including his brother John, believed that such a race would be a two-fold mistake. The campaign would
be so acrimonious that it would permanently sully Umstead's reputation
and threaten his political career. In addition, Umstead's chance for victory was too small. But Daniels fretted that should Umstead get any
substantial indication of support, he would run anyway.[26] Publicly, in an
attempt to discourage an Umstead candidacy, Daniels offered the opinion in December 1949 that Graham was unbeatable.[27]

From the American embassy in Nicaragua, Capus Waynick watched
this shadow dance as closely as the mail service would allow. He too
believed Umstead an unlikely candidate. Umstead's personal style was
too cautious, Waynick wrote T. C. Johnson, and the campaign would be
more fractious than Umstead would want. Graham was in no great
danger, Waynick concluded, provided his campaign were managed
properly.[28] Umstead himself reported, however, that he had more people
urging him to run than advising against it, although as of December 8, he
remained undecided.[29]

Anticipating opposition from Umstead, Graham's friends were urging
him to organize his campaign. Charles Tillett, whose wife Gladys was a
member of the Democratic National Committee, had combined with
Daniels, also a Democratic National Committee member, to persuade
Graham to set up his organization and begin addressing likely campaign
issues. As early as March 1949, Charles Tillett had written Graham
seeking clarification of Graham's memberships in organizations listed by
the U.S. attorney general as subversive. Tillett cautioned Graham about

joining any new organizations and advised him to reduce his memberships to two: the Presbyterian church and the Democratic party. Graham
should make certain to remove his name from the letterhead of the
Southern Conference for Human Welfare (which was now defunct) and
any other opinion organization he sponsored. He should seek the advice
of Hoey on Senate matters, Tillett wrote, and make a speech about the
contribution of capitalism to modern development and overall material
prosperity.[30] Graham paid no heed to this advice.

The Tilletts helped organize several speeches for Graham in North
Carolina. At their instigation, Graham spoke to the Men's Club of the
Myers Park Presbyterian Church and the Charlotte chapter of the Ameri-
can Association of University Women.[31] Graham also spoke in Lexing-
ton, where he praised Scott's rural electrification program and called the
Truman administration's farm price system fair, stable, and sound.[32]
Gladys Tillett and her daughter, Gladys Tillett Coddington, compiled
a list of statewide Graham supporters,[33] and Jonathan Daniels wrote
Gladys Tillett that he had continually urged Graham to appoint a campaign manager, but Graham had not acted.[34]

Eleanor Roosevelt was also concerned with Graham's chances for
election in 1950 and wrote Daniels to offer assistance.[35] In Daniels's
reply, he expressed the hope that Graham would have no significant
opposition. Daniels explained that while Graham was a wonderful natural politician, he was "a little innocent and naive in matters of political
organization." Daniels believed that the crucial danger facing Graham in
an election campaign was Truman's civil rights program. Graham's support of Truman's legislation would antagonize large numbers of people.
Daniels feared that the only possible way "they could defeat Frank, would
be in a horrible 'nigger-communist' campaign." Voters would be too
intelligent to let such a campaign succeed, Daniels wrote, but if such a
campaign were carried out there would be some dreadful months in the
state.[36]

The growing concern for Graham's apparent disinterest in campaign
organization soon reached the Scott administration. At a news conference in mid-December, Governor Scott declared his disagreement with
Jonathan Daniels's public assessment that Graham was unbeatable. "If I
were going to run," Scott told reporters, "I would certainly anticipate . . .
opposition, and would plan my campaign accordingly. No man exists on
earth who can't be beaten." Moreover, Scott remarked, if Graham did
have opposition, and a "smear" campaign ensued, Scott himself would
campaign actively for Graham.[37]

The Charlotte *Observer* interpreted Scott's statement as a friendly warning, not only to Senator Graham, but to his friends and supporters. With his own prestige and political hopes linked to Graham's Senate career, and as a sincere Graham admirer, Scott feared defeat unless Graham immediately began to plan a coordinated campaign.[38] To encourage such an effort, Scott had invited a group of influential Graham supporters to the governor's mansion in early December, primarily to discuss ways the Scott administration could aid Graham. One of those present, State Commissioner of Paroles T. C. Johnson, was shocked at the political naïveté the meeting revealed and tried to convince those present that Graham could have serious political problems.[39]

Already it was clear to some Graham friends that North Carolina farmers—Scott's major political strength—would not be Graham enthusiasts simply because Scott had appointed him. Farmers had gotten no action on specific farm problems except a promise to study those problems, and they feared and distrusted Graham's liberalism. In a similar vein, Thomas J. Pearsall and Kemp Battle, Rocky Mount attorneys, had urged Graham not to rely too heavily on labor support, in part because labor simply could not deliver a large vote in North Carolina. It was better, they counseled, to solicit more conservative groups, among them the state's farmers, who were much more numerous.[40]

Despite all the pleas from his friends, Graham still made no serious effort to organize his election campaign. He told CIO political worker Dave Burgess in a December 21 meeting that he understood that North Carolina was a basically conservative state and that he fully expected Umstead to take him on.[41] Yet he had not yet bothered to choose a campaign manager, plan strategy, or set up a campaign headquarters for the May 1950 primary, barely six months away. Nor had he given any thought to how much a Senate campaign would cost, or how the money to finance it would be raised. Recalled assistant campaign manager Kathryn N. Folger, Graham simply thought that if North Carolina voters wanted him in the Senate, they would march into polling booths on primary day and mark their ballots for him. If left up to Frank Graham, Folger observed, he probably would never have done anything to organize his campaign.[42] Graham believed in an open primary, Raleigh lawyer R. Mayne Albright remembered, and he did not want to discourage potential opponents. Graham remained unaware of the practical tasks required to construct a campaign organization.[43]

Eventually friends and supporters of Graham would assume the essential organizational tasks, and they would have to proceed to their duties almost in disregard of Graham's idea of what his campaign would need. Graham's friends, of course, were not about to abandon their candidate or let the campaign languish. Scott, Daniels, and others simply took it over, in precisely the same manner that they had managed the appointment. On January 7, 1950, Senator Graham finally announced that William W. Staton, a young Sanford attorney, would set up a campaign headquarters shortly in Raleigh. The choice of Staton was largely credited by the press to YDC President Terry Sanford, acting on instructions from Governor Scott. Sanford denied the report, insisting that the YDC would be completely neutral in the forthcoming primary.[44] At the same time, Allard Lowenstein, a recent Chapel Hill graduate and Graham apostle, joined Graham's Senate staff, primarily to do research on campaign issues.[45] Holt McPherson, editor of the Shelby *Daily Star*, was asked to become publicity director, an offer he declined.[46] Despite this belated flurry of activity, there was still no campaign manager or campaign headquarters by the end of January.

As the fledgling campaign was being shaped in early January, the first in a long sequence of improbable events occurred. Former Senator William B. Umstead, recuperating from December throat surgery, announced on January 6 that he would not oppose Graham, despite "an overwhelming promise of support from around the state." Senator Graham quickly responded to Umstead's announcement: "I am glad [he] will not run but regret very much his ill health. He would be a formidable opponent."[47] Umstead's withdrawal, of course, arched many eyebrows, for it suggested at first glance that Scott and Daniels had made the rumored deal with Umstead: no opposition to Graham in 1950 in exchange for full support for Umstead to succeed Scott as governor in 1952.[48] No documentary evidence supports such a claim, but Scott and Daniels did try everything they could short of a deal to coax Umstead out of the race.

Umstead's withdrawal was undeniably a major boost for Graham. The former senator was Graham's most threatening potential challenger. Nonetheless, he chose not to run, as he explained in letters to Hoey and former Governor R. Gregg Cherry, in part for legitimate health reasons. His surgery—to remove a small tumor in his throat—had resulted from a physical examination undertaken in anticipation of the race against Graham, and his recovery had been slower than expected. His physicians advised against the campaign, and Umstead, much disappointed, took their advice. Doubtless, too, Umstead's brother John, a close Graham friend, had argued against the contest.[49] With Umstead removed, Graham and his advisers now had reason to anticipate a primary campaign with only minimal opposition.[50] There might be some sort of race, the Raleigh *News and Observer* wrote, but the epochal Graham-Umstead contest would likely yield to a skirmish between Graham and some lightweight. That Graham would continue in office without the diversion of a difficult primary struggle now seemed a sure thing to most observers.[51]

But Governor Scott was having none of it. When asked at a subsequent press conference if Graham were a safe bet for nomination, the governor replied: "If it was me, I'd run like I was being shot at."[52] Scott had also told labor groups that Graham was the finest liberal to be found anywhere and "you folks will now have to back him up."[53]

Scott's warnings, however, still did not rouse Graham. As Scott and Daniels actively solicited support for Graham, the senator, with no opposition in sight, continued to postpone picking a campaign manager and opening a state headquarters. Speculation recommenced. Who would run against Graham? Fred Royster, perhaps, or maybe Congressman Graham Barden or former Congressman Bayard Clark. Graham would beat any of them, most analysts believed. Other names surfaced in the days ahead, among them Judge Henry L. Stevens of Warsaw, U.S. Comptroller General Lindsay Warren,[54] and State Agriculture Commissioner L. Y. "Stag" Ballentine, the best known of these three to North Carolina voters.[55]

Two minor candidates were also flirting with candidacy, Manley R. Dunaway, a Charlotte realtor (who subsequently withdrew without ever paying a filing fee, grumbling that the power of the Scott machine made Graham invincible),[56] and perennial candidate Olla Ray Boyd, pig breeder extraordinaire and the pride of Pinetown, North Carolina. Olla Ray Boyd had run for governor twice, in 1944 and 1948, amassing about two thousand votes each time. (Boyd at 6'4" and 277 pounds could rightly claim to be the "biggest hog breeder in the state.")[57] A political oddity he certainly was, but a serious candidate he would never be. But as long as Graham had no serious rivals, Boyd's antics could provide the political campaign with limited comic relief.

Boyd announced his candidacy for the Senate on January 9, 1950, as he simultaneously proclaimed his intention to seek the presidency of the United States in 1968. Shortly thereafter, to a throng of thirty-eight gathered in the cavernous 850-seat high school auditorium in Washington, North Carolina, Boyd detailed the issues he would stress in his campaign. If elected, he would support bullet-proof vests for combat troops; federal support for hogs, goats, cattle, and sheep; and "legal lynching" as the only effective method of controlling crime.[58] The heavyset hog dealer paid his filing fee March 16 in Raleigh—in anonymity—although he had wired the State Board of Elections in advance of his

Olla Ray Boyd (right), the political perennial from Pinetown, could persuade
only 5,900 Tar Heel voters to support him in the Senate race. In the early
going, he provided the campaign with limited comic relief. (North Carolina
Department of Archives and History, Raleigh)

impending arrival. Even a call by the candidate himself to the offices of the Raleigh *News and Observer* could produce neither a reporter nor a photographer, and Boyd returned to Pinetown, his candidacy unremarked.[59]

In May 1950, Boyd embarked on an uncharacteristic flurry of campaigning and planned to climax his political quest with a speech in Asheville. Accompanied by his new wife, Boyd showed up at the Buncombe County courthouse in Asheville but was met by only a single reporter. He declared the speech "rained out" and returned to Pinetown.

Ten days prior to the primary, Boyd turned in his preliminary campaign expenditure estimate, as the election statutes required. He claimed to have spent $135: $125 for the filing fee plus $10 for rental of the school auditorium. The Asheville *Citizen* used the occasion to comment that Boyd's financial report was altogether commendable. It was full and complete, an unheard-of practice in state politics. North Carolina law in 1950 limited each candidate's expenses in the first Senate primary to a maximum of $12,000. In keeping with the law, no candidate in memory had reported more, just as no serious candidate in recent years had spent less than eight to ten times the legal limit. "Candidate Boyd," observed the *Citizen*, "is expected to run fourth in a field of four but this is neither prediction nor endorsement. Pigs, as Ellis Parham Butler said, is pigs. And maybe politics is politics, and fun, at $135. Olla has announced himself for President in 1968, by which time perhaps the public may tire of pushy politicking and the lightning could strike Pinetown."[60]

Olla Ray Boyd, of course, was never a concern for Senator Graham. But as candidate Boyd cavorted, Senator Graham had to deal with a difficult and politically threatening civil rights issue: the proposal from the Truman White House to establish a federal Fair Employment Practices Commission (FEPC). The proposal would empower a federal commission to mediate disputes in which employees claimed discriminatory treatment attributable to racial, ethnic, or religious prejudice. The commission, should conciliation fail, would have enforcement powers.[61]

Graham, since his membership on the Truman Committee on Civil Rights, had always favored the concept of a federal FEPC but opposed granting it compulsory powers. He continued to stress federal legislation to outlaw the poll tax and to make lynching a federal crime as an alternative to a Senate fight over FEPC.[62]

Graham's position, consistently argued, thrust him into the center of a political gridlock. By November 1949, the NAACP, organized labor, and other liberal groups were pushing mightily for passage of an FEPC bill in the 1950 congressional session,[63] and with equal resolve, southern politicians were determined to turn them back. Graham's view on the subject therefore pleased neither side. His opposition to compulsory powers angered liberals while his support in principle for FEPC upset most southern whites. In early January, Senators Hoey, Burnett R. Maybank (D.-S.C.), and Olin D. Johnston (D.-S.C.) announced their intention to join a southern filibuster, if necessary, to defeat FEPC,[64] but Graham indicated that while he opposed the bill, he would not participate in a filibuster against it.[65] He did not intend to be merely a rubber stamp for Truman's Fair Deal legislation, Graham stated. When asked to speculate on Truman's likely response to his position on FEPC, the senator replied, "I don't think he is going to like it."[66]

As the controversy progressed, many political analysts grasped that Graham's most threatening moment on the issue would come on the question of cloture a Senate vote to limit debate, which would, if passed, terminate the southern filibuster, resulting in victory for FEPC proponents. Passage of cloture would require a two-thirds majority and would put Graham in a political quandary. Graham's Senate colleague, Clyde Hoey, who termed FEPC "unfair and vicious," was afraid that if brought to a vote, the bill would pass the Senate. Hoey had allied himself with seventeen other southern senators determined to prevent any such vote.[67]

Graham thus found himself in the company of Senators Estes Kefauver of Tennessee and Claude Pepper of Florida, the three musketeers, as it were, of southern liberalism. And when the eighteen southern senators committed to a filibuster against FEPC met in mid-February for a strategy session, they excluded the three southern nonparticipants, publicly isolating them even further from their southern colleagues.[68]

As the maneuvering over FEPC continued, the administration's forces, aware of the undying opposition of key senators, were determined to push a Senate bill that had little chance of passage. Meanwhile, the House passed an FEPC bill that removed the controversial enforcement provision. In response, the Truman White House pressed on in the Senate, undeterred by the House action, hoping to embarrass Republican senators who were up for reelection in 1950 and would oppose the Senate version of the FEPC bill.[69]

Such a strategy was not without risk for the Truman forces, and for the president as well. By pushing an unpopular bill with little chance of passage, the administration forced all senators, Democrats as well as Republicans, to declare themselves. The result was a White House ambush of Senate Democratic liberals, as FEPC became a substantive issue in the 1950 elections and in Graham's early Senate maneuverings. One constituent, J. R. Cherry, reminded Graham that his FEPC stance was being watched closely by voters back home. If Graham voted "yea" on cloture, or even if he continued to isolate himself from the majority of southern senators by giving less than wholehearted support to efforts to kill FEPC, there would be damaging repercussions in North Carolina.[70]

In January 1950, however, the FEPC issue did not appear to menace Graham—if only because stout opposition to his election seemed improbable. It even seemed to some observers that Hoey and Graham's common opposition to an FEPC with enforcement authority signaled a consensus between them on immediate civil rights issues, despite their differences in parliamentary strategy.[71] Some even thought that Graham's views were morally defensible and politically astute and that he had come out of the controversy in a stronger position than Hoey.[72]

Thus the January forecast was that neither Graham nor Hoey faced career-threatening storms. The most menacing cloud in Hoey's sky was the beaming countenance of Bob Reynolds, Hoey's most likely opponent. Few people, however, expected Reynolds to be more than a nuisance should he take on North Carolina's senior senator. Indeed, the lack of a credible opponent for Hoey was a condition still troubling to organized labor. In contrast, many of Graham's associates remained convinced that his campaign would be better served if they did not promote opposition to Hoey, on the theory that the reactionaries, anticipating a massive Hoey victory, would remain quiescent and not fight against Graham. But Dave Burgess, the CIO political factotum, continued to stress that the decision not to oppose Hoey was a tactical mistake. It suggested to voters that the Scott-Daniels forces lacked the strength—and perhaps the courage—to challenge Hoey. Moreover, if Hoey ran unopposed, the conservative moneyed interests would pour all their resources into the campaign to defeat Graham.

Graham therefore remained vulnerable to a bare-knuckle brawl, generously financed, that could turn him out of office. A better plan, Burgess argued to all who would listen, would be to test Hoey, dilute the strength of the inevitable challenge to Graham, and force the conservatives to fight on two fronts. If labor, black voters, farmers, and educators were given the opportunity to vote not only for Graham but against Hoey in the same primary, Burgess insisted, they would register in much greater numbers.[73]

Burgess, of course, believed that the decision to leave Hoey unchallenged was part of Scott and Daniels's complicated plan to pressure Umstead not to run against Graham in 1950. In short, the Scott faction would not oppose Umstead for governor in 1952, while the conservatives would be neutral in Graham's upcoming race and the Scott minions would leave Hoey alone in 1950. But Burgess was mistaken because the deal was never consummated. As Capus Waynick recalled, Governor Scott *had* urged Waynick to oppose Hoey. Scott had even sent Waynick to talk to President Truman, who wanted to see Waynick run but told him that direct White House support for an effort to ground Senator Hoey would blow up in Waynick's face. If Waynick ran, Truman counseled, he would have to run on his own.

As Waynick pondered Truman's words, who should call on him but Hoey himself. Waynick recalled the conversation. "Capus, I want to go back to the Senate," said Hoey. "I'd hate to run against you, and I know you are considering it." Hoey then observed that Waynick, not Graham, should have been appointed to succeed Broughton. Hoey told Waynick that he had a bad heart, and he doubted he would survive a second term. Should he die in office, and should Scott still be governor (Scott would have two more years in office after the 1950 primary), Waynick would certainly be Scott's choice to succeed the late Senator Hoey. Finally, the clincher: "If you don't run, I can and will help Frank Graham."[74]

While Waynick's account is not corroborated, events confirm it. On February 2, 1950, Waynick called a press conference and announced his disinclination to challenge Hoey. (Hoey claimed that Waynick withdrew because he could not win.) Waynick also made clear his intention to support Graham in his campaign.[75]

The obvious winner in these purported dealings was, of course, Clyde Hoey. He had shed his most difficult potential opponent and could anticipate an uncomplicated reelection effort, even if Bob Reynolds took him on—all for a promise to give Frank Graham clandestine assistance of an undisclosed nature. As a consequence, Hoey cruised to renomination, Graham's political opposition now was free to coalesce in exclusive opposition to Graham, and Waynick was left to limp back to Managua to await Hoey's fatal seizure (which came in 1954, two years too late to help Waynick since Umstead was in the governor's mansion).

Roughly three weeks prior to Waynick's decision not to run, Graham's associates had finally concluded that they must organize the campaign, even though Graham remained indifferent and no serious opposition existed. Organization, at the least, would be a sound prophylactic measure. And so, with four months remaining before the primary, the Graham steamroller lurched forward. Utilizing a list of Broughton county campaign managers sent her in January 1949 by Broughton's 1948 campaign manager, Clinton attorney Jefferson Deems Johnson, Jr., Gladys Tillett sent letters statewide encouraging supporters to rally to Graham's standard. She received encouraging responses from each of the state's one hundred counties.[76]

As part of a national effort, Jonathan Daniels persuaded a cooperative Drew Pearson to make Graham a featured subject of his "Washington Merry-Go-Round" column. Graham, Pearson wrote, was wonderful and "Christ-like" (quoting Senator Wayne Morse). Pearson quoted Senator Charles Tobey as saying that Graham's Senate speech on the North Atlantic Treaty—his maiden effort—had been "the greatest I have heard in the Senate." Graham, Pearson observed, was "as friendly and disarming as a puppy" and possessed a "lively twinkle in his dark eyes." Pearson, who Harry Truman had once claimed to be descended from canines, named Graham as one of the most conscientious men in Washington—a modest, unassuming person with great affection for people.[77] This column led W. T. "Tom" Bost, a Graham champion, to conclude in the Greensboro *Daily News* that Pearson's endorsement all but sealed Graham's election.[78]

Within the state, Graham's friends began to speak publicly of his virtues. Following Graham's speech to the Pinehurst Kiwanis Club, novelist Struthers Burt praised him to the Southern Pines *Pilot* as a man of "complete honesty, utmost integrity, excellent knowledge and learning, quiet brilliance, far vision and implacable courage who retained his modesty and human touch."[79]

The governor, too, in mid-January made it clear that he had decided to support Graham in a very public fashion. Speaking to a meeting of labor union representatives in Asheville, Scott once again urged them to work diligently to send liberal-thinking legislators to Washington, beginning with Senator Graham. He again reminded them: "You haven't got a better liberal in America than the Senator you've got. Don't slip up in the election."[80]

Simultaneous with his charge to labor, Scott formally announced that no state employee should instruct subordinates to support Graham. Nor should state-owned vehicles be used for the transportation of voters to the polls. Such statements were intended to suggest a fair and open election, supporting the argument that Graham was the integrity candidate. Tom Bost, who had observed state politics since the Aycock administration, reminded his readers that Scott's admonitions might sound slightly hypocritical. The governor was an active participant in the Graham campaign, his preference was clear, and certainly state employees could expect no punishment if they worked on state time for Graham. Graham would consider such an effort a great wrong, Bost observed, and would protest much more quickly if state workers labored in his behalf than if they worked against him. But Scott was hardly a political novice and doubtless would use every lever in his political gearbox to give Graham a push.[81] Perhaps Bost knew that a major component of the

Graham effort, unbeknownst to the candidate, would continue to be the State Highway and Public Works Commission, whose district supervisors were already hard at work putting together a Graham organization at the county level. Bost certainly knew, as did everyone in the state who read a newspaper, that one of Scott's first acts as governor had been to remove all the sitting commissioners (save one) and replace them with people supportive of his administration.

In addition to labor and Governor Scott, a major source of strength for Graham would likely be the state's black voters. Blacks correctly identified Graham as their best friend in the state. They had been jubilant at his appointment, and black leaders were now organizing to help the Graham campaign. At a meeting of the executive committee of the North Carolina chapter of the NAACP, the organization proposed to register 250,000 black voters during 1950.[82] While the NAACP did not by tradition endorse candidates, its efforts to increase black registration would surely be of benefit to Graham.

Graham's prospects, hopeful though they were, were scarcely of sufficient volume to hush a continuing grumble from the state's Democratic conservatives. William B. Umstead's withdrawal had clearly disoriented Graham's opponents, but the search for a formidable opponent—initiated after Umstead retired—was now underway in earnest. Moreover, the lack of a candidate in hand did nothing to discourage Graham's critics from continuing to fulminate against him. Typical was a January editorial in the High Point *Enterprise*. The campaign to come, the editorial predicted, would focus on Frank Graham's life as a social activist. Referring to Graham as North Carolina's "pink-tinted Senator," the paper suggested that the key issues in the primary, regardless of who opposed the senator, would be Graham's radicalism, his fronting for Communist organizations, and his thinly disguised enthusiasm for socialism. Graham's devotees were loudly insisting that no "mud" be thrown in the campaign, but the *Enterprise* argued that Graham's past and continuing political associations were fair game. Certainly, the editorial suggested, Graham's supporters would not object to the campaign use of a candidate's past if that candidate had been committed several times to an insane asylum. Such a candidate, however well intentioned, could hardly complain if his opponents continually reminded voters that he had a screw loose.[83]

The *Enterprise* clearly did not have Bob Reynolds in mind in its discussion of lunatic candidates. Reynolds, in his storied career, had been called many names, but no one had ever thought him crazy. He pushed Reynolds watchers to the limits of credulity, however, when he announced on January 31, 1950, that he would accept the challenge and take on not Clyde Hoey but Frank Graham.

"Our Bob" Reynolds (middle) searches for the political magic that had brought
him two earlier Senate terms. He entered the race in January 1950, but his
campaign fizzled. He made only a halfhearted effort once he realized his fate.
(North Carolina Department of Archives and History, Raleigh)

Reynolds had been a senator for two terms, from 1933 to 1945. He
had won the post in the trough of the Great Depression, when he
traveled the state in a broken-down jalopy proclaiming himself the poor
man's candidate. He had ridiculed the wealth of his opponent, Senator
Cameron Morrison, accusing him of eating "Red Russian fish eggs" in
Washington's Mayflower Hotel and of living a life of privilege and ease in
the nation's capital. In contrast, he had presented himself as the protector
of the little guy against the "rapacious greed" of large corporations.
Underestimated by his opponent, Reynolds's showmanship and underdog role caught the mood of many North Carolina voters in 1932, and he
laughed Morrison out of the Senate and into retirement. Easily reelected
in 1938, Reynolds himself "retired" in 1944 rather than face certain
defeat at the hands of Clyde Hoey, in part because Reynolds's hard-line
isolationism in the desperate years prior to Pearl Harbor and American
entry into World War II had made him an embarrassment.[84]

As noted earlier, Reynolds had seemed a likely opponent for Hoey in
1950, and, of course, had done all within his power to encourage such

speculation. When he returned to North Carolina from Washington in 1947, opening an Asheville law office, the Washington *Post* confided to its readers that Reynolds's purpose was to rebuild his political strength and take on Hoey in 1950.[85]

But Reynolds's eye was always on the main chance, and he followed the Graham appointment and resultant political intrigue with a practiced grin. He was as observant as any other Senate aspirant, and he duly noted Umstead's withdrawal from a challenge to Graham. Nor was he blind to Hoey's political strength, and the improbability of unseating the senator from Shelby.

By December 1949, Reynolds, having traveled the state, had decided to run, although against whom he was not sure.[86] Publicly, he continued the charade that he was not yet a committed candidate. In mid-January he told reporters: "I've been so busy lately building myself some fences that I haven't given much thought to what I should do. And I don't mean political fences. I mean cattle fences. And I've been working right along with the boys." He had been urged to run by poor people from all over the state, he said. They were fed up with high taxes and the all-powerful federal establishment. As a states' rights man, Reynolds would defend the poor: "You know," "Our Bob" intoned, "the federal government now takes the rich cream of a man's income, and the state comes along and takes the thin cream, and then the cities and counties get the milk, and, by George, when they're through the poor old taxpayer ain't got a thing left but blue-john." Well, was he running, reporters inquired. He did not know but acknowledged his delight in political campaigns. "They're always good for me. I get around and see the folks and have a fine time. Campaigns suit me just fine."[87]

In fact, Reynolds's campaign was already launched. He had flooded the state with Christmas cards in 1949 depicting his estate near Asheville and bearing the message: "The gate is wide open and the latch string is on the outside."[88] And in late January 1950, he mailed public letters urging an end to world government. Apparently he hoped to update his isolationist views in a way 1950 voters would embrace.[89] The message was, additionally, a signal to all world federalists and Wilsonians, notably Frank Porter Graham, that Reynolds believed he had found an issue.

Few observers were receiving Reynolds's coded messages, however; and Reynolds's announcement, when it came, shocked Graham supporters and political observers alike. It broke the east-west tradition and threatened to turn the race into a political carnival. Nor were conservative opponents of Graham pleased at Reynolds's entry. They thought he could not win, and he was not a conservative. He was simply an opportunist and a showman, "filled with the hollow ring of the phoney he is," as journalist Holt McPherson phrased it.[90]

Nonetheless, Reynolds's decision to oppose Graham was a calculated choice. Had he opposed Hoey, he would have been "running against Hoey and talking against Graham." Many people in North Carolina rejected Graham's views, reasoned Reynolds, while Hoey's views were embraced widely. Hoey and Reynolds were much closer in their political philosophies, while Graham stood for "many things that are foreign to my thinking and are not in keeping with the voters of North Carolina."[91] In his own mind, Reynolds stood a better chance of defeating the controversial Graham, whose political strength was untested, than Hoey, who was conservative, experienced, and popular.[92] Confided Reynolds to his law partner in vintage Reynoldsese, "I could never defeat Hoey. I can't beat a man who goes around the state with a Bible in one hand and his pecker in the other."[93]

Couched in his unique blend of states' rights democracy, nativism, and governmental largesse, Reynolds's campaign platform proposed limiting federal power; permitting each state to treat its own civil rights concerns; controlling foreign aid; reducing the national debt and lowering taxes; ceasing immigration, at least until unemployment fell to one million; and deporting all undesirable aliens. Reynolds remained firmly opposed to "socialized medicine" and communism, but he continued to support labor's right to bargain collectively and the closed shop. And he continued to advocate monthly pensions and medical care for everyone over sixty-five. Finally, he charged those who labeled him an isolationist with using smear tactics. He was simply heeding the advice of George Washington, he admonished his critics. Americans should see to their own affairs first, Reynolds proposed, "The time has come to look homeward."[94]

Reynolds intended a vigorous, county-by-county campaign, but he would be walking into the teeth of entrenched Democratic opposition. Most Democratic leaders, irrespective of political philosophy, had always seen Reynolds as an embarrassment, and they greeted his reentry into elective politics with loud groans. Reynolds's rival, Senator Graham, remarked simply that he intended to run on his record.[95] Jonathan Daniels airily dismissed Reynolds's candidacy; he felt Frank Graham was a "better citizen, a sounder man, and better senator" than Reynolds. This contest, wrote Daniels, gave state Democrats an easy choice.[96]

Nor was the press corps enthralled, however colorful a Reynolds candidacy might be. The Durham *Morning Herald* reminded its readers that Reynolds's earlier performance in the Senate had been a feeble effort, climaxed by his forced retirement. In a word, he must be kept out of the Senate, "where for years he was a perpetual embarrassment to North Carolina."[97] From Winston-Salem, *Journal* editorialists were somewhat amused. Reynolds was likable and genial, but he lacked a statesman's attributes. "He knows how to tickle the vanity of many voters, and in his handshaking tours may pick up quite a few votes."[98] "Candidate Reynolds," announced the Greensboro *Daily News*, "has never . . . publicly subscribed to Barnum's dictum that a sucker is born every minute, but his platform indicates that he is working on the assumption that a lot of them have come of age in North Carolina since he left the senate."[99] He was the "Same Old Bob," the Charlotte *Observer* concluded. His views had not changed, but he was a master of political psychology who could get votes.[100]

The most thoughtful assessment of Reynolds's impact came from the Washington (N.C.) *Daily News*. Reynolds's entry, said the paper, had created the opportunity for a third candidate to run against Graham and make a much stronger bid than might be made alone. Reynolds's loyal following included many people who would vote for Graham if Reynolds were not running. Because many North Carolinians could stomach neither Graham nor Reynolds, a large mass of anti-Graham conservatives still had no candidate.[101]

Graham's political advisers, principally Daniels, did not have time in January to worry about Graham's possible conservative opposition. Daniels had already devised a plan to wed southern Democrats to the national party—and Truman—by holding a Southern Regional Democratic Conference in Raleigh on January 20 to coincide with the annual Jefferson-Jackson Day dinner. This love feast, to which Daniels invited governors, party chairmen, and national committee members from the southern states, would feature Vice President Alben W. Barkley, former senator from Kentucky and a principal Truman spear-carrier.[102] Also included would be CIO Political Action Director Jack Kroll and two other labor leaders invited to consult with the southerners about election strategy.[103]

Daniels intended to build up southern support for the Fair Deal and Graham at the conference but hoped the civil rights issue would not surface.[104] Early intimations that the marriage was in trouble came when only three of the thirteen invited governors accepted Daniels's invitation. Nonetheless, Daniels pressed fearlessly forward, in part because President Truman favored the meeting and gladly sent key emissaries to shore up support from southern Democrats.[105] At the opening of the conference, administration notables, including Secretary of Agriculture Charles F. Brannan, discussed major legislative objectives of the Fair Deal, while excluding FEPC or any other civil rights matters.[106] Vice President Barkley paid lavish tribute to the Democrats and their accomplishments under Roosevelt and Truman, and when Frank Graham stood for recognition, the throng rose to cheer his name.[107]

Daniels hailed this Jefferson-Jackson Day meeting as a signal success,[108] but his delight met the scorn of several important guests. Agriculture Commissioner L. Y. Ballentine emerged as chief critic. Ballentine's wrath rose when, upon arrival at the dinner, he discovered a packed ballroom that did not have a single spare seat. His two $50 per plate tickets now rendered worthless, Ballentine turned publicly against the whole affair. The conference, Ballentine charged, had only one purpose anyway: to promote the political ambitions of Daniels and Graham.[109]

Ballentine's complaint found a receptive audience. Letters of praise filled his Raleigh office, one writer commenting that Ballentine's criticism of Daniels had been heard statewide and had been favorably received. Ballentine replied that the statement he had made about Daniels was the most popular comment he had made in recent years. He believed that many North Carolina Democrats would be delighted when Daniels's term on the Democratic National Committee expired and a more conventional North Carolinian replaced him.[110]

Daniels's tactic would not work, Truman critic and radio commentator W. E. Debnam told his eastern North Carolina audience. The event, planned to glorify Daniels and his ilk, had simply made North Carolinians aware of the "Trojan Horse of Socialism . . . wheeled inside Party walls to disgorge its army of wild-eyed apostles of a planned economy whose . . . only purpose was to perpetuate themselves in power." Debnam chastised Daniels for inviting labor representatives to the conference and ridiculed the idea that southern Democrats would unite under the Fair Deal banner. He averred that Daniels's conference would only help awaken the South to the realization that the Democrats were leading the nation down "Free-Lunch-For-Everybody street" and over the precipice of bankruptcy.[111]

In short, Daniels's soiree was a laboratory demonstration of the law of unintended result. Conservative Democrats recoiled from the Raleigh spectacle and renewed their search for somebody to run against Graham—and Daniels. Daniels himself admitted to Dave Burgess that he was in hot water over the lack of seating at the Jefferson-Jackson Day dinner and therefore probably should not take a strong stand on either candidates or issues in the forthcoming primary.[112]

In early February, the focus of the anti-Graham conservatives narrowed to three individuals: Judge Henry Stevens of Warsaw and Com-

Jonathan Daniels, Democratic National Committee member and intimate Graham adviser, at the 1950 Jefferson-Jackson Day dinner that he organized and staged. The ill-planned affair generated party dissension and criticism of Daniels's high-handed ways. (North Carolina Department of Archives and History, Raleigh)

missioner of Agriculture L. Y. Ballentine, both already mentioned, and a new entry, Raleigh lawyer Willis Smith. All were able men, and each would likely make a credible showing. Stevens, however, was little known to voters and an unlikely winner in a race against Graham. He thought about running but sensibly decided against it.[113] Ballentine, on the other hand, did not lack recognition. He was a fixture in North Carolina politics, and he could command an enthusiastic following. He received a number of letters urging him to run and expressing strong disfavor with Graham, Scott, and Daniels. "I don't believe the Scott-Daniels-Graham crowd can get enough labor and Negro votes to beat you," wrote a Reidsville car dealer. "I believe business and the farmers will send you to Washington."[114] But Ballentine did not want to go. He probably could be commissioner of agriculture for as long as he wanted to be, he enjoyed his job, and he had no desire to leave North Carolina. He could find no good reason to risk his position for a race he might not win. Accordingly, he spurned his suitors and remained in Raleigh, even though he was mindful that a strong sentiment had surfaced in the state demanding a major challenger to Graham.[115]

The anti-Scott-Daniels-Graham forces then turned in full importunity to their last best hope: Willis Smith. Smith had been a depression-era speaker of the North Carolina House of Representatives (1931–33) who had abandoned elective politics upon the expiration of his term as speaker. He had built a highly successful law practice in Raleigh and was a former president of the American Bar Association. Until his conservative Democratic friends began to apply the pressure, he had not seriously envisioned confronting Frank Graham. He did acknowledge publicly, as reporters began to sniff around him, that the Senate beckoned. "That's the only political job I would want," he told the press in early February.[116] But into the middle of the month, despite heavy pressure, he temporized. Claiming no strong appetite for the rigors and expense of a Senate campaign, Smith simultaneously remarked that he would like to serve his state and nation.[117]

As Smith pondered his future, Governor Scott once again warned Graham supporters against overconfidence. "The most dangerous statement you can make is to say you can't be beat. Folks don't like a man to say he is all-powerful."[118] Meanwhile, Graham tended to his Senate duties and made a few speeches in North Carolina and Washington on the theme of international peace. Graham favored nuclear disarmament as well as additional funding for the Voice of America in these talks and noted that the idea of the brotherhood of man had, in the atomic age, become the most necessary idea of all.[119]

Gradually, Willis Smith's associates sensed success in their effort to persuade Smith to run. By February 18, Smith was claiming statewide support should he declare, arguing that a majority of North Carolinians simply did not share Graham's views. A contest with Graham now seemed a great opportunity for "someone who wants to represent the real viewpoint of most people in the state." That "real viewpoint" to Smith meant views consonant with those of Senator Hoey. "I approve . . . Hoey's position on almost everything," he told reporters. Should he announce his candidacy, moreover, Smith now told the press, he thought he could win.[120]

Smith's musings to the press did not require a code breaker to interpret. His potential candidacy provoked fear and a note of desperation among Graham's closest friends. Not only were members of the Graham camp aware of the resources Smith could summon, but they also knew Willis Smith well, especially Graham's attorney friends, and they believed him to be a person of ability and integrity. In opposition to Graham, he would be a genuine threat, a clear contrast to Bob Reynolds's hucksterism and Graham's liberalism.

Thus, as Smith approached his Rubicon, some of Graham's lifelong friends tried desperately to talk Smith out of running. Seeking to discourage his candidacy, Charles Tillett telegraphed Smith on February 18, the day that Smith publicly discussed his potential candidacy: "Disturbed to read you are seriously considering running against Frank. . . . Should you decide to run it will put you and me on opposite sides for the first time." Smith would lose, Tillett implied, because he was not well-known to voters, while Senator Graham was known and admired throughout the state.[121] Five days later, on February 23, Smith received additional counsel from vacationing acquaintances via Western Union:

Three of your Rocky Mount friends in Ft. Lauderdale . . . have just heard with regret you considering run against Graham and urge you to stay clear. First reason, patriotism. . . . Reynolds potentially dangerous dictator and your entry would split respectable vote and put him in second primary; second, you would be heartbroken at large number of your sincerest friends who will support Graham even against you in belief North Carolina owes it to nation to keep him in Senate; third, his foreign policy is same as Hoey's and most likely to prevent final world war and a campaign against it would be a "disservice" to the world. . . . Fourth, his domestic policy votes and announcements do not warrant charging him with being radical. He is middle of the road. . . . Fifth, his opponents seeking to use you for their own purposes. Sincerely, Arthur L. Tyler, Frank E. Winslow and Millard F. Jones.[122]

These telegrams, transparently partisan, were probably not pivotal in Smith's decision whether or not to run. But they certainly revealed that those closest to Graham saw in a Smith campaign the potential to menace Graham's budding Senate career. Had Smith sought independent confirmation that he had a good chance in this effort, it is hard to imagine more reassuring words than the patronizing pleas of Graham's friends to stay out of the race.

Indeed, on February 21, when Graham finally opened his Raleigh headquarters, Smith acknowledged receiving a hundred phone calls and stacks of mail beseeching him to run. Expressing pleasure and surprise at the strength of this apparent ground swell, Smith promised a decision shortly.[123] Seventy-two hours later, he appeared at the Board of Elections office and paid the $125 filing fee. As the first candidate to file, Smith joked with reporters that perhaps no one else would run. Bob Reynolds immediately replied by welcoming Smith into the race, observing that Smith's candidacy made the race more interesting and provided the voters with greater platform variety.[124] Neither Scott nor Graham made a public comment.

It seems obvious in retrospect that Graham's tardiness in organizing his campaign had given the Smith forces encouragement. As Sam Ragan, then on the staff of the Raleigh *News and Observer*, and R. Mayne Albright have recalled, Daniels, Scott, and Graham had waited too long to choose a campaign staff and set up a headquarters.[125] If money had been raised and the campaign organization put on a viable basis prior to December 1949, potential candidates like Willis Smith might have been discouraged from entering the race. Graham would have had an insuperable head start. February 1950 was not too late to organize a winning campaign, as Kate Humphries, one of Graham's staff members, has pointed out. But it was too late to dissuade challengers.[126]

It is equally obvious that Willis Smith had yielded to an intensive, even frantic, conservative push to enlist his candidacy. Smith's conservative friends, who abhorred the specter of Frank Graham continuing in the Senate, had gone down the line searching for a credible challenger. Smith, as Clyde Hoey pointed out, was the last man in line. Had he declined, the effort to unseat Graham would have fizzled, and Graham would have walked back into the Senate.[127]

Three days before Smith filed to run, Graham had finally selected a campaign manager—after months of prodding from the Tilletts, Daniels, Scott, and others. Hoping to inherit Senator Broughton's support statewide and to reassure voters of his orthodoxy, Graham named Broughton's campaign manager, Jefferson Deems Johnson, Jr., of Clinton, to run his campaign. It was a move that delighted Graham's close advisers and heartened his supporters. In describing Johnson, Graham said he knew of "no man for whom I have a higher personal regard or in whose judgment I have greater confidence." Like Willis Smith, Johnson was a graduate of the law school at Trinity College. He had served in the state senate from 1937 to 1941 and had been a superior court judge from 1941 to 1945. Since 1945 he had been a practicing attorney in Clinton.[128]

Johnson's work in the Broughton campaign had identified him as an astute political operative. His choice reassured Graham sympathizers who were worried about Graham's political inexperience. In fact, Johnson seemed an ideal choice. As a former state legislator and jurist, he was well-known and much respected.[129] As an attorney with close ties to Broughton, and an easterner to boot, Johnson's political history placed him squarely in the ideological center of North Carolina politics. A racial moderate by North Carolina standards, Johnson nonetheless had no clearly defined public views on race. Moreover, he had no ties to Chapel Hill and bore no public identification with liberal causes. He was a well-organized manager, respected for his integrity, who could be tough when he had to.[130]

With Johnson named to head the campaign, Graham headquarters opened February 21, 1950, in room 532 of the Sir Walter Hotel. Graham flew in from Washington for the ceremony, announcing his intention to deliver as many speeches in North Carolina as his Senate duties would allow. Johnson discussed the organization of the campaign and denied that Broughton people would be running the Graham election effort. He hoped for a balance among all the groups that would support Graham. Simultaneously, Johnson, without blinking an eye, announced that Kate Humphries, secretary to Broughton for twelve years and currently Graham's Washington secretary, would be the campaign office manager in Raleigh. Johnson confirmed that Bill Staton, a young Sanford attorney and formerly director of information for the state YDC, whom Graham had named earlier to organize the Raleigh office, would be his first assistant.[131] He also named Kathryn N. Folger, a Mt. Airy native and daughter of former Congressman Lon Folger, as campaign aide responsible primarily for the piedmont and western counties.[132]

These appointments completed the paid staff, save one notable void. Johnson had named no publicity director. Several names were on the short list, among them Shelby newspaperman Holt McPherson, C. A. "Abie" Upchurch, Jr., a Scott operative and head of the Alcoholic Beverage Control Board's Division of Malt Beverages, and WRAL radio news director Jesse A. Helms. McPherson had been the first choice but had declined, apparently because he was principally a "Hoey man" in North Carolina politics and while not hostile to Graham, did not find the prospect of handling Graham's publicity irresistible. Helms too, in his own recounting, turned the job down. The Raleigh radio man was, in 1950, on good terms with Governor Scott and hence not surprised to get a call from him in late February requesting Helms's presence in Scott's office. When he arrived, Helms found Senator Graham in attendance. In the course of their conversation, Scott remarked to Helms, "You ought to get out of the radio business; there ain't no money in radio." Why not, Scott suggested, take the job as Graham's publicity director?

To the surprise of both Scott and Graham, Helms refused. In "one of . . . the most difficult statements I ever had to make in my life," Helms recalled, he tearfully told Graham of his affection for him and thanked

Graham consults with his publicity director, C. A. Upchurch, Jr. (to Graham's
right), and Capus Waynick (left front), former Scott campaign manager.
Waynick was at the time U.S. ambassador to Nicaragua and a fervent Graham
backer. (North Carolina Department of Archives and History, Raleigh)

Governor Scott for thinking of him. But he could not accept, he told
Scott and Graham, because he did not agree with the senator on some
crucial issues. Moreover, Willis Smith had indicated he might oppose
Graham, in which case, Helms would support Smith. At that moment,
Graham put his arm around Jesse and said he understood.[133] Subse-
quently, Graham named Upchurch to the post.[134]

As was obvious to all, Smith's entry changed the nature of the Senate
campaign. Smith's nineteen-year absence from elective politics was no
doubt a political disadvantage, but he was as well connected to the state's
conservative Democracy as a candidate could be. Born in Norfolk, Virginia, in 1887, the son of Willis and Mary Creecy Smith, Willis Smith's
father had died when the boy was three years old. His mother thereupon
returned to her native Elizabeth City, North Carolina, where she reared
her son, supporting herself by running a private school for neighborhood
children. Smith attended local public schools and then enrolled in
Trinity College in Durham, where, at 6'2", he played center on the
basketball team and worked his way through school. Upon graduation in

1910, he entered the Trinity College School of Law. He led his class academically, passed the bar in 1912, and began his legal practice in Raleigh. Subsequently, he served three state legislative terms as representative from Wake County, culminating in 1931 with service as speaker of the North Carolina house in a difficult depression-era session. Smith thereupon left the General Assembly, focusing his full energy on his law practice, professional associations, and civic service. Elected president of the North Carolina Bar Association in 1941, Smith became in 1945 the first North Carolinian ever to serve as president of the American Bar Association. Named by U.S. Supreme Court Justice Robert Jackson, a good friend, as an observer at the Nuremberg Trials, Smith made an important report of those proceedings to the American bar and the American people. President Truman also appointed Smith to the Amnesty Board to review cases of those convicted of violating the Selective Service Act during World War II. Smith had, in addition, remained active in Democratic party politics. He had been a precinct chairman, frequent delegate to state and county conventions, and chairman of the 1940 North Carolina Democratic Convention. Well-known to local and state politicians, Smith had been a delegate in 1944 to his party's national convention.

His record of civic involvement was equally noteworthy. He was a director of the YMCA, on the board of trustees of the Edenton Street Methodist Church, and a board member of the Wake Community Chest. He had organized the local Legal Aid clinic, had been chairman of the tuberculosis bond drive, and had served as president of the local Kiwanis Club. An active alumnus of Duke University, he was at the time of his Senate candidacy president of the university's board of trustees.

Associates described Smith as a quick study but as one who liked to think things out before beginning to work. Normally a man of even disposition, he was not without a temper. While hardly misanthropic, Smith could not be described as a glad-hander.[125] He was an attorney of note—known to his legal associates as "Big Willis"—and a man of serious disposition. He might not be well-known to the state's voters, but among attorneys, he had high visibility. The law firm he had helped found, Smith, Leach, and Anderson, was one of Raleigh's most prosperous. Its client list included a number of the state's most powerful business interests: Occidental Life Insurance Company, Wachovia Bank and Trust, Southern Railway, the North Carolina Medical Society, International Pulp and Paper Company, and numerous other insurance companies.[136]

In sum, Smith was representative of the "progressive conservative" faction Kerr Scott had taken to the woodshed in 1948—although ironically, Smith had voted for Scott in that election. In Smith, the foes of Graham and Scott had a candidate who would represent their traditional southern democratic views and who would, they devoutly hoped, depose the new liberal order in North Carolina. At least Smith might send Senator Graham into early retirement.

But Smith, for all his bona fides, was hardly the perfect candidate. Too businesslike to be identified as a man of the people, Smith was hardly a "happy warrior." Indeed, once before, in 1940, he had flirted with entering the race for governor, only to withdraw in order to avoid the physical and financial strain of statewide electioneering and the attendant neglect of his law practice.[137] Senator Hoey, in fact, had continued to believe up until Smith's formal announcement in February 1950 that he would refuse the pleas of his friends to run.[138]

Of course, Smith eventually overcame his reluctance and made the race, in part because the large number of phone calls and messages urging his candidacy, a ground swell of conservative support, convinced him he could win. Influential Democrats, including Raleigh attorney Colonel William T. Joyner, Sr., Wachovia Bank Vice President Leroy Martin, Lloyd E. Griffin, and Edwin M. Gill, among others, urged him into the contest and pledged that they would raise the funds for the campaign, thereby relieving Smith of his fear that the campaign would require huge sums of his own money, a price he simply would not pay.[139]

In addition, Saxapahaw textile executive B. Everett Jordan, a close Smith friend, business associate, and at the time, state Democratic party chairman, secured for Smith much-needed textile industry support. As state party chairman, Jordan could not work publicly for Smith, but the necessity for official neutrality did not prevent Jordan from raising money quietly and advising Smith on a regular if unofficial basis. Among other individuals and groups who pressured Smith to run and backed their promises with money and effort were the North Carolina Medical Society, judges and attorneys from throughout the state, Louis Sutton, president of Carolina Power and Light, as well as Edwin Pate and the McNair family, all wealthy Laurinburg merchants, Raleigh businessman A. J. Fletcher, and High Point newspaperman Bob Thompson.[140]

Press reaction to the Smith candidacy was predictable. At least three politicians had turned down the opportunity to face Graham, the Raleigh *News and Observer* commented, leaving Democratic conservatives frantic for a candidate. But the paper editorially accepted the challenge Smith now posed: "For nearly twenty years the same forces which have persuaded Smith to run have tried to oust Frank Graham from the presidency of the university. . . . They did not succeed then. They will not succeed now," the paper predicted.[141]

To the Durham *Morning Herald*, firmly pro-Graham, Smith's announcement represented a signal failure of the Graham forces. They had been unable to convince his opponents of Graham's invincibility, a ploy that could have scared off all serious opponents. Yet Graham remained the candidate of choice, the paper argued, in part because the liberalism that seemed to offend so many people had not yet been evident in Graham's Senate service.[142]

In Smith's birthplace, the Norfolk *Virginian-Pilot* praised his candidacy as representing the legitimate conservative view of North Carolina. Smith would prove a severe test for Graham.[143] The High Point *Enterprise* proclaimed its delight at Smith's announcement. Smith would be a strong candidate because he was a superior attorney, a progressive without a tinge of the reactionary, and an appealing personality as well. Boasted the *Enterprise*: "He is a hard fighter but a clean one; a tough opponent but a fair one; a strong man, but a gentleman." In contrast, the *Enterprise*'s Frank Graham was a starry-eyed idealist who had been used time and time again by Communist front organizations. The *Enterprise* never called Graham himself a Communist; he was instead a person of socialist tendencies who had frequently played into Communist hands. Frank Graham was a good man, the *Enterprise* wrote, but "when a good man becomes the stooge of subversive forces . . . he becomes even more dangerous than a bad man."[144]

Irrespective of viewpoint, commentators agreed that Willis Smith was a candidate around whom the heretofore diffuse Graham opposition could coalesce. Smith would certainly embolden Graham's adversaries. For political observers who loved a good fight, the Graham-Smith-Reynolds contest now loomed as the greatest battle of the century.[145] Smith's entry assured a two-primary campaign in the opinion of political writer Wade Lucas. Smith would take the middle course, between Graham and Reynolds, and would be the principal beneficiary of the sallies Reynolds could be expected to aim at Graham. For even Smith's entry had not changed the campaign's focus. This race would be a referendum on Frank Graham and the recent political changes in North Carolina. Much would depend on Graham's skills as a campaigner and Scott's ability to persuade his supporters to vote for Graham without creating a backlash to his effort. North Carolina voters were known for their independence, Lucas wrote, as witnessed by their rejection of Senate appointees in two recent episodes: Cameron Morrison in 1932 (in favor of Reynolds) and William B. Umstead in 1948 (in favor of Broughton).[146]

From the Graham group, reaction was predictably gloomy. Dave Burgess reiterated labor's view that the refusal to oppose Hoey left the conservatives free to mass their strength against Graham.[147] Jonathan

Daniels foresaw a "real fight,"[148] the embodiment of the anti-Truman resistance in the South.[149] Willis Smith, Daniels wrote President Truman, was the epitome of opposition to Truman, and this Senate campaign was therefore a national contest. Consequently, to avoid adverse reaction to "outside meddling," advised Daniels, the Democratic National Committee should not participate in the primary.[150]

Everything was changed now, Charles Tillett confided. With Smith's entry, many people were lining up against Graham. Tillett warned that thousands could be swayed by the charge of communism. Graham remained the favorite, but it would take much hard work to insure victory, the Charlotte attorney argued.[151] Capus Waynick remarked to Jonathan Daniels that, as an architect of the Graham appointment, he had a tough problem. Willis Smith was a political force, a highly intelligent man who would command enthusiastic conservative support.[152] "Willis has a lot of friends, especially among the Methodists down here," added an Aberdeen attorney.[153]

Smith's entry "tightens the contest," counseled Edenton attorney Richard Dixon in a sobering letter to Jeff Johnson. Smith's Elizabeth City background had given him "highly connected ties of relationships in several [area] counties," where he was "highly regarded and admired." Many of Johnson's Broughton supporters would embrace Smith's candidacy, Dixon stated, mentioning specifically Herbert Peele, former owner of the Elizabeth City *Daily Advance*, who had been a "big help" in the 1948 Broughton Senate campaign. Dixon, who had been Graham's friend for forty-four years, added: "I deeply regret Willis Smith's candidacy. He is a very close and valued friend . . . and has always responded promptly and cheerfully to any request I have made of him. But I have been for Graham from the appointment and I will stand for him."[154]

Only Scott remained undaunted; he insisted that Smith's candidacy would serve "to prove Frank Graham to be a very effective politician before it's over."[155] He had better be. The maneuvering was finished, and each contender was astride his stool in the curious three-cornered ring.

4 · Skirmishes

Candidate Graham, confronting the first electoral challenge of his nascent political career, seemed unperturbed at the threat posed by his three rivals. "The more the merrier," he told the Charlotte *Observer*.[1] He paid his filing fee on March 7 and began scheduling a series of speeches and appearances across the state.[2]

Simultaneously in Raleigh, Jeff Johnson and his staff began the tough task of organizing the campaign. The hard-working Johnson and his wife moved into a room at the Sir Walter Hotel, enabling him to devote sixteen hours a day to the task of Graham's election. He took no salary, except for room and board at the hotel and expenses for occasional trips home to Clinton. Beginning his day very early in the morning, he would telephone farmers and business people before they went to the fields or their offices and would end his daily effort with staff meetings that usually ran into the shank of the night.

Kate Humphries, as office manager, answered the telephone, directed all the typing and correspondence, and kept a record of campaign contributions and files on county managers. It was her task to get fliers and weekly information sheets to the county managers—all for a salary of $550 per month.

Johnson and his lieutenant Bill Staton were the principal campaign strategists, with constant advice and intervention from Scott and Daniels. Governor Scott was an active if surreptitious adviser from the outset. He mobilized his own organization on behalf of Graham and met occasionally with the campaign staff to listen to problems and make suggestions. Scott did not visit the campaign office—it was too public—but he frequently talked to Johnson by phone. Jonathan Daniels was also involved in the campaign, attending staff gatherings irregularly.[3] Daniels raised money, wrote editorial after editorial for Graham, and made additional efforts to get Graham favorable headlines. He too had regular phone chats with Johnson.[4] Charles and Gladys Tillett also offered counsel, but they directed their own ancillary efforts from their home in Charlotte. Gladys Tillett believed that women voters would determine the election, and, convinced that women would support Graham overwhelmingly, she launched a massive effort to organize women for Graham. At least one critic remembered her as enthusiastic but ineffective in her effort to persuade women to support Graham.[5] Her husband focused much of his energy on the state's lawyers, writing letters endorsing Graham and soliciting money.[6]

Johnson and Staton determined initially to present Graham as a national and international figure who commanded worldwide respect and esteem. They would stress his compassion, his integrity, and his ability, all of which he had displayed in his brief Senate tenure, and, more completely, in his Chapel Hill years.[7]

For his part, Graham attended assiduously to his Senate duties. He did not come often to his campaign headquarters and had very little to do with campaign planning. Raising campaign funds was a task he found repugnant, and he simply refused to do it. He had no idea what a Senate campaign cost, and no notion where the money would come from. Very quickly Johnson and the staff learned which tasks Graham would do— he would make speeches and shake hands—and those he would not do—he would not ask directly for votes, and he would not raise money. They planned the campaign accordingly. Nor could Graham be told what to talk about in his campaign. The staff made suggestions, but Graham insisted on writing his own speeches.[8]

With his staff in place and an overall strategy identified, Johnson picked a manager for each of North Carolina's one hundred counties[9] and began to take soundings to determine the depth of Graham's popularity.[10] He also worked to consolidate support from Graham's most likely constituencies. He contacted the CIO Political Action Committee and asked that labor gifts be given in cash directly to the campaign treasurer.[11] In addition, Dave Burgess visited John Marshall, secretary to Governor Scott, who explained that labor could also pass money to Graham through him.[12]

Smith's declaration of candidacy administered a major purgative to the Graham camp's bloated confidence. Graham's friends and associates now saw a difficult struggle, even though in their eyes, Graham remained the favorite. John Umstead envisioned stout opposition from those he labeled "mossbacks" (those opposed to all progressive ideas) but felt that Graham would win if his supporters worked constantly.[13] T. C. Johnson, a veteran political observer and staunch Scott ally, was especially enthusiastic about Graham's chances. Writing to Capus Waynick, Johnson praised Graham's splendid election staff and predicted a Graham victory in two primaries, although he regretted that Hoey had no opposition. Graham would have been helped, Johnson observed, if the moneyed interests had been compelled to divide their funds between Smith and Hoey.[14] A *Daily Tar Heel* writer argued that complacency could be a major problem for Graham. Graham would have to campaign vigorously, and all his friends would need to join him. They would need to rebut

charges of Communist sympathy by arguing that Graham was a relentless
foe of communism. On race, they had to show that Graham disagreed
with federal plans to eliminate discrimination in the South. Many people
who liked Graham, cautioned the writer, would not vote for him because
of his stands on controversial questions.[15]

Among Graham's closest advisers, a more somber mood descended as
the first reports from around the state reached headquarters. For example, Graham was not popular in the eastern town of Burgaw, in Pender
County, Daniels learned from Nellie P. Cook. Furthermore, Cook informed Jeff Johnson that when she had suggested Senator Graham as a
commencement speaker to school principal E. M. Thompson, "he turned
pale and said they already had gotten a speaker." Cook then observed
that surely the principal was supporting Graham—no educator could do
otherwise: "To this he turned even whiter and made no reply, but was in a
hurry to get back to school. Later I learned he is for Smith."[16]

Nonetheless, Daniels wrote Eleanor Roosevelt in an early March ap-
praisal that the belief that Graham was too liberal and too friendly to
black people could be overcome with hard work and careful planning.[17]
And at least one Graham advocate, Scott's secretary John Marshall, detected by March 6 that the initial excitement accompanying Smith's
announcement had subsided. Marshall believed that Jeff Johnson had
started strongly and was doing an exceptional job of persuading the
various factions in the party to work together.[18]

Even more encouraging were the Graham endorsements from prestigious and powerful North Carolinians. An early enthusiast was Burlington Industries board chairman J. Spencer Love, who had endorsed Graham on February 28.[19] He was joined on March 7 by Rocky Mount
textile manufacturer and banker Hyman L. Battle and, two days later,
industrialist J. Holmes Davis.[20]

Business endorsements made the Graham staff beam, and their grins
broadened when a past president of the North Carolina Medical Society
embraced the senator.[21] And when Mrs. O. Max Gardner, widow of the
former governor and sister-in-law of Senator Hoey, announced plans to
work for Graham because he would effectively pursue the establishment
of permanent world peace,[22] the Graham people became positively ecstatic. These endorsements from businessmen, doctors, attorneys (such
as R. Mayne Albright, who came out for Graham on March 13),[23] and
old-line political families such as the Gardners were especially useful.
They demonstrated that Graham was a patriotic, capable, middle-of-the-
road candidate who commanded broad appeal. With such support,

Graham could demonstrate the falsity of the charge that he was a dangerous radical. When added to Graham's principal constituencies—labor,
educators, and blacks—his campaign managers could claim with conviction and accuracy a deep base of Graham support throughout North
Carolina. Indeed, only one serious problem threatened the Graham
campaign in its early stages: it had too little money. In part, the problem
reflected the candidate. As national columnist Drew Pearson observed in
one of his Daniels-inspired efforts, Graham was a "babe in the woods"
now thrashing around in a political thicket. The skills of campaigning—
backslapping, logrolling, raising money—were lost upon him.[24]

As mentioned above, Graham would not solicit funds. Neither would
he discuss money with his staff nor accept money personally. He would,
instead, ask the donor to see a staff member, a practice that cost him
some large sums. One benefactor offered the campaign $500, but when
Graham would not acknowledge the gift personally, the offer was withdrawn. The senator likewise would not go out on fund-raising forays,
thus giving up the opportunity to make valuable contacts and receive
significant contributions.[25]

Graham's fund-raising aversion left his campaign short of funds at
critical times,[26] money that could have been raised in sufficiency as the
campaign began. Louis Graves, editor of the Chapel Hill *Weekly* and close
friend of Graham, thought Graham could win the election if he took
advantage of his record and integrity and impressed these qualities on
the voters, but he would need enough money for the radio broadcasts
necessary to get his message across. Charles Tillett was already trying to
raise funds for that purpose,[27] but Graves wrote Daniels that a half-hour
broadcast on statewide radio cost about $1,200, and large sums of
money needed to be raised immediately.[28]

Graves then wrote an editorial decrying Smith's handsomely financed
campaign, in contrast to Graham's meager resources. He urged Graham's
proponents to contribute generously to his campaign[29] to demonstrate
that some of Graham's supporters understood the necessity of raising
money, even if the standard-bearer remained aloof from the petty business of acquiring funds. Finally, at the insistence of his friend Maurice
Rosenblatt, Graham did agree to solicit money from University of North
Carolina alumni.[30]

Graham's willful ignorance of campaign finances meant that he could
retain an innocence of the realities of campaign expenditures. He never
asked and was never told about the raising of money. His staff in one
sense became his protectors, insulating him from all matters financial.[31]
Perhaps the most telling comment Graham made during the campaign

regarding finances came when he first announced his candidacy. Money

to finance his campaign would be no problem, he told friends; he had
$5,000 in a savings account, a sum he deemed sufficient for his Senate
race.[32] It was, of course, not nearly enough to place one penny postcard
in the hands of every Tar Heel voter.

Fund-raising therefore became the province of close advisers, notably
Governor Scott, Jonathan Daniels, Jeff Johnson, and various labor organizations.[33] They apparently did not begin a serious quest for funds until
the first week of March,[34] and even at that late date, some Graham
sympathizers noted that no one at headquarters was leaning on visitors, at least some of whom were simply waiting to be asked for contributions.[35]

Only labor seemed to understand the need for money— and lots of it.
Dave Burgess learned from Jeff Johnson that C. P. Deyton, head of the
North Carolina Teachers Retirement Administration and treasurer of
Scott's 1948 campaign, was the "money-man" for the Graham committee. Deyton, Burgess discovered, preferred cash to checks and kept the
cash in a headquarters safe. Deyton suggested to out-of-state contributors who wanted to pay by check that they should make their checks
payable either to cash or to Deyton personally. Money sent to Burgess in
this fashion would be turned over to Deyton, who would issue a receipt
for the funds. Mindful of the campaign's need for money, Burgess began
meeting weekly with Johnson, Scott, and Marshall to help raise money,
to tender advice about the campaign, and to discuss the best ways to pass
money on to Graham.[36]

The first primary spending limit was $12,000 and each candidate had
set up statewide committees required by law to file spending reports with
the secretary of state. But nothing in the law, recalled the ageless Thad
Eure in 1984, required Secretary of State Eure to police the act, which
explains in part why only Olla Ray Boyd actually complied with the law.
Most contributions simply went unreported, and campaign headquarters
customarily kept two sets of books—one for the candidate and the
public, the other for the staffers who handled expenditures.[37]

This method of bookkeeping in elective politics in North Carolina
was a subject openly discussed. Pundits estimated the cost of a heated
one-primary statewide campaign—for governor or senator—at around
$100,000.[38] Absurd though the situation may have been, practicing
politicians understood it and acquiesced in the submission of false expense reports.

All politicians, that is, except Frank Graham. Graham had no knowledge that—in a technical sense—illegal contributions financed his cam-

paign. Had he known, he would not have permitted it—even if it had meant the collapse of his campaign. He thought all the money in his election effort came from small contributors—the "common people"—a dollar or two at a time. He boasted of turning down large contributions—a vision of his campaign of which he was never disabused. Observers agreed that had he known that the law had been violated, he would never have signed the official financial report that went to the secretary of state's office.[39] Shielded by his staff from the realities of political finances, Graham went blissfully forward with his campaign for world peace and social justice. And he signed his name to the financial report sent to the secretary of state, showing total expenditures of less than $12,000, fully convinced that the report was accurate. Any major candidate who signed a report declaring less than $12,000 in expenditures obviously participated in a false report since it was impossible to run a campaign for that amount.

How Graham could imagine that a campaign for the U.S. Senate could be waged for $12,000 is inexplicable. Kate Humphries's salary for four months was $2,200 and a half hour on statewide radio cost $1,200. If one included the cost of telephone calls, rent for headquarters, salaries, postage, and local newspaper ads, that amount alone would come to over $12,000. Apparently Graham did not want to know anything about the finances so that he could remain uncorrupted and free to sign the financial reports in clear conscience. Graham was either obtuse or disingenuous in maneuvering to avoid a moral dilemma over his campaign finances.

Governor Scott was in the audience when Graham formally opened his campaign in North Wilkesboro on March 2, 1950. In an appeal to the state's farmers, he repeated his strong support of parity prices for basic agricultural commodities. In addition, Jeff Johnson, targeting farmers as the Scott faction most suspicious of Graham's candidacy, began sending press releases to all the state's weekly newspapers, reiterating Graham's stand on farm prices. In his own talks, Graham continued to press his position: "The farmer asks not for charity, but for parity; not for privilege, but for equity; and for the equal opportunity to play his indispensable role and creative part in the making of a fairer and stronger America."[40]

Graham took aim at another potential nemesis: the charge that he was an advocate of "socialized medicine." "I am not," he told press and public, "and never have been for socialized medicine." In a form letter sent to physicians in the state, Graham explained his position against federal control of medicine. Accompanying the letter was a statement from Dr. Hamilton W. McKay, president of the Southern Medical Association, pledging McKay's support for Graham as an opponent of nationalized medical care.[41]

Graham argued that federalizing medical care would increase the demand for services without correspondingly increasing the supply.[42] He proposed instead a program patterned after the North Carolina Medical Care Plan, which he had helped implement, that functioned on a voluntary local-state-federal basis to increase the supply of doctors, nurses, and facilities and to improve medical education.[43] It was an idea press editorials cheered. North Carolinians did not want "socialized medicine," the Kinston *Daily Free Press* wrote, as it lauded Graham's position.[44]

While trying to defuse criticism on several issues, Graham also appealed to two of his most ardent constituencies for help, namely students and the state's black citizens. Campaign staffs organized Students for Frank Graham committees on nearly every college campus in the state, coordinated by former University of North Carolina students Lindsay Tate and Allard Lowenstein.[45] From Chapel Hill, Graham Jones, publicity director of Students for Frank Porter Graham, sent five thousand letters to University of North Carolina students, urging them to talk to parents, relatives, and friends about "Dr. Frank."[46]

No effort was necessary to convince the state's black voters to support Graham. They were already Graham advocates of long standing. The campaign effort, therefore, focused on ways to translate that advocacy into a massive vote for Graham. Jeff Johnson consulted frequently with black leaders, especially Kelly M. Alexander, Jr., of Charlotte.[47] Johnson conferred as well with T. A. Hamme, superintendent of the Colored Orphanage in Oxford, J. W. Jeffries at North Carolina Agricultural and Technical College in Greensboro, and a group of active supporters in Durham.[48]

A number of blacks wrote to Graham and Johnson offering to help in any way they could. One backer, citing a lasting friendship with Graham, wrote that he was doing all he could to get out the Negro vote.[49] Jesse Stroud, the black bellman at the Carolina Inn in Chapel Hill, had known and loved Graham for many years and offered his help, noting that Graham's announced opposition to FEPC would not diminish his cause among Chapel Hill Negroes.[50]

Black ministers likewise were excited to have Graham in the Senate. They understood as well the delicate touch necessary to support Graham without triggering a white reaction that would imperil their candidate. One minister told Johnson that blacks would have to run a new type of campaign, "quiet and intelligent, do a lot and say a little."[51] This concern led Johnson, in one instance, to urge Kelly M. Alexander, Jr., to restrain the flamboyant statements of Reverend Joseph Fraylon, who had arranged "mammoth singing gatherings" in a divinely dictated plan to get blacks to participate "in this Holy War." Johnson wanted Alexander to coordinate Fraylon's campaign activities. He knew that Graham needed black support but that such support was a political tinderbox and could ignite the racial resentment of white voters if publicized.[52]

Nonetheless, it was impossible for Alexander and the NAACP to push for increased black voter registration out of the public eye. At a meeting of the nonpartisan Voter Registration Committee of the NAACP in Durham on March 4, attended by two hundred black leaders, Alexander announced a goal of registering 250,000 North Carolina black voters in 1950.[53] The 1950 election was critical, Alexander told his audience, and Negroes in the state must become more active politically. In order to recruit new voters, he recommended the establishment of an information committee, a finance committee, and local voting committees. Alexander urged blacks to notify him if they were denied registration. He then added that the committee would not endorse candidates,[54] a guise that did not obscure the reality that these ambitious plans, if realized even partially, would be a significant boon for Frank Graham.[55]

Reports recurred throughout the campaign that blacks were being refused registration in various areas of eastern North Carolina. J. R. Scott wrote Graham, complaining of systematic discrimination by eastern county registrars. He urged Graham to report the situation to the proper authorities so that blacks could register and vote for him.[56] Already the State Board of Elections had heard appeals from Negro voters, charging discrimination. Registrars were unfair in the test on constitutional interpretation, complainants charged, and in some rural areas, black college graduates had difficulty satisfying local registrars.[57] Responding to these complaints, the State Board of Elections included in its pamphlet of instructions to county registrars the admonition that registrars must not act arbitrarily in giving the literacy test then required for registration.[58] At best, the board's action produced limited results and was frequently ignored in eastern North Carolina, as continued complaints throughout the campaign attest.

In his effort to mobilize the state's political center, Graham announced on March 29 a fifteen-point platform that featured an affirmation of his belief in the "American way of life." He called for economy in government and the strengthening of free enterprise as the best answer to socialism, communism, and fascism. He advocated "working toward" a balanced budget and the elimination of deficit spending. Proclaiming his opposition to "government waste," he reminded voters that he had supported

the first seven recommendations of the Hoover Commission, a body
created by Truman to study government efficiency. Graham further proposed "intelligent reduction of Marshall Plan aid," while opposing "drastic cuts" that might threaten American and European security. He repeated his support for federal aid to education, with funds under state
and local control. For farmers, he reembraced parity and, for labor,
advocated "equality of bargaining" between responsible workers and
responsible management. He endorsed "reasonable" minimum wages
and social security as a cushion against the hazards of old age but
emphatically opposed the use of federal power in race relations, a position he had always advocated. Only religion and education, he repeated,
could lead to permanent racial changes. He did want the poll tax eliminated and measures enacted to eliminate lynching in the United States.
He also repeated his opposition to all forms of "socialized medicine."
Finally, he endorsed rural electrification, rural telephone service, more
adequate housing for veterans and low-income earners, a strong national
defense, and leadership by the United States in the United Nations,
especially on disarmament and peace issues.[59]

The platform, in sum, identified Graham as a conventional Truman
Democrat but challenged the Fair Deal on some points. On civil rights
and health care, for instance, Graham clearly disagreed with the administration. His platform, moreover, presented a specific refutation of most of
the anticipated charges that could be made against him. In his speeches
and campaign appearances, he would reiterate these points again and
again in order that voters would know precisely his positions.

In Asheville and Brevard the week prior to releasing his fifteen-point
platform, Graham stressed the main themes of his election effort. He
expressed his desire that the United States have a strong voice to equal
the "communist thunder" coming out of Moscow. Additionally, he advocated inspection and control of atomic defenses.[60]

From Asheville and Brevard, Graham then moved across the state to
his birthplace, Fayetteville. He was learning about the rigors of elective
politics as he struggled to participate in every important Senate vote and
tried to traverse the state "from Manteo to Murphy."[61]

Several hundred enthusiastic followers were on hand to hear his Fayetteville talk. Graham told the crowd he did not seek the aid of the
mighty or the powerful. He had been rebuked in his career by both
Montgomery Ward's Sewell Avery and the United Mine Workers' John L.
Lewis (Lewis once characterized Graham in his War Labor Board days as
"that sweet little son-of-a-bitch"). He had been denounced, said Graham,

by isolationists Fulton Lewis, Jr., and John T. Flynn, and, of course, by Moscow (as a tool of capitalism). Through it all, he said, he had come to believe that the people of North Carolina stood for the principles he had always upheld—strength in freedom, democracy, and spiritual power; strength in industrial and commercial power; and strength in military and scientific power, all of which made the United States a bulwark for freedom and the hope for peace in the world.[62]

Graham's idealistic speeches found their match in Bob Reynolds's delight that he was once again on a political quest. Visiting Washington on March 7, Reynolds said he was more concerned about his daughter Mamie's chicken pox than about the campaign, but he expected to return to the nation's capital in January 1951 for a four-year visit.[63]

Shortly after Reynolds's Washington visit, his former Senate aide Wesley McDonald announced that he was sponsoring a Reynolds-for-Senator Club in Washington.[64] In a speech to 150 hard-core supporters, McDonald lashed out at Frank Graham, promising that "Our Bob" would oust him from the Senate. McDonald foresaw a two-issue campaign: Americanism versus communism and states' rights versus civil rights. Reynolds, McDonald claimed, was an eternal foe of communism, one of the original discoverers of the menace. Men in high places who knowingly or unknowingly gave communists aid and comfort were a fit target for Bob Reynolds, McDonald warned.[65]

Johnston Avery, Jonathan Daniels's eyes and ears in Washington, heard the McDonald performance and gave Daniels a full accounting. The Reynolds-for-Senate organization was of little import, Avery wrote, since most who attended the meeting were not even registered in North Carolina. Nor was much money likely to flow from the meeting. It was just a chance for Wesley McDonald to reestablish his political presence.[66]

As McDonald was delivering this oratorical frenzy, Reynolds told reporters he would file against Graham on March 17. Rumors that he would switch to a campaign against Hoey were in error, he said, since Graham was his "natural adversary." He vowed to campaign in every county.[67]

As promised, Reynolds filed on March 17, plunking down 125 one dollar bills while declaring that he was "one of the best friends labor ever had." When asked to confirm his intention to highlight the Communist issue by donning a red suit, a red hat, and riding the campaign trail in a red car, Reynolds denied the report. Seemingly offended by the rumor, Reynolds said he had never had the slightest intention of doing such a ridiculous stunt. It would be beneath the dignity of the office of senator. Breezy and jovial as usual, Reynolds did repeat his campaign platform, emphasizing that old age pensions for everyone over sixty could be funded easily if the United States would stop giving money abroad in a futile effort to buy friendship. Had his bill, which required all aliens to be fingerprinted, been passed ten years earlier when he proposed it, "we would not have the 54,000 Russian Communists we have now."[68]

Reynolds decided to forego a Raleigh headquarters office—it was "too expensive," he said. "I need money for postage."[69] He wanted to start campaigning, to hit every dirt road in North Carolina, devoting his time to "some politicking, some handshaking, some requesting of votes."[70] Unlike Graham, Reynolds had never found it difficult to ask people to vote for him.

He told a Raleigh radio audience on March 18 that he had taken on Graham because Graham stood for programs Reynolds could not accept. He then leaped into a cream-colored Studebaker convertible bound for Pittsboro, where he spoke to the Lion's Club. Then he continued on to Elizabeth City, where he stressed the issues of excessive taxes and deficit spending.[71]

He returned to Asheville on March 29, claiming to have logged one thousand exhausting miles. In and out of the Studebaker hundreds of times, Reynolds realized in short order that this was not 1932. He planned to stay at home for a time, he told reporters, catching up on his correspondence and drafting campaign literature.[72] Voters did not yet know it, but Reynolds's active effort to return to the Senate was now largely spent. His future activities would be haphazard and, at best, lackluster. Reynolds at sixty-five was simply too old and too tired for the rigors of intensive electioneering. He had little campaign money, and his meandering down dirt roads had raised only random clouds of red clay dust. Voters had reacted to his call with the most dismissive response in public life—indifference. As a seasoned vote seeker, Reynolds understood his plight, but he would not withdraw. Committed to the race, he would see it through, savor whatever public attention he could claim, and smile just to have the flashbulbs once again in his face.

Reynolds's early failure was not so evident to Jonathan Daniels and company, who were hardly ready to dismiss him. In an election, anything was possible, and "Bumptious Bob," as Daniels called him, might get hot and win. Daniels unleashed a bitter editorial broadside denouncing Reynolds in late March, while privately pursuing nasty rumors about Reynolds's World War I military record. Reynolds's request for Tar Heel money to finance a return to the Senate "where he disgraced North Carolina before in order that he may disgrace it again is . . . unmitigated gall," Daniels wrote. In the Senate, Reynolds had consorted with Nazi sympathizers in World War II, Daniels reminded his readers, when American security was at stake. Surely voters would remember why Reynolds had retired in 1944 and not be suckered into contributing to their own shame by supporting "Our Bob."[73]

At the suggestion of Johnston Avery, Daniels wrote Truman military aide Harry H. Vaughan, suggesting that Reynolds, who did not fight in World War I, was possibly afraid of his war record—or lack thereof. For campaign use, Daniels asked Vaughan to investigate.[74] Within a week, Vaughan replied. Reynolds had no federal service; he had registered for the second draft in September 1918 but simply had not been called. Obviously, there was nothing questionable in such a record, and Daniels's foray into the lower depths of political intrigue came to naught. Daniels, of course, kept this effort from Senator Graham.[75]

Daniels's principal focus in late March was not Reynolds, in any case, but Willis Smith. In all likelihood, if Graham lost the race, Smith, not Reynolds, would be taking his place. But Smith, having entered the race late, was slow to set up his campaign organization. Not until March 10 did he name Charles P. Green to be his campaign manager and Alice Edwards to run his Raleigh office. On March 12, workmen began moving desks and typewriters into Smith headquarters at the Sir Walter Hotel.[76]

Charles Green was a thirty-nine-year-old Louisburg lawyer and World War II veteran who was active in Franklin County politics but had no experience in statewide campaigning. Perplexed at Smith's organizational confusion, one observer, Raleigh attorney Allen Langston, thought Green a poor choice, characterizing him as a "political tyro" with few statewide acquaintances and no political judgment.[77] But J. C. B. Ehringhaus, Jr., a Smith confidant, approved the choice of Green, praising his organizational skills and his state contacts.[78]

Green did not have the burden of fashioning Smith's comprehensive strategy. That task fell to Smith's inner circle, a group of attorneys, businessmen, and conservative Democrats. Chief among them was Colonel William T. Joyner, Sr., son of educational statesman and ardent Grahamite James Yadkin Joyner. Colonel Joyner, a respected Raleigh attorney, was a former chairman of the State Highway Commission and a vital Smith supporter. Other key associates were Smith's law partner John Anderson, attorney and owner of WRAL radio A. J. Fletcher, Ehringhaus, and longtime Democrat Banks Arendell. Two young Raleigh attorneys, William T. Joyner, Jr., and Tom Ellis, were important staff operatives, and the young news director of WRAL radio, Jesse A. Helms, while not an official staffer, was a stout Smith backer who frequented Smith headquarters to do what he could to assist the campaign.[79]

Green, as campaign director, ran Smith's day-to-day operations. Once strategic decisions were made, state headquarters informed county managers, who would then implement the decisions. Smith's late start meant that the Smith organization did not always get its first choices for county managers—some had already committed to Graham—but the organization nevertheless delegated authority to local directors, who raised their own money and sometimes printed their own ads.[80]

Smith chose Hoover Adams, the thirty-year-old editor of the Dunn *Dispatch*, as his publicity director.[81] According to a Graham supporter, Smith enticed Adams with the promise that in regard to salary, "you can write your own ticket."[82] Adams announced immediately that Smith's campaign theme would be the Frank Capra–Jimmy Stewart inspired "Mr. Smith Goes to Washington."[83] But before Washington there was Raleigh, a task accomplished when Smith headquarters opened on March 14. Rebutting claims that he was handicapped by a late start, Smith stated that more work had been done than people knew, and in time observers would realize that the campaign was well launched.[84]

Smith's brave effort to overcome the disadvantage of a late announcement could not, however, hide the clear liability that his delayed entry had created. Graham was much better known, had opened his headquarters two weeks ahead of Smith, and had the support of both Governor Scott and President Truman. Initially, Smith had to achieve name recognition by introducing himself to the voters, which he began to do in massive mailings from Raleigh. These mailings emphasized Smith's service to the Democratic party, both in the state house and as a stalwart party member, in contrast to the picture of Frank Graham as a newcomer to party politics and undeserving of a Senate nomination.[85]

Smith's strategy, as he described it to Allen Langston, would be opportunistic. Smith would exploit any mistakes Graham might make and capitalize on Scott's aggressive seizure of the party and the accompanying resentment of many party regulars. Smith's forces intended to twist every pronouncement the free-talking governor might make, tying dislike for Scott to his Senate appointee. Smith intended also to set up a straw man called "socialism" and pummel him from one end of the state to another. Between rounds with the straw man, he would seek the support of the medical profession with fulminations against "socialized medicine." Smith did not intend to state that Graham favored "socialized medicine"; he would only claim to be more attuned to the political sentiments of doctors. Finally, Smith intended to use his presidency of the American Bar Association and his Nuremberg war trials experience to argue that as a lawyer with an international reputation, he would have great influence in the Senate's deliberations on foreign affairs.

This campaign, Allen Langston wrote on March 22, would not be

Smith confers with campaign manager Charles P. Green (to his right) and pub-
licity director Hoover Adams (on the telephone). Adams's broadsides against
Graham were a highlight of the Smith effort. (North Carolina Department of
Archives and History, Raleigh)

decided on basic issues; nor would the character or capacities of the two
leading candidates be decisive. Rather, the outcome would hinge on
Smith's ability to blow small things into major issues. Graham faced a
real fight for reelection, Langston predicted, not because substantive
issues would threaten him but because the campaign would see "a lot of
whispering and street corner gabbling about socialism, communism, and
'niggers.' "[86]

From the outset, the Graham forces believed that the Smith camp was
knee-deep in money, especially from big business contributions. But
Allen Langston thought otherwise. Clearly Smith had been promised big
money as an inducement to declare, but his hesitation in setting up his
organization indicated some problems in converting pledges to cash.
Smith, Langston wrote, had difficulty getting the money to pay printing
costs for his initial mailings.[87]

One pledge made prior to entering the race Smith was determined to
keep. He would spend very little of his own money in his senatorial
effort. Realizing that he was a reluctant candidate anyway, campaign

aides knew that he would accept defeat rather than impoverish himself or imperil his family's economic future. He had been promised money to run his campaign, and if people wanted him to express their political views, they had to pay their pledges. The Smith campaign therefore was not awash in money, in its initial phase, and Smith occasionally threatened to withdraw because of inadequate finances.[88]

Some Smith supporters apparently thought that Smith was personally wealthy, had huge sums pledged to him, and therefore did not need more money, a predicament that explained the early lack of postage money. But Tom Ellis and others got busy. Ellis collected money from everyone he could find,[89] and substantial sums came in anonymously. Once, a man dumped $6,000 in Hoover Adams's lap and said, "Use it to beat that man Graham." On another occasion, two older ladies, who would not give their names, gave Adams $500 to defeat Graham. Numerous others gave time and money. Nathan M. Johnson, owner of a farmer's supply store chain based in Dunn (Johnson Cotton Company), discontinued his regular advertising and used his radio spots to support Smith. Edwin Pate of Laurinburg used the local radio station and newspaper that he owned to assist Smith's campaign. Although the campaign never had limitless resources, eventually the Smith people solved their money problems and as the campaign intensified, they spent heavily.[90]

Amid the turmoil of organization and acquiring finances, Smith announced his official platform on March 19. His objective would be "to keep America liberal, Progressive and yet sane in its Progress." Rejecting the extremes of either left or right, he denounced socialistic and communistic trends in government, focusing his ire on socialist planners as threats to liberty: "Planners may soon become plotters, and the plotters the masters of the people unless we stop them where they are." In office, he would bar from federal employment anyone possessed of "foreign ideologies" and would oppose anyone in high office who would "condone such employment, or give aid, encouragement and comfort to Socialists, Communists, and their sympathizers and fellow travelers." This was an obvious rebuke to Senator Graham, although Smith did not mention him by name.

The remainder of Smith's platform was mild. He favored continued parity programs for tobacco and other crops, a balanced budget, no deficit financing, an end to government waste, and continued improvement in the good racial relations for which North Carolina was noted. He favored high wages but did not want workers to be represented by "labor racketeers." Regarding FEPC, he opposed it, not only because it would corrode race relations, but also because it threatened states' rights. Law and force could not produce harmony in race relations, the platform argued. The power of the churches and schools must be utilized to produce fair and impartial treatment of minorities.

The platform included a brief candidate biography, emphasizing Smith's impressive climb from humble circumstances to professional prominence. Inheriting neither wealth nor privilege, Smith had become successful through his hard work and strong character. A self-made man whose rise the American system had made possible, Smith now was portrayed as fighting to preserve that system for future generations.[91]

Smith's platform, as poorly written and as cliché-ridden as one expects of such documents, was aimed at conservative voters. Its most remarkable quality was its similarity to the Graham campaign document. Both candidates opposed "socialized medicine," both proclaimed their fidelity to the principle of balanced budgets, both opposed FEPC, and both professed similar views on solving racial problems, although Graham specifically condemned the poll tax and lynching. Graham also stressed more federal aid for education, more federal housing expenditures, higher minimum wages, and increased social security coverage. Smith made no specific mention of these issues. Smith decried the advance of socialism and communism in the United States; Graham wanted to fight communism in Europe. Smith made no mention of national defense, while Graham advocated a strong military defense and active participation in the United Nations. Clearly then, both platforms were sufficiently muddled to appeal, their authors hoped, to the largest number of voters without offending anyone. But the platforms did not obscure significant substantive differences. Graham was more liberal on race, more internationally oriented, and more an advocate of federal spending, all differences that would become clearer as the campaign proceeded.

Smith chose his hometown, Elizabeth City, for his first major campaign speech. Speaking from the courthouse, he urged his listeners to stand against socialist planners before it was too late. Many Americans who paraded as liberals moved on to socialism and then to communism, and they must be stopped. He then reiterated the need for a balanced budget and expressed his opposition to the Brannan Plan, a policy proposed by Agriculture Secretary Charles Brannan in April 1949. The plan aimed to eliminate agricultural price supports—parity—and move toward market pricing for farm products while supporting farm income by direct payment to farmers.[92]

Smith spoke to a huge assemblage, the largest gathering in Elizabeth City in years, according to the local newspaper. His audience found his speech impressive, his plainspoken style appealing. A consensus of those present concluded that Smith would wage a strong battle, and the *Daily Advance* predicted a second primary.[93]

From Elizabeth City, Smith headed west, all the way to Waynesville, Brevard, Forest City, and Asheville, constantly warning his audiences to keep socialist planners out of government and predicting victory for his campaign. At Charlotte he reminded voters that he had been long in the fight against socialism, communism, and other ideologies, citing his service as general counsel to the North Carolina Medical Society and his role in opposing "socialized medicine."[94] As he campaigned, his confidants began their public endorsements. J. C. B. Ehringhaus, Jr., Colonel William T. Joyner, Sr., and former state representative Wilbur Bunn all committed publicly to Smith. They wrote letters to the far corners of the state hailing Smith's candidacy and arguing that Smith's beliefs and convictions represented the thinking of the majority of North Carolinians.[95]

On the stump, Smith proved a bit stiff—"too lawyerlike." His talks did not arouse strong emotions, and he proved to be only an average campaigner. But he had a knack for names and faces—seemingly he remembered everyone he had ever met. He was, in addition, a husky (6'2", 210 lbs.), well-kempt figure, possessed of an imposing mien. Strongly self-confident, his bearing drew peoples' eyes when he entered a room or hall, and he was undeniably a man of conviction and integrity. Intelligent, compelling, forceful, and articulate, the "average campaigner" was an imposing candidate.[96]

While on his western swing, traveling, as all the candidates did, by car, Smith made a slashing attack on Graham without once mentioning the senator's name. He charged that "one of his opponents" favored FEPC because it had been endorsed by the President's Committee on Civil Rights (the Truman-appointed group on which Graham had served), which had produced the controversial report *To Secure These Rights*. Graham had stated several times that although he did sign the committee report, he had authored a minority report within the overall document opposing the establishment of a compulsory FEPC. In his charge, Smith told his listeners that they would search in vain for any "minority report." It was "only a figment of the imagination of a far-seeing friend who realized that the committee had gone too far."[97]

Smith's issue was timely and well chosen. FEPC was under debate in the Senate as he spoke, and Smith intended to turn the screw on Graham to force an admission that he had favored it in 1947, only to temporize under the heat of voter scrutiny in 1950.[98] His bowshot also served notice that he meant to swarm Graham with pointed questions that would require direct denial or rejoinder or astute counterattack. Smith had thus taken an offensive posture and was bent on holding it.

Smith's FEPC charge at first tied every tongue in the Graham camp. Jeff Johnson did reply with one of the limpest rebuttals in the annals of politics: "Mr. Smith is doing the talking. He did not mention the name of the candidate he refers to, and we do not know who he was talking about."[99] Olla Ray Boyd, perhaps? For certain, it was not "Our Bob."

Jonathan Daniels knew that it was Graham. And it was trouble. In the next day's Raleigh News and Observer, Daniels deplored Smith's raising this issue. Both candidates had clearly stated their opposition to FEPC, Daniels insisted. Smith was striving "to stir up the furies of racial prejudice as a means of getting votes." The tactic was beneath Willis Smith, a gentleman who had never shown any inclination to foment race angers in North Carolina. No profit could come from it. Graham's dissent on FEPC, Daniels argued, was "as clear as type and ink," right there on page 167 of the civil rights report. On that page (actually page 168), under the subject of education, the southerners on the Committee on Civil Rights had written their disapproval of federal intervention in racial matters. Daniels quoted the section in full, attributing the opposition to federal force to Frank Graham. Daniels further explained Graham's belief that segregation could only be ended through religious teaching and through improved education. Graham was fighting against the zealots eager to use federal force to impose racial change, Daniels wrote. "FEPC is not involved in this campaign," Daniels claimed, hoping that his declaration would defuse the issue.[100]

Four days after Smith's initial FEPC broadside, the Greensboro Daily News joined Daniels in Graham's defense. If Graham were not opposed to federal intervention to end segregation, why was the state attorney general citing him as an opponent of federal force? Referring to North Carolina's amicus curiae brief in the then pending case of Sweatt v. Painter, Attorney General Harry McMullan had pointed out that Graham and other fair-minded southern liberals favored the eventual end of segregation but not as a consequence of federal force. Smith could not have it both ways, the Daily News argued. If Graham's view in the Committee on Civil Rights report could be cited to argue against federal intrusion in a court case on segregated education, he could not fairly be pilloried by his critics as an integrationist firebrand.[101]

The Durham Sun agreed that Graham was one of the signers of a minority report that opposed an immediate end to racial segregation,[102] while the New York Times reported substantially the same conclusion.[103] North Carolinians, explained Harold Martin in the Saturday Evening Post, had read the report and were not disturbed by Graham's stand because he had dissented from the antisegregation recommendations.[104]

It made no difference anyway, added the Durham *Morning Herald.* Graham opposed FEPC now, and as a Senate liberal in opposition to the bill, he would likely carry more weight in the matter than a southern diehard. The paper suggested that Graham speak directly to the issue, especially since his friends, in defending him, had made a poor case. They had taken a demurrer from the section on education in the Truman report and applied it to the section in the report discussing FEPC, where no dissent appeared. Such a defense only made the issue more lively, concluded the *Morning Herald*, and more difficult for the senator.[105]

Certainly the issue was lively to conservative WRAL radio commentator Alvin Wingfield, Jr. A Smith adviser and advocate, Wingfield had been after Graham on FEPC since early March. Wingfield, like Smith, assailed the idea that the "so-called minority report," which Graham kept referring to, in any way modified or challenged the committee position on FEPC. The "minority report," argued Wingfield, applied only to the issue of segregation and could not be interpreted as modifying the paragraph on FEPC. The report indicated lack of unanimity in only two places, and neither place referred to FEPC. Wingfield told his radio audience that his reading of the report convinced him that Graham favored an FEPC with full compulsory power. Even if Graham now repudiated the former position, Wingfield argued, he was still at odds with North Carolina voters who would oppose FEPC in any form.[106]

The High Point *Enterprise*, like Wingfield, could find no record that Graham wrote or signed a "minority report" in his service on the Truman committee. If Graham had opposed the committee FEPC position, the paper could find no reference to it. It called on Graham to reveal the location of the minority report, or to produce the "hidden record of his minority report, if there is such a thing."[107]

Graham, of course, had never advocated an FEPC with full compulsory power. He had long favored the eventual and voluntary elimination of racial segregation in the South as a goal, but he had always been aware that the race issue was an incendiary question. He well knew that when racial violence occurred in the South of the 1930s and 1940s, blacks were its victims. Hence, he was always cautious in endorsing domestic measures that threatened what he saw as a delicate balance in racial matters. His concerns had influenced *To Secure These Rights* specifically in the report's discussion of segregation on page 167 and in the recommendations on the admission and treatment of students in public and private educational institutions on page 168. University of North Carolina

Comptroller William D. "Billy" Carmichael, Jr., had confirmed Graham's claim of opposition to the use of federal force in both instances when he conferred with Dr. Robert Carr of Dartmouth College, the secretary of the Committee on Civil Rights, and committee member Mrs. M. E. Tilly of Atlanta. Both Carr and Tilly recalled that the opposition to federal intervention expressed in the two places was Graham's exact position.[108]

Graham expressed his view on the matter most cogently in a letter to Pauli Murray dated March 6, 1950. Before he could sign the official report, Graham recalled, he had asked that a statement be included under the heading "In General," in the "Recommendations" section of the report. This statement set forth "my objections to the use of federal sanctions in matters of discrimination and prejudice. This statement of the views of a minority of the Commission was inserted under the section 'In General' to make it unnecessary to repeat the same thought after each of several individual recommendations."[109]

This position was entirely consistent with Graham's racial posture over the years. Federal sanctions, he believed, would only intensify opposition to racial change and prolong segregation. Yet he remained more liberal on race issues than his senatorial opponents, despite his position against arbitrary federal power. Graham had opposed the poll tax, endorsed full voting equality for blacks, recommended more equal employment practices, and advocated admission of qualified blacks to southern state graduate schools where no separate provision for blacks had been made.[110] These positions clearly distinguished Graham from his opponents and exposed him to attack. D. Hiden Ramsey urged Graham to meet this attack by advocating, in a campaign speech, complete equality of education within the pattern of segregation. Voters feared the breakdown of school segregation as they feared nothing else, Ramsey wrote.[111] But Graham thought his position already clear and chose not to address the question further. His refusal to discuss it only fed his critics' fury. Perhaps a stronger, more lucid response in the manner of his letter to Pauli Murray would have helped; certainly early signs indicated that the race issue could not be circumvented.

Nor could the issue of communism and the related question of Graham's social activism be sidestepped. Indeed, Smith's focus in the first primary was Graham's career as an activist liberal and his association with controversial organizations and causes—"subversive organizations" in the argot of the House Un-American Activities Committee (HUAC). Smith told one of his audiences, "I can say to you . . . that I do not now nor have I ever belonged to any subversive organizations and that as a United States senator I shall never allow myself to be duped into the use

of my name for propaganda or other purposes of those types of organizations. The unwary cause just as much harm as the unscrupulous in the
days that are at hand."[112] This testament of Willis Smith was a representative sample of the language he employed in his effort to paint Graham
as a red hot pink, a muddle-headed academic who could not tell Joe
Stalin from Joe DiMaggio.

The issue of communism and the broader theme of subversion had, of
course, been primary domestic questions in American life since the latter
part of 1949. In a succession of sensational disclosures, Americans had
been bombarded with stories that seemed to suggest a concerted, highly
effective, systematic effort to compromise American national security
and cripple the government internationally. Against the background of
the cold war, containment, and deepening tension between the United
States and Stalin's Soviet Union, the American people had been stunned
by a series of dramatic events: the Communist victory in the Chinese civil
war, Stalinist control of eastern Europe, and the Soviet explosion of a
nuclear bomb. They were further gripped by the melodrama of the Hiss-
Chambers case. That affair, arguably the most publicized espionage/
perjury case in U.S. history, had been in clear view since Whittaker
Chambers first made his charges against Alger Hiss public on August 3,
1948, in testimony before the HUAC.[113] The perjury case that grew out
of this affair came to a conclusion on January 21, 1950, when, in the
second trial, Hiss was found guilty on two counts of perjury.[114]

As the Hiss-Chambers case unfolded, the FBI arrested Judith Coplon
in March 1949, and she began her active life as an ex-Communist
witness.[115] In February 1950, British nuclear physicist Klaus Fuchs sur-
rendered to authorities on charges of passing American atomic secrets to
Soviet operatives. Fuchs, as it turned out, was a Soviet agent who had
kept Soviet authorities fully apprised of the work at Los Alamos, New
Mexico, and other secret U.S. nuclear installations. Following Fuchs's
confession, nine Americans, including Julius and Ethel Rosenberg, were
arrested and linked by the Justice Department to Klaus Fuchs. The Fuchs
case, which alarmed Americans, was in the headlines of all the state's
dailies. The papers recounted in detail the coverage of Fuchs's trial, the
most spectacular of its kind in British history.[116]

The sensational revelations from the Hiss-Chambers, Rosenberg, and
Fuchs cases were laden with domestic political implications, and the
national Republican party, desperately seeking a path to power, sensed a
surefire campaign issue: the Communist menace. The cold war and its
attendant complexity had cast widespread suspicion upon American
Communists and Soviet sympathizers as disloyal. The sensational disclo-

sures of treachery in high places generated a highly charged political atmosphere and gave credibility to the claim that the national Democrats were either blind to the threat of communism or subversive dupes. While charges of softness on communism against Democratic administrations were a routine feature of right-wing Republican rhetoric, the accusations gained new prominence with the emergence of Wisconsin Senator Joseph R. McCarthy as the nation's premier anti-Communist. In speeches at Wheeling, West Virginia, on February 9, 1950, and at Reno, Nevada, two days later, McCarthy called on Truman to ask the State Department for the names of its employees who were Communists, after alleging that he had a list of State Department Reds.[117] Both speeches were widely reported in North Carolina.[118]

McCarthyism, as it developed, became a politics of revenge, practiced by groups resentful of American social policy since the New Deal, angered by communism's seemingly relentless advance since the end of World War II, and opposed to a European-centered foreign policy. McCarthyites were livid at what they saw as Truman's arrogant dismissal of the Hiss-Chambers case as a "red herring." These frustrations made McCarthyism a convenient and apparently effective bludgeon with which to assault Democrats.[119] Republicans around the country made communism their number one campaign issue.[120]

Jonathan Daniels, of all of Graham's advisers, understood most clearly the emerging Republican strategy, especially as it would affect the upcoming election in North Carolina. He knew as well that conservative southern Democrats, sensing an effective vote-getting tactic, would attack Frank Graham by taking "the straight Republican anti-Truman line."[121] The case against Graham would likely be built on his membership in Communist front organizations.[122]

Daniels's prediction proved prophetic; congressional candidates nationwide worked to exploit the Communist issue to the fullest. Willis Smith, of course, had already sounded the clarion against Graham on March 23, challenging many of Graham's political associations. Smith's headquarters then assigned William T. Joyner, Jr., and Tom Ellis to trace the path of Graham's life as a social activist. Ellis and Joyner worked diligently at their task, composed memoranda summarizing their findings, and gave the memos to Hoover Adams. Ellis and Joyner wrote ads attacking Graham's political associations and his political judgment, had them approved by Adams, and then published them in major dailies, principally the Raleigh *News and Observer*. The Ellis-Joyner material set the basic themes for Smith's first primary attack.[123]

Pro-Smith newspapers supported in editorial commentary the themes

Smith headquarters developed. Without question Bob Thompson's High Point *Enterprise* made the case against Graham with more consistency and vigor than any other anti-Graham daily. Thompson always professed that he liked Graham personally but believed him "soft-hearted" and a fall guy who had been falling for phonies all his life. This characterization explained why Graham had allowed so many subversive and Communist front organizations to use his name. "This nation, in these times, can't afford to have such a man, regardless of the good intentions, in the United States Senate." Those who supported Graham were allowing personal friendship to blind them, "They, too, are fall guys," Thompson insisted.[124]

One principal source for the volleys Smith partisans aimed at Graham was anti-Roosevelt ideologue John T. Flynn. Thompson, who at times referred to Graham as "Frank the Front," and others had been disseminating material from Flynn's most recent broadside, *The Road Ahead*. As he had done in a widely read earlier work, *The Roosevelt Myth*, Flynn argued in his more recent work that the road ahead under present Democratic policy was a socialist quagmire. Published under the auspices of the Committee for Constitutional Government, and supported by newspaper magnate Frank Gannett,[125] *The Road Ahead* specifically attacked Frank Graham's affiliation with Communist front groups, referring to Graham as a "national socialist planner" and a "hooded Socialist."[126] The book inspired Graham's opponents and was a persistent problem for Graham forces. Perhaps it would defuse Flynn's charges, Mrs. Paul P. McCain wrote Vice President Alben Barkley, to point out that Flynn was a reactionary Republican bent on smearing Democratic candidates.[127]

Graham's opponents also circulated a Flynn-inspired sermon, authored by Nashville, Tennessee, Presbyterian minister Walter R. Courtenay, first delivered on Lincoln's birthday, 1950. Courtenay praised *The Road Ahead* from his pulpit, defended free enterprise capitalism, and warned that socialism was the sickness of the twentieth century. Many educators, clergymen, and senators, Courtenay lamented, thought pink and talked pink. They were neither Communists nor vicious people; they simply preferred the socialist state to the American system. Courtenay decried the influence of the Americans for Democratic Action, a group he identified as "about as Democratic as Stalin." Its backers, among them Senator Graham, leaned far to the left of the American system and were intent on destroying free enterprise. A socialist planner in Washington did not differ at all from one in Moscow, Courtenay argued. They both were enemies of the basic liberties of men.[128]

The spreading of this antisocialist literature struck a raw nerve among some Tar Heel voters. Franz H. Krebs, in a letter published in the Charlotte *Observer*, identified Graham as a socialist planner and thought him "more dangerous to our country than all the communists tried and convicted." When a person joined several front groups, wrote Krebs, it seemed logical to assume that he knew what he was doing, and anyone who participated in such groups should be viewed with suspicion.[129] Another complainant, writing to Senator Hoey, feared that if Jonathan Daniels, Graham, and other socialists had their way, America's heritage would be debt, socialism, and integration of the races.[130]

Graham forces scurried to their candidate's defense as their worst fears about the campaign began to materialize. Jeff Johnson noted that even though Smith was unwilling to call Graham a Communist, he was nonetheless willing to twist any information he could get from whatever discredited source to make people think Graham was a Communist. Such guilt by association tactics, Johnson charged, should be beneath the dignity of a former American Bar Association president, whose campaign ethics should be above reproach. Apparently Smith believed that a lie told often enough would become truth, even from a source as compromised as John Flynn, whom Johnson labeled the number one Republican character assassin.[131]

Of course Graham's friends had long anticipated this line of attack and had warned the senator. Now supporters renewed their counsel. North Carolina was massively anti-Communist, wrote one Grahamite, and many voters were wary of Graham's record on the Communist issue. They could not tell a liberal from a Communist, and Graham would have to overcome their prejudice against him by making several strong anti-Communist speeches.[132] Another writer similarly urged Graham to bury this charge with strong anti-Communist language.[133]

Heeding this advice, Graham answered his critics with an explanatory pamphlet and a speech to the Dunn Rotary Club on March 24. He denied that he had ever been a Communist or a socialist and asserted that he had never been "a member of any organization known or suspected by me of being controlled by Communists or socialists." Denouncing both socialism and communism, Graham proclaimed his devotion to the American free enterprise system for all people, pointing out that he had always fought all forms of totalitarianism. He claimed that he was a loyal Democrat and that he had never scratched a Democratic ticket in his life, implying of course that Willis Smith had done exactly that. He had been active in public affairs for thirty years, Graham continued, and in that time, he had sponsored or contributed to scores of movements and organizations devoted to a variety of interests: religion, health, educa-

tion, labor, social security, social well-being, and world peace. "I felt that
by uniting my efforts with thousands of other forward-thinking and
progressive citizens I could be more effective."

Concluding his rebuttal, Graham acknowledged that he had once
belonged to a committee on the attorney general's list of subversive
organizations—the American Committee for the Protection of the Foreign Born—from which he had resigned in 1941, seven years before
the attorney general identified it as "subversive." He had never been a
member of any organization after it made the list, he told the Dunn
Rotarians.[134]

Graham's speech was a positive and emphatic denial of Smith's
charges. Without mentioning his opponent's name or the specific allega-
tions emanating from the Smith camp, he had defended both his integrity and his patriotism effectively. But the question the Smith forces
sought to stress was the issue of Graham's political judgment, and on this
subject, Graham's reply was general and at best disingenuous. Graham
had been fully informed in 1938 that Communist party members had
insinuated themselves into the Southern Conference for Human Wel
fare—indeed, he knew quite clearly who they were—and the issue had
nagged at him throughout his association with the SCHW. As his liberal
friends and colleagues quit the organization at varying intervals throughout its chaotic history, they kept Graham fully apprised of their reasons
for leaving, as did southern liberals and radicals who had kept the
SCHW at arm's length from its beginning. Graham in 1970 admitted in
an interview, "Well, I now know that there were far leftists in the conference, but whenever we brought an issue to the floor we always beat
them."[135] In addition, his acknowledgment that he had resigned from an
organization later cited by the attorney general as subversive confirmed
to his critics that Graham had been careless, foolish, or gullible in his
political associations.

Graham's advocates nonetheless were quite pleased with his Dunn
speech. Graham had set the charges to rest, the Raleigh *News and Observer* wrote. His statement proved that there was never any validity to
the argument that linked Graham either directly or indirectly to Communists. The charges, coming from those who knew better, had confused
some well-meaning people. "The meanest man who walks the earth," the
paper quoted House Speaker Sam Rayburn, "is the man who goes all out
and spreads unjustified fears and fills the people with unhappiness and
discontent and distrust."[136] The entire controversy, added the St. Louis
Post-Dispatch from afar, was incredible and even more abhorrent because

the tawdry charges came not from Bob Reynolds but from Smith, from whom more was expected. Graham was clearly the best candidate in the field, opined the paper, and "no more a Communist than they [Smith supporters] are fair fighters." Many Americans, the paper added, hoped North Carolina would send Graham back to Washington.[137]

Charles Tillett and Senator Graham had already initiated a letter-writing campaign to contain possible damage from the Communist issue. Tillett argued in a letter to a Charlotte citizen that characterizing Graham's views as leftist was a complete misrepresentation. Graham's policies were constructive, designed to maintain free enterprise capitalism.[138] In another letter, Tillett explained that socialism was the nationalization of a country's principal industries in certain circumstances, a concept Graham opposed. Graham did favor the use of federal authority under some conditions, for example, the Federal Deposit Insurance Corporation's (FDIC) protection of bank deposits. No one would condemn the FDIC as socialistic. Tillett wrote that he knew of no one more completely devoted to American capitalism than Frank Graham.[139]

The Raleigh campaign staff had prepared a "socialism form letter" to rebut any presumption that Graham was anything but a fervent capitalist. Graham's commitment to free enterprise was unequivocal, the letter maintained. It pledged Graham's continued vigilance to oppose trends or policies that might result in socialization of the United States.[140] These views Graham echoed in a series of personal letters, such as one penned to Mrs. Dudley Bagley in which he expressed his appreciation for her political support and for her aid in the fight against Fascist and Communist tyranny.[141]

Another campaign booklet, aimed at confronting Smith charges directly, offered a precise explanation of Graham's views and history over the years. The document claimed that the charge that Graham sponsored organizations devoted to undermining the U.S. government "was a vicious libel on one of the most patriotic Americans of our times." Omitting the negative findings of the Atomic Energy Commission's Security Board, the pamphlet cited Graham's unanimous selection by the commission to serve as the first president of the Oak Ridge Institute of Nuclear Studies as evidence of his high esteem and trustworthiness.

The pamphlet then listed the five (of 159) organizations cited by the attorney general as subversive to which Graham allegedly had belonged. Of the five, the pamphlet explained, Graham had never joined or sponsored the International Labor Defense, and he had withdrawn from the American Committee for the Protection of the Foreign Born in 1941. As for the China Aid Council, a group affiliated with the American League

for Peace and Democracy, Graham's connection consisted of sending a
contribution for a Shanghai hospital that cared for the wounded of
Chiang Kai-shek's nationalist army. Graham had also contributed money
to a hospital in Madrid through the Medical Bureau, which was affiliated
with the North American Committee to Aid Spanish Democracy, an
organization that had expired in 1939. Finally, the pamphlet concluded,
Graham had never joined the Citizens Committee to Free Earl Browder
but was instead one of hundreds of patriotic Americans who had signed a
petition for Browder's release from prison because they felt he had served
enough time for the offense for which he had been convicted. All of these
organizations, including the Southern Conference for Human Welfare,
the pamphlet pointed out, had been defunct for some time, and "the
groups Frank Graham helped were not subversive."[142]

In the political climate of 1950, nonetheless, subversion was to some
extent in the eye of the beholder. The Browder committee, the North
American Committee to Aid Spanish Democracy, the American Committee for the Protection of the Foreign Born, and the American League for
Peace and Democracy had been declared subversive by the U.S. attorney
general, and Graham clearly was affiliated in some way with each of these
organizations. The associations were, at best, unusual for a U.S. senator
and unheard of for any other North Carolina politician.

In defending Graham's activist past, the pamphlet also included several Graham speeches, beginning in 1931, reiterating his stand against
communism and fascism and his support of "liberty and freedom." It
cited public attacks on Graham as an American imperialist published in
Tass and in *Pravda*.[143]

The pamphlet, of course, could not hide the specter of Communist
affiliations. The issue continued to impede the Graham campaign. Writing to Graham's wife Marian in March 1950, Charles Tillett—who had
told Graham one year earlier to resign from everything except the Presbyterian church and the Democratic party—expressed his dismay at a
recent Greensboro *Daily News* report that Graham remained honorary
cochairman of the National Council against Conscription. The *Daily
News* itself had editorialized, as an ardent Graham ally, that he should
disassociate himself from all legislative pressure groups, and it lamented
the seemingly endless exploitation of Graham's good name. Had Graham
in fact withdrawn from this group and others like it, Tillett asked Mrs.
Graham.[144] Well, no, she responded. "Knowing Frank as you and I do, I
am sure he will not get off this committee right now."[145] Other close
friends, *Carolina Israelite* editor Harry Golden, for example, who tirelessly defended Graham as a patriotic and great American, had to admit

that Graham might have been too enthusiastic in his idealism, lending his name to controversial groups subsequently cited as subversive by various critics.[146]

Other controversies, some minor and some major, added to the growing sense of consternation in the heretofore optimistic Graham camp. One political imbroglio proved especially troublesome. On March 18, 1950, the Scott-appointed State Board of Elections, chaired by Charles M. Britt, ignored the recommendations of State Democratic party chairman B. Everett Jordan (based on names submitted to Jordan by the county Democratic Executive Committees) and named election board members of its own choosing in eight western North Carolina counties. It was an action without recent precedent, and it outraged local politicians, who vowed to fight in court if necessary to rescind this highhanded maneuver. Asked if he had the right to ignore the Democratic party chairman's recommendations, Britt responded that it was "for a good cause." He admitted he had talked things over with Governor Scott, and despite party leaders' fears that the furor would affect the Senate race, he had gone ahead with his decision.[147]

Reaction was nasty and not confined to the eight affected counties. Britt's action, charged the Asheville *Citizen*, was illegal, and worse, Britt must have known that it was illegal. As for the governor, "Kerr Scott's air of injured innocence," the paper observed, "is a little too transparent to make us believe that he, also, was ignorant of an established procedure." Such chicanery undercut public confidence in the political process. Perhaps it was mere coincidence, the paper scolded, that seven of the eight counties affected had voted for Scott's opponents in both 1948 gubernatorial primaries and all eight had opposed Scott in the runoff.[148]

That the State Board of Elections had violated the law was not in doubt. Section eleven of the state election laws provided that county election boards be named for two-year terms beginning on the tenth Saturday before each election. The state chairman of each party could recommend three electors in each county, from among whom the State Board of Elections could choose one.[149]

Not even the Raleigh *News and Observer* could swallow this deed whole. According to state law, the board at least had to show cause and make its findings public before removing election officials. If the board had acted solely out of suspicion of some wrongdoing, it should rescind its removals, the paper counseled.[150]

Willis Smith, no doubt grateful for the chance to bash the Scott administration directly, asserted that Britt's action was not only outrageous, it was a plain violation of statute. Any county desirous of challenging the ruling could obtain the services of his law firm without charge, Smith told reporters.

Governor Scott, besieged by newsmen for an explanation of this action, lamely declared that the matter was in the hands of Britt and the Board of Elections. Scott supposed that Britt had felt justified in making the decision because of reports of rigged elections and ballot tampering in the eight affected counties.[151] Scott, however, had stated a month previously that large segments of the population (specifically farmers) were not represented on such boards, a situation he intended to change.[152]

On March 22, Attorney General Harry McMullan ruled that the State Board of Elections had exceeded its authority when it appointed members of the eight county boards, ignoring the state chairman's recommendations.[153] The next day, the board rescinded its appointments and appointed new board members chosen from the names recommended by the state party chairman. But the board made clear its intention to remove any appointees who might be implicated in election fraud by ongoing State Bureau of Investigation inquiries.[154] Eventually, one Swain County board member was removed in April, but no more was heard about additional removals.[155]

The effect of the political gaffe by Scott forces lingered, in part because nearly every newspaper in the state denounced the election board action in often bitter editorials. The Scott tactics, protested the Asheville *Citizen*, a Scott friend, bore the earmarks of justice in a totalitarian state. Scott, the Tar Heel dictator who had previously abhorred political machines, now was using the influence of his office to get his favorites elected.[156]

Tom Bost in the Greensboro *Daily News* observed that the flap had given Willis Smith a big boost in the Senate race.[157] The Goldsboro *News-Argus* concurred, suggesting that the board's action had maligned all election officials in western North Carolina. Graham had been hurt by the arbitrary power play, which had done so much damage that it made most of Graham's ardent supporters really sick.[158]

Political observer Allen Langston saw strong indications that the blunder by Britt and Scott could be made into important campaign material. The chairman of the State Board of Elections had been "successfully tagged taking too long a lead off first base." Scott and Britt had committed a serious political error "both in what was done and in the way they have each handled the matter."[159] C. M. Douglas, secretary of the Western North Carolina Associated Communities, informed Jeff Johnson that the elections board mix-up had hurt Graham in the west, because Scott had tried to ram the changes down people's throats.[160]

Brevard College President Eugene T. Coltrane, a strong Grahamite, now wrote that many voters in Asheville who were expected to support Graham would have nothing to do with the Scott organization. Since they thought Scott and Graham were in the same boat, they used the furor as a good excuse for supporting Smith. The anger and resentment would subside, Coltrane predicted, without serious consequences, but "some way must be found to keep the governor from doing things that are damaging to Senator Graham."[161]

Coltrane had put his finger on a campaign issue that would never die: Graham's relationship with the controversial and partisan Scott. Graham supporters had come to Scott to appeal the election board decision, but Scott had ignored them even though he knew Graham might be damaged. He did acknowledge that Graham's opponents were attempting to make Scott a major issue in the campaign, but Scott insisted he was not the issue—the records of the contestants were most important. According to the governor, big corporations in North Carolina were still trying to elect the next senator, as they were accustomed to doing, but voters were now "fed up" with this kind of influence.[162]

The North Carolina newspapers favorable to Smith continued to keep up a drumroll of anti-Scott invective, even after the election board controversy subsided. After all, noted the Durham *Sun*, Scott was backing Graham in every way he could, as was the state Democratic leadership in the person of Jonathan Daniels. Scott and Daniels had abandoned any pretense of maintaining the Democratic party leadership's traditional stance of neutrality. Scott was an issue, the paper remarked, because of his purges and pressures and because he was trying to be North Carolina's little Napoleon. Switching comparisons, the *Sun* suggested that as the Huey Long of Haw River, Scott was doing Graham no good.[163]

Hoover Adams's Dunn *Dispatch* likewise repeatedly pilloried the governor. Scott had kicked over the traces and was doing his all for Graham, as was Daniels. The Raleigh *News and Observer*, the *Dispatch* complained, was now the official organ of the Graham campaign. Gladys Tillett, national vice-chairman of the Democratic National Committee, had also abandoned her neutrality and was writing letters for Graham. Their actions, the *Dispatch* warned, might be the "kiss of death" and could "prove to be the greatest obstacle which Senator Graham has to overcome."[164] Certainly the obstacle would be great if the High Point *Enterprise* had its way. It chided state Democratic officials for failing to observe the proprieties and ethics of party politics. Scott's effort, the *Enterprise* wrote, included using state employees, on state time, in state-owned vehicles. The governor's crowd even ignored a state election law. They were acting in a desperate manner.[165] None of Scott's appointees could

be expected to be neutral in the race, added the Greensboro *Daily News*, as Scott's prestige was on the line.[166]

The race had indeed presented Scott with a delicate dilemma. He was reluctant to go all out with his public support for the senator, realizing that outright and overt assistance carried a political risk. As late as March 28, he claimed he had no plan to stump extensively for Graham.[167] But many Graham supporters, such as F. E. Edwards, a shoe salesman for Knapp Brothers, demanded that Scott intervene directly, with the full force of his prestige and power, even though others continued to caution that open support could backfire.[168] On balance, Graham's inner circle believed they had more to gain than lose by inviting Scott's open intervention and continued to urge Scott to help Graham in every way possible.

The national administration likewise threw its full weight behind Senator Graham. The party sent House Speaker Sam Rayburn to Asheville where he spoke at a YDC rally of fifteen hundred people. The gathering was one of three such meetings held across the state, the other two hosting Vice President Alben Barkley and Tennessee Senator Estes Kefauver. Ostensibly, the meetings were to be neutral toward competing Senate candidates, although the choice of speakers gave the meetings a distinctly pro-Graham cast. In his effort to maintain a neutral stance, YDC President Terry Sanford even refused to honor Willis Smith's request to have "Dixie" played when Smith was introduced to the audience.[169]

In his speech, Speaker Rayburn defended Truman policies and denounced the practice of pinning Communist labels on innocent persons, saying that it was "unfair for a man in a responsible position to make irresponsible statements." An obvious reference to the tactics of Wisconsin Senator Joe McCarthy, Barkley's statement, in the context of North Carolina's Senate race, could have applied as easily to Willis Smith.

All three major candidates were present in Asheville, and each made a speech. In his remarks to the assembled Democrats, Senator Graham spoke for the continuation of race progress without the compulsory powers of any government agency. He advocated aid and support to the "700 million people who are wavering between communism and democracy." Smith, on the other hand, again raised the question of Graham's affiliations while proclaiming his opposition to anyone in high office who allowed his name to be used by subversive organizations. "We can't afford to let the unwary or the well-wishers take us to the four corners of the earth. We should take care of America and our liberties first." If elected, Smith promised, he would march in the Senate in lockstep with Senator Hoey. Agreeing with Smith, Bob Reynolds said that gifts to foreign nations should be halted immediately: "We should look homeward and provide for the needy millions in America."[170]

A mountain-style square dance followed the speech-making at this late March affair, and Bob Reynolds at last had a forum in which his folksy style was without peer. Even though he had been reduced to a position of third in a three-candidate race, at this event he exuded a winner's ebullience, confiding to the crowd that he felt "as spry as a grasshopper." On the marquee of the George Vanderbilt Hotel, Smith supporters had positioned a banner promising that "Mr. Smith Is Going to Washington." Reynolds's crew had interposed, above it, that "'Our Bob' Will Be in Washington to Receive Mr. Smith."[171]

If so, he would be there merely as a spectator. The race had narrowed to Smith and Graham, and Reynolds knew it. His bravado was simply his last hurrah. Willis Smith, however, took full advantage of the news interviews at the conference to disclose his campaign design. He would take his case against foreign ideologies into every section of the state, he promised. Once again, Smith condemned FEPC, civil rights legislation, and the like. Such bills would mean federal officials in the state enforcing laws that should not be on the statute books.[172]

The YDC convention in Asheville marked the end of the first phase of the contest. A momentary lull descended prior to the eight chaotic weeks before first primary balloting on May 27. In the meeting's wake, political analysts and editorialists assessed the race and each of the candidates' prospects. Most believed Graham to be the clear front-runner, Smith in an obvious second place, and Reynolds reduced to the role of spoiler, the potential cause of a now likely second primary. Nell Battle Lewis wrote that Reynolds would not be a serious contender but in a liberal-conservative race, could well tip the balance.[173]

Wade Lucas, writing in the Charlotte *Observer*, stressed the importance of a Graham majority in the first primary, the principal objective of Graham strategists. In a second primary, a candidate as controversial as Graham would have a tough time, Lucas believed.[174] His fourth-estate colleague, New York *Times* reporter William H. Lawrence, suggested that the Graham race would have national importance as an early test of the political expediency of widespread use of the Communist issue as a vote-getting tactic. The response of Tar Heel voters to the issue of "liberty vs. socialism" would provide an important clue to Democratic vulnerability to Republicans on this issue nationwide, Lawrence observed. North Carolina, after all, had remained loyal to Truman even in the difficult year of 1948, and Graham's defeat would be a body blow to the Truman administration. Graham had the support of labor, blacks, teachers, and the Raleigh *News and Observer*, but his key to victory, Lawrence believed, would lie in his ability to convince eastern farmers to transfer their Scott allegiance to his Senate candidacy and in his success in overcoming the hostility of party regulars to the emergence into power of the Scott-Daniels wing of the party. This hostility, Lawrence concluded, gave Smith a base of solid support, especially from industrialists and the medical profession.[175]

Graham would have difficulty sustaining his early lead, C. A. Mc-Knight of the Charlotte *News* told his readers. The vigor, viciousness, and determination of his adversaries would threaten Graham's initial advantage. He was vulnerable to attacks on the race issue, his prolabor attitude, his lack of concern for economy in government, his seeming indifference to communism combined with his willingness to associate his name with organizations of questionable merit, and his alleged support of "socialized medicine." Hence, McKnight predicted, the election would turn on Graham's skill at answering the charges thrust at him. His assets were, after all, tremendous: he was known, admired, and often revered in the state and outside it; he was forceful and persuasive before small groups; he was deeply religious and courageous; and he was a novelty in politics—"a man who appears to act and vote according to his conscience rather than the dictates of pressure groups."[176]

Nearly every analyst concluded that Smith, after a short flurry of activity, had successfully established himself as a serious threat to Graham. Nonetheless, the High Point *Enterprise* admonished Smith campaign strategists to be wary of overdoing the assault on Graham and minimizing Smith's eminent senatorial qualifications. Graham's perceived weaknesses should not be ignored, the *Enterprise* reminded the Smith forces, but Smith's strengths were an important asset for anti-Graham forces.[177]

As part of its effort to foil Smith's attack strategy, the Graham organization once again called on national columnist Drew Pearson, who was willing to help in any way he could.[178] Pearson wrote a column in mid-March that stressed Graham's favorable initial impression on his new Senate colleagues. Graham was a senator, Pearson wrote, who stayed true to his ideals no matter how many votes it cost: "His heart is as big as his size is small, and his votes are always on the side of the common people." In his current election fight, Graham was being battered by big money interests in North Carolina, Pearson charged, and he was being smeared with the Red brush, but he was too deeply rooted in North Carolina tradition to be smeared successfully.[179]

Graham and his strategists would have been wise to heed the counsel of Johnston Avery as the campaign proceeded. Avery reminded Daniels that one of Graham's signal assets was his warm, friendly nature. Graham should emphasize that dimension of his personality, Avery counseled, and place less emphasis on the statesman's attitude. In many of his campaign addresses, Graham seemed a bit out of touch as he talked of the philosophy of democracy—a complaint Graham's advisers heard repeatedly.[180] Too much abstract rhetoric did not strengthen Graham's case, Avery wrote. People were going to vote in this election for the candidate they liked best, and that was definitely Graham, provided he would just "be himself." Let the people see "that he was sweet and gentle and one of them."[181] No doubt he was, but whether he could campaign without heavy reliance on platitudes remained to be seen.

5 · *Round One*

April

Whether Graham discussed political philosophy or tobacco support prices, the most pressing need of his campaign, as Johnston Avery indicated, was greater visibility. As a political newcomer, he must meet with as many voters—in groups and individually—as possible. Yet his campaign staff, in the pivotal April weeks while Smith labored to organize his challenge, failed to plan or provide the exposure Graham needed. In the first ten days of the month, the senator was scarcely seen in the state, and from April 10 to 16, he had only three scheduled appearances: on April 13 before the combined Goldsboro civic clubs, on April 15 in Rural Hall (near Winston-Salem) to dedicate the Rural Hall American Legion Hut, and on April 16, a Sunday night, in Greensboro to talk to the annual convention of the North Carolina Association of Jewish Women, Men, and Youth.[1]

His Senate duties often kept him in Washington, but even when he was in the state, his schedule was poorly planned. His appearance before the Jewish group in Greensboro, for example, exposed him to a statistically insignificant group of voters who were already committed to him. In addition, he campaigned at a leisurely pace in April. His speech in Goldsboro on April 13 left him with nothing scheduled the following day. His next appearance was a full forty-eight hours after his Goldsboro visit. Nor did he fill in his schedule with informal stops. As a rule, he had only one official appearance each day. There seemed to be no overall plan for working the state's urban areas or the eastern farming communities where Graham's support was suspect. Moreover, the campaign's substantive focus remained hazy, as various self-appointed advisers inundated the candidate with election advice.[2]

Graham's old friend Kemp Battle wrote Marian Graham and urged her to persuade her husband to abandon the effort to stay in Washington to tend to Senate business. Graham should naturally be present for important Senate votes but should spend most of his time campaigning in North Carolina. In fact, Battle proposed, the Grahams should live in Raleigh and commute to Washington instead of the reverse. Battle, while admitting that Jeff Johnson was an excellent man, thought he moved too slowly and lacked sufficient drive. Johnson had not appointed enough county managers. Graham could win only if the campaign were waged aggressively.[3] Eula Nixon Greenwood, in her "Raleigh Roundup" column, agreed with Battle that Johnson needed to be more aggressive to counterbalance Graham's shyness.[4] A Hertford County man wrote Johnson to express the hope that Graham would once ask someone to vote for, him—when he campaigned, "he never mentions he is running for office."[5]

Harry Golden advised Graham that he should make an out-and-out Roosevelt New Deal speech and identify himself with the political largesse that had flowed to North Carolina under New Deal auspices. Graham should not waste "one minute" answering falsehoods and "McCarthyisms," Golden counseled, and should not overestimate the power of the conservative businessmen and editors who supported Smith.[6] Other friends urged Graham to rebut every specific charge hurled at him and to do so repeatedly. Some stressed the importance of the piedmont towns and cities, while others focused on the farm vote. All of the writers assumed a political omniscience and believed their own counsel superior to Johnson's, a condition that made the campaign manager's task a forbidding one indeed.

As a consequence, the campaign was slow to develop coherence, if indeed it ever did. To add to his problems, Graham's respective staffs were poorly coordinated. His Washington office often was at odds with the Raleigh campaign headquarters. One Graham adviser had written Allard Lowenstein urging him to explain to Graham that his Washington office had serious problems and needed reorganization. The office desperately needed a publicist, who would see that Graham's Senate accomplishments were reported at home. Should Lowenstein fail to tell Graham of the problem, "Dr. Frank will go on thinking that all is running smoothly," the writer concluded.[7] Others, notably Kathryn Folger, have concurred that Graham's Washington staff was less than sensational.[8] It was a problem that concerned even Governor Scott, and he outlined his displeasure to Graham on April 19. Scott was especially upset that Graham's Washington associates had failed to disseminate in western North Carolina information detailing Graham's work to speed completion of the Blue Ridge Parkway. "It is important," Scott wrote, "that these stories be kept coming out just as fast as they can."[9]

Nor was the Raleigh staff without flaw. Staffers faltered in the pursuit of uncommitted voters, and at least one county manager, disgusted at the torpor in the Raleigh office, resigned his duties.[10] There was a continuing buzz of dismay at what observers labeled the slow pace of campaign organization and scheduling.

The candidate continued to exercise very little control over his campaign. Bill Staton illustrated the point in a memorandum sent to Graham

in mid-April. The memo contained precise instructions about a speech
Graham was to deliver. The senator was to make a positive speech on
medical care, FEPC, civil rights, and the farm program.[11] Despite close
instruction, however, electoral politics remained a bewilderment to
Frank Graham. When asked by reporters in mid-April how the campaign
was going, Graham replied, with typical candor, "I don't know. They tell
me I am doing all right. You know I am no judge."[12] Graham seldom gave
campaign strategy a passing thought, nor did he ever devote a moment of
reflection to the kind of campaign strategy he intended to employ. In all
of the voluminous records Graham left, one finds little documentary
evidence that he even bothered to respond to advice tendered by friends.
He kept no journal, wrote few notes or messages, and made limited use
of the telephone. The Washington and Raleigh campaign people, principally Jeff Johnson and his staff, assumed control over almost every
dimension of Graham's state campaign. Locally, county managers retained much latitude.

Perhaps the most important element in this confusing scene was
overconfidence. As late as May 3, Charles Tillett, one of many managers
without a portfolio, thought Smith was in retreat even though Tillett
admitted that the Graham campaign had inadequate funds.[13] Jeff Johnson confidently wrote Highway Commissioner Mark Goforth, a key
campaign operative (as were all the highway commissioners), that only
overconfidence could deny Graham his victory.[14] From Brevard, Eugene
T. Coltrane reported that farmers, working people, women, and blacks
were sixty to forty for Graham.[15] And Newsweek, in a mid-April prognos-
tication, wrote that the soft-spoken Graham "seemed a sure bet for reelection."[16] It is hardly surprising, with so many favorable reports, that
staffers became guilty of the very overconfidence they feared.

Doubtless the best example of that overconfidence can be found in
Mecklenburg County and its county seat, Charlotte, the largest city in the
state. Graham, of course, had grown up in Charlotte where his father had
been a pioneer public educator. Here Graham had a powerful network of
family friends and associates, including such notables as former governor and Senator Cameron Morrison and merchant prince Henry Belk.
Both Belk and Morrison were enthusiastic and generous Graham supporters. Charlotte, in addition, was a Presbyterian and Chapel Hill
alumni stronghold, a city in which Graham seemed invincible.[17]

David M. McConnell, general counsel for the Belk stores and a prominent Charlotte Democrat, ran Graham's campaign in Mecklenburg. In
few other counties did Graham forces have a more able leader than

McConnell. A skillful organizer and Democratic centrist friendly to the Scott and Truman administrations, McConnell had a strong personal commitment to Graham's candidacy.[18] He planned for the campaign to be aggressive and enthusiastic. Generously bankrolled by Belk, Morrison, and others, McConnell and Harry Golden wrote many of the campaign ads themselves. Their original theme drew on Graham's Mecklenburg roots: "Charlotte Raised Him—Let's Elect Him." The ads highlighted Graham's life of service, his career as an educator, his diplomatic experience, especially in Indonesia, his commitment to Truman's foreign policy, his marine service in World War I, and his opposition to the use of federal power in race relations. The ads further explained that Graham was "not a buffoon—not a professional hater" (obvious references to his opponents) and "not a scare artist. He has faith in the people."[19]

The mayor, the police chief, and 60 percent of Charlotte's lawyers supported Graham, McConnell wrote Jeff Johnson. Labor and the Jewish vote were solidly for Graham, and the "colored vote" was nearly unanimous for the senator, with its leaders' attitudes ranging from worshipful to ecstatic.[20] Blacks in Mecklenburg worked in overwhelming percentages for "Dr. Frank," remembered the state NAACP leader Kelly M. Alexander, Jr.,[21] while McConnell got important labor help in distributing fliers and watching polls on election day.[22]

Yet Graham lost Mecklenburg County in the first primary. Assuming that Graham "could not lose" Charlotte, his advisers sent him there sparingly in the final two months of the campaign.[23] Smith campaigned constantly in this key area and spent heavily on both radio and newspaper ads. But Graham's advisers, assuming Mecklenburg "safe," sent him elsewhere. He could carry the state's most populous county with only infrequent visits, his managers thought.

They thought wrong. As they learned too late, Graham had serious problems not only in Mecklenburg but in all of McConnell's district. Many new residents in Charlotte and the surrounding area had no memory of Frank Graham or his family. Large numbers of mill workers were hostile to Graham because of his racial views,[24] and textile manufacturers, led by David Clark and his *Southern Textile Bulletin*, had for years been among Graham's most vitriolic critics because of his labor stands. Clark in particular had never forgiven Graham for his actions during the Gastonia textile strike of 1929. When McConnell tried to distribute Graham pamphlets in nearby Kannapolis, Charlie Cannon, who owned Cannon Mills and controlled the town, had McConnell's campaign worker arrested at the mill gate for loitering. The second Graham representative was arrested for vagrancy, and the third distributor was arrested for littering the streets. Finally, in desperation,

McConnell hired an airplane and dropped the circulars on the exiting mill workers. "Charlie Cannon had missed the boat," McConnell recalled. "He forgot to install anti-aircraft devices."

David McConnell always believed that his major problem in combating the textile owners' opposition was an inadequacy of campaign money while Smith had large contributions from textile interests and banks. With additional funds, McConnell thought he could have won the county for Graham. Yet these shortages were in themselves an example of overconfidence. With a more determined effort, the Charlotte headquarters could have raised more money.[25]

The contrast of the Smith effort to the Graham effort in Mecklenburg is instructive. Richard Thigpen, Sr., Smith's Mecklenburg manager, organized the county precinct by precinct. One of his precinct chairmen claimed it was the best job of political organization in the county's history. Thigpen ignored the black vote, concentrating on textile workers and farmers. Graham, in Thigpen's view, was vulnerable on the issues of race and socialism, and Graham's labor support hurt him in Charlotte. Thigpen raised $15,510 locally for Smith and worked full-time on the campaign. He had help from a large number of people and organizations, the key to Smith's Charlotte success.[26] In short, Smith forces outhustled, outorganized, and outspent Graham's Mecklenburg contingent, and the Graham camp seemed unaware that Charlotte was slipping away.

The attention of the Graham advisers instead was focused on other concerns: the effort of Smith forces to make an issue of the open partisanship of both Gladys Tillett and Jonathan Daniels, the unsubtle use of the Scott administration to help elect Graham, and the senator's ties to the Truman presidency. Candidate Smith, speaking to the YDC in Mount Holly on April 6, charged that certain top Democratic officials had "violated traditional neutrality" in the Senate race. The duty of party officials, Smith declared, was to promote party harmony, directing their efforts "against the common enemy in the general elections." In their support for Graham, "certain party officials" were rendering a great disservice. "These party officials I refer to are operating so vigorously and vehemently that it is not necessary for me to call names because the people of the state know who they are." Two of them were traveling the state, Smith continued, telling audiences that Graham could not be defeated. Yet his opponent, Smith proclaimed, had never been elected to any public office; he had been appointed to every office he had held. The citizens of North Carolina were not going to permit would-be political bosses (i.e., Daniels and Gladys Tillett) to tell them how to vote.[27]

That Charles and Gladys Tillett were fully committed to Graham's candidacy was hardly a secret. Charles Tillett, as indicated earlier, had written speeches and position papers—all unsolicited—for Graham, raised money, and canvassed for voters. In one of his stratagems, Tillett had decided to capitalize on alumni affection for Graham and requested University of North Carolina alumni mailing lists from Alumni Secretary J. Maryon Saunders. But Saunders refused Tillett's request, stating that the lists could not be used for political purposes. Peeved at Saunders's refusal, lawyer Tillett wrote acting University of North Carolina President William D. "Billy" Carmichael, Jr., to press his claim. The lists, Tillett argued, should be available to any state citizen. Tillett understood that Senator Graham would personally oppose such use of the lists but wrote that Graham's wishes on the matter were not relevant. Graham, as a candidate in a legal primary, was powerless to control any citizen who wanted to engage in the campaign. Tillett felt that his actions were none of Graham's business. Nonetheless, the university president refused to surrender the lists. The alumnae secretary at the Woman's College in Greensboro, part of the university system, refused a similar request from Gladys Tillett Coddington, the Tilletts' daughter.[28]

Such activities, combined with periodic public attacks on Smith, did not endear Tillett to Graham's Raleigh headquarters. To Jeff Johnson and Jonathan Daniels, Tillett's broadsides were more of a hindrance than a help. In an unauthorized speech on April 15, Tillett had suggested that Smith should run for the Senate as a reactionary Republican, since he talked just like Thomas E. Dewey. Tillett also assailed Smith for using scare tactics.[29]

Tillett should refrain from such attacks, counseled the Greensboro *Daily News*. They were unworthy of Frank Graham's high-mindedness.[30] Bob Thompson, in the High Point *Enterprise*, took a different view. Thompson acknowledged that on some issues Smith did have a Republican viewpoint. And if Tillett insisted on calling Smith a Republican, then it was hardly improper for Thompson to charge that Frank Graham "thinks and acts like a member of the socialist party."[31]

Such exchanges and criticisms persuaded Gladys Tillettt to resign her post as vice-chairman of the Democratic National Committee. She announced her resignation on April 17 to become "a volunteer worker in the ranks" for Frank Graham. She would work to enlist North Carolina women in Graham's cause, convinced that their highest duty was to elect Graham. His diplomatic experience as an international peacemaker, Tillett argued, "qualified him beyond any other candidate to deal with [the] threat" of atomic war.[32]

Smith's campaign manager, Charles Green, responded to Tillett's resignation by saying that it was several months overdue. She had resigned,

Green explained, because she could no longer look the state's Democrats in the face, having wrongfully used her position for partisan purposes. Green also called on Jonathan Daniels and other top officials who had violated traditional neutrality to resign their posts as well.

Jonathan Daniels quickly made it clear that he had no intention of following Gladys Tillett. He noted that criticism of his support for Graham originated with people (i.e., Smith) who did not vote the Democratic ticket in 1948. As a historical matter, continued Daniels, predecessors in his current post during the past twenty years either had actively supported candidates or had been candidates themselves. His position, Daniels explained, was not the same as Gladys Tillett's. He was not a member of the central staff of the national party and had no duties in any state except North Carolina.[33]

Daniels's response, though correct historically, aggravated rather than concluded the controversy concerning his campaign role. Smith's headquarters now accused Daniels of being Graham's "real, behind the scenes campaign manager"—his "undisputed boss." Daniels was a political opportunist, Charles Green charged, who thought he should run and control North Carolina politics. Many of the state's Democrats, Green argued, felt that Daniels should resign because of the dissension he was creating. But no one, Green concluded, expected him to do so.[34] Daniels's role in the campaign thus remained a controversial subject.

Daniels was not without his defenders, among them Governor Scott. Indeed, Scott announced on April 19 that he intended to speak publicly on behalf of Graham in the campaign's latter phase. Those who were asking for Daniels's resignation, he told reporters, "might say the same thing about me."[35] Which, of course, they did.

Scott's statement was precisely to the point. Smith's claims that the Tilletts, Daniels, and Scott were aligned in a power pact to cram Frank Graham down the throats of voters was having its effect. As Sam Ragan, managing editor of the Raleigh *News and Observer* in 1950, has recalled, all, including Graham, had become symbols for views that many North Carolina Democrats loathed. The *News and Observer*'s editorial support for Graham was unprecedented, and many of its readers resented the shrill advocacy of the "Nuisance and Disturber" in this campaign. In one personal incident, a Raleigh woman, distressed at the paper's fervent advocacy of Graham, spied Frank Daniels, Jonathan's brother, at the Carolina Country Club, approached him, and spat in his face. Ragan himself received a number of telephone threats and verbal harassments. Within the offices of the paper, emotions occasionally got out of hand. At one point, Nell Battle Lewis, author of the Sunday column "Incidentally," and a fervent Smithite, screamed at Jonathan Daniels in the newsroom, "I hope all your children have nigger babies."[36]

One pro-Graham paper, the Durham *Morning Herald*, reflected on the divisive effect that Scott and Daniels's advocacy had on Graham's election bid. Daniels, the paper observed, could not be expected to write impartial editorials because of his political post; nor could Governor Scott, Graham's appointer, be expected to remain neutral. "And who knows?" the paper asked. "The opposition of those two might be more of a help [to Smith] than a hindrance." Smith's charge that Graham was Daniels's man, the paper noted in a later editorial, was nonetheless ridiculous. "Frank Graham is nobody's man."[37]

Smith's advocates were obviously pleased that their complaints had forced Gladys Tillett's resignation from the Democratic National Committee. But her decision redoubled their effort to capitalize on Daniels's partisanship. His resignation from the state committee was long overdue, the High Point *Enterprise* claimed on April 17. Comparing Daniels to state Democratic party chairman B. Everett Jordan, a Willis Smith business partner who maintained public neutrality (while surreptitiously laboring for Smith), the *Enterprise* praised Jordan's public posture. The paper also echoed the Durham *Morning Herald*'s view that Daniels's open support had become a Graham liability: "We think that Daniels antagonizes two voters for every one he attracts." Nonetheless, the paper claimed that it hated to see Daniels's high party office prostituted so blatantly.[38]

Throughout this affray, Daniels ably defended himself and Gladys Tillett. In his editorials, Daniels pointed out that Tillett did not resign due to criticism but only because she wanted to work full-time for Graham. And Daniels continued to argue, correctly, that party officials had always participated in factional fights. Senator Hoey, for example, had run for the Senate in 1944 while serving as a national committeeman.[39] Confirming Daniels's contemporary observation, Thad Eure recalled in 1984 that party officials were frequently involved in primary struggles hip and thigh, raising money and giving open endorsements.[40] The fact that Daniels was correct historically, however, did not prevent Smith from making his partisanship a campaign issue of some importance.

Even more nettlesome was Governor Scott's involvement. T. W. Allen, a Granville County tobacco grower, reiterated the Smith position in late April, issuing a statement decrying the governor's partisanship. Voters, Allen complained, should be able to vote their convictions without political pressure from the governor or other high officials.[41]

The "Know the Truth" Committee, an arm of the Smith campaign, produced
this cartoon, and many similar ones, stressing Graham's left-wing affiliations
and the influence of Jonathan Daniels and W. Kerr Scott on Graham's political
life. (Harry S Truman Papers, Harry S Truman Library, Independence, Mo.)

Even though no one claimed historic neutrality for governors in state
politics, Smith's effort to tie Graham to the controversial Scott and his
insurgent administration was a clever stroke. Scott already understood
that he was an issue in the campaign, and he finally began to wonder
whether he was a liability or an asset. Attacked as the head of a powerful
machine and as a lackey for Jonathan Daniels, Scott was advised by some

field managers to put distance between himself and Graham. One method, suggested Graham supporter W. Banks Shepherd in a letter to Johnson, would be for Graham to refer publicly to his political independence from Scott. Such a statement would help eliminate the governor as a campaign issue,[42] while still enabling Scott to give Graham the support he needed in the east.[43]

Johnson and Scott ignored Shepherd's counsel. Scott's personal support and the perquisites of his office were too important to abandon. Scott's speech-making for Graham was on balance a good idea, Johnson wrote labor organizer Dave Burgess.[44] By late April, therefore, Scott became an even more outspoken Graham advocate. Moreover, in response to Smith's charges of undue Scott influence on state workers, Scott publicly hoped that state employees would support Graham, but if "they don't, it's all right with me." Asked if complaints had been heard regarding pressure to compel state employees' contributions to Graham, Scott seized the moment: "From all I've heard they [the Graham campaign] need the money mighty bad. If anyone wants to pass the hat it's okay."[45] This was a far cry from his earlier position admonishing state workers not to campaign on state time.

In one sense, Smith's strategy worked well. Scott was pugnacious, and Smith's charges made him angry. Scott went to Warrenton on April 28 and vigorously defended his appointment of Graham. He chose Graham, he told his audience, because Graham had always fought for the rights of the average man. He was the only candidate who had. The South had never had a better humanitarian, Scott argued, and Graham had done more for education in North Carolina than anyone since Charles Brantley Aycock.[46]

Willis Smith directed his campaign not only at Daniels, Tillett, and Scott, of course, but also at Graham. He continually tried to link Graham to the Truman administration. Smith claimed that the party's dominant forces were in league against him. (And he was right.) Thus, when Vice President Alben W. Barkley returned to North Carolina for a speech in late April, Smith cried foul. Barkley spoke to a YDC gathering in Greenville on April 27, which neither Smith nor Reynolds attended. Graham, however, was present. Declaring that he came to the state to make an impartial "straight Democratic speech," Barkley proceeded to give special praise to Graham for "his broad vision, his sympathy, his character, and his love for the common man." For his part, Graham spoke briefly and received a standing ovation.[47]

Barkley's speech was, Smith charged, a ruse. Barkley was there at Truman's behest to plump for Graham in a strictly partisan effort.[48] The

Durham *Sun* questioned why Smith should be surprised at Barkley's effort to help Graham. Every campaign observer knew, the paper pointed out, that both the state and national Democratic administrations were full-bore for Graham. However, the paper added, resentment against the efforts of Governor Scott and Truman was growing.[49]

Truman, in fact, continued to maintain a close personal interest in this race. He called both Graham and Jeff Johnson frequently for campaign updates, asking if they were getting adequate help from the Democratic National Committee. Truman was careful not to give Graham an open endorsement, but he did what he could short of it, as visits from Sam Rayburn and Barkley attest.[50] Increasingly, as the Washington (N.C.) *Daily News* pointed out, the campaign took on the air of a North Carolina referendum on the Truman administration,[51] a view encouraged by both Smith and Graham.

None of this criticism, as observed, discouraged Scott, Daniels, and the Tilletts from their campaign participation. But it did exacerbate tensions among various Graham factions. Daniels thought the Tilletts were of marginal assistance at best, and he hoped Gladys Tillett would remain with the national committee and stay in Washington.[52] But the Tilletts, convinced of the importance of their effort for Graham, marched steadfastly on with their crusade. Daniels, it should be pointed out, was only a part-time enlistee himself. Throughout the campaign, he was deep into writing his Truman biography (*The Man of Independence*), and he never missed a deadline, producing a manuscript that greatly pleased Truman.

Gladys Tillett directed her women's organization for Graham from her home in Charlotte. She set up a Committee of Two Thousand, using the slogan "Women Will Win This Election." Each of the two thousand committee members was charged with recruiting fifty female Graham-ites, a kind of political chain letter. Tillett drove through eastern North Carolina, holding women's meetings and talking about human rights and what Graham had meant for education in North Carolina. She also raised money, all the while claiming, no doubt correctly, that she had never worked on anything so hard in her life.[53] In one typical meeting, Gladys Tillett told a group of student hairdressers at the "Kollege of Beauty Knowledge" in Wilson to beware of candidates who went around oppos-ing without offering anything positive. She went on to reiterate the principal point in her campaign effort for Graham, namely that he was more qualified than his rivals to deal with the threat of nuclear war.[54]

Tillett's repeated claim that a vote for Graham was a vote for world peace had embroiled her directly in an exchange of charges with Smith officials. Challenging her claim, Charles Green quoted to the press the February 3, 1949, *Congressional Record*, reminding voters of the Atomic Energy Commission Security Board's denial of security clearance to Graham when he was president of the Oak Ridge Institute of Nuclear Studies. The board, in Green's words, had decided that Graham "ought not, for security reasons, be permitted to come near atomic secrets." In view of the record, Green wondered aloud, how could Gladys Tillett justify such a claim?[55] At a later date, Green initiated a series of political ads, paid for by the Women for Smith Committee, which trumpeted that Tillett was badly misinformed and confused. Graham's actual record, the ad claimed, spoke louder than campaign camouflage supplied by Tillett.[56]

Green's ads so incensed Charles Tillett that he wrote and personally paid for a rejoinder ad, which stressed Graham's achievements in Indonesia and quoted Senator Hoey's comment that Graham was as loyal as any American could be.[57] The damage was done, nonetheless. The charges were effective, as David McConnell recalled, especially since newspapers were filled with headlines and stories involving accused spies Klaus Fuchs and Alger Hiss.[58]

By mid-April, then, a rough campaign strategy had emerged for each candidate. Smith would attack, as he had planned to do from the beginning, assailing Graham's career of social activism, questioning his political judgment, and painting him as the handpicked stooge of Scott, Daniels, and Truman. He would further charge that Graham's policy views were simply incompatible with mainstream North Carolina Democrats. Smith would stress his own career accomplishments, and, in contrast to Graham, his previous experience in party politics.

Front-runner Graham would run a favorite's race. He would accent his long career of service and focus on his diplomatic and foreign policy experience. He would emphasize his moderation on sensitive questions. As Gladys Tillett had suggested, Graham would present himself as a candidate who could help maintain world peace. In this context, Graham tended to speak in generalities, as he did in an April 13 gathering of the Sons of the American Revolution, held at the Jefferson Memorial. Jefferson, he told the assembled audience, would not advise the use of compulsory federal power in an effort to abolish racial prejudice. Instead, Jefferson would strive, in Graham's view, for an America "made safe for both democracy and differences, where the answer to error is not terror; where democracy is achieved without vulgarity and excellence without arrogance, where the majority is without tyranny; the minority without fear, and all people have hope."[59]

Another example of the "peace theme" came two days later, when the Graham camp announced the senator's five-point plan for peace. This plan would encourage international disarmament, U.S. leadership in the United Nations, international control and inspection of atomic power, economic aid to the backward people of the world, and greater support for the Voice of America to combat Soviet propaganda and to convey to the Russian people the truth that the United States wanted freedom and peace.[60] Ten days later, to demonstrate his patriotism, Graham reminded listeners that "there is no substitute for Americanism."[61]

This strategy would be combined with already publicized endorsements from prominent North Carolinians. In this competition, Graham was indeed invincible. How much value could be attached to elite endorsements is, of course, difficult to say, but Graham workers were convinced that the endorsements advanced their cause. Among the first out of the chute back in February had been Burlington Industries chairman J. Spencer Love. Now Thomas A. Morgan, head of Sperry Gyroscope, and merchant Henry Belk publicly recommended Graham's election.[62] It was hardly necessary to explain to voters that business leaders and industrialists would not have embraced Graham had they believed he was the socialist and radical that Smith claimed he was. He was not opposed to big business, Graham subsequently stated in several speeches, or to capitalism. But business should grow on the basis of fair competition and not through power, privilege, and monopoly.[63]

A number of other prominent North Carolina women followed the lead of Mrs. O. Max Gardner and Gladys Tillett in their Graham endorsements. Among them were Mrs. Annie Bost, former state commissioner of public welfare, and Mrs. J. Henry Highsmith, a former president of the state federation of women's clubs. Mrs. Highsmith recognized in Graham the qualities of Christian leadership and character that all women valued.[64]

In addition to prominent women, the Graham forces counted heavily on educators. They were delighted, therefore, when octogenarian James Yadkin Joyner, of La Grange, former superintendent of public instruction and a farm leader, endorsed Graham, calling the senator "a relentless foe of Communism and the other isms brewed in Russia's hell-broth of hate behind the Iron Curtain." Graham, Joyner proclaimed, was the best-qualified Senate candidate at a critical time in U.S. history.[65] Joyner's recommendation was followed by a score of others, including a solid commitment from Jewish leaders.[66]

Graham, in addition, continued to rely on covert help from organized labor. Graham staffers understood that most North Carolinians were deeply skeptical of organized labor. Consequently, labor personnel worked quietly. The state CIO director, for example, coordinated the activities of labor officials in Mecklenburg,[67] while Dave Burgess worked with piedmont black leaders to increase black registration and get out the vote. Burgess even attended a joint American Federation of Labor–Congress of Industrial Organizations meeting in Greensboro, a rarity in 1950.[68]

As yet, however, Graham strategists had devised no overall effective plan to counter, deflect, or ignore Smith's attacks. Nor had any plan emerged—save for reliance on Governor Scott's personal intervention—to hold farmers to the Graham standard. Granted, Graham struggled to convince farmers that he was worthy of their support, but friends kept reporting that his efforts were not succeeding. Kemp Battle warned him in late April that his views were not being conveyed convincingly to farmers. Graham needed to say more about the tobacco program and to bear down on economy in government.[69] Graham had already made a statewide radio address where he pledged to continue parity price supports,[70] but he had trouble with farm support. Farmers perceived Graham as too liberal on racial and economic matters.

Graham's farmer problem was exposed dramatically when T. W. Allen announced formation of a statewide Farmers for Smith committee. Allen, a state farm leader and state representative, had served Scott as his Granville County campaign manager in 1948. His past support for Scott suggested that he would show enthusiasm for Scott's Senate appointee, but instead he publicly opposed Graham's election, claiming he resented the appointment as a Scott power move.[71] Allen's willingness to break openly with the governor should have provided another useful antidote to the overconfidence malady.

From the outset, the Graham effort had been hampered by Graham's inexperience as a campaigner. More troubling to his supporters, he did not improve as the months passed. No one ever mistook Frank Graham for an effective politician, recalled Graham supporter John Sanders in 1984. But the qualities of heart and mind that endeared Graham to so many would, his supporters believed, make him appealing to voters. His sterling qualities would override his deficiencies as a working politician.[72]

Many in Graham's circle contended that his naïveté—the foundation of much of his political difficulty—could be attributed to his steadfast insistence on human goodness. Conceding the darkness of the human soul would have menaced Graham's entire set of Christian values, contends Graham's biographer.[73] Graham's trusting and kindhearted view of his fellow human beings meant that he would refuse, in the campaign, to attack his opponents; he would, in addition, be slow to defend himself against attack. He answered specific charges with great reluctance, preferring simply to state his own views. If someone did not agree with Graham, he would not endeavor to persuade. As stated earlier, he could not bring himself to ask people to vote for him—it would be too egotistical.[74] Graham, according to friends, never acted for selfish purposes. Believing himself to be pure in motive, he imputed to others the same purity. He was, in short, a phenomenon never before seen in North Carolina politics—a candidate fired not by the desire for victory at any cost, but by the desire to win while doing the right thing as his Christian values guided him.[75]

Graham's lack of campaign experience and his unique campaign philosophy did not mean, however, that he was a political neophyte. He was not. He was naive by society's standards, but in his career, he had shown both deftness and strength: in his legislative dealings as president of the consolidated university; in his ability to survive the administrative long-knives associated with the consolidation of the university system; in his service on the War Labor Board and the Truman Committee on Civil Rights; and in literally hundreds of other such proceedings. In them all, he had displayed impressive diplomatic gifts.[76] And his courage in defending the university against outside attack was deservedly lauded. Translating these talents into a political campaign in which he was an active candidate was not, however, something he could do. In his mind, his record was clear. Voters could take it or leave it, although undoubtedly Graham believed they would take it. He thought he would win.

Part of his naïveté, or innocence, stemmed from his personal habits, habits that reflected the man. In the age of the unfiltered cigarette, he did not smoke. In the age of the three-finger bourbon shot, chased with water, he did not drink. In the glory days of fountain-mixed soft drinks, he did not partake. Indeed, on one campaign foray, an exhausted Graham shocked his companions by asking for a "dope" (a Coca-Cola), believing the beverage would pep him up. His surprised aides complied, and Graham drank his Coke. After a few minutes, a perplexed Graham approached his assistants and asked, "How long does it take for it to have an effect?"[77]

Idealistic as a politician, Graham was impractical as a campaigner. In fact, in the routines of daily life he was almost helpless without assistance. Having never learned to drive, he had to be chauffeured everywhere he went—either by campaign assistants or by his valet and personal servant Hubert Robinson. It was Robinson who put out his clothes for him each morning and helped him dress. Chronically forgetful, he might leave his hat or coat anywhere.[78] When returning from Washington to North Carolina to campaign, he sometimes lost his airline ticket. J. Melville Broughton, Jr., then a young aide to Graham, two or three times had to put him on the plane without a ticket—"the airline people knew him, and knew that he had a ticket someplace." He was chronically late for political events, usually because he would lose himself in chance conversations with old friends—and new acquaintances too, for that matter, a carryover from his Chapel Hill days.[79] Inattentive to his health, he was frequently ill, usually with respiratory problems, although his small stature did not connote frailness. Graham was physically tough, with a resilient personality and strong will. He worked hard at campaigning—although his wife protected him from being overscheduled—and he carried out his campaign duties with enthusiasm and purpose, even if it was a role he had never envisioned.[80]

Despite his campaign inexperience and unique approach to politics, Graham displayed clear political strengths. He was very effective in small groups and with individuals, and while not a magnetic stump speaker, he had extensive experience before assemblies. He could make a good speech, provided he did not talk too long or shift into his lecture mode. On occasion he could achieve eloquence, especially in describing his political ideals. Like Willis Smith, he remembered names with almost total recall, especially those of former Chapel Hill students, their parents, family members, and even hometowns.[81] Finally, he was beloved. Any town or crossroads in the state contained at least one individual who could speak proudly of having met or known "Dr. Frank." His supporters and associates accepted his eccentricities, believing that Graham's disregard for the mundane stemmed from his lifelong concern for the greater good. Graham, in their view, had spent his life helping others, disregarding any concern for personal wealth or self-aggrandizement, and they would work to carry him to victory.[82] This commitment from so many was an incalculable political asset even if Graham refused to think of it in those terms.

Working with him in the campaign was nonetheless vexatious. Graham's gentle nature and soft-spoken political speeches were too often uninspiring. Several of his associates, among them Terry Sanford, wanted Graham to be tougher in responding to Smith's attacks.[83] Bill Staton thought Graham too trusting and insufficiently political in his campaign effort. When Smith's attacks put Graham on the defensive, Staton felt he neither rebutted nor counterattacked effectively against Smith's conservatism.[84]

Although his campaign visits were not as well organized as they might have been, Graham was nonetheless effective when campaigning before smaller groups. Here he is shown waving to supporters toward the end of the first primary. (North Carolina Department of Archives and History, Raleigh)

His refusal to portray his opponent as the prince of reaction did not, however, deter his advisers. In early April, they initiated their own assault. First, they issued a press release lambasting Smith, born in Norfolk, Virginia, for his failure to be born in North Carolina. Smith's spokesman, Charles Green, replied that the Graham forces had apparently run out of campaign issues. He also charged the Graham camp with sinking "to a new low in political campaigning."[85] The "native son" issue should never have been brought into the·campaign, observed the Charlotte *Observer* and other dailies. Realizing that they had raised a foolish question, the red-faced Graham advisers retreated.[86]

Next, the Graham staff took out newspaper ads stating that Smith's current commitment to budget-balancing was a recent conversion. The "Corn Bread and Collards" Committee, in an ad entitled "Look Who's Talking," called Smith a big spender, flailing Smith's leadership of the North Carolina House in 1931 when the state budget went into deficit by $3,764,172. At the end of the biennium, the ad charged, there had been a net deficit of $6,179,172.[87] Again, state newspapers ridiculed the charge. Smith had nothing to do with the depression deficit, contrary to the claim of Dr. Calvin Rea, head of the "Corn Bread and Collards" Committee, wrote Tom Bost in the Greensboro *Daily News*.[88] Added the paper editorially, the charge was "as unfair, as unintelligible, as untruthful, and as unconscionable as charging Frank Graham with being a Communist. . . . Everybody ought to quit this business."[89]

Undeterred by two misfires, the Graham forces pressed forward. They seized onto Smith's statement that he believed in "high wage scales for the American working man." In political ads purchased all over the state, the Graham camp accused Smith of opposing a forty-cents-per-hour minimum wage scale for the same North Carolina workers he now claimed deserved high wages. The Graham ads tried to contrast Smith's position with Graham's support for a high minimum wage. Citing Smith's legal services on behalf of corporate clients (Armour and Company, Prudential Life Insurance, Wachovia Bank and Trust Company, and Southern Railway) and his services as a paid lobbyist, the ads asked voters to consider whether or not Smith's aid to special interests equipped him to be a people's representative. Further, the ads stated, Smith was a stockholder in Royal Cotton Mills of Wake Forest, a mill that paid workers lower wages than comparable mills in nearby towns. Graham, in contrast, had recently supported a federal seventy-five-cents-per-hour minimum wage bill and was a friend to labor who had long advocated improved working conditions, increased social security, and better housing for working people.[90]

Stung by these charges, Smith replied immediately with public statements and ads denouncing the attacks as half-truths and distortions. In regard to lobbying, Graham staffers charged that Smith had appeared before an open legislative committee hearing on behalf of the North Carolina Ice Manufacturers' Association, asking that, as a seasonal industry, it be excepted from the state's minimum wage law. Smith answered that he had been acting solely in a professional capacity as attorney for the association. He was not opposed to the minimum wage, he added. Furthermore, ice industry employees were paid well over forty-cents-per-hour, the state minimum. He claimed to be one of the fathers of the North Carolina workmen's compensation law. High wages, one Smith ad argued, resulted from a free competitive economic system, and as a senator, he would fight communism, socialism, and FEPC, which were the real threats to the working man.[91]

Smith's vigorous defense against this attack, and the narrowness of the specific claims against him, made this effort as unsuccessful as the other smear attempts of Graham managers. Moreover, when Frank Graham saw the ads and the fliers attacking Smith on the issue of minimum wage,

he immediately repudiated them. He thought the attacks on Smith to be wrong, Graham told Jeff Johnson, and he instructed Johnson to call in all the materials and destroy them.[92] Graham simply did not want to campaign that way: "I'm not attacking anybody. If I have to do that to get elected to the Senate, I don't want to go."[93]

Graham's distaste for political invective combined with his allies' lack of skill in employing attack techniques thus left his campaign vulnerable to the Smith charges. Manager Jeff Johnson and his aides were stuck with a strategy consisting of candidate homilies supplemented by a defense of Graham's record that utilized surrogate speakers and friendly newspapers. Graham's advocates did denounce Smith's tactics as falsehoods "from the ever-flowing cesspools of special interest propagandists"[94] and decried the dirt and slime used to crucify Frank Graham.[95] Such a strategy obviously failed to anticipate the relentless assault Smith forces envisioned. Clearly, Johnson and his staff did not grasp that their candidate's activist background, whether one saw it as heroic or deplorable, would make for an unconventional election. With the exception of Jonathan Daniels, Graham's associates in the campaign were at best meagerly informed of his various left-wing enthusiasms in the 1930s. Nor did they understand until well into the race that their candidate, his record, and what it meant would be the principal election issues.

Graham's backers, however, were no less resentful at what they deemed unfair charges and mudslinging from the Smith camp. The Raleigh *News and Observer* averred that two of Smith's charges were outrageous. Graham had never changed his beliefs for personal advantage, as the Smith camp claimed, nor was Graham under any man's control—his only boss was his conscience.[96] The Southern Pines *Pilot*, concerned about the tone of the campaign, saw in Smith's use of innuendo and the repetition of catch phrases a new political low point.[97] Jeff Johnson and Charles Tillett also charged Smith with a vicious smear campaign that would ultimately insure a victory for Graham. "A lot of folks," said Johnson, "are going to be ashamed of their part in the futile and ill-advised plot to smear one of the finest men this state . . . has ever produced." Johnson believed that people who listened to the appeals of ignorance and prejudice would, in the privacy of the voting booth, listen to their consciences and vote for Graham. Johnson warned of additional vicious material to be released by Graham's opponents but thought Graham would not be hurt by such abuse.[98]

Graham's adversaries, on the other hand, had understood from the time of his appointment that Graham and his record would be the key issue. By mid-April, they were hard at work exposing Graham's record and interpreting that record to the state's voters. In one sense, then, Graham's stated intention to run on his record played into his opponents' hands. To Frank Graham, his record meant service and sacrifice throughout his career for the good of the state and the nation, highlighted, in his view, by his concern for minorities, the less fortunate, and noble causes. To his opponents, however, his record was a dismal history of association with suspect political groups and ideas, whose purposes were to overturn southern race relations, collectivize the national economy, and cripple the country internationally. Consequently, then, to his opponents, his political judgment was so flawed that he could not be trusted with a Senate seat; his views were too much at odds with the political mainstream in North Carolina.

Graham's chief critics in the Smith camp therefore defended their assault on Graham both in public discourse and in private communications. "All we have done," Charles Green argued on April 28, "is to discuss his record." Responding to charges of mudslinging, Green retorted, "If he calls an honest and open discussion of his record mudslinging, then the record itself is mud because that's what we are dealing with." Green expected "the Graham crowd to yell mud-slinging because they have no other answers to the issues and written records." The Smith forces had only begun to plumb Graham's record, Green warned. They would be making additional disclosures in the weeks ahead.[99]

Throughout April the Smith campaign headquarters, in order to get its message across, tried to schedule Smith for as many speeches as possible (putting on a more active campaign than Graham stalwarts expected)[100] but relied most heavily on radio and newspaper ads. By the end of the month, Smith hoped to average at least one major speech per day,[101] a pace that was better than Graham was able to do.[102]

By April 24, Charles Green reported that he had set up campaign organizations in seventy-six of the one hundred counties in the state.[103] Typical of the campaign leaders was Lee County manager Harold T. Makepeace, Sr., who favored Smith because he was "a great American who believes in the American form of government and the American way of life." Makepeace promised to work hard for Smith's election.[104] Although Smith had gotten a late start and had not set up election headquarters in one-fourth of the counties barely one month prior to the first primary, the favorable talk about Smith in the state convinced some observers that he was rapidly gaining ground on Graham,[105] and more supporters were daily enlisting in his cause.[106]

Smith believed that his political success depended on conveying the strength and sincerity of his conservative beliefs. The people of North Carolina, explained Smith, were conservative, and a politician who was to win an election there had to share that same philosophy.[107] In presenting his conservative beliefs to the voters, Smith hammered away at Graham on "socialized medicine." Although Graham had frequently reiterated his opposition to a national health service,[108] Smith recognized this as a potent issue and denounced medicine controlled by the federal government. It would put an extra burden on the taxpayers and destroy the right of a person to choose his own physician.[109] Harry Golden claimed that Smith supporters set up a switchboard in Washington, D.C., and telephoned every doctor in North Carolina. The operators told the physicians that Graham was for "socialized medicine" and that they should make certain that they and their patients voted for Willis Smith.[110] Smith's use of the issue was effective; despite adamant denials, the general belief persisted that Graham stood foursquare for "socialized medicine."

Smith also tried to tie Graham to the Truman administration's Brannan Plan. The Brannan Plan was named after Secretary of Agriculture Charles F. Brannan, a militant liberal and partisan Democrat. The complex plan, as explained earlier, promised to continue high price supports, but the maintenance of farm income would be achieved by direct payments to farmers rather than through crop restriction and government purchase of crops. This idea would theoretically lead to more food at lower prices and more income for farmers. Conservatives saw the Brannan Plan as extremely costly—another example of more government control of the economy—and southern Democrats feared that large commodity producers would lose government subsidies. Because Graham favored the Fair Deal and the Brannan Plan was part of the Fair Deal, Smith charged that Graham must be for the Brannan Plan.[111] Smith cited the Brannan Plan as an example of the increasing federal encroachment on individuals' and states' rights.[112] He characterized it as a fantastic scheme that could wreck the national treasury and as a socialistic experiment that was not a fair deal for farmers.[113]

A forceful attack on Graham's idealistic foreign policy views came at Dunn, where Smith warned against the theory of international disarmament as a guarantee of peace. The United States had to be kept strong, or enemies would pounce on the unprepared country. "We cannot and must not indulge in the illusory idealistic thinking indulged in by those who seem to think that everything will be good if we only think and do good." Smith preferred the sentiments expressed in the song, "Praise the Lord and Pass the Ammunition." The United States should attempt to preserve the peace but must remember that "appeasers had never succeeded in preventing war."[114]

Smith got significant assistance in his effort from two partisan newspapers. The High Point *Enterprise*, responding to Graham's fear of "special interests" taking over Smith's campaign, pointed out that labor unions, the farmer, and Burlington Mills were all "special interests" seeking special favors. Graham's supporters were therefore just as much "special interests" as Smith's supporters.[115] The Dunn *Dispatch* lauded Smith's advocacy of budget restraints and spending limits. Had Graham ever operated a business or earned a living in private enterprise, rather than standing at the receiving end of the tax line, he might be willing to give citizens some relief from taxation and extravagance.[116]

In a statewide radio address on April 11, Smith continued to push the economic and defense issues by calling for a balanced federal budget and high wages for the working man. The United States, Smith told his audience, should spend its energy "trying to build a stronger nation from within by rooting out all the termites from the mudsills of democracy." Premier Stalin, Smith warned, would not attack the United States until he had first disorganized Americans by his usual methods of infiltration. If there were those in the United States who preferred the Russian way of life "or the Socialist life of Britain, let's give them passage to their favorite country. Let's preserve the American way of life for all those who remain."[117] Eight days later, in Southern Pines, Smith implored his audience to help nip socialist trends while time permitted. Government needed no "dreamers or visionaries," he warned; it needed practical people who would promote economy in government.[118]

In sum, the principal theme of Smith's first primary campaign—at least the first half of it—was Graham's radical past, especially his association with 1930s popular front groups influenced or controlled by Communists and fellow travelers. The Smith camp knew Graham was not a Communist—the charge was ludicrous, and they never made it. They argued instead that Graham had been suckered by the popular front ideology of the 1930s, and, in doing so, had displayed a conspicuous lack of political judgment. As William T. Joyner, Jr., has recalled, Graham's attackers did not question his loyalty. The purpose of Smith's ads was rather to paint Graham as a rabid left-winger, sympathetic to Communist causes. His critics charged that as a left-wing senator, Graham would advance the cause of labor and of blacks. His socialistic tendencies would lead to an enlarged federal government, through programs such as FEPC and "socialized medicine," accompanied by higher federal taxes. Individual liberty would thereby be imperiled.[119]

Graham always pointed out, one of Smith's ads argued, that he was not

a Communist, and his campaign materials constantly reiterated this point. Smith's ads granted that Graham was not a Communist. The real campaign issue, however, was Graham's socialistic sympathies: "Dr. Graham is able to deny that his affiliation with so many Communist front organizations means that he is a Communist. But his affiliation with them is strong and convincing proof of his belief in the socialistic measures which the Communist-front organizations always promote."

Another ad featured prominently the seventeen HUAC-named Communist front organizations to which Graham, in various capacities, had lent his name. Among them were the American League for Peace and Democracy, the Southern Conference for Human Welfare, the Citizens Committee to Free Earl Browder, the American Committee for Democracy and Intellectual Freedom, and the American Friends of Spanish Democracy. These memberships, the Smith backers claimed, indicated both a commitment to socialist principles and the senator's likely future course in policy decisions. In contrast, Smith declared his opposition to any program of socialism that would tear down the American system of government, choke industry, and destroy the American standard of living. "My views," said Smith, "are practical ones and not those of a classroom theorist."[120]

Equally dismaying to the editors of an obscure right-wing journal, the *Challenge to Socialism*, was Graham's failure to enumerate his various memberships in the *Congressional Directory*. Were these omissions evidence that Graham was ashamed of his links to these groups? "Should a man be in the United States Senate," the magazine queried, "if he cannot detect a subversive organization or a Communist sympathizer when he comes in direct contact with one?" Especially disturbing to this journal was Graham's long association with the SCHW. Graham became president, the magazine contended, when he should have been aware that something was decidedly wrong in the SCHW. One could make such a mistake occasionally, but Graham's record showed that he repeatedly sought the company of those who wished to overthrow the American government.[121]

These statements, and others in the same vein, emboldened other Graham critics. In a letter to the Charlotte *News*, University of North Carolina student J. R. Cherry, who had first disclosed foreign graduate student Hans Freistadt's Communist political affiliation at the university, suggested that any intelligent person who had not detected in twenty-five years that communism was vicious had "no business looking after the interests of the people—whether it be in the U.S. Senate or in a

The "Know the Truth" Committee produced this cartoon to stress to voters that Graham had left-wing sentiments that put him outside the mainstream of North Carolina politics. (Original in possession of the authors)

municipal dog pound. His reaction time is simply too slow for our own good."[122] Another letter writer observed, later in April, that the current Senate race marked the first time he could remember a candidate having to explain to voters that he was not a Communist. Certainly Clyde Hoey was not being pummeled with similar questions. In such a case as Graham's, it seemed unwise for North Carolina to take a chance on any candidate who might not believe "100%" in the American system. A. J.

Fletcher, the staunch supporter of Smith, wrote Senator Hoey that the people in North Carolina appreciated the efforts of Hoey to keep the country from falling into the hands of the national socialist planners. "If Truman got a few more Frank Grahams in the Senate, then the U.S. would be in as bad a fix as Great Britain."[123]

Perhaps no charge troubled the Graham office more in April than the recounting from Smith headquarters of Graham's cosponsorship, in 1935, of a summer school for American students to be held in the Soviet Union at Moscow State University. Initially, some Graham workers believed the charge to be pure invention. The entire episode was, in fact, a replay of a 1935 controversy stimulated by the Hearst newspapers. As the story developed, it turned out to be short-lived yet hurtful to Graham's campaign.

Following Franklin Roosevelt's extension of diplomatic recognition to the Soviet Union in 1933, the Institute of International Education in New York developed a summer program for American students to be held in Soviet Russia. The program was to be similar to other endeavors of the institute held throughout Europe, including Nazi Germany. With grants from the Carnegie Corporation and the Rockefeller Foundation, American students went to Moscow in 1934 to study and learn something about the Soviets, and Stephan Duggan, director of the institute, reported a "fair amount of success" in the initial program. In pursuit of the Moscow initiative, Duggan had created an Advisory Council to the institute. Graham, in the company of other distinguished educators—Harry Woodburn Chase, John Dewey, George S. Counts, Robert Hutchins, assistant institute director Edward R. Murrow, Howard Odum, and others—had served on this council in an advisory capacity.[124] As it turned out, the two hundred British and American students in the 1935 session arrived in Moscow only to be told by Soviet authorities that the faculty members who were to give the courses "had been commandeered by the Government for other purposes" and the summer school was canceled. Despite Duggan's best effort, no more complete explanation was ever offered by the Russians. Consequently, the institute abandoned its summer program in the Soviet Union and dissolved the Advisory Council to which Graham belonged, but not before Graham's name had been publicized nationwide, courtesy of the Hearst newspapers.[125]

The revival of this incident by the Smith campaign was intended, of course, to cast shadows on both Graham's politics and his judgment. Whether it succeeded or not is hard to say. Certainly the 1950 charge provoked a fierce response from the now renowned Edward R. Murrow of CBS radio and New York University President Harry W. Chase, both of whom insisted that the Moscow program had been a legitimate educational enterprise. The charge, President Chase commented, that Graham's sponsorship of the summer school indicated Communist sympathies was merely silly. The program had been an attempt to provide mature American students a chance to learn something about Stalin's Soviet Union. "I am amazed," Chase commented, "that an experiment entered into with the best of intentions fifteen years ago should at this late date be revived in an attempt to smear the name of a man who is my long time friend and the finest type of American citizen."[126]

In the face of these continuing charges, which were fresh news in the North Carolina hinterland, pressures intensified on Graham supporters statewide to explain Graham's association with the institute to voters. As April wore on, Johnson realized not only that Graham had been placed on the defensive, but also that some way had to be found, within the constraints the candidate placed on his campaign, to rebut Smith's charges. Graham was simply not a "fighting type of campaigner" and could not imagine anyone suspecting that he could be an enemy of America, but Johnson knew that campaign morale would plummet if the charges went unaddressed.[127]

Johnson's solution was to redouble the effort, already underway, to explain Graham to voters. He would issue additional pamphlets that stressed Graham's patriotism; he would continue to rely on the editorial defenses of friendly newspapers; he would use prominent endorsements to override the image of Graham as a wild-eyed social and economic radical. For even though the campaign pace had quickened, Johnson's hunch was that Graham retained a commanding lead. In the absence of reliable data, of course, Johnson could not be sure.

The April pamphlets emphasized Graham's marine service, his Christian faith, and his loyalty to the Democratic party. A fighting Christian Democrat by definition was a vigorous anti-Communist. "Vote for Frank Graham and Fight Communism," the new ads admonished. Other circulars denounced scandalmongers and professional bigots who besmirched Graham's good name. Graham, in a lifetime of service, had brought honor and prestige to North Carolina. Should voters believe the "loose-lipped character assassins," or should they believe people like George C. Marshall, Senator Clyde Hoey, Senator Wayne Morse, and Mrs. O. Max Gardner, all of whom had praised Graham's abilities? The "scare-boys" were traversing the state distributing hate literature and whispering foul words. "They cannot even lift their little pig-eyes out of the slime long enough to catch a glimpse of the character and stature of a world leader like Frank Graham." They made accusations of communism and socialism but knew in their hearts that Graham had been one of the most consistent opponents of nazism, communism, and socialism. The final in this series of ads stated that the "whispering messengers of deceit" could not fool the people of North Carolina, especially when voters were reminded that Stalin had once called Graham a "tool of American imperialism." Charles Tillett also wrote personal letters explaining that "you could not make communists out of Presbyterian elders, Marines and men who have devoted their entire lives to the service of their fellow men."[128]

Tillett, in a statewide radio speech, said that Smith was trying to frighten voters into supporting him by pointing to "goblins under the bed." The Smith forces had cruelly assaulted Graham simply because he loved everybody. The genius of America was not the fear tactics of Smith, Tillett argued, but the courage of Graham. Charles Green replied in kind, calling Tillett's speech "an utterance of misinformation, bias, vituperation, panic." Tillett had used "the typical rabble-rousing tactics of Communists and Socialists."[129]

Undoubtedly, the most important change in Graham campaign tactics was the gradual change in Frank Graham's speeches. While Graham remained faithful to his pledge not to attack his opponent, he did begin to defend his views more vigorously. Slow to anger and skillful in masking it, Graham was nonetheless stung by the effort to impugn his patriotism. In his speech at Goldsboro on April 11 he called again for strengthening the Voice of America and defended Truman's decision to build the hydrogen bomb. Simultaneously he urged as well that Americans live their lives so that all nations could see the United States as a free people advocating fairness and goodwill toward all.[130] And by the end of the month, in a speech in Rutherford County, he again proclaimed, "There is no substitute for Americanism," as he repeated his call for a strong national defense and a flourishing free enterprise system.[131]

On April 27, in his first campaign appearance in his hometown of Charlotte, Graham made a forceful answer to the charges of Communist leanings. Speaking before twenty-five hundred supporters at the Mecklenburg County courthouse, Graham again denied that he had "ever been a member of any group knowing it to be a front for Communists." In a repeat of his speech to the Dunn Rotary Club on March 24, he admitted that he had been a member of "three or four" committees later listed as fronts by the attorney general, but those committees "were sponsored by patriotic Americans for good causes and were disbanded long before they were placed on the attorney general's list." The only one that had not disbanded was an organization (SCHW) whose original purposes were recommended by an editorial in the New York *Times*. He had resigned from that organization seven years before it was placed on the subversive list, he told his Charlotte supporters. His explanation, while hardly complete, was good campaign rhetoric, and his audience interrupted him repeatedly with applause and cheers. And when he firmly stated that he would "not lose sleep over reactionaries who call me communist or over the Communists who call me a tool of the capitalists," his enthusiasts found their feet and their voices in a prolonged cheer. "I take my direction from no groups or no man," he concluded.[132]

He had not stood on the sidelines in the long struggle for human freedom, Graham observed a few days later. Consequently, he had drawn criticism from those who opposed his aims and principles. The risk of being smeared was "one of the most hazardous risks of our times," commented Graham, but he stood for the freedom of all people and fair play for minorities, and he would not change his values at this late date.[133]

Graham's defense of his career as a social activist, while incomplete and inaccurate, was nonetheless effective. It would have been foolish beyond imagining for the senator to recount point-by-point the extent of his left-wing activities in the 1930s. He would have given his critics even more ammunition to fire back at him and would have generated intense debate among his allies. Graham skillfully avoided this pitfall by simply suggesting that his concern for social justice had led him into paths that less committed men would not tread. In truth, of course, he could not recount all the causes, many short-lived, and organizations, many now defunct, to which he had lent his name. He seldom mentioned all of the specific committees so that listeners could determine whether or not they had disbanded. He did not discuss the other fourteen organizations he was accused of joining, and his statement that he had resigned from an unnamed organization (SCHW) seven years before it was listed by the HUAC was simply untrue. Symbolically, however, his willingness to take on his accusers implied that they were guilty of distortions, misrepresentations, and inventions about his social activism and suggested to his admirers that he would, after all, fight to defend his reputation. In a word, after a month of near silence, he had put the ball back in Smith's court. His return, however, while effective, was not a clear winner. Newspaper headlines continued to dramatize Senator McCarthy's persistent attacks on Democrats and the Truman administration, which charged them with frustrating McCarthy's attempts to expose Communists in government.[134] Consequently, C. A. McKnight of the Charlotte

News and others continued to write that the oncoming primary would be a North Carolina referendum on the effectiveness of McCarthyism as a 1950 political weapon.[135] Whether Graham's answers had convinced the state's voters would not be known until after the polls closed.

The Smith camp, in contrast, sensed that the gap between Graham and his challengers was not closing, or, at best, was not closing fast enough. As the first primary approached, therefore, Smith workers began gradually to shift the focus of the attack on Graham away from social activism and toward race. In a letter to Atlanta *Constitution* columnist Ralph McGill, Jonathan Daniels recognized the shift in emphasis in mid-April. He observed that the Ku Klux Klan and the Dixiecrats were trying to find respectable auspices (the Smith candidacy) to carry on the same old program of racism, but "I don't believe that will get us down."[136] Race was being used especially in eastern North Carolina, wrote Tom Bost on April 27. Farmers were being told that Graham's election would mean the abolition of segregation in public schools.[137]

The Smith people all along had hoped that Graham would be vulnerable on the race question if they could show that federal developments—judicial rulings, executive decisions, and congressional actions—posed an immediate threat to the racial status quo in North Carolina. They were excited, therefore, when U.S. Attorney General J. Howard McGrath filed an amicus curiae brief for the Truman administration in the cases of *Sweatt v. Painter* and *McLaurin v. Oklahoma State Regents*. The cases concerned racial segregation in state-supported graduate education and were then under Supreme Court review. In his brief, McGrath argued in support of the black appellants who were seeking admission to all-white graduate and professional schools in Texas and Oklahoma. The very idea of segregation, McGrath wrote in his brief, was both inequitable and discriminatory.[138]

McGrath's brief became a Smith-Graham campaign issue. Senior Senator Clyde Hoey immediately denounced McGrath's action, calling it unprecedented and indefensible. It indicated how far the federal government would go in its effort, in Hoey's words, to "utterly destroy established customs and practices throughout the South."[139] In contrast, Graham made no public mention of McGrath's brief at all.[140]

In reaction to McGrath's brief, J. C. B. Ehringhaus, Jr., a Smith adviser, told reporters that if the appellants prevailed in the Texas and Oklahoma cases, racial segregation at the University of North Carolina would be at an end.[141] North Carolina Attorney General Harry McMullan, tied like Ehringhaus to the conservative faction of North Carolina Democracy, applauded Hoey's criticism of McGrath. He told reporters that if the

Supreme Court ruled against the states in the cases at hand, it would mean an end to racial segregation in tax-supported schools in the South, in publicly owned separate playgrounds, and in transportation on common carriers.[142] Privately, McMullan believed that if the Truman administration position should prevail in the pending cases, "it will cause a political upheaval in North Carolina that could easily defeat every democrat who is known to be in any wise sympathetic with the National Administration."[143]

Willis Smith greeted this controversy as a welcome development and inveighed with an attack of his own. To Hoey he wired congratulations for his resoluteness in "upholding the time-honored traditions of the South which a few political henchmen were trying to disrupt and destroy."[144] Hoey responded on April 11, commenting that Attorney General McGrath had embarked on a very unwise course and thanking Smith for his approval.[145] Smith then publicly criticized McGrath and lit into Senator Graham for failing to defend North Carolina against attacks on its segregationist tradition. By his silence, Graham consented to McGrath's actions, Smith charged, and to the Truman administration's effort "to cram its civil rights program down the throats of the states."[146] Smith's statewide ads repeated the question: "WHY DOESN'T SENATOR GRAHAM DEFEND THE TRADITIONS OF THE SOUTH?" In addition, Smith reminded voters of Graham's service on the Committee on Civil Rights appointed by Truman in 1947 and restated his argument that Graham's claim to have dissented from the majority on the issue of FEPC was spurious. Senator Graham was now claiming he favored the "North Carolina way" in race relations, Smith argued, but Graham's record indicated that he had always favored ending segregation.[147]

Obviously, Smith's frenzied reiteration of charges he had made at the beginning of the campaign suggested to contemporaries his belief that Graham was vulnerable on the issue of race. More plausibly, however, Smith's reenforced emphasis on race can be seen as a realization that his effort to convince voters that Graham's activist past made him an unfit senator had not taken hold. Therefore, he renewed his attack on FEPC, calling it a political brainstorm by northerners who wanted to control the South,[148] and warned that FEPC meant "that a man's job can be claimed by another man just because he is of a different race or color."[149] He labored even harder to link Graham to the Committee on Civil Rights' report of 1947, and the contending camps therefore debated again the "minority report" dispute. In brief, they argued over the demurrer Graham had put into the report regarding federal coercion to force states to desegregate.

Smith's renewed racial charges did produce one important result.

They apparently convinced Graham to heed his advisers' long-standing pleas that he deliver a speech strongly supporting complete equality of educational opportunity within the pattern of segregation.[150] He also reiterated his opposition to FEPC as a coercive bill that would cause a real setback in race relations. Graham favored, as he had his whole life, the fundamental approach through religion and education to solve the complex problem of racial discrimination. In the long run, he continued to maintain, greater acceptance of fair principles would be won through this method than by federal compulsion.[151] In addition, Graham ran ads in Charlotte proclaiming in bold letters that he was against FEPC and would speak against it on the floor of the Senate. Eleven southern attorneys general, his ads instructed, had incorporated Graham's FEPC position in briefs supporting Texas and opposing desegregation in the then pending *Sweatt* case. A vote for Graham was a vote against FEPC.[152]

The most powerful parry against the minority report charges came through disclosures published initially in the Winston-Salem *Journal and Sentinel*. A. G. "Pete" Ivey, the paper's associate editor and a man with close ties to the Graham campaign, had written each member of the Truman committee and asked about Graham's FEPC position. Their answers to Ivey unanimously exonerated Graham of the charge that he favored a compulsory federal commission and verified his account of his advocacy, in the panel's deliberations, of a moderate and noncoercive policy. Johnson gratefully distributed their responses to reporters.

The most publicized letter came from Franklin D. Roosevelt, Jr., one of the fifteen signers of the report. Personally, he favored a compulsory FEPC, Roosevelt wrote Ivey, and hoped for committee unanimity on the subject. But he could never get Graham to consent. Moreover, Roosevelt stated, Graham was primarily responsible for the two minority views in the report that questioned the wisdom and effectiveness of federal sanctions and fair practices laws. The case for moderate gradualism in race relations had no more effective proponent than Frank Graham, Roosevelt concluded.[153]

Letters from other prominent members of the Committee on Civil Rights sustained Roosevelt's position. They unanimously agreed that Graham opposed FEPC and federal coercion and that he wrote the minority report.[154] The Reverend Henry Knox Sherrill further explained that the case for the minority could not be stated on every issue but appeared in the body of the report.[155]

Johnson now told reporters, "The Roosevelt statement has cut the FEPC limb out from under those who crawled out on it. It is proof that anyone linking Frank Graham to compulsory FEPC is sadly misinformed as all thinking North Carolinians have known all along."[156]

Roosevelt's letter not only absolved Graham of Smith's charge, but it gave the Graham camp an opportunity to introduce the magic initials "FDR" into the Senate campaign. Two hundred thousand reprints of a glowing Durham *Morning Herald* editorial, which stated the FEPC issue should now be closed,[157] were spread across the state. The Graham staff had reason to believe they had met Smith on this question and turned it to their advantage. Indeed, as April came to a close, Graham's election bid, for all its fits and starts and for all the senator's elective idiosyncrasies, seemed to many observers to be on course. National press observers now reassured Graham advocates that Graham's election was highly probable, a conviction the Graham camp shared.[158]

One reassuring aspect of the campaign for the Graham side was the unwavering support of black citizens for Graham's candidacy. That black voters were vital to Graham's success was obvious to Johnson and his aides. The Philadelphia *Inquirer* and the Goldsboro *News-Argus* both indicated that a Graham victory would depend largely on the black voter turnout.[159] No one understood the importance of the black vote more clearly than Kelly M. Alexander, Jr., president of the state NAACP. Alexander, however, was discouraged at the slow pace of political progress for blacks in the state, which he correctly attributed to the state's voter registration law. Applicants were required to "read and write" any section of the Constitution "to the satisfaction of the registrar," which made registration difficult if not impossible in some areas of the state. Such discrimination generated black political apathy, and blacks did not take advantage of voting opportunities even where they were more available.[160] Alexander, therefore, strongly urged blacks to register and vote in the May primary; they had much to lose if Graham failed.[161] The *Carolina Times* seconded Alexander's plea by explaining that the vote was the method with which blacks could obtain better jobs and schools.[162]

Black leaders frequently wrote Graham expressing their willingness to help. The secretary of the North Carolina College Alumni Association promised the aid of alumni "who are strategically situated throughout the state."[163] A black attorney in Henderson who wanted to campaign openly for Graham feared a too visible effort might create a white backlash and hurt Graham's chances. "I assure you," he promised, "that every Negro and friend of the democratic form of government will reply to the vicious attacks at the proper place—the polls."[164] The *Carolina Times*, regretting that Smith had injected the race issue into the campaign, believed that those who favored race baiting were outnumbered by thoughtful citizens who would judge candidates on their ability and experience.[165]

Canvassers for Frank Graham, however, had already discovered that the race issue would be a troublesome problem when approaching white voters. Mary Coker Joslin, wife of William Joslin, the Wake County chairman for Graham, approached one man and asked him to vote for Graham. She got a violent reaction: "That communist who wants to put Niggers in our schools?" Mrs. Joslin tried to explain that Graham was not a Communist and did not want to change the North Carolina way of doing things, but the man would not listen. "I ain't votin' for no Red and no Nigger lover."[166] Not all individuals responded in such a vehement manner, but this incident was not an uncommon experience for Mrs. Joslin, who saw race as the most emotional and divisive issue in the campaign.

Meanwhile, as Graham and Smith parried, the April outlook for candidate number three was much different from the other candidates. Up on Reynolds Mountain, "Our Bob" gathered his strength. After a mild flurry of activity in early April, his campaign had lapsed into somnolence.

Only a visit to Charlotte in the first week of the month suggested that Reynolds was still an active candidate. Here he repeated his five-point platform, copies of which were distributed in North Carolina by Wesley McDonald. The pamphlet again emphasized states' rights, anticommunism, and limited foreign policy expenditures.[167] He predicted victory: "I've got the masses. I've been fighting communism and this immigration business for ten years."[168] He returned to the language of his political heyday, claiming to be a poor boy from the hills without the money to set up a campaign organization. With no help from large contributors, he would have to get along as best he could.[169] But it was all for show. Reynolds did return briefly to the flowery rhetoric of 1932 when he attacked Graham's idealism and desire for one world government. "If he would come down out of those fleecy clouds of idealism, take off those golden slippers, unfurl those angelic robes from around his shoulders and put on the brogans of the world of stark reality, he would be better off."[170]

Reynolds was out of contention, and he knew it. The mayor of Dillsboro, M. Y. Jarrett, had penned a prophetic requiem for Reynolds in a letter to Graham in late February that was more true in April than it had been when it was written: "Fear not, I am with thee, O be not dismayed; 'Our Bob' will not hurt thee, He can't make the grade."[171] Reynolds continued to tell the press his election was imminent, but it was pure bravado. Asked about a statewide effort, Reynolds replied: "I'm my own campaign manager and publicity director and wherever my car happens to be parked is state headquarters."[172] His principal lieutenant, Wesley McDonald, was reduced to reassuring the Asheville *Citizen* in mid-month that rumors of Reynolds's impending withdrawal from the race were baseless.[173] Reynolds would stay in, but whatever influence he would retain would be simply as a possible spoiler. It was not a role "Our Bob" cherished. He wanted center stage. But the leads in the drama had already been cast, and the electorate had rebuked Reynolds's audition.

As April drew to a close, *The Nation* saw the North Carolina primary increasing in national significance. Graham was fighting not only for his political life but also "for the emergence of the South from its long dark era of representation by Rankins and Byrds."[174] Tom Schlesinger, also in *The Nation*, saw Graham as an unusual politician because even his enemies liked him and thought him "nature's nobleman." Graham's political future depended on how well he could sell his liberalism. Graham was "learning the hard way that mill hands in Gastonia much prefer to hear about his labor record than about his success in Indonesia."[175]

6 · *First Primary*

"Sound the Tocsin"

The absence of reliable polling data—or any other systematic analysis of voter opinion—perplexed the managers of both major contenders in 1950. It even left them confused regarding Bob Reynolds's potential impact on the election. Reliance on informal political intelligence—telephone chats with county managers, unsolicited progress reports from local "experts," and conflicting press analyses—meant that neither Graham nor Smith staffers could gauge the campaign's progress with clarity. As a consequence, no consistent consensus developed on the campaign's direction. Some Grahamites surmised in early May that their candidate had a commanding lead, buttressed by strength in the state's piedmont section.[1] Other observers believed that Graham still ran first but that Smith's campaign had made major inroads, narrowing Graham's advantage.[2] John Marshall, Governor Scott's private secretary, confessed his concerns to Ambassador Capus Waynick in early May, writing that Graham's effort was moving slowly—too slowly. Graham remained weak among rural voters, Marshall argued, and he doubted Jeff Johnson's ability to accelerate the campaign's pace. Marshall was peeved that Johnson had ignored key Scott operatives, whose names Marshall had given to Johnson, and he feared that the ineptitude of Graham's campaign had done serious damage to Scott's political network.[3]

Other Graham supporters were even more alarmed than Marshall. Graham would have a "hard, mean uphill fight" in eastern North Carolina, warned Lindsay Warren on May 4.[4] A Hamlet observer, writing to Graham, personally cautioned him not to "overlook this neck of the woods, as opponents . . . are really getting their work in."[5] Political columnist Doris Fleeson seemingly confirmed these private cautions, writing in late May that Smith's "racism and Reds" campaign had made the outcome uncertain.[6]

An ill-defined consensus thus emerged in the Graham camp that saw Graham's election as imperiled even as campaign staffers continued to warn that voter complacency was Graham's principal adversary. Supporters, fearful that Smith's attacks were dampening enthusiasm for Senator Graham, again pleaded with the candidate to parry Smith's thrusts; "Willis Smith is getting quite a grip on a certain type of people, of whom there are too many who don't think," one voter informed Graham.

Graham must act to combat Smith's misinformation, the writer coun-
seled,[7] an admonition seconded by many other Graham advocates. Harry
Truman's 1948 attack on the Republican Congress provided the example
Graham should copy, wrote another friend.[8]

Graham, as usual, paid little heed to this counsel. He did not notice-
ably increase the level of his campaign rhetoric in early May, a response
that vexed and frustrated his advocates. Graham's manager in Guilford
County, L. P. McLendon, Jr., remembered that he could do little to
answer Smith's charges if Graham himself raised no serious objection.
The only recourse was to ignore the attacks and continue to stress
Graham's character and accomplishments.[9]

The Charlotte News noted that Graham was probably too honest for
his own good, a view Drew Pearson popularized as a question: was
Graham too honest to be elected? North Carolina voters would have to
take Graham straight, Pearson observed, as Graham would follow his
conscience no matter what. Graham, the Durham Sun agreed, had been
presented ample opportunity to embarrass Willis Smith but had spurned
every opening. He obviously would rather lose than stoop to political
expediency. Such integrity was admirable, the Sun continued, but it
made Graham the despair of those experienced politicians who supported him.[10]

Consequently, the Graham campaign continued to bound along the
high road, trumpeting Graham's character and national reputation. Jeff
Johnson and his associates initiated an extensive statewide newspaper
and radio advertising campaign praising Graham as "the Little Giant of
Democracy" and recalling his achievement in bringing peace and democracy to Indonesia. The ads also reminded voters that Graham had supported the Hoover Commission proposals to make federal government
more efficient, and they boasted that he represented no special interests.[11] Johnson spent heavily for these ads;[12] he believed they were very
effective and urged local campaign managers to use them.[13]

Not all Graham supporters followed Johnson's example and refrained
from attack. A cartoon, "Willis Smith Goes to Washington," apparently
not published but circulated by the Graham people, showed Smith at a
train station waiting for the "Senate Special" to Washington. Loaded
down with bags and suitcases full of money, Smith waited while power
company executives and other big businessmen argued over who would
pay for his ticket to Washington. In the background, sometime radio
editorialist Bob Thompson, referred to as a "common-tater," urged Smith
to hurry since the folks were getting wise.[14]

Whether the Graham strategy would have continued in this vein is

While Smith consistently attacked Graham's liberalism, the Graham forces replied in kind in this cartoon, denouncing Smith for being in the grip of power companies and other big business interests. The cartoon was also directed at High Point *Enterprise* editor Robert Thompson, an ardent Smith supporter and radio commentator. (Daniel Augustus Powell Papers, Southern Historical Collection, University of North Carolina at Chapel Hill)

difficult to say, however, for in early May, two events changed the course of the campaign. First, on May 5 word reached the state that Florida voters had changed their state's Senate delegation. The liberal New Dealer Claude Pepper had run into a political buzz saw named George Smathers who had sliced Pepper into early retirement. Newspapers in North Carolina gave the Florida contest their full attention, and both the Smith and Graham camps looked for omens in the sunshine state race.

Smathers had assailed Pepper in a heated battle, condemning Pepper's labor support, maligning his popularity among black voters, and ridiculing Pepper as "an apologist for Stalin, an associate of fellow travelers and a sponsor for Communist front organizations." Smathers celebrated his opposition to FEPC and "socialized medicine," claiming that Pepper championed both as a stalwart loyalist of the Fair Deal. A vigorous and appealing young congressman, Smathers found an eager audience for his anti-Pepper attacks, and he buried the senator by a sixty-thousand-vote majority.[15]

Every political expert in North Carolina and many outside the state sought possible parallels to Pepper's defeat in the Smith-Graham contest. National Republicans, ignoring Truman's dislike of Pepper (who had favored the replacement of Truman in 1948 with Dwight Eisenhower), saw the race as an anti-Truman referendum. Candidate Smith called the outcome a "great victory for level headed citizens"[16] and drew obvious encouragement from Pepper's demise.

The Charlotte *Observer* also saw Pepper's rude treatment in Florida as evidence of growing anti-Truman sentiment. Florida voters, the *Observer* noted, had renounced Truman's socialistic practice of deficit spending, and their rejection signaled a national move to conservatism.[17] Columnist Thomas Stokes suggested that this evidence of Fair Deal rejection would generate much increased financial support for candidates with views similar to Smathers.[18] Marquis Childs believed that the "Red" charges against Pepper had united Florida voters from varied economic backgrounds.[19] *U.S. News and World Report* stressed voters' concerns over federal interference in race relations (FEPC) and deficit spending as major forces in Pepper's undoing. Rural areas went strongly against Pepper, and the charge that Pepper used bloc voting by blacks turned many whites into the Smathers camp.[20] The nation was growing more conservative, *Life* magazine concluded. Pepper's labor support had proved more damaging than helpful, and the "Communist" issue had become increasingly important, *Life* argued.[21]

Pepper's defeat thus emboldened Smith forces and alarmed Graham's advocates. Jonathan Daniels put the best face on the Florida primary that he could, writing that the Florida results did not help Graham but that Graham would win despite Pepper's defeat.[22] Daniels argued that the Florida primary was not important in itself and would assume importance only if it invited tactics similar to those used against Pepper.[23] *The Nation's* response was more somber: the defeat of Pepper, in large measure on the race issue, was menacing to other Senate liberals and should alert candidates to shun "the besetting sin of overconfidence."[24]

Willis Smith thought Smathers's campaign pointed the way to his success. The Florida primary energized Smith's boosters, who had understood from the beginning that Smith's chances of beating Graham were a long shot. They seized on the Pepper defeat as proof that Frank Graham could be beaten.

As for Graham personally, the Pepper ouster had little effect on his campaign strategy. His plan was to increase his appearances in the state in May as his advertising and publicity efforts peaked. In early May, he went to Laurinburg, a small community in eastern North Carolina where his campaign had been reported to be "in trouble." During his visit, he answered charges about affiliation with Communist-linked groups and claimed that he was a tool of no one.[25] During the trip, he developed a sore throat, and when his party returned to Raleigh, a physician examined the senator and diagnosed pneumonia. Graham's illness would require that he be confined to his room in the Sir Walter Hotel for about ten days, the physician told reporters.[26] By May 20, the senator's physician could report that Graham had no fever and was recovering, but would not be able to resume campaigning until May 24. Consequently, from May 12 until three days before the voting, Senator Graham was hors de combat.[27]

Graham's illness, coming at the peak of the primary, threw his campaign into new disarray. With the candidate at rest for two weeks, his election effort was without its most effective weapon—the senator himself moving around the state, meeting voters and campaign workers, and reassuring North Carolinians that he would be a responsible and productive public official. And because Graham's role in organizing the campaign was minimal, his effort to work out of his hotel room was of little benefit. In a sense, the campaign now became Jeff Johnson's to win or lose. Graham could not win the race over the telephone, nor were his amateurish radio ads a useful substitute for personal appearances. (Television was still an oddity in North Carolina and played no significant role in the campaign.)

No one can measure the cost of Graham's illness in votes. It can even be argued that his illness aroused sympathy and made some voters more disposed to support him. Since no polling figures exist to suggest Graham's strength in the campaign before, during, or after his illness, any observation is speculative.[28] Nonetheless, his illness undoubtedly complicated his campaign staff's task.

Graham's respiratory difficulties not only took him off the campaign trail but also required him to be absent from the Senate just as a critical vote loomed. A cloture motion, designed to cut off a southern filibuster to talk to death the Truman-led bill to create a federal Fair Employment Practices Commission, was imminent. Graham had not yet registered any official opinion on the civil rights question, and his response to the effort to cut off the filibuster would be menacing to his election chances unless he supported the southern position.[29]

Since Graham could not vote against cloture if absent from the Senate floor, his staff developed a strategy that would enable Graham to align himself with other southern senators and blunt the Smith camp's criticism of Graham's civil rights record. In his absence, Graham was to authorize Senator Hoey, as Hoey cast his vote against cloture (against cutting off debate), to tell the assembled senators, "And if my colleague Senator Graham were here, he likewise would vote nay." Senate liberals, particularly Paul H. Douglas of Illinois, implored Graham to embrace this strategy. According to Hoey, that simple act would be worth fifty thousand votes to Graham. It would be interpreted as a statement that Graham had embraced the position of the white South and opposed a compulsory FEPC, as he had always maintained.[30]

But to the surprise of his friends, Graham balked at the maneuver. Allard Lowenstein, Graham's energetic young aide in Washington, sought the support of other senators to persuade Graham to follow the plan. In addition, Graham was besieged with requests from county chairmen all over the state to make a stand against cloture. If he did so, the county managers argued, it would insure his victory. Both Jeff Johnson and Jonathan Daniels took up the cause of the county managers, arguing that the vote against cloture was perfectly consistent with Graham's lifelong advocacy of free speech. "Yes," Graham answered their plea, "but I'm against filibustering, too, against preventing a vote by speech that is not debate. Have they had a fair debate yet? I'm not there so I don't know. How can I say I would do something if I were there when the simple truth is that without being there I can't possibly know what I would do?"

Graham anguished over this decision. Lying on a sickbed, he simply did not know what his judgment would lead him to do were he on the Senate floor. He did not want to betray his friends and supporters, who thought a simple declaration from Senator Hoey's lips would win Graham the election; neither did he want to betray—or seem to betray—his own conscience or principles. Graham asked Lowenstein, who was much like a son to Graham, "What would you do if you were in my place?" Knowing Graham's commitment to his conscience, Lowenstein replied, "That's not fair to ask. I'm not the Senator. You're the Senator." Eventually, Graham decided he could not ask Hoey to speak for him.[31]

Graham's decision was distressing to his allies and inexplicable to experienced politicians. But to Graham, apparently, the act would have

reeked of expediency and opportunism, even if it were philosophically
correct. As one contemporary observer, R. Mayne Albright, remarked,
the worst thing Graham's counselors could have done would be to tell
Graham that the "correct" decision would be worth fifty thousand votes.
Graham, as his biographer has commented, would do nothing he regarded as self-serving, in part because he had a touch of the martyr in
him. In any event, this episode, like Graham's illness, was one in a
progression of campaign actions, any one of which could lose a close
election. Graham simply would not see the world through the eyes of a
practical politician. Conscience and principle were his guiding stars, and
his actions would follow the path they marked for him, irrespective,
apparently, of consequence.[32]

Graham's position on cloture becomes even more perplexing in light
of the fact that he had already announced that he would speak and work
against a compulsory FEPC when it came to the floor of the Senate.
Graham distinguished his effort from the southern filibuster, from which
he remained aloof, but his position against a compulsory FEPC was
nonetheless consistent with a view he had publicly stated for several
years.

His refusal to join his southern colleagues in their filibuster against
FEPC had already brought criticism from his campaign foes. The High
Point *Enterprise* observed editorially that Senator Hoey and all twelve
North Carolina congressmen opposed FEPC in any form whatsoever,
while Graham only opposed an FEPC with federal enforcement provisions.[33] The *Enterprise* wanted Graham to participate in the filibuster and
to align himself with conservative southern resistance,[34] a resistance best
expressed in a statement from South Carolina Senator Olin D. Johnston
that passage of such a bill would constitute a "Pearl Harbor for the
South."[35] Graham's rejection of the plan to have Hoey tell the Senate
what he would have done had he not been ill thus seemed to his political
advisers a dangerous mistake. Perhaps Graham simply could not decide
what to do and, in the heat of the political moment, wilted. Certainly his
claim that his illness denied him the complete information he needed to
make up his mind satisfied no one and cost him heavily in the first
primary.

Into this breach rushed Jonathan Daniels, who had a reputation as a
southern liberal on matters of race, albeit a liberal whose racial moderation remained under firm control. As Charles Eagles has shown, Daniels's
views were clearly at odds with majority sentiment in his native state.[36]
Two days after the Senate debate on FEPC began on May 8, Daniels

blasted the proposal in a Raleigh *News and Observer* editorial. He argued
that the measure would do more harm than good, that it was a dangerous
tool, and that progress on racial matters could only come through education and religion, the familiar theme of the Graham campaign.[37]

As Graham languished in his sickbed, Daniels next appeared at a mid-
term meeting of the Democratic party in Chicago, where he was a witness
before a civil rights panel of the Democratic National Committee. Daniels was not an invited witness but insisted on speaking to the panel. He
made a strong denunciation of the Truman FEPC bill. Reminding the
panel that he was a Truman enthusiast, Daniels nonetheless condemned
FEPC as a "faulty device" that not only would fail to end employment
discrimination, but also would interrupt progress in southern race relations. The measure would strengthen the Dixiecrat position and would
arouse strong reaction to all civil rights measures. FEPC allowed anti-
Truman southerners to "hide behind the civil rights issue while they fight
every progressive measure," Daniels told the panel.[38]

Daniels's statement on FEPC was consistent with his long-held views
on a compulsory federal FEPC. But, as the New York *Times* observed in
commenting on his remarks, Daniels's outspokenness was a direct result
of his zeal for Graham's election,[39] a view endorsed in the Baltimore
Evening Sun by editorial writer Gerald Johnson. Daniels's surprise testimony to the civil rights panel, the *Evening Sun* made clear, was in part an
act of political expediency, since the "announcement was directed more
at winning votes in North Carolina than in pronouncing national principles."[40] Daniels's statement would certainly help Graham's election effort,
Kenneth Royall wrote Daniels.[41] Candidate Smith called Daniels's testimony, and his animosity toward FEPC, "the most miraculous conversion
I ever heard tell of in my life," although the Raleigh *News and Observer*
reported accurately that Daniels had come out against FEPC in an editorial on November 19, 1949.[42] Daniels later recalled the circumstances
and the purpose of his outburst against FEPC, confirming that his objective had indeed been political. Daniels remembered that the day after his
testimony, he had seen President Truman, who grinned at him and said,
"I've had a candidate to support too, like you have with Graham." This
view was confirmed by candidate Willis Smith, who called Daniels's
denunciation of FEPC a "great grandstand play." Daniels insisted that he
did not say anything he did not believe but took the position because he
was one of Graham's key supporters. Because both Truman and Smith
thought the testimony a grandstand play, Daniels acknowledged, "maybe
it was. At the time the thing that I was most interested in was the election
of Frank Graham."[43]

The Smith forces, however, had the last word on FEPC. Although Graham insisted both publicly[44] and privately that he was now and had always been against FEPC,[45] one Smith lieutenant wondered if farmers would understand the distinction between getting rid of segregation by education or by force. Graham favored eventual elimination of segregation. When would this occur, never or next year?[46]

Other Smith boosters pursued the issue even more vigorously. The Raleigh *Times* saw FEPC as promoted by the Communist party to stir up racial discord and weaken the country. Smith would save the working man from such a fate.[47] J. C. B. Ehringhaus, Jr., declared Graham to be in favor of FEPC and the mixing of races while demonstrating a "shocking exhibition of side-stepping and political shenanigans" in an attempt to mislead people on his racial views.[48] Ehringhaus saw Senator Hoey as upholding the traditions of the South while Graham tried to tear down those traditions.[49]

In Graham's absence from the campaign, Jonathan Daniels was hardly the only supporter who took on a more visible role. Jeff Johnson announced immediately that Graham's schedule of speeches would be filled by friends while Daniels in his newspaper bemoaned Graham's forced furlough. The senator would need his friends now as he had never needed them before, warned Daniels.[50]

A pressing concern to Johnson was the annual gathering of the North Carolina Democratic party. The convention opened just as Graham fell ill, and he could not attend. With twenty-five hundred party loyalists in session, the Raleigh meeting had two functions: first, to tend to the formal business of declaring the state party's fealty to national Democratic policy and the Truman administration; second, to meet the informal requirements of state politics, whose primary focus in 1950 was the Senate race. Johnson's understandable hope was to do everything possible to advance his candidate among the attending delegates.

The state organization, controlled by Governor Scott, national committeeman Daniels, and their allies, commended the national Democratic administration and President Truman's progressive leadership. The convention endorsed Governor Scott's "Go Forward" program as well, while calling simultaneously for a balanced national budget and no increase in taxes. Controversial questions—civil rights, federally financed medical insurance, the Brannan Plan—were simply omitted from the state organization's platform.[51] In the statement Graham sent to the convention, he emphasized that as a lifelong Democrat he had always voted a straight ticket and was in general agreement with the party's principles.[52]

As was customary at state conventions, supporters of Smith, Graham, and Reynolds used the proceedings to promote their respective candidates. For Smith, such promotion was no easy task, even in Graham's absence. Hampered by the Scott administration's control of the party and unseasonable ninety-degree heat, Smith forces nonetheless gave their best effort. They organized a rally and parade just prior to the official convention opening, with "Smith girls" marching down the aisles of Raleigh's unair-conditioned municipal auditorium to the accompaniment of whoops and yells from Smith stalwarts. Graham enthusiasts retorted with boos, frantic waving of "Graham for Senate" posters, and chants of "We Want Graham." Smith himself attended the convention with the Wake County delegation, while a strangely subdued Bob Reynolds put in a brief appearance.[53]

The intent of the Scott administration, of course, was to produce an uneventful meeting, harmonious in appearance and noncontroversial in substance. Most journalists reported that the administration had achieved these objectives, and Ford Worthy wrote that Graham's headquarters was optimistic because the convention crowd was for Graham. "But badges don't count in elections," Worthy warned. While the meeting was bland, it was also a Graham convention from "A to izzard," wrote Eula Nixon Greenwood. Secretary of State Thad Eure's keynote speech, she observed, had all the sparkle of an attorney addressing a jury in a utility case. As the proceeding had been plotted in advance in every dreary detail, it had "about as much flavor as branch water,"[54] precisely the result Scott and Johnson had sought.

The one-day convention successfully concluded, Johnson and Daniels now turned their full attention to the final campaign push, even as Graham recuperated. They presented a succession of Graham's friends to take his place on the hustings. John W. Umstead, a prominent member of the General Assembly, praised Graham's contribution to the state and claimed Graham had "conducted the cleanest campaign ever witnessed by . . . this state in the face of absurd and baseless charges." He proclaimed his faith in Tar Heel voters, arguing that they could see through the truthless statements made against the senator.[55] Repudiating the charge that Graham advocated either socialism or communism, he implored voters to retain a senator "who is humanely minded and not dollar minded."[56] Taking the message to eastern North Carolina, R. Mayne Albright told his audiences that when Frank Graham said he was against FEPC, the Brannan Plan, and "socialized medicine," he meant what he said.[57]

Some of Graham's surrogates were not content simply to praise their

Willis Smith supporters demonstrate their enthusiasm for their candidate at the North Carolina Democratic Convention, held in Raleigh in May 1950. (North Carolina Department of Archives and History, Raleigh)

candidate. They initiated stern rebukes to Smith's campaign, rebukes that Graham had not authorized. These attacks changed the tone of Graham's campaign. In a radio address, George Maurice Hill apologized to Graham for answering his critics with blunt language, and then told the Smith backers that what they were doing to Graham was ugly, vicious, and transcended the bounds of partisanship. They had raised "the black banner of bigotry and racial hatred for political gain." Hill claimed that he had thought originally that the attacks on Graham came from local Smith workers, but after reading the vicious propaganda postmarked from Smith headquarters, he now believed that Smith had "put off the cloak of respectability [and] . . . dropped his reputed record of truth and high ethics to pick up the tools of the demagogue in an attempt to reach the high position to which he aspires."[58]

But it was left for D. Hiden Ramsey, stout Graham friend and Asheville *Citizen* editor, to issue the most blistering anti-Smith remarks. In a radio talk on May 16, Ramsey noted that Willis Smith had borrowed most of his campaign ammunition from the Republican armory, and had presented an entirely negative platform. Smith appealed to fear, arousing it with inflammatory statements intended to discredit Graham at any cost.

Graham loathed communism, Ramsey explained, because it enslaved the individual, threatened world peace, and was anti-Christian. Graham was incapable of practicing the deceptive arts of the demagogue and was a compassionate man who would wittingly do no man the slightest injustice. As to charges that Senator Graham would be the tool of Governor Scott or Jonathan Daniels, all who knew Graham realized that no man could boss him or control his vote. Graham acknowledged only the sovereignty of his conscience, concluded the Asheville editor.[59]

Graham stalwarts acclaimed Ramsey's speech. One writer told Ramsey that he had never heard a more effective political utterance. "Though Frank Graham is sick at this time—his cause is safe with you on the stump in his stead."[60] In response, Ramsey judged that the advantage in the race had shifted to Graham. If the fight were pressed, Graham should win the first primary outright.[61]

Jeff Johnson, as he wrote Ramsey congratulations, agreed that the balance was turning in Graham's favor. Johnson told the Asheville editor that he intended to rebroadcast Ramsey's remarks frequently.[62] Encouraged by the favorable response to his first effort, Ramsey delivered another broadside against Smith on May 24. He could understand a congenital liar, Ramsey commented, but he could never understand one who slandered a good man for political preferment. Ramsey called such conduct loathsome and criminal. He called on the people of North Carolina to elect Graham in order to "rebuke that kind of slimy, despicable conduct."[63]

Most of Graham's advocates during his illness were public men and women, few of whom were controversial figures. The overwhelming exception was the governor. Debate had raged from the beginning among Graham staffers over the wisdom of high profile gubernatorial support. The debate regarding his role became academic, however, when Graham's illness took him off the stump, and the opposition began including the governor as a target in its attacks on Graham.[64] The campaign needed Scott's experience, contacts, and organizational skill. No one ever accused Kerr Scott of being above the battle, and as the attacks mounted, his advocacy of Graham became more direct and more partisan.

Even antedating Graham's illness, Scott could not resist making his best "private" effort to aid Graham. In early May, his advisers "cut the Governor loose" and encouraged his informal support for his Senate appointee. Scott wrote letters to political allies, explaining that he was "extremely interested" in electing Graham and seeking their active assistance on the senator's behalf.[65] While not actually stumping for Graham, the governor did take pains to explain in public talks why he had appointed him. He traced Graham's efforts over many years to encourage improved health care and education for all North Carolinians. In a speech before seven hundred Sampson County farmers in early May, Scott was surprised when, at the first mention of Graham's name, the audience rose as one and applauded—"the first time this has happened in the campaign," the governor's secretary informed Capus Waynick. Scott's effort, in other words, seemed to be of considerable assistance.[66]

Yet Scott's help did have a negative dimension. It reminded groups opposed to the governor—business interests and conservative Democrats—of the link being forged between the maverick governor and his liberal Senate appointee. Scott's visible role in the campaign warned his opponents that his effort would enthrone those groups he claimed to represent, specifically farmers and common people.[67]

Characteristically, Scott discounted the risk that he would do more harm than good and forged ahead. In early May, he had openly denounced "corporate interests," observing that North Carolina had sent corporate lawyers to the Senate for fifty years. The state should have a liberal layman representing it for a change. Hoey and Graham, Scott claimed, made a fair Senate team—Hoey speaking for conservative interests, Graham for the liberals, "and I don't mean any wild liberal either," he added. He was not politicking or not asking anyone to vote for Graham, he explained, merely articulating his reasons for appointing the University of North Carolina president.[68] Naturally, no sensible person saw Scott's activities as anything other than what they were: active campaigning for Graham.

In the face of Graham's illness and the accelerated pace of the campaign in mid-May, Scott pressed his case. Graham's campaign, said the governor, was a "continuation of my program to give the party back to the people," especially since monopolies, through corporate lawyers, had dominated politics and thwarted progress in North Carolina. Graham was a humanitarian, Scott explained, and it would be all right to have a humanitarian in the Senate once every fifty years.[69]

Mindful that the bedrock of his support was in rural North Carolina, Scott confined his "visits" to areas where he was much in favor. In Goldsboro, he defended Graham when he stated that voters had no need to fear socialism. "If you call hot lunches for school children socialistic, then I say let it be."[70] In Carthage and Pittsboro, Scott praised Graham's hard work for improved education and better health care. From a list of fifty-four candidates, he had chosen the one he thought was the best "and never had reason to change my mind."[71]

On May 22, Scott told a radio audience that the U.S. Senate needed a man who would concern himself with the hopes and aspirations of people rather than cold-blooded bank balances and lobbying fees. He charged, in addition, that Graham's rival had spread misinformation about Graham and had mocked and demeaned the Truman administration.[72]

Scott's jabs delighted his rural audiences. "I have heard nothing but favorable comments on your speech," wrote one enthusiast. But his remarks also elicited an immediate and heated reply from Smith. The claim that his charges against Graham were false was a slander, Smith argued, declaring that he had been factually accurate in every statement he had made about Graham. He dared Scott to point out one bit of factual misinformation. Scott was simply trying to divert attention from the facts by crying smear: "They have attempted to hide the truth by hurling epithets." Graham's leftist record should not be obscured by this smoke screen, Smith stated. Moreover, Smith pointed out that Scott's opposition to his candidacy seemed odd in that Scott had himself asked Smith to seek the governor's office with his backing in 1948. Finally, Smith denounced the governor's use of state cars and state employees in the effort to elect Graham. In response, Scott acknowledged that he had suggested to Smith in 1948 that Smith run for governor. He had not been aware at the time, Scott stated, that Smith was opposed to the national administration. Further, if state cars and state employees were being used to aid Graham, such acts were "without my knowledge or consent." Of course, Scott told reporters, he appreciated the loyalty of state workers who supported Graham, but if anyone in state government wanted to vote otherwise, they were free to do so.[73]

Backers of Smith would, obviously, have to buck considerable Graham strength within state government. As was customary, Scott used whatever influence he had with state employees to get them to vote for Graham. In addition, the great purge of state government that Scott had initiated upon assuming office was largely complete by 1950, hence state workers subject to gubernatorial appointment were overwhelmingly pro-Scott. Scott probably threatened no one outright, nor would he be foolish enough to give anyone time off to campaign, but he did use his considerable powers of persuasion to turn out a large state government vote for Graham. For example, the superintendent of prison camp number 1003 wrote Graham: "Prison Department is one hundred percent for you and stands ready to 'go down the road' for you." And Scott most certainly used the promise of delivery of state services—especially road paving—to enlist support for Graham. Such leverage was standard procedure for the state highway department, no less for Scott than for any previous administration. The reorganized department, headed by stout

Scott ally Dr. Henry Jordan, was the vanguard of the Scott machine statewide and had been at work since late 1949 organizing the state for Graham.[74]

As voting day approached, the Graham staff became convinced that Scott's assistance had helped their cause, even if his critics were dismayed at his overt partisanship. Graham supporters now believed that Scott's influence was the key element to Graham's hopes for a first primary majority.[75] The Durham *Morning Herald* gave editorial assent to this view, pointing out that even though many voters resented Scott's partisanship, in rural North Carolina Scott was undeniably the most favored politician. His endorsement of Graham meant that rural people would look to Graham with the same confidence they had placed in the governor.[76]

Other political forces were summoned to aid Senator Graham's May push, including the White House staff. With much more subtlety and much less publicity than the Scott administration, Harry Truman did what he could for Graham. Truman threw many important favors in North Carolina's direction, including the award of a surplus floating dry dock, courtesy of the U.S. Navy, to Wilmington. The dock was a source of employment and revenue and was highly coveted by several East Coast cities. Once awarded, Graham could use the dry dock as proof of his national clout. He could also rebut critics who charged he was spending too much time on foreign affairs, characterizing him as "the senator for Indonesia." To the dismay of his staff, however, Graham would not permit his office to publicize his pork barrel achievements. Governor Scott had to credit Graham with the dry dock acquisition in order for voters to make any association between the dock and Graham's office.[77]

Not every effort to enlist national support achieved success. Allard Lowenstein and John D. McConnell, Graham Senate aides, tried mightily—unbeknownst to Graham—to elicit a statement from General George C. Marshall asserting Graham's loyalty and praising his accomplishments in Indonesia. But General Marshall, who had warmly endorsed Graham's appointment in a private message, refused to budge from his lifelong practice of not endorsing political candidates.[78]

McConnell and Lowenstein also sought a statement from FBI Director J. Edgar Hoover, which they believed would rebut all the Smith camp's charges concerning Graham's activist involvement. In a Washington meeting with agent L. B. Nichols, McConnell noted that the FBI had investigated Graham (before he joined the War Labor Board). Would the director, asked McConnell, be willing to issue a statement that acknowledged the investigation and reported that the FBI "had found him [Graham] to be a law-abiding, patriotic citizen?"[79]

Nichols replied that such a statement could not be issued. It would "necessitate the Director's departing from a traditional policy of not evaluating [publicly] results of investigations." Undeterred, McConnell then approached the attorney general whose office called Nichols, acknowledging that the FBI probably could not help McConnell but urging that "if there was anything we could do . . . the General would want you to do it." There was no way, Nichols wrote, a conclusion Hoover noted on Nichols's memorandum as "absolutely correct."[80]

While neither Marshall nor Hoover would intervene, organized labor had no such reluctance. Labor's May push coincided with the efforts of Graham's friends, Governor Scott, and the Senate staff. Textile unions informed Graham of their activity in his behalf in early May, and the national CIO Political Action Committee publicly endorsed the senator on May 9.[81] As in the case of Governor Scott, the CIO's support carried political liability, in no small part because of its enthusiastic support of the Brannan Plan, FEPC, and national health insurance—all proposals Graham had opposed publicly. This policy conflict led Graham's opponents to question the sincerity of his opposition to labor's positions. The CIO, they argued, would not back Graham unless, in reality, Graham agreed with the CIO's views. Never would he vote for a candidate who had CIO support, one man wrote the editor of the Winston-Salem *Journal*, because the union was loaded with Communists.[82]

The CIO, of course, had much more to offer than mere endorsement. William J. Smith, state director of the CIO Organizing Committee, summoned all North Carolina staff members to a May 22 meeting in Charlotte and instructed them to "throw everything we can into the Graham campaign."[83] In Durham, labor planned to mail ninety-five hundred postcards to all county precincts and distribute thirty thousand "mill leaflets" to working-class districts, thirty-four hundred "Graham leaflets" to middle-class districts, and two thousand "FEPC leaflets" to middle- and working-class precincts. The CIO also continued to push black registration in the eastern part of the state.[84]

In related activity, Dave Burgess accelerated his already vigorous effort for Graham. The week of May 7–13 found him in Charlotte, Raleigh, Greensboro, and High Point, focusing on voter turnout and the distribution of leaflets to mill workers, especially those at Kannapolis's Cannon Mills.[85] Subsequent trips convinced Burgess that Smith was gaining ground, and he reported that the Smith people had bought off some black voters. He also stated that in Rockingham Smith forces were hiring drivers at $30 to $50 each and that a large, well-bribed vote was poised to deliver the town to Smith. He expressed fear that antiblack sentiment might lead the Railroad Brotherhood in Hamlet to work against Graham.[86]

Burgess steadily forwarded advice and money to Graham's Raleigh headquarters. In a mid-May letter to Johnson, Burgess hoped that Graham would get mad at the charges leveled against him, retaliate in righteous indignation, and "Attack Smith!" The CIO would help in any way possible in the campaign's final frenzy.[87] Johnson responded that the CIO was "sparking the drive immeasurably" and informed Burgess that the Raleigh *News and Observer* would soon launch a series of strong attacks against Smith, as Burgess had counseled.[88]

Labor's effort for Graham found its complement in the unprecedented mobilization of black voters in late May. From Durham, North Carolina College Dean James T. Taylor, a key black political operative, provided Johnson with a constant flow of political intelligence in the first primary's later stages. Trying to work inconspicuously, Taylor predicted that Graham would get seventy-five thousand black votes. Smith support among blacks was nonexistent, which meant Graham would get 99 percent of the black vote, the largest in the history of the state. This outcome was not in doubt, Taylor confided to Graham: "You can give your attention to other matters."[89]

A black Graham worker in Gastonia verified Taylor's claim, writing that the considerable number of "colored voters" in Gaston County were 100 percent for Senator Graham.[90] Similar letters came into headquarters from all over North Carolina. Willie Jacobs, who identified himself as a sixty-year-old father of fourteen children, wrote Graham in a painstaking scrawl that twenty-seven hundred outstanding black citizens in his county would vote for Graham. "We feel you are a good and honor-[able] man and mean freedom for all people of the world."[91]

Such reassurances, however, were not interpreted to mean that the black vote could be taken for granted. Johnson wrote T. A. Hamme, superintendent of the Oxford Colored Orphanage and a key Graham ally, that black voters must not fall victim to overconfidence in what was a very hard fight.[92] Black Democrats also circulated statewide an organizing pamphlet that stressed the importance of registering as many black voters as possible. Anticipating resistance to their efforts, the pamphlet advised appointing observers who were to contact state NAACP President Kelly M. Alexander, Jr., if problems arose in registration or voting.[93] *The Carolinian*, Raleigh's black newspaper, argued editorially that black voters would decide the first primary. Voter registration drives had been successful in Durham, Greensboro, and other cities, the paper reported, and legal action had been initiated in Nash and Warren counties, where blacks had been denied registration.[94]

Such success, *The Carolinian* added, did not mean discrimination against blacks had ceased. Intimidation remained a major impediment to aspiring black voters, who were subjected to a variety of tactics. In one instance, a registrar was approached by several blacks who wished to register. He fled to his house, where he was believed to have registered whites privately. In many areas, blacks lived in perpetual fear of reprisal, and *The Carolinian* urged blacks to raise money with which to prosecute one of these cases to establish black voting rights.[95]

Throughout the campaign, *The Carolinian* joined ranks with the state's other black newspapers to urge Graham's election. Columnist W. L. Greene identified Graham as a gradualist who would accept change in race relations. Contrasted with the traditional status quo position of his opponent, Graham was an appealing candidate, even though, Greene remarked, Graham's gradualism made him less than the ideal candidate.[96] The Wake County Committee for Graham even put an ad in *The Carolinian* touting Graham as a champion of democracy but waited until May 27 to run the ad.[97]

The imponderable element for Graham organizers remained rural folk. "The farm vote" was crucial to Graham's success, and he had tried throughout May to reassert his support for agricultural parity support programs. On May 5, before his illness, speaking to seventy-five hundred people at the Wallace Strawberry Festival, he explained the necessity of keeping the farmer on the same economic level as other elements of society. Government assisted industry with tariffs and land grants, Graham told his audience, but when aid such as farm price supports was extended to the little people, "some call it socialism."[98]

Seeking to reassure farmers in the face of Smith's attacks, Jeff Johnson asked the general manager of the Farmers' Cooperative Exchange to send a letter to all members explaining that Graham was not a Communist, that he understood the farm problem, and that he would give farmers a "square deal."[99] Press releases restated Graham's opposition to the Brannan Plan, and the staff circulated letters from former Agriculture Secretary Clinton P. Anderson and southern senators Richard Russell and Lister Hill that praised Graham's efforts on behalf of high price supports for cotton and tobacco.[100] But none of these measures produced the fervent pledges of support for Graham that were so characteristic of state labor leaders and black political workers. Graham's farm support, especially in eastern North Carolina, remained the campaign's biggest puzzle.

The combination of Graham's illness, Smith's attacks, and the push by both candidates to close the campaign in a spectacular fashion led the Graham entourage to a late effort to impugn Smith's character and professional integrity. The focus of this effort was voters in the east. Beginning on May 16, ads appeared in the Raleigh *News and Observer* under the headline "MR. SMITH WENT TO MOREHEAD CITY." The ads assailed Smith's role as court-appointed receivership trustee for the Madix Asphalt Roofing Corporation, located in Morehead City, and were allegedly funded by a disgruntled stockholder of that company. They pictured Smith as a high-pressure, greedy corporation lawyer. One ad charged that Smith collected a fee of $23,137.77 for his services while 137 unsecured creditors and thirty-nine holders of common stock got nothing. Smith, whom the ad represented as opposing a seventy-cents-per-hour minimum wage for North Carolina workers, labored ninety-eight days at a daily rate of $219.25, a princely sum indeed in 1950 North Carolina.[101] Drew Pearson repeated the ad in his "Washington Merry-Go-Round" on May 18,[102] and another ad followed on May 20, showing a beach scene crowded with unidentifiable sunbathers. Signed "Beachcombers Committee for Graham," the ad offered a $25 reward to the first person who located in the beach scene "an unsecured creditor or stockholder of the Madix Corporation."[103]

While some Graham stalwarts cheered this venture as a masterpiece of political assassination,[104] a number of commentators severely criticized the attack on Smith. The cries of "smear campaign," trumpeted by Graham people against Smith forces, would hereafter have a hollow ring, wrote Carl Horn, Jr., in a letter to the Charlotte *Observer*. Horn, an attorney familiar with bankruptcy law, assailed the ads' unfairness. State law required trustees and receivers to hire attorneys to assist them in liquidation, Horn noted, and attorneys, by law, were allowed a fee of 5 percent of receipts and 5 percent of disbursements made by the bankruptcy referee. Attorneys' fees were costs of the administration of the estate and, as a matter of law, had priority over all other claims against the corporation. Stockholders were last on the list for distribution of assets because they had invested in the corporation as a risk. U.S. District Judge Don Gilliam, continued Horn, found that Smith had spent 275–300 days working on the case (not the 98 days claimed in the ad). Judge Gilliam had deemed Smith's fees and expenses "fair, just and proper." The ad was a slur on the integrity of both Smith and Judge Gilliam, Horn asserted. That Smith's opponent could find nothing in his record to criticize save a trivial situation involving a disgruntled stockholder in a bankruptcy proceeding seemed to Horn "a tribute to Smith's character."[105] Moreover, as James K. Dorsett, Jr., later recalled, the ads failed to acknowledge that Smith's legal work helped the business stay alive financially.[106] Dr. Calvin Rea, of the "Corn Bread and Collards" Committee, attempted to blunt Horn's dissection of the ad, but his refutation merely accused Horn of "shedding crocodile tears" for Smith after his allies had

The Graham headquarters lashed out at Smith in this ad for receiving a huge payoff in a Morehead City bankruptcy proceeding, while the unsecured creditors got nothing. This was a campaign charge that misfired. (Raleigh *News and Observer*, May 16, 1950)

gone all over the state besmirching Graham's character. The fee paid to

Smith, Rea wrote, was not his idea of fairness, especially since the stockholders got nothing. "The poor can starve while he [Smith] waxes fat," Rea concluded.[107]

The Morehead City ads did not have their intended effect, in part because their basic claims were clearly rebuttable. The ads did reveal that the Graham forces, as the campaign approached primary day, were on edge. They still hoped and believed that Graham held his lead, but they feared that a first ballot majority was now at risk. Consequently, they attacked Smith along a broad front.

First, they assailed his use of guilt by association. An ad in the Charlotte *Observer* explained that by Smith's logic Winston Churchill was a Communist since he was a member of the Church of England and one of the church's high officials was a fellow traveler. The ad wanted to know why the "smear boys" sought to tear down North Carolina's racial amity. It called members of the Smith organization the lackeys of greed and privilege, who sought to revert to wages of less than forty cents per hour. "THEY MUST NOT CRUCIFY NORTH CAROLINA and its half century of progress in economics and racial amity, on the cross of bigotry, hate and greed," the ad concluded.[108]

On May 22, another Graham ad asked, "MR. SMITH—WHERE WERE YOU WHEN WE NEEDED YOU?" Where was Smith when farmers were trying to get electricity through the Rural Electrification Administration and better roads from state government? Where was he in campaigns for better schools and increased pay for teachers? He was too busy taking care of the affairs of the thirty-six corporations he represented as a lawyer, while Frank Graham was in the forefront of the battle for schools, better roads, and a better life for all people.[109]

Two other Graham ads explained that both Graham and Smith opposed communism and socialism, as well as FEPC. But Graham, the ads argued, was responsible for the minority report of the Truman Committee on Civil Rights that objected to federal compulsion in such a program. Moreover, their records of community service left no doubt which of the two candidates was a more committed public servant. Smith was a corporate lawyer, uninterested in the plight of common folk, whose career had been devoted to advocating measures to expand the privileges of the few; Graham's lifework had been a struggle on behalf of the dispossessed. Finally, claimed Graham ads, the senator had refused to smear his opponent even though Smith waged a negative "I'm against everything" campaign.[110]

The Graham counterattack continued until the ballots were cast on

May 27. In an ad entitled "They've Sold You Down the River, Mr. Smith," the Wake County Committee for Graham wondered if a corporation lawyer whose advisers were Dixiecrats and Roosevelt haters, and whose clients comprised a fat stable of corporations, could represent the people. Or would he instead instinctively favor his corporate clients?[111] C. A. Upchurch, Jr., encouraged Allard Lowenstein to pass material to Drew Pearson, who would continue to emphasize Smith's corporate affiliations.[112] Finally, in Mecklenburg County, David M. McConnell argued that the Senate did not need another "knocker and smearer" like Senator Joe McCarthy. North Carolina needed Frank Graham for "cool, considerate, level-headed leadership in world affairs."[113]

Denying Graham a first-ballot victory was, of course, the basic objective for Willis Smith's campaign. Smith forces, heartened by Claude Pepper's defeat in Florida, had pressed their campaign with renewed enthusiasm in May, and as they headed into the final weeks of the race, they professed hope of victory. So did the candidate. On May 1, even before the Florida news, Smith wrote a backer that the campaign was "progressing nicely." He had never dared hope to have such an encouraging situation, Smith noted.[114] The zeal of Smith's advocates had never been in question, but their numbers remained unknown. Further, Smith's political intelligence was no more reliable than Graham's.

On the basis of his impressions, Smith was convinced in early May that his tide was surging, and he campaigned with increasing fervor and energy. Warming to his role as a candidate, he stressed his announced campaign themes, with minor emendations. He attacked international communism and "internal crackpotism" again and again, and he reiterated the charge that Scott and Daniels wanted to be the political dictators of North Carolina.[115]

In a western swing at the beginning of the month, he told a Morganton audience that the crucial issue was whether voters wanted to go to the left with Graham or stay safe-and-sound in the middle of the road with Smith. Their decision on this question, Smith warned, would determine if a free America would survive.[116] In Waynesville on May 6, he lambasted Graham for favoring "Truman socialism" and questioned again Graham's claim that he opposed FEPC and the Brannan Plan. Smith promised to stop the ultraliberals in Washington and to throw out traitors and disloyal government employees. He chided Graham for allowing Red-tinged organizations to use his name and position. "Do you want someone in Washington so unwary, who can be led and swayed?" Moreover, if government spending were not curtailed, he warned, Truman would bankrupt the nation. As a parting shot, he reminded his Haywood

County audience of an earlier contretemps when Governor Scott had tried to take their elections board from them, and he urged his listeners to reject dictation from any government.[117]

Jonathan Daniels found Smith's reference to "traitors in government" especially offensive. In making such a charge, Daniels wrote, Smith had "out-McCarthied" the Wisconsin senator. If Smith knew of traitors in government, he should name names and present evidence. Otherwise there was no justification for such charges.[118] But some North Carolinians, at least, felt that Smith's fulminations against Graham's "Communist sympathies" and socialist tendencies were not baseless. Ruth Swisher wondered, in a letter to the Southern Pines *Pilot*, how Graham could claim he was unknowingly involved in Communist front organizations. She knew they were Communist fronts, Swisher wrote; it was inconceivable that Graham did not.[119] David Clark, Graham's long-time critic, cheered Smith's attacks and repeated most of them in his *Southern Textile Bulletin*. Graham's views meant, in Clark's opinion, that he could never be a true and honest representative of North Carolina.[120]

When the CIO Political Action Committee endorsed Graham publicly, Smith used the endorsement to substantiate his case against Graham. Labor supported Graham because "he would carry out their program of socialization" in its "full range of horrors": the Brannan Plan, FEPC, and "socialized medicine."[121] Smith publicist Charles Green simultaneously accused the CIO of rushing "propaganda experts and rabble rousers" into North Carolina to help elect Graham.[122]

Throughout May Smith continued to criticize Governor Scott's open effort to elect his senatorial nominee. Scott's use of his office to pressure state employees to back Graham was contrary to law and a sense of fair play, Smith complained. In a Wilmington address on May 13, Smith reported that Scott and Daniels were even bringing into North Carolina a lot of "smart boys" from Washington and New York (Kenneth Royall and Sperry Corporation President Thomas Morgan) to control affairs from outside the state. Their support, Smith proclaimed, "was the greatest demonstration of outside interference that has ever appeared on the political scene in North Carolina."[123] Indeed, Smith warned, democracy itself would be threatened if only a few people controlled the state's Democratic party. There were many different points of view among North Carolina Democrats, Smith stated, and he had entered the race to give middle-of-the-roaders a chance to express their views.

Smith's strategy encouraged conservative Democrats troubled by Graham's candidacy. Smith's chairman in Lee County, Harold Makepeace, Sr., observed that the Graham forces were stating that they "did not want another conservative and half-Republican. Every time they use that expression," Makepeace wrote Senator Hoey (the obvious target of the derision), "it means another vote for Mr. Smith."[124]

By mid-May Smith had found another target for his attacks: Graham's alleged vacillations. Graham had changed his mind on several questions, Smith claimed, chief among them the trio of uglies: the Brannan Plan, FEPC, and "socialized medicine."[125] On the subject of national defense, Smith argued, Graham one moment would advocate a strong defense and then seem to be for national disarmament: "Consequently, I don't know where he stands on that subject . . . as is the case on many other issues in the campaign." Pledging his own support for a strong national defense, Smith promised that he would never vote to disarm America.[126]

The challenger also worked to turn Graham's attacks to his advantage. Graham backers, Smith charged, had made "abusive and misrepresentative speeches about me." Moreover, "vicious, libelous and scurrilous cartoons" had been passed around in a desperate attempt to prejudice voters. Smith claimed that he had made no personal attacks on Senator Graham—a claim from which he never retreated. He was only discussing issues and Graham's record on those issues. Smith stated publicly his belief that Graham had no intention of attacking him personally, but he knew that a political contest provided opportunity for the "mean, the little, and the vicious to use their powers in great measure." He would not hold against Graham the things said and done by his proponents.[127]

Meanwhile, Smith's advocates pressed the attack, however clumsily. Friends like former Governor R. Gregg Cherry made speeches for Smith, while the "Know the Truth" Committee circulated cartoon ads depicting Scott and Daniels manipulating the strings attached to a Frank Graham puppet. Graham would do their bidding, the puppeteers said to each other, and he would obey the commands of northern politicians. Daniels, talking on a telephone, was shown saying, "Hold on, here's another order from Washington." The puppet Graham simultaneously was pictured as saying he had always been for FEPC, "socialized medicine," and the end of segregation, even though as a political candidate, he had to change his tune to get elected. He did not want to let Jonathan and Kerr down.[128]

Such tactics, practiced by both camps, produced a spate of newspaper criticism condemning the campaign's descent into insult. Smith's tactics of distortion and implication, observed the Durham *Morning Herald*, merited "complete contempt," even though Smith denied that his attacks were personal. The Graham ads attacking Smith for his legal work in Morehead City were similarly objectionable, the paper wrote. They served not to guide the voter but only to confuse.[129]

In any event, by mid-May the Smith campaign was in full stride,

ripping Graham daily. It appeared more energetic, better organized, and much more aggressive than Graham's forces. The volume of campaign materials gushing from Smith's headquarters seemed, at least to some observers, to have no modern parallel.[130] The Raleigh News and Observer insisted that Smith had more money behind him than did Graham, as evidenced by his expensive newspaper ads and more frequent radio speeches.[131]

Whether true or not, the News and Observer's claim cannot be measured with accuracy. Certainly Smith had sufficient resources, but, as stated earlier, the Graham campaign was hardly penurious. Clearly the Smith effort was more focused, and, at first primary flood tide, the major emphasis continued to be Graham's past affiliations with alleged popular front or Communist-dominated groups and causes.

In ad after ad, Smith forces reviewed Graham's activist past and attacked Graham's record. Smith's materials, hoping to raise questions regarding the senator's judgment and political balance, condemned Graham as an inveterate joiner of suspect organizations. Smith hoped to show that Graham's political beliefs were far removed from the sentiments of heartland North Carolina.

An ad that appeared in the Raleigh News and Observer on May 16 reminded readers that Graham had acknowledged his role as an active organizer of the Southern Conference for Human Welfare. The conference, of course, had been labeled by the House Un-American Activities Committee as a Communist front organization both in 1944 and in 1947. While Graham had identified the organization's purpose as providing a forum in which southerners could address southern problems, the ad contained a picture of a New York rally for SCHW that featured black performer Paul Robeson and James Dombrowski, a former SCHW president, both closely linked to Communist party activities. One purpose of the rally, the Smith ad advised, was to raise money to unionize the South.[132] Another ad linked the SCHW with FEPC, abolition of segregation, and other radical racial ideas, arguing that Graham, the organization's honorary president, had neither resigned his position nor renounced its policy objectives. How was it possible, the ad queried, that Graham never suspected that the SCHW was controlled by Communists and socialists?[133]

An ad released on election eve attacked Graham's many affiliations, pointing out once again that Graham had formal associations with eighteen groups identified by the HUAC as Communist front organizations, and named all eighteen.[134] Attacks of this kind continued unabated

The Smith forces, in several ads, listed many of the left-wing organizations with
which Graham had been linked. This ad focused on the Southern Conference
for Human Welfare and Graham's long association with it. (Raleigh *News and
Observer*, May 19, 1950)

throughout the first primary. Believing that Graham's political associations were a legitimate campaign issue, Smith's "Read the Record" Committee refused to relent when Graham forces cried foul. On a daily basis, Smith ads listed Graham's numerous memberships, petition signatures, and political endorsements, among them the American Committee for Democracy and Intellectual Freedom and the American Committee for the Protection of the Foreign Born. The ads disclosed Graham's sponsorship of a 1944 dinner to honor the Red Army and his signing of a petition to secure the release from jail of Communist party leader Earl Browder. In each instance, the ads asked rhetorically if Graham had been fooled into supporting such activities. Did he not suspect what was going on?[135]

In response to these attacks, Graham continued to opt, as he had throughout the campaign, for a general defense. He trusted the state's voters, he was proud of his record and career, and he was simply incapable of attacking his opponent. Additionally, he had no desire to plumb publicly the full range of his 1930s activism. As a practical matter, such discussion would have mired him hopelessly in detail. Politically, a full discussion would have revealed some instances causing acute embarrassment and discomfiture. General rebuttal was for Frank Graham the only possible response. It was, in addition, the shrewdest response he could have given.

Smith's focus on Graham's activist past continued to be his principal campaign emphasis. On May 19, however, that focus was joined by a new charge from the Smith side. Lynn Nisbet, Raleigh correspondent for the North Carolina Association of Afternoon Dailies, whose column was distributed in various papers statewide, accused John Marshall, Governor Scott's private secretary, and Carl Williamson, former chairman of the state Alcoholic Beverage Control Board, of soliciting out-of-state liquor distillers and suppliers for contributions to Graham's campaign fund. In pursuit of liquor dollars, the pro-Smith Nisbet wrote, Marshall and Williamson had visited Washington, Philadelphia, and New York.

Nisbet's charge elicited a vehement denial from Marshall. He had contacted no distillers nor asked any liquor interest for money. Senator Graham commented that the charge sounded fantastic to him and that he did not believe a word of it. Nor would the abstemious Graham accept liquor money if offered. When reporters confronted Scott with Nisbet's claim, the governor professed ignorance. All he knew, he told reporters, was that Marshall had asked for a vacation, and he had told Marshall to go ahead. Liquor dealers had offered him money in 1948, the governor revealed, but he had refused the offers, and he knew that Graham would never knowingly take liquor money. When asked if there were things going on in the campaign that Graham did not know about, Scott replied, "Oh, Lord, yes. There's a lot going on Dr. Graham doesn't know about."

The demurrers, however, did not deter correspondent Nisbet. Spokesmen for the distillers had confirmed his story, he insisted, and it would withstand close scrutiny. Nor would the demurrers deter Smith headquarters. On May 20, the same day Nisbet published the story, Smith forces published a full-page ad under the headline "Liquor Money for Graham." The ad claimed that the liquor companies that sold their product for distribution in state-run liquor stores in North Carolina were afraid not to pitch in. Responding to John Marshall's claim that he had gone fishing on his "vacation," the ad observed, "that's right, fishing in liquor ponds for goldfish."[136]

The simultaneous appearance of Nisbet's column and the Smith ad led the Raleigh *News and Observer* to charge that Nisbet had given the liquor story to the Smith camp before he published it. How else could the ad have run simultaneously with the column? Moreover, the "Old Reliable" complained that Marshall had been shadowed in his travels by a private detective. Campaign director Charles Green insisted that he knew nothing about private detectives, while Nisbet insisted that his story had news value and was not a plant.[137]

Smith's supporters, of course, were delighted with Nisbet's story. It provided, in their view, clear evidence of their claim that the nefarious Governor Scott was in control of the Graham campaign. And no Smith advocate was more pleased with Nisbet's exposé than the High Point *Enterprise*. Bob Thompson asked Nisbet to recount the complete story of the affair, which Thompson gleefully published.

Word had come to Smith headquarters that Marshall and Williamson were to undertake the trip, and the Smith staff had indeed employed a gumshoe to follow the two men. Marshall and Williamson flew to Philadelphia together, where they conferred with officials of the Publicher Alcohol and Chemical Sales Corporation. They went on to New York and visited the American Distilling Company's Park Avenue offices, concluding their junket with a tour of the Distilled Spirits Institute in Washington. Nisbet's account was replete with trip details, including time of entry and departure from each building in each city. But neither the *Enterprise* nor Nisbet could produce sufficiently strong proof to link Governor Scott directly to the activities of his secretary. Moreover, the paper accepted Senator Graham's protestations of ignorance regarding the incident. Such a posture was, in the *Enterprise*'s view, consistent with Graham's life history. After all, he had not known the organizations he joined year after year were Communist fronts. "What reason," argued the *Enter-*

prise, "is there to keep such a naïve man—such a sucker for shady
characters—in office? At best he is a front man who doesn't know what it
is all about."[138]

Despite Thompson's best effort, however, the story did little damage to
Graham. The Kinston *Daily Free Press* thought the reports ridiculous,[139]
and the Durham *Sun* wrote that Graham would never have permitted any
such solicitation.[140] Whatever criticism that came of the episode was
directed at the governor's office. In the closing days of the first primary,
the issue of liquor money solicitation simply did not attach to Graham,
even though the report was essentially correct and clearly Scott knew all
about it. Scott had managed to keep himself at finger's length from the
deal, and his stout denial of any knowledge of the solicitation caused the
press to lose interest in the story. The governor's brother remembered in
an interview years later that such a solicitation was hardly uncommon for
the governor, although in most cases Scott would simply call people
rather than solicit through subordinates.[141] In this instance, however,
Scott wanted to remain aloof from the actual arm-twisting so that he
could deny either knowledge of or complicity in the deal.

The failure of this effort to sully the Graham campaign did not, of
course, diminish in any way the zeal of Smith staffers. In the campaign's
final two weeks, Smith intensified his effort to paint Graham as a racial
radical who would work to overthrow segregation. Smith continued to
rail about FEPC and Graham's membership on the Truman Committee
on Civil Rights. The FEPC controversy elicited considerable correspondence suggesting that it was a potent issue for Smith. "Thank heaven, we
have at least one real man in North Carolina who has the backbone to
fight such a measure," one voter wrote Senator Hoey,[142] a consistent
FEPC critic. Graham campaign workers in Bertie and Hertford counties
reported, in addition, that the issue they were asked to explain most
often was FEPC,[143] and J. S. Liles wrote from Wadesboro that FEPC
charges by Smith were hurting Graham's campaign. Some Graham supporters were wavering, Liles warned, under Smith's attack.[144]

Another Smith charge painted Graham as having favored the abolition
of segregation in the District of Columbia's public schools. In 1949 the
Senate had debated a "home rule" bill for the district. Among the bill's
provisions was a proposal to give the city council the power to abolish
existing segregation in the schools. Mississippi Senator James O. Eastland proposed an amendment to the bill that would give district voters
the right to a referendum on whether they desired to abolish school
segregation. Every southern senator, with the exception of Estes Ke-

fauver, Claude Pepper, and Frank Graham, had voted for the amendment. While Graham glibly talked about handling race problems the "North Carolina way," Smith ads charged, he had voted to deny the people of Washington the same rights that he guaranteed to North Carolinians.[145]

Graham had voted against the Eastland amendment, Jeff Johnson responded in a convoluted explanation lost on North Carolina voters, because he believed that the District of Columbia City Council, not the U.S. Senate, should decide if such a vote would be held. For the Senate to order the district to hold a new vote would violate completely the concept of home rule.[146] The ad headlines claiming that Graham favored the abolition of segregation in District of Columbia schools were much more effective, however, than Johnson's rebuttal. Graham's vote against the Eastland amendment, of course, did not necessarily suggest that he favored desegregation in the capital's public schools, but the vote against the amendment nonetheless put Graham on record once again in opposition to the southern bloc. The charge stung and was not easily explained.

Even more difficult for Graham forces to rebut were local ads and circulars, many of which were far more incendiary than anything emanating from Smith's Raleigh headquarters. One ad, published by the Scotland County Friends of Segregation, pictured the black members of the 1868 South Carolina Reconstruction legislature and wondered in the caption if history would repeat itself.[147] One infamous handbill, never published but distributed anonymously in parts of rural North Carolina, pictured black GI's dancing with white women in England during World War II, complete with a caption stating that Frank Graham favored such activities for North Carolina.[148]

Vicious rumors often accompanied the handbills, and they were nearly impossible to rebut. However ridiculous, such charges might influence ignorant people to vote against Graham, one observer related. For example, textile workers were told that a vote for Graham would mean "a nigger at a machine next to a white woman."[149] Smith supporters had "gone all out in their denunciation of Frank," one friend of Graham's wrote Jeff Johnson, and had openly made unbelievable and unspeakable remarks about the senator.[150]

Although countering such claims was difficult, Johnson ran ads condemning Willis Smith for appealing to prejudice and reminded voters once again that Graham had always opposed federal compulsion in matters of race.[151] But the more outrageous racial rumors were too fantastic to yield to rational rebuttal. Either North Carolinians would believe them, or they would dismiss them as absurd.

Perhaps the best example of this level of effort came on May 22, when

unidentified agents, presumably Smith supporters, mailed hundreds of postcards to state residents from New York City: "Dear Voter: Your vote and active support of Senator Frank Graham in the North Carolina Primary, May 27, will be greatly appreciated. You know, just as we do, that 'Dr. Frank' has done much to advance the place of the Negro in North Carolina. The Negro is a useful, tax-paying citizen! [signed] W. Wite, Executive Secretary, National Society for the Advancement of Colored People."[152]

Johnson, speaking for the Graham forces, charged that the "inflammatory postcards" were "crude frauds and I don't believe any North Carolinians can be so easily taken in." There was an NAACP, with Walter *White* as its executive secretary, Johnson explained, but the official NAACP organization was not campaigning for any candidate.[153] "A scurvy and contemptible fraud" was the Raleigh *News and Observer*'s description of this base effort at race baiting. The cards were mailed too late in the campaign for the poisonous charges to be rebutted. "Any Senator nominated by . . . men using such tactics would be ashamed along with the state."[154] Indeed, condemnation of the ploy was nearly unanimous, and Smith forces took pains to disassociate themselves from such activity. Years later, Smith campaign participants continued to deny having had any hand in this scheme.[155]

Publicity Director Hoover Adams remembered that the campaign had been the dirtiest and meanest he had ever seen but insisted that Willis Smith bore no responsibility for the baser tactics used against Graham. The Smith campaign simply could not control supporters who were doing such things. The tactics so upset Smith, Adams recalled, that the candidate demanded to know if any of the racial trash was coming from Smith headquarters. If so, Adams remembered, Smith told Adams he would be fired and Smith would withdraw from the race.[156] Campaign staffer James K. Dorsett, Jr., agreed, in another interview, that such surreptitious activity was not Smith's way and that he would have fired anyone who took such action.[157] Hoover Adams recalled Smith declaring, "I don't want to be Senator badly enough to be elected on that issue."[158] Nonetheless, not once during the campaign did Willis Smith publicly denounce the gutter tactics employed against Graham. Nor did he take specific steps to eliminate such reprehensible practices. Admonitions to campaign staffers were not enough. If he benefited from such tactics, apparently he was willing to accept the benefit.

The postcard campaign was such a crude fraud, and raised such a brief controversy, that it did Graham little harm. Far more threatening was the rumor, floated statewide, that Graham had appointed a black youth to

30 W. 40th St.   May 22, 1950
New York 18, N. Y.

DEAR VOTER:

   YOUR VOTE AND ACTIVE SUPPORT OF SENATOR FRANK
GRAHAM IN THE NORTH CAROLINA PRIMARY MAY 27 WILL BE
GREATLY APPRECIATED. YOU KNOW, JUST AS WE DO, THAT
"DR. FRANK" HAS DONE MUCH TO ADVANCE THE PLACE OF •
THE NEGRO IN NORTH CAROLINA. THE NEGRO IS A USEFUL,
TAX-PAYING CITIZEN!

                    W. WITE, Executive Secretary,
                    National Society for the Advancement of Colored People

This postcard, sent to North Carolinians from a nonexistent New York City address on May 22, 1950, purported to be from NAACP director Walter White,
urging support for Graham. The mailing was an effort to link Graham's candidacy with the NAACP. (Daniel Augustus Powell Papers, Southern Historical
Collection, University of North Carolina at Chapel Hill)

West Point. In this instance, there was just enough truth to the rumor to
give it life. The story would haunt Graham for the balance of the contest.
In early May, handbills began to appear bearing a picture of a young
black man named Leroy Jones that was captioned, "This is what Frank
Graham appointed to West Point." In the handbills, Jones's photograph
had been retouched to make his hair seem more frizzy than it actually
was.[159]

   Leroy Jones had begun his quest for an appointment to West Point well
before Frank Graham went to the Senate. In May 1948, he had written to
then Democratic nominee J. Melville Broughton expressing a strong
desire to attend the military academy.[160] Broughton had not acted on
Jones's inquiries, however, and following Broughton's death, the service
academy files were in due course turned over to his successor. Graham,
concerned that North Carolina service academy appointments in recent
years had a high rate of failure, decided to change his appointment
procedure after consultation with his Senate peers. Hereafter he would
make his appointments not through political favor but through a competitive civil service examination open to all applicants. He therefore
wrote Jones, a student at St. Augustine's College in Raleigh, and offered
him the opportunity to sit for the exam, to be administered July 11,
1949.[161] Jones replied with enthusiasm that he was honored by Gra-

ham's letter and appreciated the chance to compete.[162] He took the civil service examination in Kinston and scored a rating of 78.13, an excellent score that placed him fifth overall in a field of forty candidates.[163]

Graham's procedure ranked the top six finishers, in order of their scores, as eligible for appointment to West Point and the U.S. Naval Academy. Senator Graham therefore named Jones as second alternate for the appointment to West Point behind first-place finisher William L. Hauser and runner-up Malcolm Gambill, the first alternate. Graham's administrative assistant John D. McConnell then telegraphed Jones of his selection, informing him that if Hauser and Gambill failed the army physical to be given March 6, 1950, Jones would be entitled to the appointment. Senator Graham congratulated Jones on the excellent grade he had achieved on the qualifying exam, and Graham's office released the names of all three appointees to the press.[164]

As word spread through the state that one of the names on Graham's military academy appointment list was a black youth, a mild sensation ensued. The appointment of a black youth as second alternate to West Point was, after all, a first for a southern senator. Commented one anti-Graham member of the state's congressional delegation, "We won't have to worry about beating him next year." "I would feel mighty bad about my chances of renomination next year if I had appointed that boy," seconded another southern politician.[165] Tom Bost, in his Greensboro *Daily News* column, wrote in early October that Graham's action was so controversial that Graham had not made a scheduled public appearance at the North Carolina–Georgia football game for fear of being booed by the Kenan Stadium crowd [166]

Nonetheless, Graham's Senate mail regarding Leroy Jones was overwhelmingly favorable. Wrote John Sanders: "Your appointment has made me extremely proud of being a North Carolinian."[167] And North Carolina College Dean James T. Taylor predicted that the appointment of Jones as an alternate would cause an immediate flutter but have no long-term consequences.[168] The Gastonia *Gazette* praised Graham for having the courage of his convictions, even though the decision could cost him his seat in the Senate.[169]

Taylor's observation seemed accurate enough, especially after William Hauser passed all the required examinations and was admitted to West Point. Hauser's acceptance of the appointment meant, of course, that Leroy Jones was never admitted to West Point and never attended the military academy. The initial controversy thus faded. But the May campaign push gave it new life, as rumors and the Jones handbill circulated statewide.

Throughout the controversy, Smith headquarters denied having sent the anonymous fliers. In a 1983 interview, Hoover Adams named Graham's nemesis David Clark as the person responsible. Adams explained that when word first spread that Graham had put Jones on his appointment list, Clark determined to publicize the act: "Let's tell the people how Frank Graham appointed a nigger to West Point." Smith would not cooperate with the plan, according to Adams, whereupon Clark went to Kinston, Jones's hometown, got a picture of Jones from his mother, printed fifty thousand fliers, and sent them all over the state.[170]

R. Mayne Albright later recalled the impact of the Jones issue on the final days of the first primary. Jones's listing as second alternate meant that if both individuals ahead of him should bow out for some reason, Jones would be Graham's West Point appointee. The situation enabled Graham's adversaries to twist the issue so that, in Albright's words, "you could not get the phrase 'he appointed a nigger' out of the minds of the people."[171] And whether or not Willis Smith headquarters participated directly in or encouraged the distribution of the handbill, the issue was potentially harmful to Graham's election bid.

The controversy did give Graham advocates an opportunity to make a stinging response. In a radio speech on May 18, George Maurice Hill castigated the people responsible for the unsigned circular. They had used the tool of the blackmailer, he told his audience, having sent the circular in an unmarked envelope. For his part in the episode, Leroy Jones had done nothing except take a civil service exam graded by examiners who did not know his race. He had not received the appointment, Hill stated, "but Frank Graham left the colored boy's name on the list to show what he had done—a fine and decent thing to do—the only thing which a man like Frank Graham could do." Now Graham's enemies, continued Hill, would defame Graham's act of decency. Hill placed the blame for the racial attacks on Willis Smith and labeled Smith a demagogue.[172]

While Graham and Smith bore in on each other, monopolizing the campaign's spotlight, candidate number three sat quietly on Reynolds Mountain. "Our Bob" continued to predict victory, acting as if he knew a secret no one else could understand, even though his campaign remained somnolent. At the state Democratic convention in mid-May, he had told Governor Scott, "Governor, somebody told me I ought to tell you that you are too active for Graham, so I am telling you." Reynolds then added: "I told this man that's to be expected. After all, you appointed Graham. . . . But it's all right with me. I'm going to beat him anyway."[173]

Such braggadocio was the substance of the Reynolds effort. In early
May, he had addressed fifteen hundred stalwarts in Charlotte, where, to
audience exhortations of "go ahead, boy," he reiterated his stand against
immigration, world federalism, and the Marshall Plan. "You tell 'em,
Bob," his audience yelled, as he reported that the country was "honey-
combed with spies and Russian agents, and the ideal of one world was
ridiculous since the Communists had already enslaved half the world."
Reynolds claimed he would win the May 27 primary and denied persistent rumors that he would withdraw from the race. His opponents were
worried, he observed, because "I'm working while they're jawing. I'm
getting the votes while they're making the noise."[174]

Again, on May 10, Reynolds predicted he would win the primary by
twenty-five thousand votes. He had received more encouragement, he
added, than in any previous election. He was "pleased to see Smith at
Graham's throat, and Graham attacking Smith. It's pie for me."[175] In fact,
to exploit the respective assaults Smith and Graham forces were ex-
changing, Reynolds ran one of the campaign's cleverest newspaper ads in
late May. "If Frank Graham is what the Willis Smith supporters say he is
. . . and if Willis Smith is what Frank Graham's supporters say he is, then
vote for Robert R. Reynolds."[176]

Reynolds's sporadic efforts continued until primary day. He had no set
schedule for the final weeks of the campaign, having devised instead a
program of "spot talking." He did place one series of newspaper ads that
appeared in the final week of the campaign, urging people to "vote
American" and reminding them that he favored a strong national defense
and aid to farmers, veterans, and organized labor. He opposed all things
"which have a red or pink or a socialistic tinge." When elected he would
insist that all alien enemies and Communists be apprehended and de-
ported.[177] The old fire had flared briefly in a Raleigh "spot talk" in late
May. Reynolds, his face flushed and hands waving, railed against U.S. aid
to Europe. "Paris hotels," he raved, "are filled with French tourists having
a helluva good time on your hard-earned money. Those European gals,
loaded down with jewelry . . . make the girls in our own Stork Club look
like orphans."[178] Reynolds's amorous past apparently had made him
something of an expert on the subject, but his attack claimed attention
only because it was bizarre.

It had been apparent for two months or more that Reynolds's campaign role would be as a spoiler. Roy Wilder, Jr., then a Graham campaign aide, remembered that in mid-May Graham publicist C. A. Upchurch, Jr., had approached Reynolds's associate Wesley McDonald to
persuade Reynolds to withdraw from the race. Such an action would save

Reynolds the embarrassment of a mediocre showing, argued Upchurch, and would likely insure Graham's victory. But Reynolds would not withdraw.[179] Reynolds did propose that the three aspirants agree that the high man be the nominee if no one had a majority, binding them to the results of the first primary. Graham, the acknowledged front-runner, agreed forthwith, but Smith balked, claiming through campaign spokesmen that the idea originated not with Reynolds but with Graham and was a sign of the senator's desperation.[180]

Serene in the heat of battle—he truly had nothing to lose—Reynolds predicted his victory by a margin of fifteen thousand to forty thousand votes in a "whirlwind finish." He said in Winston-Salem on election eve that the nomination was "in the bag," and after returning home to Asheville to await the results, he told the press: "Victory is ours. The bag is tied up. It merely remains for us to keep the bag tied."[181] It was all a sham, of course, mere bluster. Reynolds's political career—the most unusual in modern North Carolina history—was finished, and he knew it.

The campaign thus approached its denouement. The candidates, with their massive effort and strong rhetoric, had roused voter interest like no political campaign in a generation. Moreover, the race had captured national attention as a southern referendum on the Truman administration, a litmus test on the status of race relations in the upper South and the effectiveness of Communist bashing. It was, additionally, a critical test of Governor Scott's ability to strengthen his grip on North Carolina Democracy, with the steadfast aid of aspiring kingmaker Jonathan Daniels. Finally, it was a public referendum on the career of Frank Porter Graham. In sum, it was a pivotal election that could fix the North Carolina political compass for years to come.

The press had sensed from the moment of Scott's startling announcement that he was attempting to reshape North Carolina politics. Graham in the Senate was a new departure in Tar Heel political life. In their election eve endorsements and editorial commentary, the state's papers, large and small, grasped the momentous character of the decision at hand. Whether they endorsed Graham, as did the Raleigh News and Observer and the Durham Morning Herald, among other dailies, or Smith, as did dailies such as the High Point Enterprise and the Raleigh Times, or whether they remained neutral like the Goldsboro News-Argus (no daily paper endorsed Reynolds), all papers understood the election's impact. Their various analyses reflected the campaign's divergent themes and vantage points.

Louis Austin's Carolina Times beseeched its readers to embrace the cause of Senator Graham. Abandoning the reserve that had characterized the black paper's previous coverage, Austin called on his readers to let nothing deter them from supporting Graham. To send Willis Smith to Washington "would be to turn . . . the clock back in North Carolina to the dark days of racial bigotry, deceit, and hatred."[182]

Surprisingly, two of the state's most influential papers, the Charlotte *Observer* and the pro-Graham Asheville *Citizen*, endorsed neither candidate. They simply urged voters to exercise caution and good judgment.[183] The Charlotte *News*, while critical of Smith's campaign tactics and charges against Graham, nonetheless urged Smith's election as a way to rebuke the Truman Fair Deal, to unify North Carolina's voice in the Senate, and to lessen the power of Governor Scott and Jonathan Daniels.[184]

The state's small-town press likewise divided. The Southern Pines *Pilot* endorsed Graham because of his more extensive national experience,[185] while the Washington (N.C.) *Daily News* recommended Smith, noting that Graham's failure to explain satisfactorily his long history of association with suspect groups made him unacceptable. Smith was more practical, the paper argued, more firmly opposed to the Brannan Plan and "socialized medicine," and not under the influence of the Scott machine.[186]

"Sound the Tocsin," Jonathan Daniels proclaimed on May 26, invoking the ancient word for an alarm bell that is rung for the protection of the people. Daniels warned about the falsifiers who were trying to destroy a good man and mislead the state's voters. Frank Graham was a man of such character and ability, Daniels told the Raleigh *News and Observer's* readers, that his ouster from the Senate would be nothing short of a tragedy for the nation and for North Carolina. It would be, in addition, a major personal disappointment for Daniels, who had committed himself to this effort as he had never done in state politics before. Invoking the memory of his father, the *News and Observer's* patriarch Josephus Daniels, Daniels told his subscribers that his father had charged all his sons to devote themselves and the paper to policies that championed the common people and the less privileged. Thus, if the paper failed to stand behind Frank Graham, it would be untrue to its history.[187] For the first time, the *News and Observer* editorially endorsed a Democratic primary candidate. At the same time, the paper condemned the Willis Smith campaign. Daniels found it hard to believe that Smith personally condoned the "abuse, race hatred, . . . lies, and insinuation" spread in his service. Nonetheless, in a campaign that tried to prove Graham guilty by association with evil men, Smith could not escape his association with liars and defamers. Anti-Semitism (in cartoons picturing Daniels as a Jew) and race hatred had no place in the campaign, Daniels wrote, yet Smith had never repudiated or rebuked these snide tricks nor restrained his staff from an effort to destroy the character of Frank Graham in order to get to the U.S. Senate.[188]

Nor was the election's importance lost on the national press. Indeed, the publicity accompanying the contest may well have made the election seem more critical than it really was, although such an argument would have been lost on the competing partisans. The campaign, New York *Times* reporter William H. Lawrence wrote, would be a southern referendum on Harry Truman.[189] The New York *Herald Tribune* agreed, figuring the election to be a test of the leftist Fair Deal. A Graham defeat, the New York paper concluded, would be a major reversal for Truman.[190]

Marquis Childs, in the Richmond *Times-Dispatch*, guessed that Graham would lead the first primary but would be forced into a runoff with Smith. Reynolds, wrote Childs, would finish a poor third. His demagoguery was dated, "its edges curled with a weary cynicism lacking the gusto that 'Ouah Bob' once put into it." Graham's boosters feared that in a second primary, Smith would get a majority of Reynolds's votes, and Graham's defeat, if it materialized, would insure the success of the Dixiecrats in the South. For Childs, the larger question was whether men "of Graham's progressive intentions and essential goodwill can find acceptance within the framework of the party. It may well be," Childs concluded, "that controls are passing into the stout apostles of things as they are."[191]

Perhaps so, but not without a battle. Graham forces girded themselves for the final forty-eight hours, with rallies and a statewide radio hookup, which they called the "Victory Round-Up." Featured speakers included Judge Hubert Olive, James Yadkin Joyner, Jeff Johnson, and the candidate, not fully recuperated but campaigning actively. Johnson also alerted his county managers to report returns as soon as possible and to be on guard to counteract desperate, last-minute rumors and false statements designed to discredit Graham. Predicting victory to his county directors, Johnson warned against overconfidence and urged a mighty effort on primary day.[192]

Senator Graham, after being inactive for two weeks, returned to active campaigning with renewed zeal. In a spirited rally at Lexington, Graham summed up his campaign and his hopes for the United States. In a passionate speech, he called for the attainment of democracy in the United States without vulgarity and tyranny. Graham declared himself forever American; he hoped for a country where differences could be resolved without hate, "where respect for the past is not reaction, and where hope for the future is not revolution." Graham's vision was paired with Hiden Ramsey's biting indictment of the personally abusive tactics of Smith's supporters. He could not understand, Ramsey remarked again, a man who would slander another for political preference, and he hoped North Carolinians would rebuke that kind of despicable performance.[193] Similarly, J. O. Talley, Jr., of Fayetteville, speaking on the radio for Graham on May 26, lambasted Smith for what Talley regarded as the most bitter, most unethical race in North Carolina's modern history. And he laid full responsibility on the Smith headquarters. "Where the campaign should have been based on principles, they have attempted to assault personalities. Where the people needed light, they have brought a great darkness. Where they should have debated, they have debased. . . . Where reason was needed, they have goaded emotion. Where they should have invoked inspiration, they have whistled for the hounds of hate."[194]

In his final radio appeal on the May 27 "Victory Round-Up," Graham kept to the high road. He thanked those who had fought for the cause of human justice and world peace. He would, he promised, continue to fight all his life for the goals he had espoused in the campaign. He urged every citizen to vote, "whether for me or against me," as an expression of the American heritage of freedom. Despite the attacks leveled at him, Graham observed, he maintained his faith in democracy. "In the long run, truth prevails because there is freedom in the minds and fairness in the hearts of people. Freedom has a way of balancing the scales for fairness." Graham, Jeff Johnson prophesied on the same program, was on the verge of a "righteous victory."[195]

On election day, Graham returned to Chapel Hill to vote. He and Marian Graham rode in a convertible at the head of a long motorcade and were cheered enthusiastically by well-wishers as they drove down Franklin Street to their voting precinct at Chapel Hill High School. After voting, the Grahams greeted friends and talked informally with towns-people and students.[196]

Not to be outdone as the campaign crested, Willis Smith increased his already furious pace during the final week. He focused on the piedmont, returning to Raleigh for a statewide radio address to conclude his effort.[197] Smith's campaign lieutenants, remarked the pro-Smith Raleigh Times, had clearly outdone the Graham camp. Their endless activity made Graham's assistants seem to be asleep.[198]

Smith did believe that he had turned the campaign in his favor. He flatly predicted that he would lead the field with 60 percent of the vote:

"The rapid and increasing trend in my behalf has been nothing short of amazing."[199] His accuracy as a prophet was about to be tested, but irrespective of the results, none could fault him for lack of effort. Smith had combed the state for votes (no mean feat in the days before interstate highways and routine air travel), shaken thousands of hands, made scores of speeches, talked to reporters endlessly, all in a display of political stamina that seemed to have no point of exhaustion. And he had succeeded in making himself known to the state's voters in the weeks available to him. His views on the issues of the campaign had likewise saturated the state.

As the first primary concluded, Smith continued to deny the charge, leveled by Governor Scott among many others, that he had slandered his Senate opponent. He had made, Smith insisted, "an honest and sincere effort to be absolutely factually accurate in every statement I have made about Dr. Graham's record." He again challenged Scott to point out one bit of factual misinformation. In addition, Smith believed that he had been abused by the Graham forces, as Graham's "high command" tried to divert attention from the facts by crying smear.[200] No charge confounded and angered Graham admirers more than Smith's claim that *he* had been smeared.

Smith continued on the offensive through his final appeal on primary eve. He asked Tar Heel voters to check the swing of the United States and the Democratic party toward socialism. He attacked for the final time Graham's association with left-wing organizations, and he repeated his claim that he had been insulted by his opponent's hatchet men for pointing out Graham's true record.[201]

Thus did the primary conclude, with a final broadside of charges from each side, while Bob Reynolds stayed above the fray, predicting victory for himself. Most pundits saw the race as very close between Graham and Smith, with Reynolds a distant third.[202] Voter turnout, reporter Wade Lucas estimated, would range between 425,000 and 475,000. A Graham majority in the first ballot was unlikely, Lucas believed. His estimated breakdown would have Graham leading with 235,000 votes, Smith second with 205,000, and Reynolds third with 58,000.[203] Lynn Nisbet agreed with the Lucas estimates, predicting that Graham would show strength in the west and that Smith would win eastern North Carolina. A sizable Reynolds vote would likely deny any candidate a clear first primary majority, Nisbet added.[204]

Some Graham supporters were confident to the point of gloating. Mr. Smith, wrote one Graham celebrant to Daniels, would have to eat crow when the results were known.[205] But Senator Hoey, whose role in this campaign remains elusive, foresaw a second primary, provided Bob Reynolds got a respectable number of votes.[206] In short, the outcome was anyone's guess, and all guessers were self-proclaimed experts—no one knew what North Carolina's voters were going to do.

On election night, throngs of supporters overran both contenders' headquarters in the Sir Walter Hotel. Smith's people pressed into the Manteo Room while Graham's backers jammed themselves into his fifth-floor quarters. Both camps anticipated victory.[207]

From the first precinct report, however, everyone could see two clear results. First, Tar Heels had voted in larger numbers than anyone had foreseen—the heaviest primary turnout in the state's history. Second, they had given Graham a ringing endorsement. The avalanche of ballots, which in most precincts had to be hand-counted, meant that results came in slowly. Not until early Sunday morning would a nearly complete canvas be available; final unofficial figures would take almost three days.

Sunday papers carried reports with roughly half the precincts reporting. But the primary's result was never in doubt. Graham took a commanding lead from the beginning and held it throughout the night. He scored a strong victory all across the state, displaying a consistency of appeal that confounded expert and amateur alike. Before midnight, the only question observers could ponder concerned a possible runoff. Graham would win big, but would he claim a majority and eliminate a second primary? If he won impressively but barely lacked a majority, would Smith call a runoff? These questions could be discussed, but the primary winner was not debatable.

As the vote came in, the Graham camp's excitement and delight continued to mount—"a study in jubilation," as the Raleigh News and Observer described it. The senator himself remained in his private quarters, propped in bed on two pillows, still recuperating from the pneumonia that had sidelined him. In this pose, he greeted ecstatic well-wishers, who trekked into his room throughout the evening and well into the night. And while many of Graham's loyal friends were on hand to cheer his victory—Capus Waynick, Kemp Battle, Charles and Gladys Tillett, state politicians, judges and attorneys—one element often seen at political gatherings was conspicuous in its absence. In the eyes of News and Observer reporter Jack Riley, one looked in vain for the "jewel-studded, French cuff set born to privilege and sustained by privilege." Moreover, the predominantly young crowd was stone-cold sober. "There was no liquor drinking in the headquarters," Riley wrote, and "remarkably few traces of whiskey on the breaths of the visitors." As for the teetotaling Senator Graham, "his victory drink was buttermilk."[208]

Graham's campaign staff celebrates his decisive victory in the first primary.
Graham was but 5,634 votes short of a clear majority in the four-candidate
field. (North Carolina Department of Archives and History, Raleigh)

Among "the privileged" in Smith's camp, spirits were sagging. Graham's early lead, initiated by easy-to-count returns from rural areas, increased as larger precincts and more densely populated areas began to report. Even eastern North Carolina followed Governor Scott's urging and gave Graham its support. When final totals were at last tabulated, Graham had 303,605 votes (48.9 percent), Smith 250,222 (40.5 percent), Reynolds 58,752 (9.3 percent), and Boyd 5,900 (1.3 percent).[209] A grand total of 618,479 Tar Heels had cast ballots.[210] Graham was agonizingly close (5,634 votes) to a clear majority, but he had failed to win the first primary outright.

Magnanimous in victory, Graham simply thanked Tar Heel voters for "their faith and loyalty." Willis Smith, election night disappointment chiseled into his face, would only respond with a terse "no comment" when asked if he would call a second primary. Publicity director Hoover Adams, however, predicted that Smith would indeed send voters back to the polls in June and reminded reporters that Smith had until June 12 to make up his mind.[211] But Smith himself made no such avowal.

In the midst of the euphoria and depression of election night, political realists for both candidates understood all too well that this election might not be over. Johnson dispatched telegrams to Graham supporters statewide, thanking them for their loyalty and devotion but urging them to keep their political organizations intact. Graham would have to assume that a second primary was in the offing; "We cannot afford to let up one bit until the job is done," Johnson warned his associates in the field.[212]

Both victory and defeat, of course, can breed disarray, and it was clear that Graham forces, never very coherent, could possibly become confused, disorganized, and dulled by Graham's big lead. But it was equally clear that Smith's prospects were even more forbidding. "The bitter fact," a chastened Bob Thompson wrote at midnight on election day, "is that Graham ran a better race, or Smith and Reynolds ran a worse race—than we had expected." Even if Smith should call a second primary—and Thompson urged such a course—it would be "an uphill fight for Willis Smith and for those of us who believe in him—and believe Frank Graham is unfit for the United States Senate. . . . We admit without question that our side took a shellacking."[213]

7 · Decision

"Don't Be Surprised If I Go with You"

Campaign planners and political analysts began their first primary post-mortems even before the election night jubilation and lamentation subsided. As is usually the case when political entrails are read, the quality of the examiners' questions determined the first primary's meaning. The campaign's only surprise, aside from the record-setting turnout, commented the Charlotte *Observer*, was the size of Graham's lead. The victory was a testament to the popularity of both Graham and Governor Scott, the paper concluded.[1] The Greensboro *Daily News* agreed, stating that the outcome was evidence of Scott's perseverance, particularly in the rural areas of the state.[2] The New York *Times* saw the election as a vindication of North Carolina's progressive past. Graham had won approval of his liberal views and seemed to have turned back a resurgent tide of racial prejudice.[3]

Other observers saw Graham's victory exclusively in personal terms, an affirmation of the senator as a decent and honorable man. How else, queried the Washington (N.C.) *Daily News*, could one explain Graham's victory in Wake County, Willis Smith's home base?[4] Any conclusion that the campaign produced a mandate on specific issues, added the Atlanta *Journal*, would have to be balanced with an understanding that Graham possessed a unique personality and a following that outweighed the importance of substantive questions of public policy.[5] "I have just voted for you," one physician friend from Mt. Airy wrote Graham on election day. "The vote was cast by my heart more than my head. It was not a vote for the current [Truman] Administration. . . . What happened happily in the recent senatorial election in Florida would happen here but for the wide popular knowledge of your personal excellence."[6]

Of course instead of asking why Graham won, one could ask why he had failed to win a majority. George Rothwell Brown, political columnist for the New York *Journal-American*, saw in Graham's failure to win a majority a rebuke by Tar Heel voters "for Truman's dizzy dance down the primrose path of state socialism." The coming runoff, Brown predicted, would bring victory for Willis Smith.[7] In a less splenetic vein, the Baltimore *Sun* thought Graham's vote was impressive evidence of a progressive bent in North Carolina's thinking. But the *Sun* also saw in his failure to gain a majority a sign that North Carolina still retained its traditional attitudes on race and economic individualism. After all, the *Sun* reminded its readers, 51 percent of all votes cast went to Graham's opponents.[8]

The strong sentiment of several Graham lieutenants in the field, however, argued for a different interpretation: Graham had been denied a first primary majority because of the eleventh-hour focus by Smith field people on the race issue. David McConnell, Graham's Mecklenburg manager, told Dave Burgess that such an appeal in Charlotte's blue-collar precincts had hurt the Graham campaign. On election eve, related McConnell, every mailbox was filled with "racial junk," and on the day of the election, Smith zealots displayed a picture of Leroy Jones within fifty feet of every polling place.[9]

Graham precinct workers likewise complained about the racial tactics of Smith's supporters. From Chowan County, A. B. Harless named the Brannan Plan, deficit spending, and especially FEPC as the issues that denied Graham a majority. Moreover, warned Harless, a second primary would give Smith an even larger majority in Chowan if Graham did not clarify his stand on these issues.[10] Edward B. Clark, reporting from Elizabethtown, cited the Leroy Jones pamphlets as damaging to Graham. In addition, he said that Smith workers used three auto agencies to transport voters to the polls. Intimidation on voting day was so strong, wrote Clark, that one "former friend" refused to help because he feared his participation in support of Graham would hurt his business.[11] From Scotland County came the view that "the 'nigger' issue was our downfall,"[12] and from Warren County the conclusion was similar: "the race question hurt."[13]

Mrs. W. P. Childers of Louisburg said Smith had run the dirtiest campaign she had ever seen: "Some people were drug to the polls who have never thought of voting until the dirty Smith campaigh [sic] started. They were so ignorant that some of them voted for three sheriffs. . . . Some could not read."[14]

Understandably, Smith's proponents denied that he had slandered Graham, although the ever loyal High Point *Enterprise* acknowledged that scum on both sides had resorted to anonymous mail communications that were slanderous. But neither headquarters, claimed the paper, was in any way responsible for such materials.[15]

The Fayetteville *Observer* saw the race issue from an entirely different perspective. The decisive element in the election, the paper argued, was the black vote, and its massive support for Graham was responsible for his large plurality. Moreover, such bloc voting would make blacks a broad political target in a second primary.[16] Columnist Lynn Nisbet also noted that Durham's all black Hillside precinct had cast 1,514 votes for

Graham, 7 for Smith, 6 for Reynolds, and 1 for Boyd. This startling result—startling to Smith people—was repeated in black precincts all over the state.[17] Such results confirmed some voters' worst fears: black voters might hold the balance not only in a close election but within the Democratic party itself.

Some analysts, however, dismissed the racial interpretation of Graham's failure to get a majority of the votes. Instead, they blamed Bob Reynolds. Without candidate Reynolds pulling 58,752 votes, Graham would have been the clear winner, R. Mayne Albright believed.[18] John Sanders, Terry Sanford, T. Clyde Auman, William D. Snider, and others agreed that Reynolds was the first primary spoiler.[19] Without him, the race would have ended with the first primary. Graham's failure to win a majority, therefore, was due to the presence of a third candidate.

Reynolds himself was "more than pleased" with the primary result, arguing that it was a victory for Americanism. He gave no clue, however, whether he would endorse either candidate should Smith demand a rematch. He did reiterate his belief that the high man in the primary should get the nomination.[20]

The varying analyses soon yielded to a more immediate question: would Smith call a runoff? The question became a conversational centerpiece in parlors, gas stations, and country stores throughout the state. Candidate Smith, however, remained noncommittal, the stance he had embraced on election night.[21] Certainly, the Goldsboro News-Argus observed, Smith had several major questions to ponder. He had to consider what Reynolds might do, and where those nearly fifty-nine thousand votes might go, where he could get the money for a second campaign, and whether he had any realistic possibility of overcoming the big lead of a rival who commanded the passionate loyalty of a large group of Tar Heel voters.[22] In addition, Smith had to determine if he had the stomach for such an uphill struggle. As the Durham Sun commented, Smith did not need the salary, did not relish the abuse, and did not covet the glory. Having been reluctant to run in the first place, he might not "think the game worth the candle." But he had to square those considerations with the trust that over 250,000 voters had thrust upon him.[23] It was not an enviable decision.

While Smith deliberated, Senator Graham went with his wife for a week's rest to their accustomed summer retreat, the Drane cottage at Nags Head. Graham hoped to regain the strength lost to the viral pneumonia that had sent him to his sickbed at the end of the first primary. He announced his pleasure with the huge turnout, again thanked his supporters, and departed for the isolation of the seashore.[24]

Jeff Johnson, in contrast, did not budge from the Sir Walter. He had to anticipate a second primary, and he targeted FEPC as the issue likely to be paramount in the contest. Therefore, he again instructed all local managers to hold their organizations in place and to intensify their activity for the likely showdown on June 24.[25] He and others also advised Graham to make an immediate statement declaring his intention to oppose cloture on the FEPC Senate debate when the next opportunity came. Such a statement, Johnson believed, might discourage Smith from calling a runoff.[26] Graham ignored his manager's counsel.

With Graham at the beach, his camp could not resist speculating on Smith's course of action. David McConnell was convinced Smith would proceed and wrote Johnson that he was anticipating another ballot.[27] Governor Scott refused to make a public prediction but announced that the first primary results were "very pleasing." When reporters asked Scott if blacks now held the balance of power in North Carolina politics, he hedged, commenting that no more than half the registered blacks had cast ballots on May 27.[28]

Other Graham stalwarts, however, foresaw no runoff. Graham's lead was insurmountable, concluded Winston-Salem *Journal* editor Santford Martin.[29] Assistant CIO Political Action Committee Director Tilford E. Dudley likewise believed Smith would withdraw, principally because a division of the Reynolds vote would doom Smith's candidacy.[30] The longer Smith waited to announce his decision, the less likely a runoff became, wrote Hiden Ramsey to Johnson on June 3, because delay meant disintegration within Smith's campaign organization. Should a runoff be called, Ramsey predicted Graham would get 55–60 percent of the vote.[31]

Smith's delay gave the press a free hand—and much column space—for speculation. Generally, the Graham press argued that a runoff was unlikely. Tom Schlesinger, in his "Report from Washington," revealed that Capitol Hill sources believed there would be no rematch. Smith was short of money and unsure that he could win the Reynolds vote.[32] The Raleigh *News and Observer* argued that another round was improbable. Smith, the paper commented, had no chance to defeat Graham. The paper reprinted a Richmond *Times-Dispatch* editorial that rated Smith's chance for success as virtually nil.[33] In the same issue, the *News and Observer* pointed out that no second primary had ever been called in the history of state politics after such a long (one week) delay. Should a runoff materialize, Graham would get most of the Reynolds votes, the paper concluded. Smith's prospects were bleak indeed.[34]

The *Carolina Times* likewise argued against a Smith-Graham rematch. Decent citizens of both races already had their stomachs full of the Smith forces' race-baiting tactics, Louis Austin commented. Blacks did not want to dominate North Carolina politics; they only wanted the opportunity to vote and to express their political opinions, the paper deduced.[35] *The Nation* expected Smith to continue but thought Graham would win despite the liabilities of his stance on FEPC and his Communist affiliations. Graham had achieved a near majority even though handicapped with pneumonia and political inexperience. He should win a second primary.[36]

Among Smith's press partisans, however, the urge for a second crack at Senator Graham was unremitting. Smith had an obligation to his over 250,000 voters, the Charlotte *News* argued.[37] The High Point *Enterprise*, Raleigh *Times*, and Fayetteville *Observer* all joined the *News* in urging Smith to see the race through to the bitter end. They all insisted that Smith would win a second primary.

Meantime, the Graham camp was doing all it could to convince Smith that the cause was lost. Focusing on the Reynolds votes, Graham headquarters summoned reporters on May 31 to announce that prominent Reynolds supporter Haywood Robbins of Charlotte and Reynolds's Mecklenburg County manager Ray Owen would both back Graham in a second primary. These endorsements, Graham proponents claimed, pointed to a pronounced swing of Reynolds supporters to the Graham standard. Robbins, a close Reynolds adviser, repeated Reynolds's oftstated opposition to a second primary. It would be a needless, expensive, and bitter process that would leave deep scars on the North Carolina Democratic party.[38]

Yet Smith made no move. On May 29, Hoover Adams had disclosed that Smith's Raleigh staff was reporting to work as usual,[39] and the following day Adams told the press that he was confident Smith would call a runoff.[40] But Smith himself was content to express his gratitude for the support he received from voters and to thank his workers. He also expressed appreciation to the hundreds of citizens who had called and telegraphed him asking that he enter a second primary. He huddled with a group of advisers on May 29, among whom were Hoover Adams, Banks Arendell, L. Y. Ballentine, Bill Sharpe, Alvin Wingfield, and columnist Lynn Nisbet. Smith hinted that he was anxious to run against Graham, pending the promise of sufficient money. Additionally, Smith was searching for a campaign plan—a strategy—that would bring voters to his side.[41] Provided Smith could raise the money, the Raleigh *News and Observer* expected him to base his hopes primarily on the Negro issue, and Hoover Adams predicted that in a second primary voters would leave Frank Graham "like rats deserting a sinking ship."[42]

Still, Smith stalled, and on May 31, the Charlotte *Observer* reported that Smith was having trouble raising money.[43] Governor Scott commented, in response to the *Observer's* report, on the high cost of state campaigns. Smith's delay would hurt his chances, Scott observed, but would allow him to get the money he needed.[44] The High Point *Enterprise*, still pitching for a runoff, reminded its readers that North Carolina blacks held the balance in the first primary and had used their power for Graham. This realization, the paper hoped, would awaken Smith supporters to the realities of the new state politics.[45] But press speculation would not move Willis Smith. He remained silent and continued his conferences with aides, while his headquarters admitted that the candidate still lacked sufficient financial backing to make another race.[46]

Significant developments in the first days in June, however, seemed to satisfy some of Smith's principal concerns. Graham headquarters put its managers on immediate alert for a runoff, having learned from "reliable sources" that Smith now had financial pledges adequate for the campaign.[47] Smith's campaign workers also were certain their candidate was ready to sound the call.[48]

Certainly Smith did not lack encouragement. In addition to his aides' urgings, hundreds of telegrams, letters, and telephone calls had deluged the candidate's Raleigh offices, imploring him to run.[49] He represented the safe and sane side of the campaign, wrote Nell Battle Lewis to Smith. If he saw the slightest chance of winning, Lewis urged, he should stay in the race.[50] Hundreds of messages duplicated the plea of "Battlin' Nell." But despite it all, Smith refused to commit to a runoff. He was indeed reluctant to run, Raleigh attorney Allen Langston remarked, despite the fervent urgings of his acolytes.[51]

On June 5, the sweep of national events reached into the state and changed the character of the Smith-Graham Senate race. As Smith deliberated, the U.S. Supreme Court ruled in three critical civil rights cases that promised to alter significantly the state's race relations. In one instance, the Court's rulings would change the nature and heighten the importance of a case then pending in federal district court in Durham, brought by black students seeking admission to graduate study at the University of North Carolina.

In the three civil rights cases, all brought by blacks challenging various types of statutory racial segregation, the Supreme Court made the strongest statement on the separate but equal principle since an earlier Court had embraced the doctrine in 1896. When the Court was through, statutory segregation in state-supported graduate higher education was all but finished, railroad dining car segregation in the South was struck down, and the principle of separate but equal treatment in public life was gravely weakened.

Of the three cases, the most significant for North Carolina was the case

of *Sweatt v. Painter*. In this case, Chief Justice Fred Vinson, speaking for a
unanimous Court, found that Texas must admit Houston mail carrier
Heman Marion Sweatt to the all-white University of Texas Law School
even though Texas had established a separate black law school at Prairie
View Agricultural and Mechanical University. Vinson concluded that the
law school at Prairie View was in no way equal to its University of Texas
counterpart, a finding that should have surprised no one but astounded
an entire region. In reaching this conclusion, Vinson and his brethren
redefined the concept of separate but equal in such a way as to make the
principle unattainable, at least in graduate education in public universities. Equality now meant "reputation of the faculty, experience of the
administration, position and influence of the alumni, standing in the
community, tradition and prestige," when comparing state-supported
segregated law schools. No black southern law school supported by state
funds could meet that test, including the best of those schools, the law
school at North Carolina College for Negroes in Durham, established in
1942.[52]

The Court also ruled, in *McLaurin v. Oklahoma State Regents*, that the
University of Oklahoma must end its torment of black graduate student
G. W. McLaurin, whom it had reluctantly admitted to classes under court
order. The university had attempted to enshroud McLaurin in the segregationist equivalent of a plastic bubble, designating a separate desk,
cafeteria table, and library study area for McLaurin's exclusive use. Such
restrictions, the Court found, were inequitable and impermissible.[53]
Finally, in *Henderson v. United States*, the Court barred railroads from the
policy of separating blacks and whites in dining cars.[54]

These cases, while not a clear repudiation of the general principle of
statutory segregation, were nonetheless indisputable evidence that the
legal assault on racial separation begun in the 1930s was continuing
apace and indeed gaining momentum. The Court's rulings pushed civil
rights news to the front pages of the state's dailies and alarmed white
politicians and public officials who had been working for fifteen years to
sustain the separate but equal principle in the courts. Hence, the reaction
in North Carolina to the cases was both immediate and ominous. North
Carolina had filed an amicus curiae brief in the *Sweatt* case supporting
Texas and, as previously noted, had a federal district case pending similar
to the *Sweatt* case.[55]

The Rocky Mount *Telegram* commented that North Carolina had been
making tremendous strides in race relations under segregation, strides
that would be preserved if blacks did not use the courts to force the
issue.[56] But the Charlotte *News* more realistically observed that *Sweatt*

was "the handwriting on the wall" for the principle of separate but equal. The paper acknowledged that segregation could not be defended as an abstract moral principle.[57] "Like it or not," the Henderson *Daily Dispatch* confirmed, "segregation is fading. It is on the way out."[58]

The High Point *Enterprise* did not mince words in attempting to point out the connection between the decisions and the still-pending Senate race. The decisions, observed the paper, marked a new era in the Supreme Court's involvement in racial segregation cases. The first step, argued Bob Thompson, had come with the Truman Committee on Civil Rights, of which Frank Graham was a member. The Court's rulings, Thompson concluded, had given new impetus to the movement for racial integration.[59] The *Sweatt* case, stated the Charlotte *Observer*, made it impossible for any state hereafter to maintain separate but equal facilities in graduate education.[60]

Privately, some North Carolina attorneys confirmed the hopelessness of the forthcoming University of North Carolina Law School litigation. Writing to Attorney General Harry McMullan, Winston-Salem lawyer Irving Carlyle argued that the desegregation of the University of North Carolina Law School was now "inescapable,"[61] a view Attorney General McMullan all but conceded publicly on June 7—even though he had argued initially that *Sweatt* would have no effect on the pending North Carolina case.[62]

In his response to the decisions, Senator Clyde Hoey blasted the Supreme Court. The end of segregated dining cars would only cause confusion and irritation, he argued. The *Sweatt* case, actively championed by the Truman Justice Department, was to Hoey part of the overall plan of the president to abrogate all segregation laws.[63]

Senator Graham's reaction, in contrast to Hoey, was measured. He continued to oppose the use of federal pressure in imposing "non-segregation," he stated. But he understood that states that embraced a separate but equal philosophy must accept the heavy responsibility of insuring that the doctrine was faithfully administered. The *Sweatt* and *McLaurin* cases applied to only two states, he suggested, and would have no effect on North Carolina. And he reminded reporters that the southern attorneys general had used his arguments against compulsory abolition of segregation in presenting their briefs to the Supreme Court. But he did not attack the Court as Hoey had done, and he stressed the need for continued goodwill and racial cooperation.[64] The Raleigh *News and Observer*, putting the best face possible on the rulings, said the cases set no precedents and would not affect the situation in North Carolina because the state had made a good faith effort to provide equal facilities.[65]

Improbable as it may seem to later observers, most white North Carolinians were only dimly aware that segregated public education had been under legal assault for nearly two decades prior to *Sweatt* and that the principle of legal segregation was crumbling in the courts. Many Tar Heels still clung to the belief that North Carolina's race relations constituted something of a national model of harmonious coexistence, when, in fact, racial tension was becoming more pronounced and more open, as witnessed by impending law suits. The *Sweatt* and *McLaurin* decisions thus disabused many whites of the belief that segregation was eternal.

Although the rulings were unanticipated by many whites, however, they clearly animated the Smith camp. Smith's backers, claimed the Greensboro *Daily News*, had been praying for just such a decision, as it would surely compel Smith to call a runoff. Believing that the race issue had been largely responsible for getting Smith this far, Smith supporters, according to the *Daily News*, now believed that fear of school integration would provide their candidate with the issue and the impetus he needed to win a second contest.[66]

Yet Smith himself continued to resist the call. Although he was still consulting advisers,[67] he told *Charlotte Observer* reporter Wade Lucas on June 6 that he was on the verge of withdrawing. He feared that if he called for a second primary immediately after the Supreme Court rulings, he would be charged with agitating the race issue, which he did not want to do.[68] Despite numerous additional telegrams and telephone calls from supporters urging him to run,[69] Smith summoned publicity director Hoover Adams on the morning of June 6 to tell him that he had decided to withdraw, recalled Adams, and Smith dictated a telegram congratulating Graham on his victory. He asked Adams to send the telegram immediately, but Adams disobeyed his boss. Hoping to dissuade Smith, he stuck the telegram in his pocket, where it remained.[70] Only Adams knew of Smith's resignation telegram, but several of Smith's advisers—Jesse Helms, James K. Dorsett, Jr., William T. Joyner, Jr., and J. C. B. Ehringhaus, Jr.—later agreed that Smith had decided not to run. Not even a final conference that afternoon, held at Smith's law offices, could shake Smith's decision. Upset by the lack of active support from people who had promised to rally to his side, Smith restated his intention to withdraw.[71]

Smith's decision was apparently a product of genuine soul-searching. Two nights after the primary, according to insiders, Smith had concluded that Graham's plurality was insuperable. Smith's campaign was out of money and Smith was out of energy. A devoted father and husband, he had little desire for the rigors of another statewide campaign, and his determination not to mortgage his family's financial future for a Senate seat remained fixed. Finally, he derived no pleasure from the seamy side of the campaign, and the attacks upon him that Graham forces had leveled left him weary of the effort and upset because he did not want his family to bear the hurt of slander.[72]

But in a surprising reprise of the manner in which Jonathan Daniels and Kerr Scott had persuaded Frank Graham to accept the Senate seat in the first place, Smith's friends would not let the matter drop. Hoover Adams called Alvin Wingfield, Bob Thompson, and Jesse Helms on the afternoon of June 6, following the conference at Smith's law office, and urged them somehow to change Smith's mind. Helms decided that the best plan would be to appeal to the people of Raleigh, urging them to mass at Smith's house and show their support for a runoff.[73]

Helms, at the time news director of WRAL radio, then contacted A. J. Fletcher, who owned the station, and asked to buy some airtime. He intended, Helms explained, to record a thirty-second spot and broadcast it every ten to fifteen minutes during the evening. Fletcher, also a strong Smith advocate, agreed but insisted that Helms would have to pay for the airtime. Helms consented, although Fletcher ended up splitting the cost. The spots ran eight to ten times between 6:00 and 9:00 P.M., with a staff announcer, not Helms, reading the copy.

Fearful that the appeal might fall flat—proving that no one listened to WRAL—Helms drove over to Smith's home near the corner of St. Mary's Street and Glenwood Avenue early that evening to see if anything was happening. He found a mob scene: the street jammed with cars and a crowd of two hundred to five hundred people (the reports vary) mill-ing about.[74] Helms's immediate concern was horticultural: he feared the crowd would crush Mrs. Smith's flowers. But as his initial concern subsided, Helms observed former North Carolina State College cheer-leader Billy Ward leading the crowd in cries of "We Want Smith" and "All the Way with Willis." Helms, Alvin Wingfield, J. C. B. Ehringhaus, Jr., and other Smith associates then addressed the crowd, pumping for a runoff.[75]

Word of the rally reached Graham headquarters, and Jeff Johnson dispatched young John Sanders to observe the activity at Smith's home. Sanders heard Godfrey Cheshire, a Raleigh businessman and Smith supporter, speak to the crowd and argue that the *Sweatt* decision would be worth thousands of votes for the Smith cause.[76]

Three times Smith came out of the house to address the crowd. He first expressed his appreciation but then stated his intention not to run. As the crowd grew in number and became more vocal, he admitted that the demonstration of support might cause him to reconsider. Finally, he asked the boisterous gathering, in a joking manner, to give him some peace and quiet and let him think about his decision, which he promised the following day. "Don't be surprised if I go with you," he told his partisans. At this point, the crowd dispersed. As he left the Smith home, William T. Joyner, Jr., was convinced the runoff was on.[77]

Privately, however, Smith remained troubled at the prospect of a second primary. He did not know what to do, Smith confided to LeGette Blythe of the Charlotte *Observer*. Having thought the issue settled, "this mob of people came out and demanded that I stay in the race. . . . They seemed determined that I will run, but I don't know." Smith recounted to Blythe his judgment, made that morning, not to ask for a rematch. After the Supreme Court decisions, he repeated, he did not want to do anything to inflame the race issue. "I have never injected any of these racial issues into the race. I have been charged with having done so, but haven't and I did not want to do anything that might tend to cause any bad racial feeling." Nonetheless, the evening's display of loyalty and support had touched Smith.[78]

During the rally, Smith had asked Hoover Adams whether he had sent the concession telegram. Adams would not answer, realizing that Smith was being swayed by the crowd. Finally, Adams confessed that the telegram was still in his pocket, and Smith acknowledged that he might be changing his mind.[79] If Adams had obeyed his boss's order, and if Jesse Helms and Alvin Wingfield had been less persistent, the second primary might never have occurred. But Smith's unrelenting advisers, convinced that he could win, would not let him withdraw. It was equally obvious that Smith, hardly an indecisive man, had never fully settled the issue in his own mind.

Thus, on June 7, eleven days after the first ballot, Smith, who had one day earlier been unwilling to thrust himself into a situation in which racial bitterness would be inevitable, announced that he would call for a second primary. His decision came one day before the twelve-day deadline to call a runoff. He publicly reviewed his near-decision to withdraw and acknowledged that he was yielding to what he perceived as massive public pressure for a second ballot. If he were to win, he told reporters, he would need the support of every citizen who believed in constitutional democracy. He was the underdog, he acknowledged, and he called on his advocates to work tirelessly. "With faith and hard work, we can win."[80]

From the Graham camp came a muted response. "Mr. Smith was within his right in calling for a second primary. That is part of our democratic system. We welcome the challenge," Senator Graham commented, a sentiment echoed by Governor Scott.[81] Privately, however, Graham was more rueful—and more candid about his view of the Court

Smith greets supporters, who later rallied at his residence to urge him to call a second primary. (North Carolina Department of Archives and History, Raleigh)

rulings. "While I am in absolute sympathy with the Court," he told *Carolina Israelite* editor Harry Golden, "I do wish they could have waited one more day."[82]

In recollection, Smith's advisers agreed that he decided to try again because his friends were so insistent. Smith told Wade Lucas that he had been visibly moved by the crowd's support at his home; nothing comparable had ever happened to him in his sixty-two years on earth.[83] His advisers, moreover, were joined in their attempts to persuade him by other prominent citizens. Smith doubtless took to heart a call, placed as he was making his runoff decision, from North Carolina Supreme Court Chief Justice Walter P. Stacy. Stacy, who told Smith that his call did not mean that the chief justice was meddling in politics, offered his opinion that Smith would be making a mistake if he did not let voters have another say on the issues. And clearly, at the last minute, some people came forward promising to work for Smith who were disturbed by the Supreme Court's recent rulings and the prospect of someone as liberal as Graham occupying a U.S. Senate seat.[84] Even though Smith's compatriots have denied that the Court's rulings weighed heavily,[85] evidence to the contrary simply overrules their denial. With *Sweatt* and the related rulings, everything fell into place: money, organization, urgency, and issues. Smith could now emphasize bloc voting and the race issue, although he had stated that he did not want to stir up racial animosity.[86]

Developments after the first primary made credible Richard Thigpen's claim that if Smith could carry Mecklenburg in the first primary, he could carry North Carolina in the second.[87]

From the Graham side, Smith's delay seemed quite calculated—a deliberate tactic to build tension and interest in Smith. It was obvious to Bill Staton that Smith had intended from the beginning to run again and that he had adroitly orchestrated his decision to appear to be yielding to a ground swell of citizen support. Smith's hesitation had coincidentally kept the Graham forces from campaigning, while Smith actively sought money and improved his organizational structure. And even though this interpretation is strained, the results of the delay did have the effect Staton identified. It put Graham, despite his big first primary lead, in a hole that was eleven days deep.[88]

Smith's press gallery, of course, greeted his decision with exultation. Smith could win, the Charlotte *Observer* predicted, because he would claim a majority of the Reynolds votes. The campaign would be "the most vigorous and heated" in the state's history, but the *Observer* hoped for a fair and clean contest.[89] Others, the ever-faithful High Point *Enterprise* among them, believed Smith's prospects were bright,[90] while the Charlotte *News* saw Smith facing an uphill fight. The *News* stated that the primary would offer a clear-cut choice between the conservatism of Smith and the "super welfare state" favored by Graham.[91]

The Raleigh *News and Observer* was considerably less pleased. Smith's decision meant that North Carolina was now on trial, the paper stated. The reputation of the state as a leader of the enlightened South now hinged on Graham voters returning to the polls on June 24.[92] The Greensboro *Daily News* had preferred that the state be spared the rigors of a rematch, but now that the race was on, the paper hoped the candidates could avoid smear tactics and appeals to prejudice.[93]

The Durham *Sun* foresaw a campaign in which fewer voters would cast ballots. A smaller turnout would benefit Graham, the paper believed, because his was a personal following, in contrast to Smith's voters, who were naysayers or protest voters. The *Sun* acknowledged, however, that normal political circumstances would hardly prevail in this contest. Any unusual development on the issue of race might well nullify conventional political wisdom.[94] Lynn Nisbet correctly predicted that an important element of Smith's new campaign tactic would be an emphasis on first primary bloc voting in black precincts.[95] And irrespective of personal preference, reporters knew that the political moment of their lifetimes was at hand.

8 · *Runoff*

"White People Wake Up!"

The second primary, which would last only seventeen days, began slowly, but from the first day, patterns developed that persisted throughout the contest. The most obvious of these was the general complacency of Graham forces statewide, although some groups, notably David McConnell's organization in Charlotte, were already hard at work by June 7.[1] The ubiquitous Lynn Nisbet, in early June, visited several counties to get a feel for the race. He found acute interest among voters, but he also reported that Graham workers were listless, secure in the belief that Graham's huge lead could not be overcome, while Smith people harbored no such illusion about their candidate. Smith's backers intended to cut into Graham's cushion, particularly in the piedmont, Nisbet wrote. He explained that large groups of Graham voters had been "herded to the polls" to cast ballots "on orders from out-of-state race or labor 'bosses.'" These "controlled" and "manipulated" votes would become a Smith campaign theme, Nisbet predicted,[2] a position Smith soon developed.[3]

The campaign's slow pace in the first week could be explained in part by the feverish activity on both sides to raise the $200,000 each candidate needed for a second primary and to file the required reports on first primary expenditures. In accord with the state's Corrupt Practices Act of 1931, candidates for federal office had to file an itemized statement of all campaign expenses and contributions by June 16. The term "contribution" meant any gift, payment, or loan for the candidate's benefit paid to any organization or group for the purpose of influencing the election. These reports substantiated the preliminary statements turned in ten days prior to voting.[4] The law set a spending cap of $12,000 for first primary expenses, as noted earlier, and $6,000 for a runoff.

A violation of the election laws—such as making a false statement about the amount of funds—could be prosecuted as a felony, while publishing or circulating any derogatory report about a candidate with the knowledge that the report was false was a misdemeanor. It was also a misdemeanor for a corporation doing business with the state to contribute to a political campaign.[5]

The final reports of the candidates' first primary expenses were enlightening. Olla Ray Boyd named no contributors and spent $135,[6] while Bob Reynolds collected $1,008 and spent $4,415.[7] Willis Smith listed contributions of $9,783 and expenditures of $11,961. Smith contributors hailed largely from Charlotte and Raleigh. Smith's law partners, John H. Anderson and James K. Dorsett, Jr., gave $1,000 and $500 respectively, while J. M. Peden of Raleigh gave $890 and Lee Gravely of Rocky Mount, $1,300.[8]

Every campaign source has acknowledged that the McNair and Pate families of Laurinburg and Johnson Cotton Company in Dunn were deep Smith pockets, but their aid went unreported. Richard Thigpen claimed to have raised $15,000 in Mecklenburg County alone for the first primary, but the prevailing practice permitted "local money" to be excluded from the "official" reports.[9]

Smith's listed expenditures were for conventional campaign costs: newspaper and radio advertising, staff salaries, and office expenses. The $12,000 limit was, of course, a continuing joke. In Smith's report, he did not even list the salaries of campaign manager Charles Green or publicity director Hoover Adams.

Some of Smith's advisers maintain that the campaign was perpetually short of money, but the scope of the Smith effort clearly rebuts the idea of chronic money problems.[10] And certainly, from the Graham side, the Smith forces seemed awash in funds. Field managers from various parts of the state wrote Graham headquarters repeatedly that their Smith rivals had all the money they wanted.[11] Both Harold Makepeace, Smith's Lee County manager, and Richard Thigpen acknowledge that they had enough money.[12]

It is much less clear whether large sums flowed to Smith from out-of-state conservatives and right-wingers, as Graham supporters have always maintained. There were groups working to elect Republicans and conservatives nationwide in 1950, but how much money they sent into North Carolina to assist a conservative Democrat is unclear. Sam Ragan, then of the Raleigh *News and Observer*, and other Graham partisans insist, nonetheless, that large unreported sums came to Smith from outside the state.[13]

In the second primary, as in the first, Smith had intermittent "cash flow" problems, especially in the early stages. The High Point *Enterprise* correctly observed that Smith ended his first primary race in the red. To the *Enterprise*, the debit meant that Smith did not get the huge sums Grahamites "knew" he received, especially from corporations and wealthy individuals.[14] The money problems were finally solved, but the source of much of Smith's financial support in either primary cannot be determined. Unless his personal correspondence contains complete financial records, and until that correspondence is opened to scholars, his actual contributions and his expenditures will remain unknown.

Assessing Graham's finances is much easier, although the picture that emerges is hardly complete. In his official report, Graham listed contributions of $11,941 and expenditures of $11,700. Major contributors to Graham were Kemp Battle, $500, Jonathan Daniels, $250, Worth Daniels, $250, syndicated columnist Robert S. Allen, $250, and Katherine Boyd, owner of the Southern Pines *Pilot*, $1,000. The financial contribution of Charles and Gladys Tillett was not given.[15]

Everyone who knew Frank Graham has testified that he signed his candidate's statement under oath with the firm assurance that it was complete and correct. He was as uninformed regarding finances after the first primary as he had been when he signed the preliminary report. Nor did his interest in the methods that financed his race intensify in the second primary. Graham's staffers and confidants have confirmed that local supporters raised thousands of dollars that they never reported to central headquarters.[16] Wake County manager William Joslin estimated that he raised $2,500 in the first primary.[17] In compiling the aggregate figures, Kate Humphries simply entered the sums furnished to her for the official report, knowing that much larger funds had been raised and spent.[18] Senator Graham, who had no specific knowledge of the raising and spending of campaign funds, never questioned the official figures.

Graham's campaign also had major contributors whose donations went unreported. Ralph W. Gardner of Shelby, son of former governor O. Max Gardner, gave the campaign $5,006 in the first primary and $5,140 in the second. Gardner would literally buy Cleveland County for Graham if he could, remarked Dave Burgess.[19] Graham staffers, without the senator's knowledge, also established another effective system for collecting money clandestinely. Jonathan Daniels would solicit funds, which would then be sent to Dr. Will Alexander, an old Graham friend and coworker for racial betterment. If the money were contributed by check, as in the cases of Marshall Field ($2,000) and Phillip M. Stern ($500), Alexander would deposit the money, cash his personal check off the recent deposits, and send the money to Daniels, who would then send a note of thanks to the contributor. In addition, Alexander collected several thousand dollars in cash, which he forwarded directly to Graham headquarters.[20] Other large contributors included Edgar B. Stern, who sent Alexander $2,000 on May 18, 1950, and later matched his gift to offset second primary costs as well. He sent the second primary check directly to Daniels.[21] Charles Tillett was also a conduit. "I enclose cashier's checks in exchange for the two checks I received from you this morning," he wrote Daniels on June 19.[22] In addition, money came directly to Graham headquarters from a variety of out-of-state contributors, ranging in denominations from $10 to $500. Former Interior Secretary Harold L. Ickes sent $250, Max Ascoli, editor of *The Reporter* magazine, $500, the Committee on National Affairs, $500. Various union locals and national union headquarters also sent donations,[23] and Dave Burgess continued to pass cash through John Marshall.[24]

It is not possible, of course, to know with certainty how much money came into the Graham camp. Some field-workers complained loudly that they lacked funds to pay precinct workers,[25] while others reported that they had raised locally all the money they needed.[26] In estimating Graham's funding, Terry Sanford offered perhaps the soundest assessment: Graham forces had enough money to win. Lack of money was not the decisive element in either the first primary or the runoff.[27] Nor can it be plausibly argued that Graham lacked either supporters with deep pockets or "special interests" who worked for him. He had broad support from a variety of corporations, labor, and other organizations, many of whom had substantial resources.

In regard to North Carolina's unenforceable election spending laws, both camps simply followed tradition. They ignored both the letter and spirit of the law with impunity, while observing its formal requirements, and everyone in the state, with the possible exception of Frank Graham himself, understood the way things worked.[28]

Willis Smith's indecision in calling for a second primary mirrored his reluctance to challenge Graham in the first place. Even after he announced his intention to call for a runoff, he did not immediately begin campaigning. He waited a week. As noted, in that time he raised money and conferred with campaign aides, shored up his statewide organization, and prepared himself for the ordeal to come. In addition, Smith worked to get an endorsement from Bob Reynolds. Finally, he hoped to stun the Graham camp by pulling off what would have been the political coup of the entire campaign: an open endorsement from Senator Clyde Hoey.[29]

The Reynolds endorsement Smith sought was not long in coming. On June 8, "Our Bob," exulting in his presumed role as kingmaker, embraced Smith's candidacy and promised his complete support. Speaking to the press via long distance from Hot Springs, Arkansas, where he was taking the waters, Reynolds not only endorsed Smith but also disclosed his intention to campaign actively on Smith's behalf. In a statement issued by Smith headquarters, Reynolds warned, "Perilous times face our great nation, and forces inimical to its well-being are striking from within and from without." The country needed a man with the character and ability of Smith, Reynolds stated. Simultaneously, Reynolds's former secretary and political confidant, Wesley McDonald, also endorsed Smith and publicly implored all of Reynolds's voters to do likewise.[30] McDonald would later join Smith's staff and work tirelessly for Graham's defeat.[31] Other admirers of Reynolds now came out for Smith, among them Mrs. P. R. Rankin, past president of the North Carolina Federation of Women's Clubs, and Pierce C. Rucker, Jr., who had managed Reynolds's successful 1938 Senate campaign.[32]

Not all of Reynolds's followers obeyed their leader. Some Reynolds people had already endorsed Graham. Charlotte attorney Haywood Robbins, a key Reynolds adviser in the first primary, expressed his keen disappointment in Reynolds's embrace of Smith and openly rebuked Reynolds: "Bob had bungled his own campaign from the very beginning. . . . Now he has followed through and bungled Willis Smith's." Robbins pointed out in the Charlotte *Observer* that several times during the first primary, Reynolds had argued for a winner-take-all agreement in the race. Now Reynolds endorsed the runner-up. All through the campaign, Robbins observed, Reynolds's camp had labored to prevent Bob from appearing the buffoon, but "now he goes out to Hot Springs and puts himself on record as being one."[33] Another Reynolds partisan, Ray Owen, Mecklenburg campaign manager, agreed that Reynolds's supporters felt betrayed and would no longer follow his lead. Many, Owen believed, would work for Graham.[34]

The Reynolds endorsement was therefore a wash. It would have little impact, the High Point *Enterprise* wrote, because the campaign had already turned in Smith's favor.[35] Graham's backers, moreover, had secured the support of Reynolds's field staff, the Durham *Sun* added, hence, Reynolds's endorsement amounted to little.[36] There was, in addition, a significant anti-Reynolds sentiment in the state, and a prominent Reynolds role in Smith's campaign could boomerang. Nonetheless, Smith's backers were elated with the endorsement, and Smith wrote a letter to Reynolds's constituents reminding them of Reynolds's endorsement and asking for their vote.[37]

Eventually Reynolds made a transcribed radio speech for Smith in which he attacked Graham for supporting legislation that would allow 240,000 immigrants into the United States. Reynolds declared that he was "wholeheartedly and unequivocally" for Smith and had made his choice free from any coercion or promise of political reward. Smith was a true believer in states' rights and opposed the "bending of the knee to certain minority groups for purely political purposes," Reynolds claimed. The Raleigh attorney would protect the rights of majorities.[38]

The wooing of Senator Hoey, unlike that of Reynolds, if successful, would have critical consequences. An open endorsement from North Carolina's senior senator would give Smith a lift no other individual could provide. Even Hoey's clandestine assistance would be a major boost. Smith advocates, in letters and phone calls, urged Hoey to endorse Smith. Smith even asked his close friend and law partner, John H. Anderson, to intercede on his behalf. Smith and Hoey, argued Anderson, shared a belief in a common core of political principles. The Graham forces, moreover, had used Hoey's words in their advertisements to promote the notion that Hoey favored Graham's election. At the least, Anderson argued, Hoey should clarify his position in a public statement and endorse Smith to the same degree that his words had been used to endorse Graham.[39] Anderson and other Smith advisers knew, as did all political observers, that Hoey was closer to Smith on the issues of the day than he was to Graham. They knew that Hoey opposed the Scott organization, distrusted labor unions, and was a staunch segregationist. He had delighted privately in Claude Pepper's defeat and hoped to see sober-minded southerners in the Senate who could hold the liberals in check.[40] A Smith endorsement would therefore seem to make sound political sense, especially since Hoey's own reelection was now a certainty.

Hoey would have none of it. Whether he was holding to the deal he had apparently made with Capus Waynick to help Graham if Waynick did not run against Hoey or was simply maintaining his time-honored practice of minding his own political business is impossible to say. In either case, he endorsed no one. He pointed out to the Smith people that whatever false impression Graham's staff had created by suggesting that Hoey supported Graham had been rebutted in Smith's own ads. Hoey would work for Hoey.[41]

Smith forces received Hoey's polite brush-off with disappointment, mindful that his neutrality was an aid to Graham. But they did not linger over their failure. Smith's field staff was hard at work, especially in the east, and reports reaching the Raleigh headquarters convinced campaign strategists that a major shift of opinion in Smith's favor was underway.[42]

Smith began active campaigning on June 13, only eleven days before election day. In his initial public appearance, Smith set the tone for his runoff race. He assailed what he called bloc voting by blacks for Graham in the first primary and declared his steadfast commitment to the principle of separate but equal school facilities for different races. Where they were not equal, he added, he would work to improve them in order that all children could have the full benefit of democracy. In other words, he reinforced his position as defender of the racial status quo. Victory in the coming runoff, he predicted, was certain—"a victory which I did not have the right to deny the people who were willing to work for it."[43]

At first Smith's campaign seemed simply a reprise of his May performance. He did remind voters that in calling for a second primary he was doing exactly what Kerr Scott had done two years earlier. He argued that he would have to whip several political machines in order to win: the Scott machine, the national Democratic (Truman) machine, the CIO Political Action Committee, the NAACP, and those loyal to the University of North Carolina.[44] Pro-Smith newspapers picked up this refrain, the Fayetteville *Observer* stating that the key campaign issue now was the "hard-boiled political machines which have adopted Frank Graham and labeled him as their man."[45] It was Smith against the machines, echoed the Rocky Mount *Telegram*; the paper wondered if Smith could defeat the machines' money and the huge blocs of votes they commanded.[46]

But Smith's main campaign themes were leftovers from round one. He attacked Graham on FEPC and the Brannan Plan, while repudiating the Graham charge that he was a Republican in disguise. His opposition to both proposals hardly made Smith a Republican, argued the Charlotte *News*. The *News* added that Graham also opposed both plans. There were honest differences within the Democratic party and they ought to be settled within the party, the paper determined.[47] To call southern whites "Republicans" in 1950 was to label them with an inflammatory epithet, and if Smith were a Republican, wrote one correspondent to the Charlotte *Observer*, what of the 250,000 voters who had backed him in May? Were they also disloyal Democrats?[48]

And what of Senator Hoey? Was he likewise disloyal to the Democratic party? He and Smith shared political values, J. C. B. Ehringhaus, Jr., wrote the Charlotte *Observer* on June 16. Those who attacked Smith and Hoey, Ehringhaus charged, were a "group of surly malcontents who are bent on realigning and reconstructing in a day those basic principles which one-hundred and fifty years of sober and deliberate effort has built."[49] Smith ads cleverly tied the candidate to the popular Hoey and the conservative wing of the Democratic party and explained that the liberal Graham had voted against Hoey sixty-four times in the Senate, effectively killing Hoey's vote and leaving North Carolina without any real representation.[50]

Senator Graham, too, began the runoff in much the same fashion that he had ended the May campaign. As in the first primary, candidate Graham had very little to do with setting the strategy or timetable for his effort. All planning remained the prerogative of Jeff Johnson, Governor

Smith, in the second primary, continued to hammer at Graham, assailing his affiliations with suspect groups and attacking him as a racial extremist. (North Carolina Department of Archives and History, Raleigh)

Scott, Jonathan Daniels, and, to a lesser extent, Harry Truman. The president was deeply concerned about the outcome and wrote Daniels: "I'll have another conversation with Bill [?] and I think you will find his intention is to get some individuals to help a little with your campaign. Graham must win—we can't possibly have a loss there."[51] When Truman was told that Graham's victory depended on a large vote (a spurious analysis), White House insiders quietly took measures to drum up a big ballot.[52]

The president, of course, was not alone in his concern. A steady supply of advice rained in upon Johnson from insiders, concerned precinct workers, former University of North Carolina students, and citizens at large. They forecast that Graham faced a difficult campaign against a tough challenger and needed to revitalize his followers. A father and his son, law partners in Rockingham, North Carolina, wrote that Smith's mudslinging in late May had cost Smith thousands of votes, which meant that Graham should maintain his effort "on a high level." Johnson should stress Graham's lifelong accomplishments in education under the separate but equal doctrine to counter concerns about the recent Court decisions, the attorneys suggested. Finally, Johnson should emphasize

Graham's opposition to "socialized medicine," FEPC, deficit spending,

and foreign aid, while restating Graham's commitment to free enterprise.[53] That was precisely what he intended to do, Johnson responded,
and he would also use local people in radio spots to answer local attacks
on Graham.[54]

Meanwhile, the ever-helpful Charles Tillett told the campaign director
that the best way to answer vicious attacks on Graham would be to
mention casually that publication of anonymous handbills was against
the law. Such violations, upon conviction, carried sentences of not more
than $1,000 in fines or one year in jail, or both.[55] How such a tactic
would stop the unsigned pamphlets, Tillett did not specify. Allen
Langston likewise urged strong action against the Hoover Adams–
Charles Green tactic "of pointing the finger and yelling at the top of their
voices in the hope that there are enough moonstruck idiots around to
create the impression that the mere pointing and screaming is somehow
derogatory."[56]

Some early field reports depicted a vigorous and successful effort to
hold farmers and low-income voters in support of Graham.[57] Others,
however, were not so upbeat and warned of overconfidence. A. L.
Fletcher warned state headquarters that Smith had unlimited funds that
were being spent without fanfare at the grass roots. If the Graham
headquarters thought Graham "was in, without further effort, may God
help him. At this point [June 13] he looks like a loser to me."[58] Graham
leaders in Buncombe County said the same thing. If Graham folks
thought the election was in the bag and did not turn out the vote, the
result would be disastrous.[59]

Yet many Graham insiders blithely believed the issue already decided.
Capus Waynick recalled visiting Jonathan Daniels and reporter Fleet
Williams at the Raleigh *News and Observer* headquarters in early June.
He told them Graham was going to get beat. Daniels assured Waynick
that no one could beat Graham—his lead was insurmountable. When
Waynick expressed the same sentiment at the White House, presidential
aide Charles Murphy of North Carolina told him he was out of touch
with Tar Heel politics; Graham was a shoo-in. Waynick's reaction, which
he kept to himself, was that such a view was a disservice to Graham. With
such an attitude, Graham's friends "were going to get the hell beat out of
him [Graham]."[60]

Indeed, Graham himself endorsed his invincibility. In a startling departure from his usual stance of modesty and humility, he predicted on
June 15 that he would win handily. Speaking in Charlotte—where Smith
had beaten him in May—he said: "Many of my friends who failed to get

to the polls in the first primary, they'll be there June 24. They say we are going to win by a fine majority."[61] Someone at headquarters apparently choked on these words, because the next day the senator recanted, blaming his statement on press misinterpretation. His supporters had given him encouraging reports, he stated, but he knew the election was not in the bag and he realized that much work remained to be done.[62] Nonetheless, the sense of overconfidence was scarcely allayed.

Furthermore, Graham failed to stump with increased aggressiveness. As a political campaigner, Graham never seemed to get the hang of it. Not only did he continue to refuse to attack his opponent, he even resisted the idea that he should become an aggressive candidate. "I never said a word against my opponent," he recounted with some pride in a 1970 interview.[63] Once again his advocates were forced to mount the attack for him, repeating the charge, for example, that Smith delighted in seeing cotton mill workers earn forty cents per hour. The claim, of course, was a first primary holdover, and when the leaflet once again came to Graham's attention in June, he denied it came from Graham headquarters. As in the first primary, he ordered it stopped and repudiated its message. "I just don't want to campaign like that," he told his staff.[64] (Nonetheless, the leaflet did not disappear.)

Such conduct understandably earned him press accolades. The Durham *Morning Herald* praised Graham as a man who disavowed half-truths,[65] and the Raleigh *News and Observer* wrote that he refused to be the beneficiary of anything he considered unfair.[66] This charitable attitude influenced not only the preparation of Graham campaign circulars but also some more important efforts to assist him as well. For example, Louisville *Courier-Journal* editor Mark Ethridge, a longtime Graham ally in a variety of endeavors, including the Southern Conference for Human Welfare, offered to compose an open letter to answer criticisms of Graham, but Graham turned him down. It was not his policy to reply to criticism directly, he told Ethridge; he would simply restate his position in positive terms.[67] That other friends had lambasted Smith in the first primary seemed to be lost on Graham in his reply, but the statement nonetheless reflected an attitude that made aggressive campaigning for Graham a problematical enterprise. "I don't want to be expedient, I want to be honest," he told campaign audiences, defining a position that led the Kinston *Daily Free Press* to observe, as other pro-Graham papers had done, that Graham never assumed attitudes for political preference.[68]

As a consequence, Graham continued to be an inviting target. However refreshing and praiseworthy his refusal to participate in orthodox campaign repartee, that refusal gave comfort to his critics and encouraged campaign excesses from the Smith camp. If he suffered outrageous charges without reply, the cost of such tactics to his detractors was substantially reduced. As is obvious, his attitude did not make him responsible for the attacks that came, but clearly he encouraged his opponents by refusing to protest their tactics. Had he defended himself vigorously against Smith's charges, especially on matters of race, the campaign might have turned out quite differently in the runoff, as Terry Sanford has argued.[69]

Even more direct was Graham publicity director C. A. Upchurch, Jr., who bemoaned "Dr. Graham's refusal to make use of practical political expediency." Graham continued to write all his speeches and often dawdled over them. Once, Upchurch recounted, Graham spent several hours rewriting a ten-minute radio spot, only to arrive at the station too late to broadcast it. He would not allow others to write for him "even when they used his own words and phrases." Often, Upchurch told J. Covington Parham in a 1951 interview, Graham would be off at some school "making speeches about Indonesia and world brotherhood when he should have been out talking to the farmers." Upchurch never overcame his puzzlement at Graham's refusal to issue a statement of his opposition to cloture in May, which would have won the first primary for Graham outright. Graham, he concluded, was "just not a politician." They could have won, Upchurch believed, "if the 'Doc' had not been so stubborn."[70]

One consequence of Graham's independence, of course, was to make Jeff Johnson's runoff duties difficult to the point of being almost unmanageable. To his credit, Johnson never wavered. Hampered by the continuing disarray in Graham's Washington office and the perpetual meddling of a host of self-appointed political experts, Johnson struggled in the second primary to organize a coherent campaign. On June 7, immediately after Smith announced his decision to run again, Johnson implored Graham workers statewide to devote every ounce of their energy to get out the vote and to redouble their efforts to get labor votes in the piedmont that had apparently gone to Smith in May. Smith's people would bear down on the race issue, he warned, and workers would have to go house to house to combat sensational charges.[71]

Johnson's overall strategy, therefore, varied little from the plan of the first primary. He would utilize the Scott organization and remnants of his old Broughton alliance along with labor, blacks, and groups favorable to the national administration. The overall emphasis would remain defensive and positive, at Senator Graham's insistence. The attacks on Smith and affirmative defenses of Graham would again have to come from prominent citizens, who would speak publicly in response to Smith's attacks.

Labor continued to work diligently for Graham. The CIO in particular hoped to use economic issues to persuade workers to vote for Graham. It supplied Graham headquarters with suggestions on getting out the vote and on campaign strategy and was especially helpful in circulating pamphlets and fliers.[72] Dave Burgess, continuing his active involvement, urged Graham staffers to make certain that textile union members voted on June 24; equally important, Burgess argued, was a heavy black turnout, especially in Charlotte and Greensboro. Only about half of registered black voters had cast ballots in the first primary, he stated. And Burgess continued to plead, as he had done throughout the first primary, that Graham take the offensive, attack Smith, and stress Smith's antilabor positions.[73] The state textile union director Lewis Conn likewise urged his membership to go all out for Graham, delivering handbills, working the polls, and transporting voters, to insure that the union vote came through for Graham.[74]

In pursuit of the black vote, Burgess met several times with David M. McConnell and state NAACP leader Kelly M. Alexander, Jr., in Charlotte. Burgess agreed to fund some black precinct workers and urged that ministers be utilized to overcome mill worker opposition to Graham's racial views, at least as Smith presented those views. Ministers, Burgess believed, could best repudiate the most repugnant of the Smith campaign's racial charges.[75]

In his work for Graham, Burgess faced continuing frustration. He wrote that in addition to being cursed several times for working for that "nigger-lover" Graham, Graham's Cumberland County manager was lazy and had not even bothered to contact Fayetteville's black leadership in the first primary.[76] In Cabarrus County, Burgess felt the organization had been painfully slow and unprofessional,[77] and in Charlotte, Burgess found confusion and too much dependence on "political hacks."[78]

Such frustration did not prevent a massive labor effort. The CIO delivered twenty-seven thousand campaign circulars in Cabarrus County alone and worked mills at shift changes in much of the piedmont.[79] On balance, however, such labor support for Graham remained a risky venture. Burgess admitted that the mill worker–black coalition they were attempting to forge was a very fragile foundation for a political campaign. The black vote was not as significant as it might have been, and many mill workers would simply not ally themselves politically with blacks.[80]

Labor also sensed that Smith had made significant inroads into its constituency. It accused the Smith forces of vote-buying and of offering $70 a day to people who would help Smith.[81] One North Carolina man reported a $25 offer to change his vote, while another warned of vote-buying by the Smith forces in Robeson and Brunswick counties.[82] Smith people in Lenoir County, Graham worker Will England wrote Governor

Scott, were using both liquor and bribes to make deals out in the open.[83]

The major problem of the Graham campaign, therefore, continued to be the difficulty of holding together the disparate groups that had supported the senator in the first primary but were not themselves political allies. In regard to the black vote, Johnson's dilemma now was to generate a large turnout and yet avoid substantiating the Smith claim that massive black support for Graham was a threat to the racial status quo.

Johnson never found an answer to that dilemma, but he did continue to do all he could to insure a large black turnout. Black voters, in cooperation with the Graham staff, continued to work quietly but effectively to sustain support for Graham.[84] North Carolina Mutual Life Insurance Company executive Asa T. Spaulding helped raise money for Graham in the second primary,[85] and the Durham Committee on Negro Affairs, chaired by Charles Clinton Spaulding, the company's founder, urged black voters to rally to Graham; "Remember," the committee counseled, "A VOTELESS PERSON IS A USELESS PERSON!"[86]

Other efforts to secure a large black turnout were more visible and more controversial. Kelly M. Alexander, Jr., and the state NAACP promoted a statewide meeting on June 1 that urged greater political involvement by the state's black voters. Alexander claimed that the recent NAACP efforts had doubled black voter registration in North Carolina, raising it from 50,000 to 100,000. The increase, Alexander noted, worried white politicians, who wanted black political participation held to a minimum. But blacks in North Carolina, Alexander told his audience, would continue to work for their political objectives.

National NAACP official Roy Wilkins, addressing the meeting, noted that southern politicians complained that blacks voted as a bloc. But in racially charged campaigns, Wilkins observed, blacks had no choice. Wilkins denied any direct NAACP participation in the first Smith-Graham primary, specifically repudiating the spurious "Walter White" postcards that had been sent from New York. "I did not come here to tell you how to vote," Wilkins told his Fayetteville audience, ". . . but considering the record of Graham and that of Smith, if you don't know how to vote, then shame on you."[87] Black voter apathy nonetheless remained a problem despite Wilkins's entreaty. Had black voters been able to overcome barriers to registration, and their own inertia, Graham would have won decisively.[88]

The NAACP rally came as Smith was trying to decide whether a second primary should be held and had only limited effect on the campaign to come. But to some whites in the area, the meeting was confrontational in tone and altogether an outrage. It likely increased the resolve of Smith followers to use all the resources at their command to defeat Graham.

One such individual, with significant resources at his command, was Nathan M. Johnson of Dunn, president and owner of Johnson Cotton Company, a farm implement retail company with stores in many eastern North Carolina towns. As the second primary intensified, Johnson wrote to all store managers in his company, explaining that he endorsed Smith. He acknowledged Graham to be a high-toned Christian, "possibly too good to be in politics." But Johnson feared the imposition of FEPC if Graham were elected. Under FEPC, he wrote his managers, "your children will be going to school with the good little colored boys and girls. This may be o.k. but it is not the way we have been raised." Since Smith would work for the South, Johnson insisted, his managers should not only vote for Smith but also work for him as well. "On June 24, I want you to make your car and the company car available. Furnish drivers if necessary to get the Smith votes."[89] Johnson also wrote letters to individuals outside his company and distributed Smith campaign materials denouncing FEPC and detailing the menace of socialism. He stressed his antipathy to bloc voting by blacks and his fear that race mixing in the schools and intermarriage were just around the corner.[90]

Such activity bore out Jeff Johnson's belief that race would be the primary's principal focus. The runoff's first stirrings indicated that the recent Court decisions had given racial issues a renewed urgency among white voters statewide but especially among those living in eastern North Carolina. More importantly, Willis Smith could now tie nearly every campaign question to race, including the impact on state politics that would accompany the growth of the black franchise. Did blacks now hold the balance of power in North Carolina?

Candidate Smith seemed genuinely perplexed that blacks would reject en masse a political candidate committed to segregation in a contest with a rival who had worked for years to bring about peaceful change in southern race relations. In short, Smith was slow to accept the idea that blacks in North Carolina were no longer willing to accept a segregated society on any terms. His puzzlement and alarm typified a majority of white North Carolinians in 1950 and explain in part why race became such a compelling question in the Smith-Graham runoff.

Campaigning in his home county of Wake on June 16, as his challenge was beginning again, Smith addressed a courthouse rally. Before five hundred cheering supporters, in what observers called his most spirited speech of the campaign, Smith declared it his duty "to stand up and fight the insidious forces that are trying to destroy our form of government." Smith repeated his assertion that a vote for Graham was a vote for an

FEPC with full enforcement power, the view he claimed Graham had held before the Senate campaign began.[91]

The following day, Smith toured Wake County, as did his rival. Smith led a motorcade of seventy-five cars, riding in a sleek Pontiac convertible equipped with a loudspeaker heralding his arrival. Completing the entourage was a flatbed truck transporting Homer Briarhopper's hillbilly band, sent ahead to each of the sixteen stops to draw a crowd. As he arrived at each rallying point, Smith would climb on the truck bed, festooned with a banner reading "Save Our South—Get on the Smith Bandwagon," and recite a litany of campaign themes. His theme song was "Dixie," and wherever his show performed, young women would circulate, distributing campaign literature.

At every stop, Smith denounced the Brannan Plan as a "crackpot scheme." He was especially piqued at a recent comment by Governor Scott, who had told a press conference that, like Jesus, Graham was being crucified by his opponents. "I am not trying to crucify anybody," Smith shot back, "but I am opposing with all the strength I have any effort to crucify our country on the cross of socialism." It was he who was being vilified, Smith complained, because he had challenged the authority of three or four men who wanted to dictate to North Carolina its Senate composition.

In Zebulon, he personalized his FEPC attack by remarking that one man in the crowd, a local furniture store owner whom he called by name, would be required to hire the first person of either race who applied for any job opening he might have at his store, should FEPC be enacted. He even told a group of blacks that FEPC would be "just as bad for Negroes as for whites." Later, at Wendell, Smith remarked that he could not understand how Frank Graham had gotten mixed up with so many sinister organizations. Senator Hoey had never associated with such groups, Smith observed.

At Fuquay Springs, Smith received a rare campaign comeuppance. A Graham partisan queried Smith as to "why a big man like you is afraid of the Negroes when they make up only fifteen per cent of the population?" A heated exchange ensued between the questioner and the candidate and concluded when an agitated Smith walked away from his persistent examiner.[92] At Knightdale, still on the grand tour of Wake, the Smith caravan came into sight just as Frank Graham was finishing a speech on his swing around the Raleigh circle. With Smith horns blaring, Graham stopped his speech. "Guess my time is up," he told the crowd. "There comes American prosperity up the road." With a wave to the Smith caravan, Graham drove off to Wake Forest.[93]

Smith's reception in Wake County, boisterous and enthusiastic, added

Smith as he tours his home county of Wake in a determined effort to reclaim
it in the second primary. (North Carolina Department of Archives and
History, Raleigh)

to his advisers' belief that he could win the runoff. And the campaign got
an additional boost when the Charlotte *Observer* abandoned its first
primary neutrality and endorsed Smith on the same day he toured his
home county. Both aspirants for the Senate seat were distinguished
citizens, the paper commented, but Graham would support deficit
spending and increased government control. Smith, in contrast, advocated a balanced federal budget and local self-government and opposed
the welfare state. He would best serve the state's interests and was the
safer of the two candidates, the paper concluded.[94]

Coincident with his Wake tour, Smith also launched a massive newspaper barrage using full-page messages to make his case against Graham.
His ads limned in great detail his staff's assessment of the fundamental
issues that divided him from his opponent. Senator Graham, the ads
proclaimed, would speed the state and nation down the socialist road,
"the road to the All-Powerful State, planning every man's business, regu-
lating every man's life, exhausting every man's pocket in taxes."[95] Another broadside reminded voters again of Graham's association with a
variety of "Communist front groups" and contrasted the candidates'
personal histories: Smith the private attorney, advocate of free enterprise,

and self-made man as compared to Graham the social planner who had

spent his life on the public payroll. Smith also had much longer service as an active Democrat. "Smith or Graham? Which will vote in Washington as you would vote?"[96] The ad was used with special effectiveness in Mecklenburg County. Smith strategists also sent form letters around the state touting Smith as a believer in American democracy, free of any taint of socialism, and they circulated, as in the first primary, a four-page pamphlet, "Challenge to Socialism," written by former Republican National Committee staffer Marjorie Shearon, who accused Graham of working to lead the country to socialism.[97]

Far more effective for Smith, however, were the efforts of local campaign committees and individuals who were now warning voters of an impending racial Armageddon. These local groups employed an endless array of campaign tactics, including whispers, rumors, dirty tricks, deception, and fraud. One of the first of these episodes occurred in Washington, North Carolina. On June 14, a black man walked into *Daily News* editor Ashley Futrell's office with a political ad and the money to finance its publication. Requesting anonymity "because the white folks might get mad at me," the unnamed man placed the ad that was addressed "To the Colored Voters" and signed, "Colored Committee for Dr. Frank Graham." Commenting on the recent Supreme Court decisions outlawing "Segregation of Negroes" in two southern state universities, the ad stated: "These and other liberal rulings will mean nothing unless we have farsighted, honest and fair administrators. We think Dr. Frank Graham has all the qualities." Runoff turnout was usually light, the ad continued, therefore, "the Colored vote will count more than ever. Go to the polls and support 'DR. FRANK.' . . . WE DID IT BEFORE—WE CAN DO IT AGAIN."[98] A local attorney wrote Jeff Johnson that the ad was a "put-up job"; he had checked with local black leaders and they knew nothing about it.[99] The Raleigh *News and Observer* denounced the ad, arguing that its clear purpose "was to stir the prejudice of white voters." It had been prepared "by men who would loose every tragic fury in North Carolina in order to elect [Smith]."[100]

On another occasion, well-dressed blacks, wearing large hats and conspicuous jewelry, rode through small towns in eastern North Carolina in a sedan emblazoned with "Graham for Senate" banners. The riders were in the employ of local Smith backers hoping to create white resentment against the Graham candidacy.[101] Smith supporters also printed 100,000 copies of the May 27 front page of The *Carolina Times*, which exhorted black people to vote for Graham, under a headline that proclaimed "Negro Registration over 100,000." "THE NEGRO PRESS ENDORSES

TO THE

Colored Voters

Last week the U. S. Supreme court OUTLAWED "Segregation of Negroes" as practiced by two Southern State Universities and in dining cars on railroads.

These and other liberal rulings will mean nothing unless we have far-sighted, honest and fair administrators. We think Dr. Frank Graham has all the qualities.

His record is good. Go to the polls and Vote for HIM on June 24th.

The second primary vote is usually light. The Colored vote will count more than ever. Go to the polls and support "DR. FRANK" on Saturday, June 24th.

Our Vote counted in the last primary.

WE DID IT BEFORE - - WE CAN DO IT AGAIN

Colored Committee for Dr. Frank Graham

Another example of the effort by Smith stalwarts to depict Graham as a captive of black voters. Smith supporters placed this ad—complete with staged photograph—in the Washington (N.C.) *Daily News* in a crude effort to embarrass and discredit Graham. (Frank Porter Graham Papers, Southern Historical Collection, University of North Carolina at Chapel Hill)

GRAHAM," the unsigned circular announced. On the back side of the flier were reprints of various pieces from the paper condemning the attacks on Graham and another article critical of Senator Hoey. Smith supporters distributed the circulars in Raleigh and other parts of the state. Charles Green disclaimed any knowledge of the leaflet, but in Cleveland County, the circular went to voters from Smith's county headquarters, accompanied by a letter on official Smith campaign stationery with the names of Carlos Young and Willis McMurry, Smith's county chairmen, typed in.[102]

Other circulars appeared in various sections of the state, some of them repeats from the first primary. The photograph showing black representation in the 1868 South Carolina Reconstruction legislature reappeared, as did the photograph of black soldiers dancing with white women, taken in England during World War II, accompanied by a warning that a

desegregated society would produce commingling of the races. The ads indicated that while Graham did not want to force segregation, he was not adverse to white women dancing with blacks. "Remember, these . . . could be your sisters or daughters," the ads warned.[103] Marian Graham's photograph was superimposed on the figure of one of the women in the circular, Grahamites have recounted. Such materials were not generally circulated but were pulled from pockets and flashed to individuals[104]— political pornography, as it were. The Marian Graham circular has not survived, although numerous individuals claim to have seen it. Kathryn N. Folger has recalled a labor representative showing the flier to Senator Graham, who remarked that such tactics, directed against his wife, were contemptible but made no public protest.[105]

One week before election day, one of the more frenzied documents of the campaign appeared in Raleigh and spread to High Point, Shelby, Fayetteville, Durham, and elsewhere in the final week. "WHITE PEOPLE WAKE UP!" voters were admonished. "DO YOU WANT," the ad asked, "Negroes working beside you, your wife and daughters in your mills and factories? Negroes eating beside you in all public eating places? Negroes riding beside you, your wife and your daughters in buses, cabs and trains? Negroes sleeping in the same hotels and rooming houses? Negroes teaching and disciplining your children in school? . . . Negroes going to white schools and white children going to Negro schools? Negroes to occupy the same hospital rooms with you and your wife and daughters? Negroes as your foremen and overseers in the mills? Negroes using your toilet facilities?" If so, the "Know the Truth" Committee implored, "Vote for Frank Graham. But if you don't, vote for and help elect WILLIS SMITH for SENATOR. He will uphold the traditions of the South."[106] Another flier displayed the following headline: "Did you know over 28% of the population in North Carolina is COLORED?" With FEPC, in a plant of 375 people, 105 of the workers would be black workers forced on the plant by FEPC.[107] The same ad was frequently repeated over the radio.[108]

As this attack intensified, Graham forces strained to deflect it. State representative John Umstead denounced Smith supporters for their "despicable" activities and their misrepresentations of Graham's views on segregation. In Southern Pines, in the last days of the campaign, Umstead reminded listeners that Graham had lived his life in the service of others and was the best man who had "ever offered for public office in our State."[109] The Reverend Edwin McNeill Poteat wrote a "Dear Brethren" letter reminding fellow Baptist ministers that race prejudice for

Another effort by Smith supporters designed to stir racial fears featured this
photograph of white women dancing with black GI's in London, during World
War II, evoking the specter of miscegenation. (Allard Kenneth Lowenstein
Papers, Southern Historical Collection, University of North Carolina at
Chapel Hill)

political ends deserved the rebuke of those who believed that in Christ
all were brothers,[110] while Gerald W. Johnson, writing from Baltimore,
denounced the tactics of Smith supporters. "There has not been such a
spewing up of sewer rats in North Carolina for at least fifty years,"
Johnson wrote. "The worst of the stuff I have seen does not bear Smith's
name," but because it was distributed to advance his candidacy, "the filth
with which it drips inevitably sticks to him." When the Smith literature
shouted "Nigger" and "Red," "the inference is inescapable that the candidate has not much to recommend him."[111]

Other prominent individuals again spoke out for Graham, on the
stump and on the radio. I. Beverly Lake, Wake Forest College law
professor and constitutional authority, argued in a radio address that
Graham could best wage the fight against FEPC. The senator had always

WHITE PEOPLE
WAKE UP

BEFORE IT'S TOO LATE

YOU MAY NOT HAVE ANOTHER CHANCE

DO YOU WANT?

Negroes working beside you, your wife and daughters in your mills and factories?

Negroes eating beside you in all public eating places?

Negroes riding beside you, your wife and your daughters in buses, cabs and trains?

Negroes sleeping in the same hotels and rooming houses?

Negroes teaching and disciplining your children in school?

Negroes sitting with you and your family at all public meetings?

Negroes Going to white schools and white children going to Negro schools?

Negroes to occupy the same hospital rooms with you and your wife and daughters?

Negroes as your foremen and overseers in the mills?

Negroes using your toilet facilities?

> **Northern political labor leaders have recently ordered that all doors be opened to Negroes on union property. This will lead to whites and Negroes working and living together in the South as they do in the North. Do you want that?**

FRANK GRAHAM FAVORS MINGLING OF THE RACES

HE ADMITS THAT HE FAVORS MIXING NEGROES AND WHITES — HE SAYS SO IN THE REPORT HE SIGNED. (For Proof of This, Read Page 167, Civil Rights Report.)

DO YOU FAVOR THIS -- WANT SOME MORE OF IT?
IF YOU DO, VOTE FOR FRANK GRAHAM

BUT IF YOU DON'T

VOTE FOR AND HELP ELECT

WILLIS SMITH for SENATOR

HE WILL UPHOLD THE TRADITIONS OF THE SOUTH

KNOW THE TRUTH COMMITTEE

Certainly the most widely remembered campaign flier, and arguably the most incendiary, this flier depicted a society in the throes of an integrationist nightmare. The handbill accused Graham of advocating nearly every imaginable dimension of an unsegregated social order and was widely disseminated prior to the second primary voting. (Daniel Augustus Powell Papers, Southern Historical Collection, University of North Carolina at Chapel Hill)

Did YOU know

Over 28% of the population of North Carolina is COLORED

FEPC, if enacted, means more than that you might be working next to and sharing facilities with some one not of your choice . . . and probably not of your employer's choice, either.

It means that if you are working in a plant that employs 1,000 people, 280 of them will be someone besides you or your friends.

If you work in a plant employing 375 people, 105 of them won't be you or your friends.

Or, if you just work where there are three people, one of them won't be you or your present associates.

This is not a pretty picture . . . but these are the facts.

Do not be fooled . . . most of all, do not be lulled by sweet words of high-flown idealists.

The SOUTHERN WORKING MAN MUST NOT BE SACRIFICED to vote-getting ambitions of political bosses!

A Vote for *Willis Smith* | SATURDAY JUNE 24th | is a Vote for *Your* Freedom

WORKING MEN FOR SMITH COMMITTEE

JOHN M. CULP

This Smith flier attacked Graham for his alleged support of a federal Fair Employment Practices Commission by appealing to white workers who might face an integrated workplace controlled by federal edict. (Daniel Augustus Powell Papers, Southern Historical Collection, University of North Carolina at Chapel Hill)

opposed it, Lake argued, and because he had wide influence among his Senate colleagues, Graham would be FEPC's most effective critic: "No one who knows Senator Graham believes for a moment he would deceive the people of North Carolina for a senatorship. Senator Graham says he is opposed to FEPC. That settles it."[112] D. Hiden Ramsey,[113] L. P. McLendon, James Yadkin Joyner, Kemp Battle, and a long list of other prominent citizens added their voices to the din, but whether voters were listening to their often dolorous pleas was unclear.

Graham's campaign staff also quoted national and state figures who had made public statements praising Graham and his work, even when their words were not specific campaign endorsements: Senator Wayne Morse on Graham's Christlike qualities, Senator Clyde Hoey on his patriotism and loyalty, and Mrs. O. Max Gardner on his talents. They even used a statement from General George C. Marshall that praised Graham's Indonesian mission as a "diplomatic miracle,"[114] even though Marshall had not authorized the use of his name for political purposes and had, indeed, refused to endorse Graham's candidacy,[115] as had Hoey. In fact, Hoey, seeking to protect his public neutrality, asked one Graham supporter to include a reference to his impartiality in any additional ads that used his name to avoid any false impression that he backed Graham.[116]

Jeff Johnson, resentful that Willis Smith presented himself as "the veteran's veteran," attacked Smith's service record. In a message to county managers, he pointed out that Smith had waited to be drafted one year and three months after the United States entered World War I and served only four months. Frank Graham enlisted in the marines three months after war was declared and served two years. In view of the record, it was clear, Johnson argued, that Graham was really the veteran's veteran.[117]

Other Graham ads stressed Graham's large plurality in the first primary, "Smith and His Leaders Know They Cannot Overcome This Simple Arithmetic,"[118] and also played up Graham's overwhelming vote in Orange County in the first primary, "With Those Who Know Best—It's Frank Graham 4 to 1."[119] In addition, other ads proclaimed that Graham's hometown of Chapel Hill gave him 91.6 percent of its votes, while Raleigh, Smith's hometown, gave him only 45.8 percent of its votes—"By Their Fruits Ye Shall Know Them."[120]

Governor Scott had again brought all his influence to bear the moment Smith called the runoff. One partisan wrote Scott on June 10, urging him to send the word down "in your usual discreet manner" to all state employees to do all they could to elect Graham on June 24.[121] Scott was only too glad to comply. Predictably, Scott's partisanship continued to create controversy. One persistent critic, Fitz Hoyle, wrote the governor complaining that dozens of his friends who were state employees had told Hoyle that they would lose their jobs if they refused to support Graham.[122] Scott replied by asking for sworn affidavits proving Hoyle's charges and told Hoyle, "So far as I am concerned, they are free to do as they wish."[123] Other citizens were angered that Scott used a state car and state telephones to campaign against Smith, a fellow Democrat. Taxpayers should not have to foot the bill for such expenses, they argued.[124]

Scott brushed aside these remonstrances. "Naturally, I'm going to stand by my man," he proclaimed as he forecast a Graham victory. "Mr. Smith is interested in going to Washington, but his train is late."[125] Graham's first primary lead would hold, the governor predicted on June 10.[126] He then proceeded to infuriate Smith backers when, in a news conference, he denounced Smith for attacking both state and national administrations. "The Republicans ought not to be allowed to run a candidate in this campaign," he told reporters.[127]

The Henderson *Daily Dispatch* thereupon blasted the governor for slurring Democrats who bucked the "Scott-Truman-Daniels triumvirate."

It was not the middle-of-the-road Smith campaign that had "strayed off the reservation," the paper argued, but those who were advocating social- ism. Nor was the triumvirate empowered to do the thinking for all Democrats.[128] The Kannapolis *Daily Independent* thought Scott was guilty of playing cheap politics by ruling out of the party all those opposed to Scott and Truman. Notable Democrats like Hoey would therefore be forced out of the party.[129]

Undeterred, Scott worked vigorously for Graham, both in person and on the radio. He gave special attention to the eastern part of the state, where he had his greatest strength. Here he pictured Smith as the corporate candidate, opposed to the welfare of the people.[130] In Eliza- beth City, he used the analogy of a horse trader who sought always to buy not a "has been" or a "gonna be" but an "izzer." Graham was an "izzer," he told his farm audience, "in there right now fighting the battles of the plain people for a more abundant life."[131] In Edenton, Scott acknowl- edged that in many places the fight was against Kerr Scott and not Frank Graham. Nonetheless, North Carolina needed a great humanitarian and not a corporation lawyer in the Senate. Smith's proper place, the gover- nor argued, was with the Dixiecrats.[132]

As the racial invective mounted, Scott did what he could to stifle it. Scott still believed that the people of North Carolina would not be misled by such tactics.[133] He again described Graham as a great humanitarian who was being persecuted like Jesus had been two thousand years ago.[134] Graham's record could not be tarnished by reckless charges, he told a statewide radio audience on June 20, nor did the recent Supreme Court decisions have any bearing on North Carolina's Senate race, since a senator could do nothing about Supreme Court decisions. Scott con- tended, in addition, that the recent rulings did not extend any new principle of law, hence the injection of the race issue was but an insult to the intelligence of voters and an effort to confuse them. Graham was no socialist, the governor proclaimed. He opposed FEPC, and he was no one's tool: "He fights for the rights of labor, but he is not a tool of the unions. I appointed him to the Senate, but he is no tool of mine."[135]

But Scott's words did not soothe. The strident tone of the campaign had induced a full-blown racial panic. Numerous reports from the field mirrored the comment of a Graham advocate in the Bladen County community of Tar Heel, an eastern Scott stronghold: "Folks here are so hot about the Negro question I can't even talk to them about it."[136] With "open volleys of recrimination and innuendo" exchanged daily on the stump and in the press, rumor and fantasy took hold in many areas of the state. In some rural counties, there were campaign canards that Graham

favored permitting black teachers in white schools.[137] Smith men, according to Graham supporter Willis P. Holmes, Jr., were telling voters
that if they did not want their children going to school with blacks, they
had better not vote for Graham. "Lots of laboring people with whom I
talked," Holmes reported, "told me that they had much rather work for
lower wages than to have their children going to school with Negroes."[138]
To Tom Bost, the base fiction "[is] too stupid for even a low-grade moron,
but unfortunately it is believed by people who aren't stupid."[139] Bost was
right. In one instance, Eva Cooper wrote Jonathan Daniels that in Nashville, North Carolina, young people whose parents were known to have
voted for Graham were called "Negro lovers."[140]

The Graham forces had expected racial attacks but were not prepared
for the viciousness and anger of the racial slurs. Dave Burgess feared that
Jeff Johnson did not understand the full impact of the race issue.[141]
Johnson, however, knew well the seriousness of the situation. He talked
to people in the field almost hourly. Johnson was told that a foreman at
Cannon Mills had told his workers that if they voted for Graham, many
of them would soon be replaced by blacks.[142] From Shelby, Johnson
heard that a car with "Vote for Graham" banners on each side, complete
with a black driver, had made its way slowly through Shelby's mill
villages. In Duplin County, a black man drove up to the county seat in a
Cadillac and pointedly asked directions to Graham headquarters. A
similar story came from Vance County.[143] Horace Stacy of Lumberton
told of the fifteen-year-old daughter of a Graham supporter whose school
chum told her by telephone that if her daddy voted for Graham, "you'll
be sitting by Negroes in school," and hung up.[144]

Most of this activity was local, carried out by rumormongers and
frightened people beyond the reach of logic and reason. So far as can be
determined, it was neither countenanced nor controlled by Smith headquarters.[145] The Smith organization did use racial issues with much
effectiveness, however, and focused voter attention on racial questions.
Smith people sent letters all around the state, for example, explaining the
significance of the recent Supreme Court rulings and stressing the need
to elect senators committed to the fight against such changes in the
pattern of North Carolina and southern race relations.[146]

It was in this context that Graham went forth to make his case to the
people of North Carolina. His advisers were convinced that their major
asset was the senator himself and that the best way to persuade voters
was to get Graham on the stump where he could convince audiences
of his integrity and decency. His headquarters therefore announced "a
handshaking and whistlestop-type of campaign, with no set speeches,"

just Graham, out to "mingle with the folks."[147] He left Raleigh on June 11 for a three-day trip to western North Carolina, visiting a dozen counties.[148] Initially, he stressed the themes of his first primary campaign: his opposition to federal fiats to end segregation, his commitment to the "North Carolina way" on race relations, and his continued opposition to "socialized medicine" and the Brannan Plan.[149]

From Graham's first talk, audiences displayed a different mood than they had shown in May. Wherever he went, Graham was dogged by persistent questions probing his racial attitudes. He was especially haunted by the specter of Leroy Jones. Graham supporter Worth B. Folger emphasized this difficulty when he wrote Bill Staton that he was having "a hell of a lot of trouble over this West Point appointee." Smith people were relying on it heavily in several counties and were using it to change people's allegiances. Folger wanted a complete explanation so he could answer questions as they arose.[150] Even Leroy Jones wrote Senator Graham to commiserate and to encourage Graham not to relax his guard.[151]

Repeatedly, Graham explained about Leroy Jones. "I've seen pictures from the ocean to the mountains of a Negro boy I'm supposed to have sent to West Point. He is not there." Jones had not placed first in the competitive exam, Graham explained again and again, and the white boy who had finished first was now a cadet. "You would have thought I had made him [Jones] commandant of West Point," recalled Graham in 1969.[152]

Graham reiterated his reasons for adopting the competitive system. He explained that applicants were identified by numbers on the test so that all would have a fair chance, irrespective of social station or political connection. His appointee, Graham reminded voters, was a young man from Fayetteville, whose ancestors had helped found the University of North Carolina, and the second-place finisher was now a student at Yale, while Leroy Jones had finished third and never attended West Point.[153]

Graham headquarters meanwhile ran ads statewide under the headline, "Do You Want Your Son to Have a Chance?" Candidate Smith, the ads claimed, would, if elected, return to the old system of political favoritism where only the sons of rich and powerful men would have a chance for service academy appointments. "Are you ignorant or prejudiced?" the ad concluded. "If so, you are the person at whom the phony race issue is aimed. The Jones case is just one example of how candidate Smith has permitted his campaign lieutenants to appeal to race prejudice in North Carolina." It was an insult to voter intelligence and a disservice to the state, the ad concluded.[154] But neither the ad nor Senator Graham's explanation could defuse the issue. The controversy raged on.

Back in Raleigh following his three-day trip to the west, Graham next spent a day in Wake County, inadvertently butting heads with his challenger, where, as noted earlier, their paths criss-crossed on one occasion. Like Smith, Graham visited every town and every hamlet in sprawling Wake County, slowing down at crossroads to wave at obviously astonished farmers. He started at Millbrook with a breakfast rally and made his way around the county in sultry ninety-degree weather. Wherever he stopped, he shook hands, talked from a truck flatbed, and visited service stations, food stores, and country emporiums. At Falls of the Neuse, he even took the time to toss a ball with a three-year-old. One little girl claimed she had jumped out of bed especially early, "just so I can eat a piece of cantaloupe and see Frank Graham."[155]

Mary Coker Joslin, who accompanied him on the tour, wrote that faces in Graham's audiences were filled with anxiety. They seemed to seek reassurance from Graham that he did not favor an end to segregation. In response to the inevitable questions about Leroy Jones, Graham changed his emphasis. He had been advised at the time of the appointment, Graham stated, to announce the names of only the top two candidates and ignore Leroy Jones. He declined the advice, the senator remarked, because the people of North Carolina had a right to know that a black youth, trained in segregated schools, could do well enough to finish third in a competitive exam for West Point. The people of Jones's hometown, Kinston, were proud of Jones and held nothing against Graham, the senator pointed out. They had given Graham a majority of their votes in May.[156]

In Fuquay local bank president Robert E. Prince introduced Graham to the crowd and observed, "If you are a Communist, then I would like to be a Communist. If you are guilty of un-American activity, then I would like to bear your guilt." Those assembled applauded appreciatively. In Holly Springs, Graham called his wife Marian to his side. "She's been a member of the same church for fifty-six years. Does she look like a woman who would marry a Communist?"[157]

At one stop, an enthused listener shouted, "Isn't Willis Smith the biggest liar in North Carolina?" "No," Graham responded quietly, "I never said that. I wouldn't say that about him," refusing as always to attack Smith personally.[158] But everywhere he went, he did caution his supporters against overconfidence and asked them to help get out the vote on primary day.[159]

As Graham left Wake County, where his reception had been relatively cordial, and continued to tour around the state, evidence mounted that his campaign was in deep trouble. He was scheduled to speak to the Elizabeth City Rotary Club, but when he arrived, no one wanted to

On June 17, the same day Smith was in Wake County, Graham spent the day there also. On one occasion, Graham barely missed being overtaken by the Smith entourage. (North Carolina Department of Archives and History, Raleigh)

introduce him. Rotary officials turned to a local Baptist minister who was present, W. W. Finlator, to present Graham, but many people left the dining room before Graham spoke.

On the stump, the crowds were unresponsive, often sullen. So persistent were the questions concerning Leroy Jones and Graham's appointment process that Allard Lowenstein suggested a bold move: fetch William L. Hauser, the West Point appointee, at home in Fayetteville for the summer, and have him accompany Graham. Fayetteville mayor Joe Talley broached the idea to young Hauser, and Lowenstein convinced the cadet designate that it was his duty to campaign with the senator who appointed him. After a day's deliberation, Hauser consented and traveled with the Graham entourage for the campaign's final hectic fortnight. In addition, the staff dispatched J. Melville Broughton, Jr., to assist the senator and to provide help in the event Graham's audiences should become surly or unruly, which seemed a distinct possibility in some areas. Broughton would also have the responsibility of trying to keep Graham, who was time deaf, on schedule and to prevent him from putting his arm around blacks. "Dr. Frank," Broughton recalls, "was too naive and trusting to campaign by himself." Marian Graham would continue to see to her husband's personal needs, insuring that he ate

Graham explains his political views to a pair of well-wishers. (North Carolina
Department of Archives and History, Raleigh)

regularly, had pocket money, and got some rest. She "nursed him like a
child," Broughton recounted.[160]

This modest assemblage, convened for the campaign's final push, set
off for the east, seeking to shore up Graham's suspect support there.
They toured first through Fayetteville and Cumberland County, where
Graham repeated his campaign positions and urged a balanced federal
budget.[161] When asked about race mixing in the public schools, Graham
answered that such a policy would be a great mistake and would threaten
improvements in race relations that had been made in recent years.[162]
Whenever his audience asked about Leroy Jones, Graham proudly displayed his prize exhibit, William Hauser, planted in the crowd. Calling
him forward, Graham would remark: "There's the boy who's going to
West Point. He was the number one boy. You haven't seen his picture?
Well, take a look at him now." Leroy Jones was not going to West Point,
Graham continued, Bill Hauser was. He had not appointed the number
three boy or the number two boy, "I appointed the #1 boy."[163]

Wherever he went in his eastern travels, Graham introduced young
Hauser. He found defending his appointment process distasteful, but he
never apologized for having made the process open to all. He praised
Jones for his excellent score on the exam as an example of the quality of
North Carolina's segregated schools. Nonetheless, he found audiences
skeptical of his explanation. At Chinquapin, in Duplin County, one

Opponents accused Graham of appointing a black Kinston youth, Leroy Jones, to West Point and circulated this picture of Jones statewide. Even though Graham took his real appointee, William Hauser of Fayetteville, with him on the stump to prove his point, by the second primary the racial invective had become so charged that many listeners refused to believe his explanation. (North Carolina Department of Archives and History, Raleigh)

doubter asked, "Now, Dr. Graham, is that the *only* boy you've sent to West Point?" Graham grinned and nodded yes.[164] After Graham had introduced Hauser and concluded his remarks in Beulahville, an angry murmur surged through the crowd: "Why didn't he bring the nigger he appointed? Who was he trying to fool, showing us that white boy?"[165] Others gazed upon Hauser and remarked to no one in particular, "He's mighty light, ain't he?"[166] Hauser, for his part, became an exuberant campaigner and wanted to speak for Graham, until a Graham staffer remonstrated: "Look here, boy. We haven't got you out here but for one thing—that's to prove you ain't a nigger."[167]

When asked by farmers about the various charges the Smith camp had leveled at him, Graham continued to refuse to call them lies, even when friends suggested that he should. Instead, he waved them down with a calm admonition: "I would rather fight for causes than attack anybody. If attacking a man is the way to get elected, then I don't want to get elected."[168]

His calming words, however, did not reassure voters about the charges that had been leveled against him. Late in the campaign (June 23), he

was in Guilford County accompanied by a flamboyant local figure, tobacco auctioneer George Penny. At one mill village, when Graham rose to
speak, several people began blowing their car horns and Graham could
not be heard. The senator did nothing, but Penny grabbed the micro-
phone and told the horn blowers that Graham was entitled to be heard
and was going to be heard. The disruption finally stopped, and Graham
went on with his speech. He made no remonstrance, although his wife
was visibly upset by the incident. Jeff Johnson, upon hearing of the
situation, implored Graham to react more strongly to such affronts,
reminding him that even Jesus had thrown the money changers out the
temple,[169] but his counsel was unavailing. Graham would not lash out at
his attackers.

Such incidents became commonplace in that final week. Often, textile
workers, believing that Graham was promoting integration, would not
look Graham in the eye; some even spat at him.[170] At a service station
outside High Point, Graham introduced himself to five mill workers and
extended his hand only to be told, as the workers turned their backs on
him, "We're all Willis Smith men here. We'll have nothing to do with
nigger lovers here."[171] In High Point itself, Graham faced crowds of small
children who chanted "no school with niggers, no school with niggers."
His larger audiences were likewise sullen and rude. Many individuals
would not shake his hand, and when he tried to introduce Marian, they
turned aside.[172]

The Smith campaign, in contrast, was at full throttle. In Asheville, on a
final western swing, Smith addressed a small but enthusiastic crowd on
June 21. Using ridicule and humor, he skewered Graham for not standing shoulder to shoulder with Senator Hoey in fighting FEPC and lambasted Graham's CIO support.[173] He also attacked Graham for refusing to join other southern senators in fighting the proposed cloture
rule enforcement. "Northern labor dictators," added campaign manager
Green, were trying to force Graham on North Carolina voters.[174] The
Southern Textile Bulletin added its opinion that big labor had distributed
over a million circulars for Graham and had been pivotal in the senator's
first primary victory.[175]

In attacking FEPC, Smith pointed out that black newspaper columnist
Gordon B. Hancock had told his readers that, in reality, Graham supported FEPC but had retreated in the current campaign as a matter of
political expediency. Since Graham's heart was in the right place, black
voters, Hancock had written, could condone Graham's "strategic retreat"
in order to win over those who were opposed to "Negro advance." Smith
used the column to validate his claim that Graham favored FEPC and
that Graham's claim of opposition to a compulsory FEPC was a cha-

rade, a distinction without a difference. Smith ads also reproduced the Hancock column, which had run in both the *Carolina Times* and *The Carolinian.*

As he had on June 11, Smith argued that the black vote against him in the first primary was an example of "bloc voting to a most iniquitous degree." He did not know, Smith stated, what kind of deal Graham had made with state black leaders, but the raising of the race issue by the opposition had "produced results for Dr. Graham." He then cited Graham's attendance at an unsegregated meeting of the SCHW in 1947 and reminded his audience that Graham and Henry Wallace, the "darling of the Communists," had on occasion exchanged public praises.[176]

As Smith ripped Graham in Asheville, his headquarters came out with a more traditional charge, claiming that district highway commissioner Wilbur Clark was using road bond money as a "political football." Seeking to discredit the Scott administration and to emphasize yet again Graham's tie to it, Charles Green had secured an affidavit from a Sampson County farmer who swore that Clark had told him that unless he and his friends supported Graham in the first primary, no new roads would be built in Sampson County, and those already under construction would not be finished. The incident, Green charged, was "just one of countless instances where Kerr Scott and his appointees have used state employees and state funds on behalf of Frank Graham. Never before in the history of the State," Green claimed, "has any Governor so used the whip to force people to the polls and to require those on the State payroll to campaign actively."[177]

The Smith forces also sought to remind voters, as the campaign reached its apogee, that Senator Graham was continuing to play the role of social activist. "Frank Graham Joins Another," blared full-page ads in papers statewide on June 22. The ad informed voters that in June 1950 Senator Graham had become a member of the national committee of the American Civil Liberties Union (ACLU). The association of Graham with ACLU chairman Roger Baldwin, the ad charged, was vintage Graham. Roger Baldwin, the ad reminded North Carolinians, was an atheist, had been convicted under the Selective Service Act for refusing the draft, and had spent a year in jail in 1918–19. A onetime International Workers of the World member, Baldwin had recorded in his 1935 Harvard Class Book that he opposed production for private profit and advocated socialism and disarmament. He also wanted to abolish the state as an instrument of violence: "I seek . . . abolition of the propertied class—COMMUNISM IS THE GOAL," Baldwin concluded. That Graham, who told voters he opposed communism, would serve in an organization headed by Baldwin "should cause voters to pause and think," the ad admonished.[178]

Graham made no response to the disclosure that he belonged to the ACLU and its national committee. Jeff Johnson, however, struck back, labeling the ad libelous and a reflection on the ACLU, an organization dedicated to upholding the constitutional rights of all citizens. The ACLU had been absolved of any Communist affiliation, Johnson related, by the HUAC itself.[179] Roger Baldwin credited the attack to his political enemies and, in a public letter, labeled the ad a smear, based on ancient and discredited sources. It was preposterous, he charged, to believe that Frank Graham was bound by the personal view of anyone in the ACLU.[180]

Hoover Adams got in the last word, however, defending the ad as factually accurate. Adams was correct. Baldwin had indeed spent a year in jail for draft evasion during World War I (he was a pacifist), and he had once been an International Workers of the World member. Baldwin also acknowledged that the statement in the Harvard Class Book accurately reflected his political views. Baldwin, of course, had never been a party member, but he was a lifelong socialist, and for a time, a fellow traveler. The communism he sought was not Stalinism but a more pure philosophical strain whose outlines were always ambiguous.[181] In short, as Adams insisted, the ad contained no factual inaccuracy. Voters who viewed membership in the ACLU with suspicion could therefore condemn Graham for being a member of the organization's national committee, while Graham's defenders could charge the Smith camp with a classic case of guilt by association, which, of course, they did.

The episode, however inflammatory, was brief. Far more persistent— and damaging—were the charges of bloc voting by blacks for Graham that candidate Smith continued to raise. In his ads and in his travels, Smith stressed that Frank Graham had won nearly unanimous support from black voters. Wherever he went, Smith carried handbills of six clearly identifiable black precincts and their first primary voting totals:

	Graham	Smith
Raleigh number 10	493	9
Raleigh number 16	518	18
Durham Hillside	1,514	7
Durham Pearson School	1,187	8
Greensboro number 5	1,231	12
Charlotte number 2	512	11
	5,455	65

```
          EXAMPLES OF BLOCK VOTING BY NEGROES IN NORTH CAROLINA:

                        (OFFICIAL RETURNS)


                    PRECINCT            GRAHAM        SMITH

     RALEIGH        No. 10               493            9

                    No. 16               518           18


     DURHAM         Hillside            1514            7

                    Pearson School      1187            8


     GREENSBORO     No. 5               1231           12


     CHARLOTTE      No. 2                512           11


          THESE ARE RETURNS FROM SIX WELL-KNOWN NEGRO PRECINCTS

                         WAKE COUNTY COMMITTEE FOR SMITH
                         411 Fayetteville St., Raleigh, N. C.
```

In the second primary, Smith and his staff distributed fliers that showed the voting totals from several all-black precincts that gave Graham nearly unanimous support in the first primary. On the reverse side of the circular was a reprint from the black newspaper in Raleigh, *The Carolinian.* In its editorial endorsement, the paper argued that Graham's denial of support for a federal FEPC was merely campaign rhetoric and should be discounted. (Daniel Augustus Powell Papers, Southern Historical Collection, University of North Carolina at Chapel Hill)

Such voter totals, Smith and his aides declaimed, were a menace to democracy. Perhaps more importantly, they suggested that black voters now were challenging for control of the state Democratic party. Such lopsided voter totals, Smith's ads argued, "didn't just happen. There must be a reason. Did someone make a deal?" Those loyal to Smith must bestir themselves in order to save the state from the reintroduction of carpetbag rule, the Smith faction warned.[182]

The Graham camp cried foul, but Smith maintained that he was not the one who had injected race into the campaign. Racial feeling had been stirred by the Committee on Civil Rights report of 1947 and by Truman's sponsorship of FEPC. In addition, it had been fanned by blacks themselves in the primary when they cast an almost solid vote for Graham.[183] A public letter on "Smith for Senate" stationery argued that the state's blacks, who had registered 100,000 voters and then voted for Graham en

"EVERYBODY knows that DR. GRAHAM is IN FAVOR of the FEPC", says NEW YORK NEGRO COLUMNIST.

THE CAROLINIAN

24 Pages | *NORTH CAROLINA'S LEADING WEEKLY* | SINGLE COPY | **10c**

VOLUME XXIX   RALEIGH, NORTH CAROLINA WEEK ENDING JUNE 17, 1950   NO XXVII

The substantial majority that Frank Graham polled in the recent primary was encouraging from many angles. In the first place Negroes supported Graham although he had to recant from some of his liberal positions; as for example the FEPC. Everybodys knows that Dr. Graham is in favor of the FEPC; but he had to back down before the terrific onslaught of his enemies who were doing some deadly gunning for the man's political life. So long as Frank Graham's heart is on the right side; Negroes can afford to let him make a "strategic retreat" if by such retreat he can win over those who are a 100 percent against Negro advance.

The Frank Graham episode should awaken Negroes to the advantage of certain strategies in the fight for liberation. To have forced Dr. Graham to stand up to his former position on th

This column, written by GORDON HANCOCK, OF THE AMERICAN NEGRO PRESS, is shown here as it was published in the CAROLINIAN, Raleigh Negro newspaper and other Negro newspapers throughout America.

masse, were themselves responsible for the rise of racial politics. "Don't you think the White should be as diligent as the negroes in exercising their obligation to vote their choice?"[184]

A full-blown debate ensued. In denying that Smith's campaign was racist, Jesse Helms later remarked that, first, Smith had no connection with the racist fliers that circulated so profusely. There was, in addition, a double standard in the charges that Smith was promoting racism. When Smith pointed out that blacks were asking their people to vote for Graham, Smith was called a racist. But somehow it was not racist for blacks to appeal for bloc voting. Publicizing the voting totals of black precincts, Helms argued, was a legitimate campaign issue.[185]

Harry Golden disagreed. It was an impertinence to denounce bloc voting since people in every race and every field of endeavor voted for their best interests and supported the candidate who was friendly to them.[186] The *Carolina Times* likewise decried the attack on bloc voting. Whites had used bloc voting for years to set up a one-party political system and to deny rights and offices to blacks. Blacks voted against Smith because he injected the race issue into the campaign with his flagrant attacks against Frank Graham and his use of racially inflammatory circulars. Blacks had to present a solid front against their enemies.[187]

The bloc voting charges were mild in comparison to the activities of some Smith enthusiasts. Almost everyone involved with the campaign on both sides believed Smith personally had nothing to do with the excessive and bigoted racial literature,[188] but Smith's state headquarters certainly set the tone for the campaign.

In stressing bloc voting, Smith continued a line of argument that dominated his second campaign. White North Carolina, Smith seemed to be saying, was a state under siege, assaulted from within and without by forces whose values, if imposed, would turn it on its ear. In this context, the agents of change were national institutions: all three branches of the federal government and their collaborators, political leaders in the state and their interest-group constituencies who were working hand in glove with both state and national leaders. The signal Smith was sending told voters that change was at hand and that it was menacing. Therefore, it must be opposed, and, if possible, arrested. The first step would be the unseating of Senator Graham in a resounding repudiation of the changes that he, Scott, and Daniels envisioned for the state.

Such a mood, in addition, was in consonance with the expressed concerns that encompassed larger national security questions. As Graham and Smith went at it in the late spring of 1950, Americans were continually bombarded with sensational headlines featuring a variety of espionage cases, among them British physicist Klaus Fuchs and Julius and Ethel Rosenberg. This siege mentality intensified as primary day drew nigh. Graham workers from various points in the state recounted any number of incidents that were either disturbing or menacing—and sometimes both. In Wilmington, a precinct worker called the Graham manager and hysterically demanded: "Come and take all your literature out of my house. My neighbors won't talk to me!" In Raleigh, an eight-year-old boy who spoke out for Graham was beaten up by schoolmates as a "nigger-lover." When a Durham election official's wife answered the phone, she was asked, "How would you like a little stewed nigger for breakfast?"[189] Jonathan Daniels reported similar harassment, replete with language so vile that the Daniels children were not permitted to answer the telephone. Some agitators even stoned Daniels's house.[190] Such racial attacks intimidated many Graham followers, and some Graham friends went fishing on election day, persuading themselves that Graham had all the votes he needed. "Why should I make enemies of the people I have to live with?" one Graham worker complained, as she described to headquarters the change in voter attitude.[191]

Other last-minute Smith ads continued the onslaught against FEPC. The Wake County Committee for Smith suggested in one pamphlet that FEPC would destroy individual freedom and the right to work where one pleased. Since the FEPC bill had been introduced by Adam Clayton Powell, a black congressman from Harlem, it was clear, the pamphlet observed, that Yankees were trying to cram the legislation down southerners' throats to win the black vote. If a white man and a black man applied for the same job, the employer would be forced to hire the black man. Blacks, in addition, would work alongside whites. They would be foremen, in control of whites, and would use the same restrooms on a basis of equality. "DO YOU WANT THIS?" this pamphlet asked.[192]

A final full-page ad, published in papers across the state the day before the election, claimed the purpose of FEPC was "to bring about the intermingling of the races by force." Black voters, the black press, and the NAACP supported Graham because they knew he would continue to support FEPC legislation. "WILLIS SMITH IS OPPOSED TO THE FEPC IN ANY AND EVERY WAY."

The ad went on to project a full panoply of horrors if FEPC were adopted and claimed that blacks would run FEPC because 88 percent of the FEPC work force established during World War II had been black. In addition, the Washington, D.C., police force would enforce the law and offenders would be presumed guilty. White unions, the ad argued, would be compelled to accept blacks as members under FEPC.[193]

This incendiary ad, although completely untrue, was highly effective, and some voters were swayed by this misinformation. Whatever its factual inaccuracies, white workers in North Carolina understood that the ads were a clear warning that federal influence in race relations was not too far in the future. The way to defeat or delay such Fair Deal interference was to elect a conservative like Willis Smith. In editorial commentary, the Charlotte *Observer* pointed out that a significant difference did exist between the FEPC positions of Smith and Graham. Graham would accept a noncompulsory FEPC, while Smith was opposed to FEPC, with or without teeth. Smith, the *Observer* believed, "knew that babes without teeth have a way of growing teeth. . . . The way to prevent that is to keep the baby from being born." Smith could accomplish that goal better than Graham, the paper argued.[194]

In the face of this racial hostility, the Graham organization did what it could, given the constraints under which it was functioning. It struggled to deflect the eleventh-hour Smith assault and pondered its response should the Smith faithful, as Graham's staff anticipated, try to intimidate blacks at polling places by asking them if they had paid their poll taxes.[195] The Raleigh headquarters tried to explain away the Supreme Court rulings, arguing that neither *Sweatt* nor *McLaurin* had struck down segregated education in North Carolina. These cases, Graham staffers wrote in a campaign statement, would have no effect on the pending North Carolina case, because North Carolina's segregated law school at Durham was fully accredited. The statement then concluded with a Graham quote again reaffirming the senator's opposition to federal force in the cause of desegregation.[196]

The pro-Graham press also got in a few last licks in the final seventy-two hours. The Raleigh *News and Observer* continued to lambaste Smith's campaign tactics, having already charged that the assault on Graham was designed to arouse the passions, furies, and fears of both whites and blacks. Smith's campaign, the "Old Reliable" had argued, was the "cold-blooded, advertising agency technique, employed to arouse prejudice for the purpose of reactionary politics . . . the naked program of the Dixiecrats."[197]

The Graham campaign also attempted to question Smith's activities in ads charging that the racial emphasis was a diversion from the real campaign issues. "WHY, MR. SMITH?", one of Graham's final ads demanded, "why do you attempt to fan the flames of race hatred?" Was Smith trying to conceal his nonparticipation in the fight for better schools? His opposition to a forty-cents-an-hour minimum wage? His absence from the fight for betterment of all people while he served his corporate clients? Did he really believe Tar Heels could be duped by such

"Talmadge tactics" to vote against their own best interests? Was Smith seeking to conceal that he was a reactionary who feared the future and the progressive programs of the Democratic party?[198] Another ad deplored that North Carolina had been dragged through the mud of hate and distortion in a desperate attempt to get votes. The ad concluded that the attacks on Graham were attacks on character, decency, and service, and they set class against class.[199]

From another direction, Jeff Johnson sought once again to tie Smith to the Republican party. He asserted that national Republican leaders had come to Smith's aid by sending a leaflet excerpting material from John T. Flynn's book *The Road Ahead*, mailed to North Carolinians under the frank of Republican Congressman Ralph W. Gwin. In addition, Johnson said he received continuing reports that northern Republicans were financing Smith, although he lacked conclusive evidence.[200]

Smith's backers had, from the outset, actively solicited support from author Flynn and a group called the Committee for Constitutional Government. Alvin Wingfield wrote Flynn in late March 1950: "Please give us any ideas you have. As you can see, we are a bunch of amateurs." Flynn immediately sent Wingfield selections from his speeches and information on Graham's affiliations with alleged Communist front groups.[201]

In his last rally, in High Point on June 23, Graham repeated for the final time his opposition to FEPC and socialism. As advocates pleaded his case on radio stations all over the state, he thanked the thousands who believed in him and had labored for him. To those who opposed him, Graham expressed "no ill will but rather an understanding of their rights in our democracy."[202] He made no reference to the personal abuses and insults visited upon him and Marian in the last days. He insisted to the end that he would rather not be in the Senate than attack his opponent or "exploit the race issue against the colored people." Nor did he ever display anger at the indignities directed at him. He did later confess that the racial controversy left him with a sense of hopelessness. He compared it to a forest fire; and once it was out of control, there was nothing he could do. Through it all, as one friend stated, he refused to consider the attacks a personal affront.[203]

While Graham's campaign ended on a subdued note, the Smith effort surged. During the final week, Smith backers flooded radio stations and newspapers with one ad after another. Several sources claimed that Smith had plenty of money—the essential ingredient—and was spending it all.[204] Hoover Adams confirmed that Smith forces spent huge sums in the last two weeks,[205] and Graham observers reported that in Wash-

(Political Advertisement)

Do You Want to Go Back to This?

HOOVERCARTS IN NORTH CAROLINA IN 1932

Fifteen million out of jobs!, Many homes and farms foreclosed! Thousands of Bank failures! 5-cent cotton! 10-cent tobacco! This was ended by Roosevelt Socialism! Truman Socialism!

GRAHAM vs. SMITH
The Deadly Parallel

GRAHAM—For 19 years as president of the University, headed State College and the Experiment Station, supported agriculture through the years.

GRAHAM—Candidate of Farmers, Labor and Little People of N. C.

GRAHAM—For Labor and record proves it, sponsored Workman's Compensation Act, Member National War Labor Board, Member War Emergency Board, Chairman Labor-Management Conference.

GRAHAM—A 40 year record of public service representing the weak, the underprivileged and little people of N. C.

GRAHAM—Headed a State-wide Campaign for a building program for State Institutions.

GRAHAM—40 years in the forefront of leadership for better schools, roads and hospitals.

GRAHAM—A great public servant who has devoted his life to the well being of others.

SMITH—No record whatsoever of interest in or support of agriculture.

SMITH—Candidate of Big Corporations, Money Interest and Special Privilege groups.

SMITH—Says he is for Labor but in 1947 appeared before Committee of the N. C. General Assembly—Fought a bill to increase Tar Heel workers to 40 cents per hour claiming that the bill was "harsh, unreasonable and unnecessary."

SMITH—Recognized throughout N. C. as a representative of big business corporations, moneyed interests and special privilege groups.

SMITH—No record of support or service to Good Health and Hospital program.

SMITH—Conspicuously absent for the past 19 years from groups, meetings and activities striving for improved schools and roads.

SMITH—A 19 year record since 1931 of being too busy representing Big Corporations, Moneyed Interests and Special Privilege groups

Graham forces attacked Smith in this ad as a secret Republican and warned Tar Heel voters that sending Smith to the Senate would mean a return to the days of the "Hoover Depression." The "deadly parallel" was found in a comparison of Smith's record in the service of corporate interests and Graham's record of service to the people. (Raleigh *News and Observer*, May 26, 1950)

ington, North Carolina, and elsewhere, the Smith forces were spending

more money and working harder than they had in May. In Forsyth County, a Graham partisan observed that while Graham's campaign lacked adequate money, "Smith had plenty."[206] On June 21, preparing for his initial television appearance in Greensboro, Smith flatly predicted victory—by a "good majority"—provided he got a "fair count," a statement that Jeff Johnson immediately characterized as a "slur on every election official in every precinct in North Carolina."[207]

In his boisterous final rally, held as in the beginning of the first primary at the Wake County courthouse, Smith touched all his political bases: FEPC, bloc voting, balanced budgets. State political dictators, he concluded, were trying to fool the people in this race, but the people of North Carolina would not be fooled.[208] In her speech of endorsement preceding Smith's final words, "Battlin' Nell" Lewis had proclaimed her intention to vote for a "man—not a god or a saint," in part because Smith would hold back the tide of socialism. The exuberant crowd cheered its assent, laughing repeatedly as an inebriated Smithite intermittently bellowed "Hold That Line."[209]

At last they would vote, it would soon be time to sweep up the paper and wait for the totals. Now it was time for the pundits to offer their final prognoses, to be read on voting day. They concluded that the election would be close. The race issue was the key, but Graham would win, Wade Lucas wrote, if his piedmont support offset Smith's strong eastern support.[210] Governor Scott, optimist and Graham loyalist to the end, anticipated a Graham victory margin of thirty-five thousand to fifty thousand votes, basing his prediction on a belief that Smith had overplayed the race issue and would be undone by a "boomerang" effect.[211]

But Smith workers, particularly county managers, understood that Smith had gained strength steadily. Prospects for victory in Buncombe County were good, one Smith manager reported,[212] while a Graham man in Avery County told Jeff Johnson that the Smith campaign had considerable money to spend and was putting it to good use.[213] Things looked so gloomy by the final day that even some of the Graham forces expected to lose.[214] Several newspapers, among them the pro-Smith Durham *Sun* and Raleigh *Times*, felt that North Carolinians did not believe Graham on FEPC and were angry about black bloc voting, and they forecast a Smith victory.[215] The Raleigh *News and Observer* made no prediction. But it reminded its readers that the election was a vote to determine if Frank Graham would receive justice or injustice from the state's voters. After this election, North Carolina would either go forward under a banner of enlightenment and tolerance or revert to prejudice and hatred.[216]

Election day temperatures matched the campaign's intensity— ninety-six degrees in some places—but over 550,000 Tar Heels cast ballots, a runoff primary record. Once again, with darkness, crowds gathered in the state's courthouses, now thick with cigarette smoke, perspiration, and chalk dust, as results were tabulated. Precinct workers busied themselves with the laborious task of hand-counting ballots.

From the beginning, the totals confirmed a monumental shift in voter allegiance. This time Smith took an early lead that he never relinquished. Graham was whipped, his brief senatorial career now brought to a painful close. Final official totals gave Smith 281,114 votes to Graham's 261,789. Smith won sixty-one of the state's one hundred counties.[217]

By 9:30 P.M., long before the unofficial returns were complete, the results were clear to the forces of both candidates, gathered again in the Sir Walter Hotel. Jubilant Smith backers shouted, whistled "Dixie," and exulted. Smith's lieutenants, family, and close friends waited in the Manteo Room for the now inevitable concession. "Tell ole' Kerr Scott to go to hell," shouted a few Smith diehards, while others sang, "We'll hang Dice Daniels from a sour apple tree, while we go marching on."[218]

Upstairs, on the sixth floor, Graham supporters choked back their bitter disappointment. Defeat was difficult to grasp and painful to accept. Shortly after 9:30 P.M., Graham came out of his room to face his anguished supporters. He mingled among them, embracing the women and encouraging the men. All were in tears except Graham, who had taken upon himself the task of comforting the aggrieved.

At 9:43 P.M., Graham, Jeff Johnson, and Bill and Mary Coker Joslin took the elevator down to Smith's headquarters to concede the election. As they approached the new senatorial nominee, Bill Joslin thought the attitude of Smith celebrants boisterous and hostile. Graham approached Smith, offered his hand, grinned, and congratulated his rival: "I wish you every success." Jeff Johnson simultaneously congratulated Charles Green. The two candidates then went out to meet photographers and Smith made a brief radio statement. He thanked his supporters and promised to carry out their wishes to the best of his ability. He knew he had Graham's good wishes, he stated, and hoped Graham knew that he had Smith's good wishes as well. To one eyewitness, Smith's statement was made in embarrassment and represented an apology to Graham for the bitterness of the campaign.[219] (But if so, these remarks were the only apology to Graham that Smith ever uttered.)

The concession ordeal concluded, Graham and his party returned to his headquarters. Only a few diehards tarried, and young William C. Friday, Graham's unofficial campaign aide, suggested that it was time for

Graham congratulates Smith on voting night. (North Carolina Department of
Archives and History, Raleigh)

Smith's backers exult in his amazing upset of the front-runner as they listen to
Smith thank his supporters and hail the successful defense of "southern traditions." (North Carolina Department of Archives and History, Raleigh)

everyone to go home. He drove Frank and Marian to her sister's Hillsboro residence, their North Carolina home since moving to Washington from the University of North Carolina president's house. They drove the entire trip in shocked silence—no postmortem, no lamentation, no anything. Friday walked the Grahams to the front steps of their Hillsboro quarters, and the defeated senator said: "Good night; I'll see you tomorrow."[220]

9 · Reflection

"Who Beat Frank Graham?"

For Graham stalwarts, the election's result brought a reckoning for which they were not prepared. Voter rejection of Frank Graham seemed to his supporters not only repudiation of a candidate they cherished but also acceptance of a race-based politics they loathed. "The evil genii of race prejudice are out of the bottle," D. Hiden Ramsey lamented to Chapel Hill *Weekly* editor Louis Graves. "The chances are that we will not get them back into the bottle in North Carolina for a long time. I fear we are in for a modified version of Bilboism."[1] Seeking to assuage their hurt and to understand the meaning of Smith's victory, Graham's discouraged army filled the mails with letters explaining the campaign to each other and extending emotionally charged commiserations. "Never forget," David M. McConnell counseled Senator Graham from his Charlotte law office, "you hold the devotion and homage of 262,000 North Carolinians. . . . In the first primary you received the greatest vote ever . . . by a North Carolinian in a political contest. . . . You are still a great North Carolinian and Southern political leader. . . . Your cause is still sacred to the hearts of tens of thousands in this state who came within the scope of your presence."[2]

"The primary brought a defeat," University of North Carolina student John Sanders reflected in a letter to Graham, "not for you or for the cause which you champion, but for the people of North Carolina, who, lacking the confidence of their own conviction, voted against their own best interests and the best interests of the nation."[3] In arguing that Graham had not lost, but that his defeat was instead a loss for the state at large, Sanders reflected a theme that many communicants to Graham repeated.

Hundreds of other citizens, distraught at Graham's rough treatment and anguished by his defeat, sought to reassure the senator that this setback had only nourished their affection for him. Typical was Judge Susie Sharp, who commented that Graham had shown the state that at least one person in politics "would rather be right than Senator. Some day the state may realize that yours was really the victory. At any rate, I would rather have lost with you."[4] "You stood up for the right and have been an inspiration to us all," Graham's old friend Francis O. Clarkson told him in October, as an "example of truly Christian charity and forgiveness."[5] "I weep," Lillian Turner wrote, not for the senator but "for the people of North Carolina . . . because they could be swayed by prejudices, lies, tactics which an intelligent people should . . . see through."[6] Such commiserations were joined by expressions of regret from a host of notables, among them George C. Marshall, Walter P. Reuther, and, in November 1950, Georgia Senator Richard B. Russell. Graham might have done some unwise things in his life, Russell wrote, but "I could never question your loyalty, patriotism and devotion to our . . . country."[7]

"It was a great fight," Governor Scott scrawled in a message to the senator on June 27. "The Supreme Court decision appearing at the time it did is what turned the tide against you. You did all you could. I'm naturally disappointed because I felt then and do now that N.C. and the U.S. needed your viewpoint."[8] And in December, Scott again paid tribute to Graham, expressing his appreciation that Graham had accepted the appointment "against your desire and preference." But Scott, given neither to introspection nor self-pity, remained unrepentant: if he had the chance, he would do it all again. "History," wrote Scott, "will record that a distinct gesture was made for representation on behalf of the masses of North Carolina."[9]

Publicly, Scott congratulated Smith and pledged his support in the November general election. More readily than any other Graham partisan, the governor mocked any appearance of postelection depression. "I've been in a lot of scraps," he reminded reporters. "It's not the first time I've been run over."[10] In western North Carolina for the annual "Singin' on the Mountain" immediately after the primary, Scott told the assembled throng, "I guess that after what happened to my friend Frank Graham, you think I'm up in these mountains looking for a place to hide, but it's not so. I never miss a chance to enjoy North Carolina's wonderful mountains."[11] A few days later, the irrepressible governor greeted reporters in his shirt sleeves, informing them, "I pulled off my coat just to show you that I had not lost my shirt."[12]

North Carolina would continue to "Go Forward," Scott pledged, in the Graham-Scott manner. He took credit for the large turnout in both primaries and claimed to have awakened the people to a heightened interest in their government. He reiterated that he did not regret the appointment. "I still think he's a good man and I still think there's a lot of misunderstanding by good people."[13]

His ebullience, however, did not mask Scott's anger at the tone of the campaign. At the annual convention of the state labor federation, which met in Winston-Salem in August, he denounced the state's white people for their part in the most bitter, racially charged campaign North Caro-

lina had seen in modern times. When black delegates applauded his
remarks, Scott turned to them and said: "I notice you colored brethren
clapping pretty hard, but you didn't do your part either. You may be
another color, but in this election you were just as yellow as the other
man"—an obvious reference to the meager black turnout. He reminded
his audience that a nation could never rise to its full height as long as its
politics were based on race prejudice.[14] As for Governor Scott, it was
clear that he would live to fight another day.

But not Jonathan Daniels. Stunned and deeply resentful of Graham's
defeat at the hands of race-baiters (and exasperated with Graham as
well), Daniels acknowledged that his views had been soundly repudiated.[15] On June 27, he wrote historian Frank Freidel that he had "just
gotten through probably the toughest political campaign I was ever
mixed up in and got badly beaten."[16] Yet he had no regrets, he wrote to
friends, and counseled as graceful an acceptance of the defeat as was
possible, while continuing to fight for the principles that had guided the
Graham campaign.[17] Nonetheless, the Graham defeat brought an end to
Daniels's brief role as an active politician. He would never again participate so directly in a North Carolina election. Hereafter, his influence
would stem principally from his command of the editorial desk at the
family newspaper, a role he would not fully relinquish until his retirement to Hilton Head, South Carolina, in 1968.[18] Unlike Governor Scott,
a thick-skinned career politician, Daniels found Graham's defeat to be a
chastening, indeed a humiliating experience, and he had no appetite for
further personal exposure to the rough and tumble of elective politics.

The other key campaign figure on the Graham side, Jeff Johnson, like
Scott a seasoned political operative, accepted defeat with the equanimity
one would expect of a veteran. He pointed his finger at no one on the
Graham side but instead wrote supporters statewide thanking them for
their help. He noted that in defeat Graham had garnered fifty-four
thousand more votes than had Senator Broughton in his 1948 victory
and forty-five thousand more than Governor Scott in his victory of the
same year. He regretted that the campaign had not achieved its ultimate
objective but saluted his associates nonetheless, telling them that they
"did a magnificent job in the face of rather unfortunate events and
unusual odds." Johnson characterized the opposition's methods as despicable and hoped there would be no recurrence. "I also sense emanating
from the ranks of the Smith people a feeling of apologetic guilt, which
may crystallize into something that will help in preventing a repetition of
Saturday's sorry performance," he concluded.[19] A number of Johnson's
campaign comrades wrote in response to assure him that Graham's

defeat in no way diminished Johnson. "You made a magnificent fight against overwhelming odds in the second campaign," Durham attorney Victor Bryant assured Johnson. "I want to congratulate you . . . on your fine conduct."[20] "You have no reason on earth to look back on this campaign with anything but satisfaction as to your part in it," echoed Frank Winslow. "Your fine work . . . opens up possibilities for you for which you are in my opinion well fitted. I hope you know what I mean. I am for you when the opportunity comes up."[21] Similarly, U.S. Eastern District clerk of the court A. Hand James told Johnson, "No other manager could have brought Senator Graham through the first campaign so well, or made the showing he made in the second primary. . . . Certainly Senator Graham's defeat does not in any way injure you. . . . I am for you and hope . . . our Party and our State [will] properly recognize your outstanding service."[22]

The Graham legions, of course, did more than commiserate. They analyzed the campaign and assessed its consequences. "The Supreme Court decision," Victor Bryant suggested, "couldn't have come at a worse time. In addition . . . the FEPC fight and other matters which paramounted the racial issue . . . reacted very strongly against Dr. Graham."[23] Bryant spoke for most Graham loyalists with these words, but others stressed the raw emotion the campaign unleashed. "People became inflamed and aroused," the Harnett County Superior Court clerk, Howard Godwin, reminded Johnson. "It was impossible to head off the stampede. . . . You could not reach them by appeals to reason, because there was no reason in them. You had as well try to beat out a forest fire with a pine bough."[24] Such observations stress the emergence of an early consensus that Graham was the victim of an unquenchable and irrational racial hysteria for which there was no rational remedy.

Some postmortems, however, while acknowledging the importance of racial issues, called attention to the significance of local questions. Had the contest been solely between Graham and Smith, Charlotte attorney Fred B. Helms counseled Graham, the senator would have "won in a walk." But in Mecklenburg County, "there was widespread opposition to the Truman Administration, in a congressional district that had voted for Republican Thomas E. Dewey in 1948." Mecklenburg, moreover, had been a stronghold of support for Scott's 1948 gubernatorial opponent, State Treasurer Charles Johnson. Johnson had taken Mecklenburg in both primaries. The county had also led the resistance to Scott's good roads program, Helms stated. Many Mecklenburg Republicans, Helms believed, had registered as Democrats to oppose Graham in the primaries.[25]

These private analyses accompanied endless rounds of press reviews and scrutiny, until finally the campaign became a centerpiece in North Carolina political folklore. Most dailies commented in several postelection editorials on various aspects of the campaign, and their political reporters did serial pieces dissecting it. In addition, columnists such as Lynn Nisbet and Tom Bost discussed the campaign's outcome for weeks. Coverage in national journals of opinion and national newspapers was likewise profuse.

The most heartfelt of the editorial assessments of the race, not surprisingly, came from the Raleigh *News and Observer*. In its initial response, the paper accepted the voters' decision but refused to regret its role in "the good fight for a great man." Summoning a theme that many would echo, the paper praised Graham for his gracious acceptance of defeat: "He will accept his defeat as he accepted the mudslinging against him, without once retaliating in kind or losing his temper." In short, if the campaign were a referendum on Graham's character, Graham had won the contest.[26] In defeat, Graham's Christian humility was victorious, as one *News and Observer* letter-writer suggested.[27]

Most of the analysis was less ethereal than Jonathan Daniels's original effort in the *News and Observer*. Indeed, Lowell Mellet, writing in the Washington, D.C., *Evening Star*, suggested that Graham's defeat was in large measure a consequence of his charitable character. The campaign in which Graham found himself, Mellet argued, could not be mastered by turning the other cheek. The attacks on Graham required spirited rebuttal and a willingness to rebuke the philosophy of the economic royalists opposing him. Graham should have defended the Roosevelt-Truman policies of the Democratic party, not apologized for them. The senator, Mellet contended, was not enough of a politician to turn Smith's arguments back on themselves.[28] The Greensboro *Daily News* agreed that Graham was undone, in part, by his "sweetness of character" as well as the restraint he placed upon his headquarters and "his failure to generate on his side anything like the emotionalism which entered into the opposition's presentation and appeal."[29] In short, Graham's campaign was pallid and continually defensive. Unquestionably, the state's black newspapers were more dismayed over Graham's loss—and the manner of it— than the white press, and they saw the campaign in starkly racial terms. "The torch of freedom has been snuffed out in North Carolina and there is a darkness all over the state," *Carolina Times* editor Louis Austin lamented. Racial hatred had defeated one of the "noblest, kindest, most loved . . . Christian gentlemen of our times." Even in defeat, however, there was hope. The 262,000 souls who voted for Graham would eventually increase in numbers and "light the torch that would send bright rays into this benighted state and teach men of all races to love each other."[30] *The Carolinian*, likewise dismayed, called Graham's loss a "jolting setback for the forces of liberalism in the South."[31]

From outside the state, journalists evaluated the campaign primarily in national terms but struck no immediate consensus. The New York *Times* saw in Graham's near victory a sign of growing liberalism in the state, an opinion few other papers endorsed.[32] The Richmond *Times-Dispatch* saw the result as a stunning rebuke to Harry Truman, his worst defeat since winning election in 1948. Graham's loss, the paper believed, would prove a turning point in the fate of the Fair Deal and had far-reaching implications for the presidential race two years hence.[33] The St. Louis *Globe-Democrat* and *Newsweek* concurred. Smith's victory was an emphatic repudiation of Truman welfarism.[34]

Smith forces and the victorious candidate himself did not, of course, accept the contention that Graham had been undone by an unconscionable racial assault. In the view of some Smith analysts, the second primary result merely confirmed their initial claim: Graham's political views were so at variance with mainstream political sentiment in North Carolina that, as voters came to understand those views, they rejected them and the candidate who advanced them. Granted, the Durham *Sun* observed in its primary reprise, Graham had repudiated a compulsory FEPC. "Perhaps he should have, if he conscientiously could have, repudiated *any* [*Sun*'s emphasis] FEPC."[35] Nor had Smith been guilty of raising the race issue. "The issue was raised by the Negroes," the *Sun* insisted. "They placed, and they still are placing, the whites on the defensive. A reaction is inevitable. They expect it and they expect many defeats before victory; and Dr. Graham was caught in the middle."[36]

On some questions, analysts from both sides agreed. The *Sun* stressed, for example, that the campaign meant a "direct rebuke to President Truman," and to "the ruthless partisanship and political opportunism of National Committeeman Daniels. . . . It was equally a vote of lack of confidence in arrogant Governor Scott."[37] All of these views, with slightly different emphases, could also be found among various Graham supporters.

In his immediate reaction to Smith's upset victory, Bob Thompson made no analysis. He simply exulted. Smith, Thompson proclaimed, was "a courageous battler who had won the greatest uphill fight in North Carolina political history." His victory was a vindication for all who abhorred the trend toward socialism and resented Scott-Daniels machine politics. Graham, a good and sincere man, stood repudiated by the state he loved.[38]

"Down East," the Elizabeth City *Daily Advance* emphasized the specific subject of a federally empowered FEPC as a major campaign question, paired with Willis Smith's moderate stand on the issues. Voters also objected to Scott's attempt to force Graham down their throats, the paper contended. The Fayetteville *Observer* likewise argued that voters resented Scott's heavy-handed machine effort on Graham's behalf and the accompanying activities of the CIO and the NAACP. North Carolina was a free state and "not a trained animal in anybody's political circus," the *Observer* admonished.[39]

With slightly more reserve, the Charlotte *News*, which had not expected Smith to win, remarked that his victory meant a return to the progressive conservatism that had characterized state government for several decades prior to the Scott upheaval. The *News* praised Smith as a "bigger man, and a better man, than he has sometimes appeared in the glare of a hot political fight." The paper hoped that the excesses of the bitter campaign would be quickly forgotten and harmony restored.[40]

It was a forlorn hope. Intermittently through the summer of 1950, the opposing camps traded blame for the campaign's excesses. Stung by the assertion of the Greensboro *Daily News* that North Carolina had regressed to "Deep South" status in its race relations, that visions of Bilbo and Talmadge now bestrode the state—and similar pronouncements by his journalistic adversaries—Bob Thompson challenged the papers' interpretation of the Senate primary.

Thompson acknowledged that race had played a big part, as the *Daily News* had argued on August 17. But not in the way the paper meant. Both sides had emphasized race, Thompson maintained. In the first primary, Smith had attacked Graham's political record and philosophy—his left-wing affiliations, his racial views, FEPC, and the Leroy Jones affair—without much success. That lack of success was highlighted by the fact that Graham won thirty-two eastern counties where racial issues were supposed to benefit Smith.

Simultaneously, Thompson argued, the Graham forces had used the race issue astutely. Following his pattern in the Broughton 1948 Senate race, Jeff Johnson had encouraged blacks to register and vote in the upcoming primary, and black leaders themselves had initiated "the greatest political organizing of Negroes this state has ever witnessed." Thompson maintained that "a great deal of it was under cover," citing the *Carolina Times's* eleventh-hour endorsement of Graham as proof. "It was the cleverest use of the race issue the state has ever seen. And it was used for Graham, not against him," Thompson argued. Moreover, it came within a hairsbreadth of giving Graham a first primary victory on the strength of black ballots.[41]

In the second primary, Thompson continued, "a series of events . . . caused the Graham use of the race issue to backfire": the Supreme Court rulings and the state NAACP convention, where blacks bragged that they had been the margin in Graham's first primary lead. Consequently, white voters reacted in the second primary, according to Thompson, especially in those thirty-two eastern counties, only nine of which stayed with Graham. "That, in a nutshell, was the part the race issue played in North Carolina," Thompson concluded. The black vote was twice as large as it had ever been before, proof that "there was no effort of any proportion to deprive the Negro citizens of their right to vote or to scare them away from the polls, as has occurred so often in the Deep South."[42]

Such an interpretation has been advanced by many Smith supporters. It has been repeated by both William T. Joyner, Jr., and Jesse Helms.[43] The analysis may be useful to convince Smith advocates that they did not use racial issues in an unfair or unethical fashion or to deflect criticism of the despicable race-baiting tactics employed against Graham, but as an explanation of the campaign, it is unconvincing. Its basic premise leads to the conclusion that any participation by black voters in North Carolina politics, in and of itself, raised the race issue in the same sense that the Leroy Jones affair or Graham's serving on the Truman Committee on Civil Rights was a racial question. Presumably, in Thompson's interpretation, the only way that blacks could vote in North Carolina elections without raising a racial issue would be to divide their votes for candidates precisely in the same proportions that white voters would do. When black citizens voted on the basis of racial questions—issues of obvious vital concern to them—they were abusing the democratic process, according to this position. Finally, Thompson's claim that black voters were neither intimidated nor discriminated against in their efforts to register and vote in many areas of North Carolina in 1950 is simply incorrect. In eastern North Carolina, blacks were too often barred from registering to vote, and numerous incidents of discrimination were reported in this campaign, as we have seen.

The victorious candidate, Willis Smith, wasted little time in postprimary analysis. Exhausted from the physical and emotional ordeal of the campaign,[44] Smith extended his thanks publicly and privately to those who had helped him, expressing his gratitude for their willingness to "Stand Up and Be Counted."[45] Addressing the state American Legion Convention in Charlotte three days after the primary, he stated that even though his wife "didn't like a lot of the things that were said about me" in the campaign, he harbored no ill feeling. He attributed his victory to the public protest against socialism and bloc voting by "certain groups," an example of controlled voting that North Carolinians resented. He also argued that his campaign organization had simply outhustled his opponent's forces. Finally, he believed that voters had been troubled by the prospect of a federal FEPC and by the recent federal Court decisions.[46] Beyond these general observations, Smith discussed the campaign very little. His comments, however, were more extensive than Frank Graham's public utterances.

Graham made no public analysis, in sharp contrast to his effusiveness at the time of his appointment. He did discuss the matter privately upon his return to the Senate in conversation with concerned Senate colleagues. An enterprising reporter pieced the conversations together to obtain a fairly clear picture of Graham's impression of his defeat. He told friends that he was beaten in the last days of the campaign by a "three-day blitz of racial propaganda" that depicted him as condoning the immediate obliteration of the color line in the South. When asked why he made no effort to counter the attacks, Graham replied, "I did not want to bring the racial issue into my own campaign." He discounted the importance of his many left-wing affiliations and observed that Smith had been aided by nearly unlimited financial resources. These remarks were the most extensive analysis of the campaign Graham ever offered, although in later years he discussed it freely, stating in 1969 that he had not taken Smith's attacks seriously.[47]

This assortment of inchoate theories and assessments, resulting from a hodgepodge of events, personalities, and opinions, were but obvious reflections of the tensions and powerful emotions the campaign had unleashed. But an enterprising and astute political journalist, Samuel Lubell, provided an arresting analysis in his book, *The Future of American Politics*, soon after the campaign ended. First published in 1951, following publication of portions of the book in *Look* magazine, Lubell's treatment quickly became the campaign's standard interpretation. Every writer who has touched on the Smith-Graham race since Lubell has relied heavily—often exclusively—on Lubell's analysis.

At the time of the primary, Samuel Lubell was launched on a major research project, seeking to explain the fundamental configuration of politics in the post–World War II United States. Indeed, Lubell intended to explain to Americans the impact that Franklin Roosevelt and a Democratic majority had made on the political culture of the United States. For a later political scholar, Lubell's subject might sound unoriginal—even clichéd—but in the shadow of Truman's amazing victory in 1948, Lubell's project seemed a fresh and intriguing enterprise.

Lubell became engrossed in the Smith-Graham primary because he

was convinced—even before the results were known—that the outcome
of the race would signal the future path of southern politics. And the
future path of southern politics, Lubell maintained, would determine
whether the emerging political strength of black voters would be a
divisive or a unifying force, not only within the Democratic party but
within the nation as a whole.[48] This process—the development of black
political strength as a regional and national force and the associated
struggle for black rights in the South—Lubell identified as one of eight
trends shaping postwar politics in the United States. Hence, for Samuel
Lubell, the question of "Who Beat Frank Graham?"—the subtitle of his
section on southern politics—was an inquiry of some moment.

Lubell was convinced that the postwar South was in the midst of a
social and economic revolution as it was rapidly urbanizing and rapidly
industrializing—hardly a prophetic insight in 1951. But the industrial
boom, Lubell insisted, was making the South more, not less, conservative. This burgeoning conservatism explained the failure of the CIO's
"Operation Dixie" (an effort to organize the southern textile industry),
signaled the rise of a new politically insurgent urban middle class, and
generated the paradox of emerging black voting strength coupled with an
intensification of the race issue as a political controversy. "The swirling of
these three trends was primarily responsible for the defeat in 1950 of
Senators Frank P. Graham . . . and Claude Pepper . . . , the most crushing
setbacks Southern liberalism has suffered since the coming of Franklin
Roosevelt," Lubell concluded.[49]

Graham's defeat was the more spectacular, Lubell wrote. Graham had
been the most visible symbol of southern liberalism throughout his
distinguished public career, including his membership on Truman's
Committee on Civil Rights. Moreover, North Carolina had long been
heralded as the southern state with the most enlightened race relations, a
reputation the first primary result seemed to confirm. Then came the
Supreme Court decisions and a last-minute racial blitz, which Lubell
detailed in gripping fashion. These events combined to unseat Scott's
appointee.

Having been in the state during and after the primaries, Lubell attributed Graham's loss to two "dramatic" reversals from the first primary: the
desertion by white voters in the eastern counties, heavily populated with
nonvoting blacks, and a major shift away from Graham in North Carolina cities.[50] It was these urban rebels, Lubell wrote, who voted against
Graham in Charlotte and Mecklenburg County. Evidence of this burgeoning conservatism could be found in areas such as affluent Myers
Park in Charlotte, where Graham got only 25 percent of the vote.[51] In

the tension between these urban insurgents and the growing political strength of blacks, Lubell believed, the political future of the South would be determined. It was this tension that had fixed the fate of Frank Graham.

Lubell's analysis, for all of its dramatic urgency, cannot withstand close examination. His major thesis explaining Graham's defeat is incorrect: its explanation of race as a fundamental issue of the campaign is imprecise, and its understanding of the changing currents of factional politics within the state—and their impact on the Smith-Graham race—is largely undeveloped. No mention is made of Graham's public career prior to his appointment as a possible political liability. Finally, Lubell simply ignores the residual conservative strength (both Democratic and Republican) in North Carolina that was a shaping element of the state's political life in the years 1932–50 (and beyond).[52] Even so, the superficial argument that Graham was undone by little more than a spewing forth of racial bile upon an unsuspecting electorate forms a principal theme of Lubell's interpretation. Equally important, the argument squares nicely with the view most Graham partisans have advanced over the years.

The conservative "revolution" that undid Frank Graham was, in fact, largely a Lubell invention. North Carolina Democrats were undoubtedly "conservative," a political stance they had maintained for most of the first half of the twentieth century. They were, in short, southern Democrats. They were not opposed to New Deal largesse—price supports for agriculture, federal grants for school construction, and many other federal assistance measures. Nor were they opposed to a Democratically controlled Congress that kept Tar Heel representatives in positions of power on Capitol Hill. As part of the New Deal coalition that reshaped the Democratic party, Tar Heel voters gave Franklin Roosevelt their enthusiastic endorsement every time they had the chance. But New Deal sentiment in North Carolina peaked in 1936, when the Gardner political organization (V. O. Key's "progressive plutocracy") fought back a fierce challenge from insurgent Ralph McDonald, who had appealed for "a New Deal for North Carolina." McDonald's opponent in that gubernatorial election was Clyde R. Hoey, Gardner's brother-in-law, who beat McDonald in a bitter two-primary race.[53] The Gardner organization thereafter held sway in North Carolina politics until 1948, when Kerr Scott, in another two-primary fight, surprised Charles Johnson and was elected governor.[53] Hence, Smith's victory in 1950 can more appropriately be seen as a triumph of tradition over insurgency—and a Scott insurgency at that—although not as a revival of the Gardner organization.

In short, Lubell had it backward. North Carolina never embraced the New Deal as completely as Lubell believed, a point V. O. Key had established in 1949, in his classic work, *Southern Politics in State and Nation*. If any kind of conservative revolution was underway in North Carolina in 1950, its evidence could be found in the defection of some conservative "Dewey Democrats" who had voted for Republican Thomas E. Dewey in 1948 and were contemplating Republican registration.

The extent of the Scott insurgency, moreover, should be fully comprehended. Kerr Scott, as we have seen, clearly intended to reshape the Democratic party in North Carolina. With the exception of one member, he made a clean sweep of the State Highway Commission[54] and appointed a new state director of purchasing, a new highway patrol commander, a new director of the budget, and a new director of the state parole commission, to mention but four of the key posts to which he sent his allies. One additional example provides clear evidence of Scott's thoroughness. He named David Coltrane, "an old crony from Scott's days as Commissioner of Agriculture," to be assistant budget director, after first firing Robert G. Deyton. Deyton had been a state employee since 1927 and had occupied the budget post for twelve years before Scott ousted him. D. Hiden Ramsey observed privately in late July 1949 that Scott was throwing out of office all who opposed him in the 1948 election, without regard for their qualifications. He was a vindictive man, Ramsey charged, and sooner or later there would be "a revulsion of public sentiment" against these firings.[55]

The governor also instituted a widespread purge of the nonpaid positions on fifty-four state boards, a vivid illustration of the extent of his insurgency. To say that this use of the governor's appointive powers generated resentment is an understatement, similar to suggesting that political considerations had some influence on new highway construction.[56] Graham's appointment needs to be understood in this context, because many party regulars who were dismayed at the governor's vigorous assertion of his appointive privileges saw his appointment of Frank Graham as the final insult. And their anger was intensified because the appointment of Graham was astute in its ability to divide the remnants of the Gardner organization itself, many of whose supporters voted for Graham out of personal admiration.

Lubell and most other scholars have largely ignored these factional struggles, which were a vital component of the forces working against Graham in both primaries. Scott's opponents, in other words, had powerful evidence to suggest that the governor intended to control the state's politics and move it to the left. Equally important, of course, Scott's bid had come just as the Gardner faction in North Carolina politics was disintegrating. Specifically, the 1948 elections had represented what would prove to be the Gardner organization's last hurrah, for neither victorious statewide candidate in that year, Scott nor Senator Broughton, was a Gardner loyalist. Nor were they political allies. The defeat of Charles Johnson for governor and William B. Umstead for senator left only Senator Hoey to uphold the Gardner tradition.

This struggle between Scott and his conservative opponents resulting in Scott's surprising emergence therefore provides a persuasive rebuttal to the Lubell argument that Graham's defeat came primarily from a conservative revolution that was overwhelming North Carolina and sweeping New Dealers from office. Further, the pattern of Graham's support in the first primary and the shift away from Graham in the second suggest a more fundamental issue at work in the Smith-Graham primary than Lubell or Graham supporters fully comprehended.

Viewed sectionally, Graham's May 27 plurality revealed statewide support for his candidacy. His strong showing in both the east and west defied the traditional division in North Carolina voting. Even though the Gardner family could not persuade the voters (especially mill workers) of Cleveland County to go with Graham, the western counties—what V. O. Key called the highlands—gave Graham an enthusiastic endorsement. Graham led in fourteen of the seventeen highland counties in the May 27 balloting and won a clear majority of votes, 35,316, compared to a combined total for his three opponents of 30,734. Smith finished a distant second with 18,600, while Reynolds, largely on the vote in his native Buncombe County, was a strong third with 11,561.[57]

In the piedmont, Graham's performance was less impressive, even though he received a plurality of votes. He led the ticket in twenty-two of the forty piedmont counties and got a majority of the votes in such populous counties as Guilford, Forsyth, and Durham. But he lost to Smith in Mecklenburg and barely carried Smith's home county of Wake. In total, Graham polled 157,392 votes in the piedmont to his opponents' combined total of 169,036, of which 137,330 were for Smith.[58]

It was in the east—the coastal plain and tidewater—where Graham scored the victory that most surprised his contemporaries. The region was, of course, strongly pro-Scott. Here were many of the farmers the governor had promised to "get out of the mud" with his good roads program. "Eastern North Carolina," according to Key, included, and extended well beyond, that group of counties "south of the Virginia border and west of Albemarle Sound that was the traditional center of Democratic insurgency in North Carolina."[59] It was, in addition, the

section of North Carolina with the highest percentage of black population, although black political participation in most of these counties was
severely limited. This combination of political insurgency and a high
percentage of black residents was, of course, a southern anomaly that
distinguished the Tar Heel "black belt" from the black belt regions of the
deep South, or even from the political alignment in neighboring Virginia.
The anomaly explains why pundits believed Graham's eastern support
was suspect and perhaps not transferable from Governor Scott. But in the
first primary, easterners gave Graham their warm endorsement. He carried twenty-seven of these forty-three overwhelmingly rural counties,
and his vote dispelled his campaign staff's greatest fear: that Governor
Scott's eastern support would not attach to an avowed racial liberal,
specifically Frank Graham. In fact, Graham polled 110,897 votes and
lacked only 2,103 ballots of having a clear majority in the region. Smith
was a weak second, with 94,292 votes. There were sixteen counties in
this region in which Smith led all candidates.[60]

The first primary, therefore, seemed an effective rejection of Smith
campaign strategy. Graham had run strong statewide and seemed invul-
nerable. Such a performance explains Smith's reluctance to challenge
Graham again. It was a sound and entirely understandable reaction to the
first primary results. Graham's strength also explains why many Graham
supporters refused throughout the second primary excesses to believe
that Smith could possibly overtake Senator Graham.

Graham's strength, nonetheless, could not be sustained. Only in the
west did his June 24 showing resemble his first primary performance. Of
the sparsely populated highland counties, Graham carried twelve and
lost five, a net loss of only two counties from his first primary performance. Moreover, with Reynolds removed from the ballot, Graham actually improved his margin of victory in the west, outpolling Smith by
30,769 to 20,499. Only the turnout in the west disappointed the Graham camp. The number of voters declined by 14,782, a turnout rate only
77.6 percent of the first primary total. On May 27, 66,050 ballots were
reported and only 51,268 were reported on June 24.[61] The decline in
turnout was especially damaging because Graham's runoff margin over
Smith was much larger than his first primary margin over Smith and
Reynolds.

It is probable that many of those westerners who sat out round two
were Reynolds backers. The Buncombe County turnout, for example,
declined by 8,673 votes (34.5 percent less than the May vote), as only
16,496 people voted after Reynolds's name was off the ballot. It seems
likely, therefore, that many of Reynolds's voters made their mark on the

runoff by abstention. The poor turnout in the west suggests the failure of either Smith or Graham to convert Reynolds's supporters.[62]

Graham's most serious second primary troubles, therefore, began in the piedmont, although here Graham's forces were able to contain their candidate's slippage. He lost a total of seven counties that he had won on May 27, including Wake, which now went decidedly for Smith. But he actually trailed Smith by only 8,514 votes out of 297,132 cast in the piedmont. Turnout in the piedmont for the second primary was heavy, 91.02 percent of the first primary totals. (The Scott-Johnson gubernatorial runoff in 1948 had generated statewide a turnout that was 94.6 percent of the first primary totals, a runoff record.)[63] Thus, Graham lost some ground on June 24 but experienced no catastrophic decline in the piedmont, where he had lukewarm support in both primaries. In mill precincts and in conservative areas such as Charlotte and Mecklenburg County, he fared badly.[64]

It was in the east, then, that Graham lost the election. Seventeen of the twenty-seven counties he had carried in May now voted for Smith. Of the forty-three tidewater and coastal plain counties, Graham could carry only ten. In the east, Graham's total shrank by 24,186 votes from May 27, while Smith's total surged by 13,505, from 94,292 on May 27 to 107,797 on June 24. Smith thus carried the east by 21,086 votes—almost precisely his statewide victory margin. In contrast, on May 27 Graham had outpolled Smith by 16,605 ballots. Graham went from a lead of 16,605 in May to a deficit of 21,086 in June, a critical loss of votes from which his middling piedmont showing and disappointing highlands turnout could not save him.[65] The vote in the east was 86.07 percent of its total in the first primary, a respectable turnout figure for a second primary but almost 5 percent lower than in the piedmont. The lower turnout suggests that Graham's eastern support in the second primary was complacent, perhaps because some eastern voters reacted to the racial invective by staying away from the polls. In contrast, Smith enthusiasts rallied to their candidate.

Such an analysis leaves little room for Samuel Lubell's "middle class conservative revolution" in the piedmont. It does suggest that piedmont voters were, from the beginning, divided over Graham's candidacy and over the Scott administration's policies—especially in those counties west of Davidson. Such a division means that through the first primary, the Graham-Smith results were a tribute to Governor Scott's grip on the east and Graham's personal popularity in the piedmont and especially in the highlands where Scott was not popular.

The second primary, however, departs significantly from the pattern of

Maps depicting primary vote by county and region.

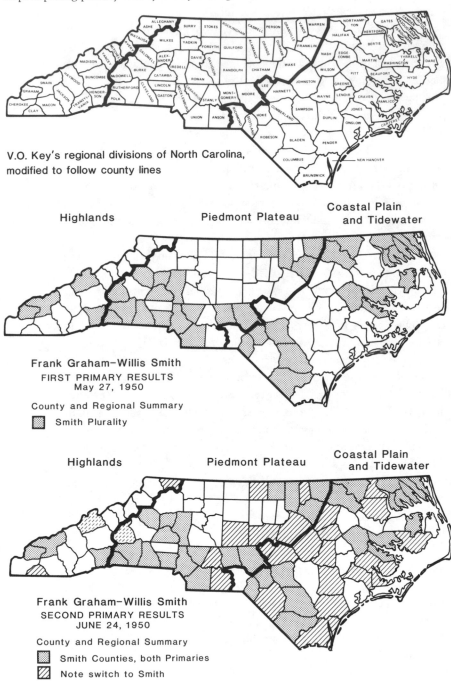

V.O. Key's regional divisions of North Carolina, modified to follow county lines

Highlands   Piedmont Plateau   Coastal Plain and Tidewater

Frank Graham–Willis Smith
FIRST PRIMARY RESULTS
May 27, 1950

County and Regional Summary

Smith Plurality

Highlands   Piedmont Plateau   Coastal Plain and Tidewater

Frank Graham–Willis Smith
SECOND PRIMARY RESULTS
JUNE 24, 1950

County and Regional Summary

Smith Counties, both Primaries

Note switch to Smith

Switch to Graham

conventional state politics in the immediate postwar era. A statistical illustration makes the point. Of the forty-five North Carolina counties with a black population of 30 percent or more, Graham won twenty-three on May 27 and nine on June 24. Of the twenty-three counties with 45 percent or more black population, Graham carried nine on May 27 and three on June 24.[66] The obvious conclusion, therefore, would be that the second primary was "about race." In Samuel Lubell's analysis, the contest was about the growing political strength of black voters, the defection of middle-class white voters in the piedmont, and the revolt against Graham in the east.

But Graham's showing in the piedmont counties, as already seen, suggests a limited desertion by middle-class whites. Many continued to support Graham because they admired his character, even if they disagreed with him on some issues. His principal problem in the piedmont was his poor showing among blue-collar whites, as in Cabarrus, Cleveland, and Rutherford counties, which he lost to Smith 10,413 to 17,738, and as in rural piedmont counties such as Caswell, Person, and Granville, which he lost to Smith 4,123 to 7,380 votes. In Forsyth, Guilford, and Durham counties, with large middle-class—and black—voting populations, Graham held his first primary leads, although by smaller margins.[67]

To suggest, therefore, that the primary was "about race" is to state the obvious and to beg the question. More precisely, what racial questions shaped this contest? What were the implications of this campaign for North Carolina politics—and perhaps for the upper South as well—as the 1950s began?

First, it is helpful to see this contest as, in reality, two distinct elections. On May 27, North Carolina voters conducted a referendum on the character of Senator Frank Graham and on the nature of his Senate appointment and his ties to Kerr Scott, Jonathan Daniels, and—more obliquely—the Truman administration. Despite Willis Smith's concerted effort to question Graham's political judgment, as revealed by his numerous left-wing associations, and to suggest that Graham's views were incompatible with mainstream North Carolina, over 49 percent of the electorate affirmed their approval of Frank Graham's character, if not his politics. They saw no threat in his continued presence in the U.S. Senate.

Yet Graham's first primary plurality did not represent voter approval of all his policy positions. Many Tar Heels voted for Graham because their approval of his character overrode their disagreement with him on policy questions. Conversely, many who opposed Graham insisted that they retained their affection for him. When an elderly woman stopped Smith publicist Hoover Adams on the street in Dunn and asked how he could campaign against the saintly "Dr. Frank," Adams replied: "I love and admire Dr. Graham. In fact, I love and respect my mother, but I wouldn't vote for her for U.S. Senate."[68] Such divided loyalties suggest that Graham's first primary lead was softer than almost anyone realized. Should the Smith camp succeed in its quest for an issue, Graham would be in trouble in a second primary.

Had Graham run a more skillful campaign—had he been a more effective campaigner—he could have won a majority on May 27 and eliminated the possibility of a runoff. His inept performance is a little-bruited subject, however, because his friends always sought to shield him from the truth of his political shortcomings and his opponents wanted to believe that his defeat was exclusively a product of their exceptional political skills. Hence, his willful refusal to accept the advice of his politically experienced friends (to resign his memberships in controversial organizations and to make his opinion on cloture public) and his determination to ignore ethical political conventions that would help his campaign (soliciting funds and asking for voters' support) played a critical role in the election's outcome.

Even with the campaign's many problems, and the candidate's other-worldly approach to politics, Graham came about as close to winning outright as was arithmetically possible. Observers and participants over the years have pointed to a variety of factors—some convincing and some fanciful—that could have turned the election in Graham's favor. (As with any election, of course, the closer the contest, the greater the elements on which the election "could have turned.")

Some people have stressed the cost of Graham's mid-May illness that idled him at the first primary's climax. Others have blamed his political inexperience, an inept staff, critical money problems, and sense of over-confidence. Any one of these reasons could have denied him the 5,634 votes he needed for a first primary majority. Other analysts point to Bob Reynolds's presence as greatly complicating Graham's election task, while some remember Graham's inexplicable vacillation on the cloture question as devastating to his cause. A number of participants believe the Leroy Jones and FEPC matters did Graham much harm, and others point to resentment at the heavy-handed support of the Scott administration and the Raleigh *News and Observer*'s abandonment of any pretense of objectivity in its campaign coverage. And, of course, Dave Burgess and other labor officials always believed the failure to run a candidate against Hoey was a major misjudgment. Further, some have faulted labor's high-profile support for Graham as damaging to his candidacy and have held that labor simply could not deliver a vote in North Carolina large enough

to offset resentment against its partisan participation. Finally, some contemporaries agree with Ben Dixon McNeill, writing from Cape Hatteras
to Daniels after the election: "If Frank Graham had, just once, riz up and
called Willis Smith a so and so—he would have been nominated."[69] In
other words, Graham would not fight.

Some of these musings are simply baseless. The effect of Graham's
illness, for example, may have been to create voter sympathy. In addition, the substitutes who filled in while Graham was sick were effective
campaigners. Also Graham did not lack for money. As we have seen, he
had enough money to win, including generous out-of-state contributions. His staff problems, moreover, did not cost him the election. Jeff
Johnson was a seasoned and effective manager, aided by a legion of
people statewide for whom politics was second nature: L. P. McLendon,
Jr., David M. McConnell, Edgar Broadhurst, Kemp Battle, William Joslin,
R. Mayne Albright, Terry Sanford, and Charles and Gladys Tillett—the
list goes on and on. In his support, one could also find most of the state's
large dailies, in Raleigh, Greensboro, Winston-Salem, Durham, and
Asheville. Many other papers were officially neutral, the Goldsboro
News-Argus, for example, while the pro-Smith Charlotte Observer was
scrupulously objective in its news coverage and did not endorse Smith
until the second primary. Graham had persistent detractors, of course:
the Raleigh Times, the Durham Sun, the Fayetteville Observer, and the
High Point Enterprise. In number and readership, however, they were no
match for the pro-Graham press.

Perhaps the hoariest legend of this campaign is the idea expressed
above by Ben Dixon McNeill: that Graham paid dearly for never attacking Smith. Graham did not, it is true, personally assail Smith for the
charges leveled against him, nor was the invective used against Smith's
platform equal in fury to the basest charges hurled at Graham. But
Graham consistently and vigorously defended his record, albeit in very
general terms. Equally important, his campaign staff and his prominent
supporters continually pummeled Smith. They tried to belittle his Virginia birth, and they charged him with being antilabor and opposed to
decent factory wages. They mocked his professional accomplishments,
ridiculed (and overstated) his self-made wealth, and condemned his
success as an attorney. They also attacked his professional integrity in the
Morehead City bankruptcy proceedings, called him a closet Republican
(strong words in North Carolina in 1950), and accused him of being
opposed to improved race relations. And they put all the blame for the
dirt hurled at Graham on Smith personally. Except on a few private

occasions and once publicly, Graham did not rebuke his troops in their attempted defamation of Smith. Even when Graham did so, his remonstrances were routinely disregarded.

Far more substantial than these arguments is the claim that Bob Reynolds's presence on the ballot denied Graham a first primary victory. A Graham-Smith contest would have been a clear mismatch that Graham would have won handily, but Reynolds's 58,752 votes deprived Graham of a first ballot majority. In addition, Graham's indecision on cloture was harmful to his cause. Senator Hoey had thought the issue worth fifty thousand votes, although such a view cannot be tested. There is universal agreement, however, that the cloture question made FEPC a more potent issue and hampered the Graham campaign.[70] The Leroy Jones incident likewise confirmed some voters' suspicions that Graham was soft on segregation. When combined with the charges relating to Graham's activist past—and the hostility directed toward Governor Scott— enough opposition coalesced to block a first primary victory for Graham but not to prevent an impressive lead in the voting. The Graham performance, moreover, profoundly dismayed the Smith people, who thought, as did their candidate, that they would lead or win the May 27 vote outright.

In addition, although Governor Scott's involvement undoubtedly hurt Graham in the western piedmont—where Charles Johnson had beaten Scott badly in 1948—his vigorous assistance gave Graham a needed boost in the east. As for Jonathan Daniels, his high profile undoubtedly cost Graham some votes, but Daniels was far enough removed from the campaign that his role did not become a critical campaign issue. Nonetheless, Scott's and Daniels's visible presence animated Graham adversaries who resented what they regarded as a clumsy and unwarranted intrusion into the Senate race. Newspaper accounts and private correspondence attest that many people feared the creation of a "liberal triumvirate" of Scott, Daniels, and Graham. Some observers even believed that the open involvement of Scott and Daniels caused some of Graham's friends to desert the senator.[71]

Overconfidence, as Jeff Johnson had feared, loomed large as a problem for Graham, especially once the results of the first primary were in. Many supporters believed that Smith simply could not overcome Graham's commanding lead, no matter what he did. Graham could not lose.[72] Even Jonathan Daniels admitted that he was surprised at Graham's loss, because he did not think that a campaign such as Smith's could succeed in North Carolina.[73] The Graham camp simply could not convince some supporters that the campaign might be in peril, even at the height of the second primary frenzy, which may help explain why the total vote declined by 75,566 in the second primary.

Whether a Scott-backed opponent for Hoey would have helped Graham is impossible to say. A "nuisance candidate" would have had little effect on the Smith-Graham race, and a strong candidate—Capus Waynick, for example—might have drained as many resources from Graham as from Smith in an almost certain losing effort against the popular Hoey. As we have seen, in this race there was no clear Hoey-Smith connection. Many of Smith's prominent supporters were not major players in the Gardner-Hoey faction in North Carolina politics, even though they were Hoey admirers, and the old Gardner group was split beyond recognition in this race. Some were strong for Graham, a few worked hard for Smith, and many others participated in this contest only as voters. Perhaps Dave Burgess was correct in his judgment that competition against Hoey would have benefited Graham, in part by blurring the focus of the campaign, but no one can know. Moreover, some able politicians, among them the governor himself, vetoed the idea as unsound. They reasoned that Graham, Scott, and Daniels had their hands full running one race, although the outcome of the second primary left at least Daniels questioning the wisdom of their decision.[74]

Graham's labor support also proved to be more harmful than helpful. Labor did not work hard enough in the first primary, Dave Burgess explained, and "failed to help the Negro leaders in time." As a consequence, Burgess maintained, black turnout was disgracefully low, a widely held view among Graham people.[75] Other Graham supporters complained that labor's support was poorly coordinated and often counterproductive. "Labor organizations were operating independent of your County Manager," Wilmington attorney Edgar L. Yow informed Jeff Johnson in a late June reprise, and labor refused to accept any supervision from Graham's New Hanover County headquarters, even though the Graham organization in New Hanover "welcomed . . . and invited their cooperation." During the final days of the runoff, Yow reported that "a white woman working under the auspices of the PAC [Political Action Committee] was openly soliciting Negro votes," an action Yow dubbed ill-advised and "absolutely unnecessary." Black voters were already committed to Graham, Yow argued, and while the incident did not do great damage (by alienating whites), it was an indication of labor's failure to exercise good judgment.[76] Labor's endorsement, Samuel Lubell concluded in an article in *Look* magazine, was the "kiss of defeat" in North Carolina, especially when racial issues turned mill workers away from labor's man.[77] Yet labor involvement did not cost Graham the election.

The black vote in this campaign, on the other hand, was potentially a clinching element. Estimates of black turnout vary widely, from as high as 100,000 to a low of 20,000 in the first primary. All were far from Kelly M. Alexander, Jr.'s, publicly declared intention in the spring of 1950 that the state NAACP would register 250,000 black voters. In fact, black turnout in both primaries was, as labor sources acknowledged, disappointingly low. The black vote, Jeff Johnson wrote in August 1951, had been greatly exaggerated. Johnson estimated that it was "consistently short of 50,000 votes, and was much lighter in the second than first primary." The bulk of the votes was cast in a few cities—Durham, Raleigh, Greensboro, Charlotte, and Asheville—Johnson reported, while in the east, the black vote was negligible: "just enough to give a touch of reality to the scare campaign and stir to fever heat the racial emotions of those most susceptible to such." One had to distinguish, Johnson remarked, between registration and voting. Many more blacks registered than actually entered polling booths in senatorial primaries. "As voting day draws near," Johnson wrote, "they [black voters] can sense and feel resistance developing," which induced insecurity and frustration, especially in those areas where blacks had only recently voted in Democratic primaries. Hence, Johnson believed that blacks played a minor role as voting participants, although the Smith forces stressed the strong black support for Graham—as bloc voting—with much effectiveness, notably in the second primary. In short, blacks who voted were nearly unanimous for Graham, yet the numbers that actually turned out were consistently overstated.[78] A higher black turnout in the first primary could well have elected Graham.

Had the same issues shaped the second primary as dominated the first, Graham would not have been beaten. But the Supreme Court rulings turned the second primary into a referendum on racial segregation. Graham forces had to pay dearly for their first primary failure; in politics as in any contest, a moment not seized is a moment lost. Intervening events imposed a validity and an urgency to the charges swirling around Graham that did not attach to him in the first primary. These events convinced many voters that Graham's liberalism, as revealed by his racial views, simply could not be forgiven. If a racial crisis were in the offing, a senator as liberal as Graham would have to go. His views, on race and other issues, were simply incompatible with the views of the majority of North Carolina voters.

In short, the Court decisions gave Willis Smith the issue and the impetus he needed to call a runoff. As Charles Tillett concluded in a reflective letter to his son, the ruling that admitted black students to white colleges in Texas "made everyone realize that 'it can happen here' and therefore, they thought every conceivable and possible step should be taken to keep out of public office folks in any sense willing to give Negroes their legal rights."[79]

The sense of panic generated by the threat of radical racial change combined with Graham's display of vote-getting power in the first primary to create in the Smith camp a climate of heroic desperation. Their candidate had no chance unless Smith's supporters bent every effort in his behalf. Convinced that they were enlisted in a struggle against overwhelming odds, they outhustled their opponents, as Smith later suggested. And when their effort got out of hand, they justified it as a dirty job that someone had to do or denied involvement in the seamier practices. "We disliked the duty of opposing [Graham]," Bob Thompson wrote in late June, but did so because " . . . to oppose him with all one's strength was the duty of every believer in the traditions and democracy of America. . . . We regret it was necessary for [Graham] to be . . . punished," Thompson concluded, in a sentiment many Graham opponents seconded, "but necessary it was . . . for the welfare of the state and nation."[80]

All the issues the Smith forces pressed in the second primary became issues of moment when tied to Court rulings and the looming threat of an immediate end to racial segregation. Especially effective was the stress on first primary support for Graham among black voters. In Cleveland County, recalled attorney and Graham manager B. T. Falls, Smith followers circulated widely the *Carolina Times* endorsement of Graham, accompanied by first primary totals from black precincts in Wake, Durham, and Guilford counties. Falls wrote that on Friday, June 23, voters were mailed the "WHITE PEOPLE WAKE UP" circular, and on Saturday morning, June 24, Smith workers in Shelby photographed black voters as they stood in precinct voting lines and had the shots developed and "rushed over the county to outlying precincts."[81] Statewide, Smith forces laid heavy stress on the catastrophe that they predicted would result if the state's public schools were desegregated.[82]

"Perhaps no . . . single issue would stir as violent an emotional storm in the South," Samuel Lubell concluded, "as to outlaw segregation in elementary schools."[83] A similar concern could be seen in the furor over Leroy Jones and his effort to win an appointment to West Point. Such attacks, widely repeated, thus triggered a wave of fear—of rapid racial change and of black citizens possessed of ready access to the polling booth. The issue of race relations was made even more menacing when tied to economic issues, as in the argument over FEPC and the desegregation of the workplace.[84]

The impact of the campaign's bitter racial invective on North Carolina was deep and long-lasting. It does much to explain the timidity of the state's elected officials (with a few exceptions) on racial questions in the decade after the 1954 *Brown v. Board of Education* decision. It may also help explain the electorate's subsequent preference for racial "moderates" in the years immediately after this brawl. Certainly, most North Carolinians hoped to avoid stirring up the acrimony that would remind them—and the nation—of the 1950 campaign.

The national press, which had been strongly pro-Graham, saw in the campaign a besmirched reputation for the state customarily hailed as the leader in southern interracial relations.[85] Many white North Carolinians, moreover, were appalled at a campaign based "solely on racial prejudice, bitterness, and bigotry."[86] "For the first time in my life, I felt ashamed of my state," wrote the dean of women at Wake Forest College, Lois Johnson, to Graham after the primary, a refrain Graham heard many times.[87]

The election demonstrated clearly that North Carolina, in fact, had never been the liberal bastion on matters of race that writers had often portrayed. All racial policies in the state had as their fundamental premise an acceptance of the principle of statutory segregation. Whatever commitment North Carolina had made to its black minority was made within the limits of the separate but equal myth. The challenge that the Graham forces could not meet was the need to convince voters that Graham was fully committed to the principle of segregation. Could a self-styled "liberal" in politics be "safe" on racial matters? In Graham's case, the voters' answer was "no." Had the first primary result prevailed, obviously the answer would have been "maybe." But in neither case would a Graham victory have signaled an abandonment by North Carolina's white population of its commitment to racial separation.

With Graham's defeat, the liberal moment passed. Subsequently, statewide candidates tagged as racial liberals—Terry Sanford as a gubernatorial candidate and Kerr Scott as a Senate candidate come immediately to mind—were careful to run as gradualists on racial matters and to focus on other issues, such as education or agriculture. They had learned their lesson well, as had Luther Hodges, who followed William B. Umstead to the governor's mansion and stayed there for six years. Hodges pleaded for voluntary segregation and focused his energy on economic development.

Statewide candidates depicted as strong segregationists, I. Beverly Lake, for example (gubernatorial candidate in 1960 and 1964), had no more success in their quest for office than Frank Graham had found as a racial liberal. North Carolinians, in short, rejected any candidate for state office identified as a racial extremist as well as any policy identified as racially radical. They neither closed their schools nor embraced full desegregation. As federal pressure mounted, however, the North Carolina commitment to statutory segregation and dual schools eventually came undone.

In political terms, the 1950 campaign was a fight for control of the Democratic party, but the result of the struggle was inconclusive. Governor Scott retained his personal political strength but failed in every instance to elect associates to statewide office. Governor Umstead, "the last Gardnerite," was elected governor in 1952 but died in office after having served less than half his term. Lieutenant Governor Luther Hodges was identified with neither wing of the party.

The most suggestive outcome of the Smith-Graham race is found in the race's meaning for North Carolina Republicans and conservative Democrats. Clearly, the Republican party benefited from the Democratic fratricide. As the national Democrats and their Tar Heel allies continued to espouse policies Willis Smith had opposed in 1950, economic conservatives—especially in the western piedmont—swallowed their history and began to vote Republican in general elections. General Dwight David Eisenhower, for example, came within 4 percentage points of carrying the state in 1952. In the same year, Charles Raper Jonas, a Republican, won a congressional seat from a district dominated by Charlotte and Mecklenburg County. He would serve ten terms, would surrender his seat to a fellow Republican, and would depend throughout his political life on Democratic votes for his margin of victory. Also, Jonas was never accused of being a race-baiter.[88]

Was Jonas's success, similar in voting pattern to Willis Smith's Mecklenburg showing, more than a local phenomenon? Perhaps not, although in hindsight it becomes clear that should the eastern counties subsequently desert the Democratic party as they deserted Graham in the second primary of the Senate campaign, the result would be a political alliance that would change the face of North Carolina politics.[89]

It is not possible to know with certainty all the sources of the basest racial propaganda that appeared in this campaign. The tracks of those who spread it have been largely obliterated, and if there are those who know, they are not talking (although some fingers point to *Southern Textile Bulletin* editor David Clark of Charlotte). But virtually every campaign participant interviewed agrees that Willis Smith was not directly responsible for the antiblack literature that appeared; he would never have sanctioned such tactics. In his own statewide effort, Smith campaigned ethically. He vigorously defended the racial status quo, challenged Graham's record, and raised reasonable questions about Graham's political judgment—questions that, privately, troubled even some of Graham's advocates. But the Smith campaign, like its Graham counterpart, was waged on two levels, state and local. In many communities, the Smith attack went beyond the bounds of fair political electioneering. Many charges were vicious, personal, unwarranted, and hateful. Smith, by all accounts, could not control all his supporters and did not condone their activities. But, as stated previously, he never publicly repudiated any of the vile statements made against Graham, and these statements did work to his political benefit. "Smith . . . kept ostentatiously aloof from these arguments," D. Hiden Ramsey wrote in the heat of postelection fury. "But the responsibility in the last analysis rests upon him. There is no moral distinction between the thief and the witting recipient of stolen property in my ethical dictionary."[90] As a consequence of the campaign, in other words, Willis Smith's political reputation was permanently besmirched.

I. Beverly Lake accurately depicted the sentiment of many North Carolinians in a postprimary letter to Graham. Lake found it hard to believe that thousands of North Carolinians would be so gullible as to be defrauded by such a campaign. "It must hurt you deeply," he consoled Graham, "to see those for whom you have worked so faithfully. . . turn to another because of a blind, unreasoning racial fear deliberately dragged in . . . by the other side." He could never understand, Lake concluded, how "informed people could stoop so low as to conduct so dishonorable a campaign."[91]

They could do so because the "evil genii of race prejudice" that D. Hiden Ramsey had believed the Smith-Graham campaign had unleashed had in fact never been secure in a segregationist vessel. Statutory segregation had only contained racial tensions; it could not resolve them. Nor did it. The 1898 and 1900 white supremacy campaigns in North Carolina had arrested Tar Heel race relations,[92] but by 1950 the effort to reexamine and redirect black-white relations in North Carolina was long overdue. The New Deal, the rise of Hitler and fascism, and World War II had all conspired to force the question of race relations back into full public view.

In a crude sense, therefore, the Smith forces correctly forecast the impending demise of statutory segregation. Those who struggled to hasten its end, and those who applauded its end, saw in segregation's overthrow a regenerative—indeed, a redemptive—act. But for those in 1950 who were threatened and frightened by the specter of desegregation, the campaign to overturn racial separation was profoundly disturbing. The Smith-Graham primary reflected that fear.

Racial segregation was a strongly held belief in white North Carolina

in 1950. The consensus supporting it was deep and powerfully felt. Despite North Carolina's cherished reputation as a beacon of enlightenment in southern race relations, that enlightenment had never included the actual ending of segregation—at least not in the immediate future. No politician could question segregation's wisdom and expect to continue his political career. Indeed, any other candidate for public office in North Carolina who held Frank Graham's racial views would have been dismissed from the first as a fringe figure, a political oddity. In his own campaign, Frank Graham was careful to appear cautious, skeptical of too rapid racial change. But events—and the logic of his public life—caught up with him in the second primary. He was undone by the panic-driven association that linked him to the effort—now fully launched in the nation—to overturn statutory segregation. The irony of the campaign rests in the realization that Graham's critics—and his defamers—correctly assessed his true racial sentiments.

Epilogue

"A Man Rejected"

In the week after his defeat, Frank Graham resumed his Senate duties. He walked forthwith into a floor fight over cloture on the same FEPC bill that had dogged him in May, eight days before the first primary ballot. Graham, of course, had been ill in Raleigh and unable to participate in the Senate's May vote. Spurning the pleas of Jeff Johnson, Jonathan Daniels, and Allard Lowenstein, Graham had refused to permit Senator Hoey, who voted against cloture, to remark that Graham would do likewise were he not ill and unable to participate.[1] On the July 12 ballot, however, when the clerk called his name, Graham spoke a forceful "Nay!" His shocked Senate friends asked him, as soon as the roll call ended, why he had not indicated his position on cloture in May. "I wasn't here," Graham responded.[2]

"I have never been able to quite forgive him," Daniels confessed in reflection a decade later. "If he could take that position when he wasn't under stress, I don't see why he couldn't take it [in the first primary], but he couldn't bear to let it seem even that he was bowing to political necessity." Daniels's displeasure even led to a rather testy exchange between the two men when they reminisced about the campaign on television for posterity in 1962.[3] C. A. "Abie" Upchurch, Jr., the Graham campaign's publicity director, was moved to write, after Graham's July vote against cloture, "If he had done it in the first primary, there would have been no second primary."[4] Newspapers also questioned Graham's vote. The Lexington (N.C.) *Dispatch* argued that his vote proved Graham was not the racial extremist he had been painted to be, while Jonathan Daniels explained that Graham's vote simply restated his refusal to take any position on the basis of political expediency.[5] Whatever the explanation—and Graham did not discuss it at the time—his vote left his supporters vexed. Years later, in his exchange with Daniels, Graham argued that at the time of the first vote, he could not vote cloture because there was no filibuster underway on the floor of the Senate. Despite his protestations, however, the circumstances of the two votes were separated by only one difference: the timing in regard to Graham's campaign.[6] He simply could not provide a sensible explanation of his action on the cloture issue.

Graham's remaining days in the Senate passed quickly. He busied himself with his duties, providing strong support for Truman's initial decisions on Korea, where hostilities had begun the day following Graham's defeat. (Some analysts speculated at the time that had the Korean War begun forty-eight hours before the June 24 vote, Graham, on the strength of his international experience, would have won his race.) He worked diligently but without success in September in opposition to the Internal Security Act that Congress passed over Truman's veto on September 23.[7] And on September 22, he inserted in the *Congressional Record* a seventeen-thousand-word "Farewell Statement," a compendium of his record on social, political, and international issues from the previous twenty years. The document was unlike any explanation of his activities Graham had ever offered before or during the campaign or would ever present again. It was specific, detailed, and defensive. In one sense, it traced the cataclysmic events of the previous twenty years—the Great Depression, the New Deal, the Japanese aggression in Asia, the rise of Hitler and Stalin, the "great debates" among American intellectuals in the 1930s and 1940s, World War II, and the early cold war—and Graham's reaction to these and other events as mirrored in his memberships and associations.

In the years 1930–50, Graham wrote, he had joined perhaps one hundred organizations (the number was actually over two hundred, as his biographer notes), only four of which, he claimed, ever made the attorney general's list of front organizations. He had "never knowingly joined a Communist-front organization," Graham insisted. He had never been a member of the International Labor Defense and had declined to sponsor the American League for Peace and Democracy, although he had signed a petition against aggression circulated by the league. Nor had he ever been a member of the Citizens Committee to Free Earl Browder, he stated, although he had urged Browder's release from prison, as had Wendell Willkie and a host of other Americans.

Graham's statement continued. He explained his association with the Southern Conference for Human Welfare, the foreign policy clashes within that body, and his reasons for remaining as honorary president throughout its existence. He discussed his role as a founding member of Americans for Democratic Action and his efforts to aid the Republican forces during the Spanish Civil War:

> I was on committees against Hitler, Mussolini and Franco . . . ; for aid to China against Japan; for civil liberties and on other such committees during [the] last score or more of years. . . . The overwhelming majority of the people along with whom I sponsored these committees were well known as loyal Americans. If members

of these committees had ulterior aims it was then without our
knowledge and has never had our approval. From past experience I
am aware of Communist techniques of infiltration into organizations which have good purposes. However, I do not now renounce
any stand I made for human freedom.[8]

"I have run the risk of taking sides," Graham wrote, "in the midst of
events which could not wait for certificates of safety and conformity
while freedom was embattled. . . . Along with countless loyal Americans
I took sides for the freedom of the human mind, the dignity of the
human being, and the autonomy of the human spirit. I took sides in the
South and in the nation for the fairer consideration of Jews, Catholics,
Negroes, and the foreign born, for fairer consideration of children, teachers, industrial workers, farmers, little business people and consumers."[9]

He concluded his apologia with a peroration that was by now familiar
to his friends and followers: "In this America of our struggles and our
hopes, the least of these our brethren has the freedom to struggle for
freedom; where the answer to error is not terror, the respect for the past
is not reaction and the hope of the future is not revolution; where the
integrity of simple people is beyond price and the daily toil of millions is
above pomp and power; where the majority is without tyranny, and the
minority without fear, and all people have hope."[10]

With that extraordinary statement, Graham closed his brief Senate
career. His purpose in entering it into the public record is not clear, but if
his message was intended for his critics, it left them unmoved. Indeed,
opponents read the statement as a confirmation of their worst suspicions:
Graham had been and remained a political innocent whose judgment
could not be trusted. Nor were his friends impressed with Graham's
Senate valedictory. They were instead saddened that Graham now found
it necessary to explain, to apologize, for his activist involvement. And
they understood that, more than anything else, the farewell revealed that
this defeat had seared his soul. In the words of Warren Ashby, "For the
first time in his life, he, who had been lavished with love, was publicly
rejected, apparently hated—and in North Carolina."[11] Graham had
never anticipated that his state's voters would reject him after he had
spent a lifetime in service to them. But they had, and the experience left
Graham dazed, even disoriented. It was a defeat that he could not turn
into victory.

Yet Graham never displayed bitterness or self-pity. Indeed, some of his
associates have argued that Graham's mauling did not have a long-term
effect on his outlook. As William C. Friday observed, Graham always
retained an ability to accept disagreement without rancor. Further, by

1950 Graham was hardly a stranger to either controversy or personal attack. Once the campaign had ended, according to Friday, neither Frank nor Marian Graham bore malice toward anyone. They went on with their lives, unburdened by either remorse or regret.[12]

Such a view could explain Graham's unwillingness to rehash publically the campaign or to utter a word of recrimination. Graham, his biographer wrote, retained a firm conviction in the rightness of all his stands—a view Graham confirmed in a 1969 interview.[13] Therefore, nothing was gained by asking what went wrong. When things were finished, they were finished (a peculiar view for a historian). Graham was simply not given to either introspection or analytical probing. Far more appealing to a man with Graham's personality and spirit, Warren Ashby has argued, was the opportunity now provided to be a magnanimous martyred Christian and to blame no one: neither himself, nor his campaign staff, nor Willis Smith and his minions.

Such a view—that Graham sustained only a glancing blow in the assault upon him—is no doubt a comfort to his friends. They suffered with him through his pummeling. But this view simply does not take into account the extent of the calumny heaped upon him. The trajectory of Graham's life after 1950 proves that the defeat—the bitter and unremitting campaign against him—had cut him to the core. It had inflicted on him a permanent hurt that went far beyond the pain accompanying a mere political defeat.[14]

Frank and Marian returned to Chapel Hill in late September 1950, and Graham supported the campaign for the November election of the full Democratic ticket—including Willis Smith. On election day, he cast a straight Democratic ballot, as always. It was an exercise his wife would not perform. Whether she actually voted for Smith's opponent is unknown, but she made it clear on the evening before the general election that no force in the world could persuade her to mark her ballot for Willis Smith.[15]

Smith, as expected, easily won election to the Senate. He defeated his Republican opponent, E. L. Gavin, 364,912 to 177,753, totals that attested to the enduring Republican strength in North Carolina. (Even Clyde Hoey's Republican foe received 171,804 votes to Hoey's 376,472.) A puny effort to revive Graham's candidacy as a write-in contender died at the borders of Chapel Hill township.[16]

Smith took his Senate oath in late November and threw himself into his Senate duties with the same resolution and drive that had characterized all his professional life. It was as if he thought he could dispel the political cloud under which he had gone to the Senate by proving through hard work his fitness for the post. He was anticipating a cam-

paign to win a full six-year Senate term when a heart attack struck on
June 24, 1953, three years to the day after his upset victory over Frank
Graham. He died on June 26 at 4:40 A.M., with his wife and four children
at his Bethesda Naval Hospital bedside. He was sixty-five years old. Some
of his family and friends have always believed that the strain of the fight
against Graham and the demands of a public career brought on his heart
attack and shortened his life.[17] To succeed him, Governor William B.
Umstead appointed Alton A. Lennon, a Wilmington attorney. In a bitter
1954 primary that also focused on the question of race relations, former
Governor Scott defeated Lennon 312,053 to 286,730. Scott served in the
Senate until his death in 1958.[18]

For Frank Graham, the years after his Senate defeat were difficult. Now
sixty-four years old, he had accumulated no significant economic assets,
not even a Chapel Hill homeplace. Consequently, he needed to work to
support himself and Marian. He could not decide what he wanted to do,
but he clearly intended to leave his native state.

He did not lack for offers. President Truman proposed the presidency
of the American Red Cross. Graham declined. Truman offered an appointment to the Civil Aeronautics Board. Graham asked not to be
considered. Truman suggested a forthcoming position as director of the
National Science Foundation. Graham was unenthusiastic but willing if
the president pressed him. While the foundation board reviewed his
candidacy, he declined a broad range of tentative and definite offers:
membership in a law firm, associate editorship of a newspaper, presidency of several colleges, and a position with the United Nations Point
Four program. But the National Science Foundation board decided
against recommending a nonscientist as its director, and Graham remained unemployed. He finally accepted appointment on March 21,
1951, to a Labor Department Defense Manpower Administration program created to ease labor problems associated with the Korean War
mobilization. But as he began his duties a call came on April 5 to serve a
three-month term as United Nations representative for India and Paki-
stan in their dispute over Kashmir. True to his Wilsonian and world
federalist impulses, he accepted the assignment and moved to New York
City.

Graham would remain at the United Nations for nineteen years, he
and Marian living for most of that time in a modest apartment located in
the Fairfax Hotel on East 56th Street. The Kashmir dispute proved
intractable, however, and after intermittent efforts at mediation, the issue
was dropped from the United Nations agenda in 1954, although Graham
retained his office. In 1957, after his duties had been temporarily
usurped by the president of the Security Council, Graham made one last

but futile effort at resolution of the Kashmir dispute. After 1958, as Warren Ashby observes, Graham was "essentially a man with an office but without a job." He continually reworked his report on Kashmir but was never permitted to present it to the Security Council, despite repeated requests. When the Security Council debated the question in 1962 and again in 1965 during the India-Pakistan War, he was on both occasions ignored. His frustration led him to offer his resignation, but both Ralph Bunche and Secretary-General U-Thant asked him to remain, and he did. He busied himself making speeches in support of the United Nations throughout the United States—over fifteen hundred talks in his nineteen years at the United Nations. For several years, he chaired the United Nations' speakers' bureau.[19]

His time at the United Nations came to a close in 1967, although he did not resign his post until 1970. Marian Graham died in April 1967, and the grief-stricken Graham suffered a heart attack the following June. He returned to Chapel Hill to live quietly in the house of his sister, visiting with friends, answering correspondence, and talking with students. His health gradually worsened, and he died quietly on February 16, 1972, in his eighty-sixth year.[20]

"In facile judgment," Jonathan Daniels wrote in his editorial eulogy, "it might be said that Frank Graham lived too long. In the last two decades of his life he moved as a man who had been rejected, in a political campaign of savage intensity, by the people he loved most." Alluding to the strife-torn United States in the era of Graham's death—the age of Vietnam, Black Power, and George Wallace—Daniels wrote that Graham had "given his life to love and seen hate triumphant. He had labored for the vision of peace on earth and seen it mocked." Yet his faith in American ideals never wavered, Daniels told his readers: "He was a little man nobody pushed around in his stubborn adherence to righteousness as he saw it. But he was sweet in the strong meaning of goodness which Southerners give to that word."[21]

His death was mourned by thousands of North Carolinians on whose lives Graham had laid a guiding hand. As they remembered his life, his mourners recounted the individual ways their own lives had intersected with Graham, and they memorialized those traits of head and heart that had endeared "Dr. Frank" to so many. They remembered the inspirational qualities with which Graham had marked their lives: the idealism, the kindness, the gentleness, the love. And they recalled the fateful campaign of 1950, the crucible through which Graham's life—and in important ways the life of their state—had passed.

Appendixes

County	Willis Smith	Frank P. Graham	Robert R. Reynolds	Olla Ray Boyd
Alamance	3,137	4,484	601	61
Alexander	687	600	126	1
Alleghany	784	1,034	299	12
Anson	2,235	2,313	407	42
Ashe	413	1,350	91	1
Avery	162	356	50	2
Beaufort	2,454	2,025	191	145
Bertie	1,380	1,610	150	18
Bladen	2,853	2,590	571	57
Brunswick	1,014	1,940	456	54
Buncombe	4,760	12,719	7,484	206
Burke	2,258	4,469	294	27
Cabarrus	5,575	4,034	1,767	209
Caldwell	2,980	2,613	534	68
Camden	869	400	111	9
Carteret	2,038	2,571	415	24
Caswell	1,193	1,265	284	43
Catawba	3,834	3,303	776	51
Chatham	1,635	1,741	529	13
Cherokee	679	1,430	290	18
Chowan	779	764	31	4
Clay	386	431	104	5
Cleveland	6,208	4,332	968	138
Columbus	4,962	3,576	833	104
Craven	2,270	3,194	895	175
Cumberland	5,055	4,067	747	60
Currituck	1,238	711	195	8
Dare	420	1,286	177	11
Davidson	2,610	4,353	492	42
Davie	312	1,137	121	11
Duplin	2,769	4,305	349	54

Appendix 1. (continued)

County	Willis Smith	Frank P. Graham	Robert R. Reynolds	Olla Ray Boyd
Durham	6,397	12,630	1,112	158
Edgecombe	2,942	4,082	423	56
Forsyth	5,219	8,894	1,144	59
Franklin	3,367	1,817	858	92
Gaston	6,701	6,072	1,473	187
Gates	834	478	101	7
Graham	376	259	70	0
Granville	2,457	1,711	567	16
Greene	695	1,584	135	25
Guilford	9,900	13,758	1,829	159
Halifax	4,457	3,584	738	121
Harnett	2,502	3,529	434	34
Haywood	2,241	5,595	606	121
Henderson	2,420	2,012	955	63
Hertford	976	1,565	230	25
Hoke	941	642	115	14
Hyde	451	738	83	28
Iredell	5,278	4,712	1,107	67
Jackson	1,549	2,249	333	43
Johnston	4,420	5,963	789	124
Jones	568	1,142	311	23
Lee	1,978	2,286	361	35
Lenoir	1,791	3,711	723	56
Lincoln	2,233	2,887	462	30
Macon	929	1,904	270	32
Madison	1,009	905	216	18
Martin	1,267	3,218	196	100
McDowell	2,067	1,906	900	27
Mecklenburg	14,963	10,245	1,364	110
Mitchell	109	393	39	1
Montgomery	1,293	971	383	11
Moore	2,548	2,281	514	31
Nash	3,934	4,464	488	118
New Hanover	5,310	6,740	2,346	124
Northampton	2,220	1,908	266	32
Onslow	1,206	2,221	660	45
Orange	1,234	5,212	443	34
Pamlico	773	823	159	33
Pasquotank	1,764	1,481	149	12
Pender	1,059	1,110	349	14
Perquimans	1,179	657	46	3

County	Willis Smith	Frank P. Graham	Robert R. Reynolds	Olla Ray Boyd
Person	2,092	2,087	500	46
Pitt	4,519	4,319	397	459
Polk	1,199	980	374	26
Randolph	2,193	2,381	342	34
Richmond	3,847	4,163	1,144	184
Robeson	4,512	6,850	704	83
Rockingham	2,652	4,937	1,339	101
Rowan	3,870	6,041	1,233	149
Rutherford	4,203	2,517	1,645	72
Sampson	842	2,943	96	13
Scotland	2,541	1,116	208	36
Stanly	2,229	2,242	559	67
Stokes	394	1,912	141	23
Surry	2,480	4,044	481	51
Swain	1,063	511	222	9
Transylvania	733	2,011	455	33
Tyrrell	548	492	138	19
Union	2,847	2,762	536	78
Vance	2,623	3,118	910	64
Wake	10,346	10,405	1,362	103
Warren	1,825	1,267	314	26
Washington	558	1,241	105	48
Watauga	514	1,217	18	4
Wayne	4,347	5,406	584	98
Wilkes	1,557	3,721	239	16
Wilson	3,204	3,465	439	79
Yadkin	499	1,238	120	13
Yancey	473	940	50	5
Totals	250,222	303,605	58,752	5,900

Appendix 2. North Carolina Manual Election Returns
Vote for United States Senator
Second Primary, June 24, 1950

County	Frank P. Graham	Willis Smith
Alamance	4,200	3,494
Alexander	975	897
Alleghany	590	1,166
Anson	2,290	2,818
Ashe	1,699	765
Avery	394	201
Beaufort	1,722	3,452
Bertie	1,242	1,454
Bladen	1,872	2,892
Brunswick	1,536	1,738
Buncombe	10,185	6,311
Burke	4,334	2,434
Cabarrus	2,852	5,664
Caldwell	1,964	2,416
Camden	321	650
Carteret	1,976	1,629
Caswell	981	1,569
Catawba	2,700	4,492
Chatham	1,354	2,217
Cherokee	1,625	760
Chowan	682	700
Clay	329	359
Cleveland	4,701	7,004
Columbus	2,770	6,000
Craven	2,176	3,205
Cumberland	3,747	6,595
Currituck	682	1,212
Dare	691	298
Davidson	4,243	2,982
Davie	1,049	313
Duplin	3,185	3,251
Durham	10,973	6,401
Edgecombe	3,497	3,271
Forsyth	8,213	5,276
Franklin	1,800	3,918
Gaston	5,975	7,279

County	Frank P. Graham	Willis Smith
Gates	437	845
Graham	329	452
Granville	1,343	2,878
Greene	1,328	921
Guilford	12,606	10,147
Halifax	2,206	3,659
Harnett	3,387	3,663
Haywood	3,974	1,719
Henderson	2,070	3,869
Hertford	997	1,056
Hoke	518	989
Hyde	553	600
Iredell	4,192	6,062
Jackson	1,293	1,186
Johnston	5,039	6,736
Jones	634	670
Lee	1,513	2,173
Lenoir	3,163	2,606
Lincoln	2,179	2,149
Macon	1,323	506
Madison	1,907	213
Martin	2,390	1,436
McDowell	2,555	2,424
Mecklenburg	9,701	15,067
Mitchell	459	136
Montgomery	1,028	1,872
Moore	2,033	2,988
Nash	3,812	4,737
New Hanover	4,761	6,284
Northampton	1,352	1,985
Onslow	1,763	1,591
Orange	4,269	1,462
Pamlico	586	852
Pasquotank	1,179	1,574
Pender	796	1,383
Perquimans	394	1,016
Person	2,099	2,933
Pitt	3,430	4,571
Polk	1,172	1,450
Randolph	2,133	2,605
Richmond	3,616	2,824

County	Frank P. Graham	Willis Smith
Robeson	4,281	4,489
Rockingham	2,879	2,110
Rowan	4,620	3,382
Rutherford	2,860	5,070
Sampson	2,880	1,444
Scotland	840	2,547
Stanly	2,334	3,100
Stokes	1,729	535
Surry	4,081	2,436
Swain	461	926
Transylvania	1,524	647
Tyrrell	414	544
Union	2,933	3,759
Vance	2,777	3,240
Wake	10,247	13,930
Warren	1,018	1,972
Washington	1,229	937
Watauga	1,434	487
Wayne	4,199	4,998
Wilkes	3,547	1,557
Wilson	2,915	4,320
Yadkin	1,307	513
Yancey	1,173	796
Totals	261,789	281,114

Notes

Introduction

1. For North Carolina and the South generally, see Kousser, *Shaping of Southern Politics*.

2. Puryear, *Democratic Party Dissension*, is both a lucid and meticulous treatment of the demise of Simmons and the rise of Gardner.

3. Key, *Southern Politics in State and Nation*, pp. 205–28, esp. p. 228.

4. Puryear, *Democratic Party Dissension*, p. 19.

Chapter 1

1. "The Oliver Max Gardner Award, 1950" typescript, North Carolina Collection, University of North Carolina at Chapel Hill.

2. Raleigh *News and Observer*, March 7, 1949; Charlotte *Observer*, March 7, 1949, p. 1.

3. Greensboro *Daily News*, March 8, 1949.

4. Lefler and Newsome, *North Carolina: The History of a Southern State*, 1963, p. 592; Bass and DeVries, *Transformation of Southern Politics*, pp. 228–29; Charlotte *Observer*, March 9, 1949, p. 1.

5. Charlotte *Observer*, March 7, 1949, p. 1.

6. Raleigh *News and Observer*, March 8, 1949, p. 1; Greensboro *Daily News*, March 7, 1949, p. 1; Charlotte *Observer*, March 7, 1949, p. 1.

7. Jonathan Daniels to Jo Rosenthal, March 9, 1949, Daniels Papers; Charlotte *Observer*, March 7, 1949, p. 1.

8. Raleigh *News and Observer*, March 8, 1949, p. 1.

9. Charlotte *Observer*, March 9, 1949, p. 4-A.

10. Wilmington *Star-News*, March 8, 1949; Charlotte *Observer*, March 9, 1949, p. 1, March 10, 1949, p. 1.

11. Charlotte *Observer*, March 9, 1949, p. 1.

12. Personal correspondence, boxes 168–71, Scott Papers.

13. Clyde R. Hoey to Henry B. Benoit, March 14, 1949, Hoey Papers.

14. Thurmond Chatham to W. Kerr Scott, March 19, 1949, Scott Papers.

15. C. A. Fink, president, North Carolina State Federation of Labor, to W. Kerr Scott, March 9, 1949, Scott Papers.

16. Richard L. Neuberger to Jonathan Daniels, March 7, 1949, Daniels Papers.

17. Jonathan Daniels to Arthur Simmons, March 10, 1949, Daniels Papers; Norfolk *Journal and Guide*, March 12, 1949.

18. Dr. Thurman Kitchin to W. Kerr Scott, March 9, 1949, Scott Papers; Greensboro *Daily News*, March 11, 1949.

19. Author's interview with J. Melville Broughton, Jr., December 12, 1984.

20. Helen Heatherly to W. Kerr Scott, March 12, 1949, Scott Papers.

21. T. Boggs Dellinger to W. Kerr Scott, March 12, 1949, Scott Papers.

22. W. L. Griffin to W. Kerr Scott, March 10, 1949, Scott Papers.

23. E. D. Craven to W. Kerr Scott, March 10, 1949, Scott Papers.

24. W. Kerr Scott to E. D. Craven, March 16, 1949, Scott Papers.

25. W. J. Armfield to W. Kerr Scott, March 16, 1949, Scott Papers.

26. Robert R. Mullikin to W. Kerr Scott, March 17, 1949, Scott Papers.

27. Norwood R. Lane to W. Kerr Scott, March 9, 1949, Scott Papers.

28. Fred W. Bonitz to W. Kerr Scott, March 12, 1949, Scott Papers.

29. Ormond Fooshee to W. Kerr Scott, March 9, 1949, Scott Papers.

30. Charlotte *Observer*, March 10, 1949, p. 17-A.

31. Greensboro *Daily News*, March 11, 1949, p. 1; Raleigh *News and Observer*, March 10, 1949, p. 17-A.

32. Interview with Capus Miller Waynick by Bill Finger, February 4, 1974, pp. 4–5, Southern Oral History Collection; interview with Capus Miller Waynick, September 19, 1979, p. 41, Waynick Papers.

33. Raleigh *News and Observer*, March 23, 1949, p. 1.

34. W. Kerr Scott, "Why I Appointed Frank Graham to the United States Senate," n.d., Coffin Papers.

35. Greensboro *Daily News*, March 18, 1949, p. 11.

36. Charlotte *Observer*, March 12, 1949, p. 1.

37. Ibid., March 13, 1949, p. 2-A.

38. Jonathan Daniels to Lindsay Warren, March 15, 1949, Warren Papers.

39. Charlotte *Observer*, March 16, 1949, p. 1.

40. "Conversation with Frank P. Graham," June 10, 1962, p. 1, transcript and film on file in Southern Oral History Collection (hereafter cited as "Conversation with Frank P. Graham"); author's telephone interview with Robert W. Scott (son of W. Kerr Scott), April 10, 1984; author's interview with Ralph W. Scott (brother of W. Kerr Scott), October 31, 1984.

41. "Conversation with Frank P. Graham," p. 1; interview with Jonathan Worth Daniels by Daniel Singal, March 22, 1972, p. 158, interview with Jonathan Worth Daniels by Charles Eagles, March 9, 1977, p. 229, Southern Oral History Collection.

42. Scott, "Why I Appointed Frank Graham," Coffin Papers; Raleigh *News and Observer*, March 24, 1949, p. 3.

43. Scott, "Why I Appointed Frank Graham," p. 3, Coffin Papers.

44. Asheville *Citizen*, March 24, 1949; *Newsweek*, April 4, 1949, p. 25; Charlotte *Observer*, March 24, 1949, p. 2.

45. Greensboro *Daily News*, March 20, 1949, p. 1; Charlotte *Observer*, March 19, 1949, p. 1.

46. Gastonia *Gazette*, March 19, 1949; Charlotte *Observer*, March 20, 1949, p. 12-A.

47. "Conversation with Frank P. Graham," p. 2.

48. Charlotte *News*, March 13, 1950.

49. Raleigh *News and Observer*, March 24, 1949.

50. Charlotte *News*, March 13, 1950.

51. Scott, "Why I Appointed Frank Graham," Coffin Papers; Asheville *Citizen*, March 24, 1949; Raleigh *News and Observer*, March 24, 1949.

52. Scott, "Why I Appointed Frank Graham," Coffin Papers; interview with Jonathan Worth Daniels by Daniel Singal, March 22, 1972, Southern Oral History Collection; Asheville *Citizen*, March 24, 1949; Charlotte *Observer*, March 24, 1949, p. 2.

53. "The Oliver Max Gardner Award, 1950"; Raleigh *News and Observer*, March 23, 1949, p. 1; New York *Times*, March 23, 1949; *Alumni Review*, University of North Carolina, February 1949, p. 147; Charlotte *Observer*, March 23, 1949, p. 1.

54. Authors' interview with William C. Friday, October 17, 1984; interview with William C. Friday by George Maurice Hill, April 17, 1974, Hill Papers; Charlotte *Observer*, March 24, 1949, p. 2.

55. Raleigh *News and Observer*, March 23, 1949, p. 1; Charlotte *Observer*, March 23, 1949, p. 1.

56. Authors' interview with William C. Friday; Charlotte *Observer*, March 23, 1949, p. 1.

57. Asheville *Citizen*, March 23, 1949, p. 1; Raleigh *News and Observer*, March 23, 1949, p. 1.

58. Scott, "Why I Appointed Frank Graham," Coffin Papers.

59. Author's interview with William D. Snider (administrative assistant to W. Kerr Scott), October 30, 1984; W. Kerr Scott to Mrs. A. P. Hedrick, June 29, 1950, Scott Papers; author's interview with Lennox Polk McLendon, Jr., November 2, 1984.

60. Author's interviews with Ralph W. Scott, J. Melville Broughton, Jr., Sam Ragan, October 25, 1984, and William C. Friday; James Free, "Under the Dome," Raleigh *News and Observer*, April 3, 1949.

61. Goldsboro *News-Argus*, n.d., quoted in Charlotte *Observer*, March 24, 1949, pp. 3–8.

62. Asheville *Citizen*, March 24, 1949.

63. New York *Times*, March 23, 1949.

64. Durham *Sun*, March 31, 1950.

65. James E. Webb to Jonathan Daniels, March 22, 1949, Jonathan Daniels to James E. Webb, March 26, 1949, Daniels Papers; interview with Capus Miller Waynick by Bill Finger, February 9, 1974, Southern Oral History Collection.

66. Newspaper clipping, n.p., n.d., Waynick Papers.

67. Frank P. Graham to Clyde R. Hoey, March 22, 1949, Hoey Papers, Frank P. Graham to John J. Parker, March 22, 1949, Parker Papers.

68. Charlotte *News*, March 13, 1950; author's interviews with R. Mayne Albright, November 30, 1984, William D. Snider, and William C. Friday; Frank P. Graham to Nell Battle Lewis, February 17, 1950, Lewis Papers.

69. "Conversation with Frank P. Graham," pp. 2–3.

70. Author's interview with Warren Ashby, October 30, 1984.

71. Interview with Mrs. Dudley Bagley by George Maurice Hill, n.d., Hill Papers.

72. Ashby, *Frank Porter Graham*, pp. 4–5.

73. Ibid., pp. 4–8.

74. Ibid., pp. 11–31; Raleigh *News and Observer*, March 27, 1949, sec. 4, p. 1.

75. Ashby, *Frank Porter Graham*, p. 20.

76. *Yackety-Yack, Yearbook of the University of North Carolina, 1909*, p. 40.

77. Ashby, *Frank Porter Graham*, pp. 26–30; Charlotte *Observer*, March 23, 1950, p. 1.

78. Frank P. Graham to Eugene Barnett, September 5, 1910, Graham Papers; Ashby, *Frank Porter Graham*, p. 34.

79. Ashby, *Frank Porter Graham*, p. 26.

80. Ibid., p. 38; "Biographical Sketch," n.d., Graham Papers.

81. Raleigh *News and Observer*, March 27, 1949; Harold H. Martin, "Fighting Half-Pint of Capitol Hill," p. 107.

82. *Time*, October 26, 1945; Ashby, *Frank Porter Graham*, pp. 49–52.

83. "Biographical Sketch," n.d., Graham Papers; Ashby, *Frank Porter Graham*, pp. 57–59.

84. Ashby, *Frank Porter Graham*, pp. 55–59.

85. Ibid., pp. 74–81; Tindall, *Emergence of the New South*, pp. 351–52; Tippett, *When Southern Labor Stirs*, pp. 286–88; David Clark to southern textile owners, January 31, 1930, Graham Papers.

86. Ashby, *Frank Porter Graham*, pp. 80–86; Morrison, *Josephus Daniels*, p. 160.

87. Tindall, *Emergence of the New South*, p. 368; Lefler and Newsome, *North Carolina: The History of a Southern State*, 1974, p. 608.

88. Ashby, *Frank Porter Graham*, pp. 90–95, 103–5.

89. Singal, *The War Within*, pp. 265–301. See "Contempo Affair," Graham Papers on Hughes's visit and Bertrand Russell file, Graham Papers, on Russell's lecture at the university.

90. Lockmiller, *Consolidation of the University of North Carolina*, pp. 86–88.

91. "Personal Security Questionnaire," August 2, 1947, Graham Papers.

92. Ashby, *Frank Porter Graham*, p. 142; Greensboro *Daily News*, September 8, 1934; interview with Rupert B. Vance by Daniel Singal, September 3, 1970, Southern Oral History Collection. The case against Lawrence was later dropped.

93. Lucy Randolph Mason to Frank P. Graham, November 24, 1938, Graham Papers; Singal, *The War Within*, pp. 191–93. This account corresponds to Singal on the origins and outcome of the SCHW rather than Krueger, *And Promises to Keep*.

94. Singal, *The War Within*, p. 291; Jonathan Daniels to Francis Winslow, December 13, 1938, Daniels Papers; Raleigh *News and Observer*, November 26, 1938.

95. Singal, *The War Within*, p. 295; Klehr, *Heyday of American Communism*, p. 277. The correspondence in the Graham Papers discussing this problem is extensive and continues throughout the life of the organization. For a small sample, see Josephine Wilkins to Frank P. Graham, October 20, 1938, Joe Tolbert to Josephine Wilkins, October 19, 1939, Frank P. Graham to Mark Ethridge, December 20, 1939, Frank McCallister to Frank P. Graham, March 18, May 11, 1940, Howard Kester to Francis P. Miller, March 19, 1939, Graham Papers.

96. Frank P. Graham to Howard Kester, December 1, 1939, Howard Kester to Frank P. Graham, December 11, 1939, Graham Papers.

97. Roger Baldwin to Frank P. Graham, January 9, 1940, Frank McCallister to Frank P. Graham, March 18, 1940, Graham Papers.

98. Frank P. Graham to Joseph Gelders, January 15, 1940, Graham Papers.

99. Joseph Gelders to Frank P. Graham, January 17, 1940, Howard Lee to Frank P. Graham, November 4, 1939, Graham Papers.

100. Frank P. Graham to Joseph Lieb, April 19, 1941, Graham Papers; interview with Clark Foreman, November 16, 1974, Southern Oral History Collection.

101. Eagles, *Jonathan Daniels and Race Relations*, pp. 72–73; "Conversation with Frank P. Graham," pp. 7–12.

102. Claude Pepper to Frank P. Graham, February 6, 1939, Graham Papers.

103. Hays, *Politics Is My Parish*, pp. 141–43; Francis Pickens Miller to Frank P. Graham, December 21, 1938, Marjorie Westgate McWhorter to Frank P. Graham, October 31, 1939, Graham Papers.

104. Krueger, *And Promises to Keep*, p. 38. Among the many who dissociated themselves after Birmingham were Lister Hill, Luther Patrick, Cooper Green, and John Bankhead.

105. Singal, *The War Within*, pp. 295–96; author's interview with William Terry Couch, August 3, 1982.

106. J. C. Cox to John B. Thompson, April 26, 1941, copy in Graham Papers; Mark Ethridge to John B. Thompson, February 28, 1941, copy in Graham Papers; Barry Bingham to Frank P. Graham, May 27, 1940, Graham Papers.

107. Krueger, *And Promises to Keep*, pp. 82–95; Singal, *The War Within*, p. 293. George Tindall has observed that the SCHW served as an epilogue for the New Deal in the South. Tindall, *Emergence of the New South*, p. 639. On John B. Thompson, see, among other letters, Barry Bingham to John B. Thompson, April 12, 1941, Graham Papers.

108. Ashby, *Frank Porter Graham*, pp. 191–239; U.S. President's Committee on Civil Rights, *To Secure These Rights*.

109. Ashby, *Frank Porter Graham*, pp. 237–39; "Excerpt from Broadcast of Fulton Lewis, Jr.," January 1949, typescript in Graham Papers and Tillett Papers.

110. Ashby, *Frank Porter Graham*, p. 238; *New York Times*, December 21, 1948, January 13, 1949.

111. Other members of the security board were former Undersecretary of State Joseph C. Grew, physicist Karl Compton, H. W. Prentiss, president of Armstrong Cork Company, and George Humphrey, president of the M. A. Hannah Coal Company of Cleveland. Ashby, *Frank Porter Graham*, p. 238; *New York Times*, December 21, 1948.

112. Frank P. Graham to Fulton Lewis, Jr., January 13, 1949, typescript copy in Graham Papers and Tillett Papers; "Broadcast of Fulton Lewis, Jr.," January 1949, Graham Papers and Tillett Papers.

113. "Broadcast of Fulton Lewis, Jr.," January 1949, Graham Papers and Tillett Papers.

114. Ashby, *Frank Porter Graham*, p. 239; *Congressional Record*, 81st Cong., 1st sess., 1949, 95, pt. 1:1814–18.

115. Kemp Battle to Frank P. Graham, February 9, 1949, Graham Papers.

116. Harry S Truman to Frank P. Graham, February 17, 1949, Graham Papers.

117. Frank P. Graham to Howard W. Odum, June 15, 1940, notary seal, February 9, 1949, Frank P. Graham to Frank McCallister, June 6, 1940, notary seal, February 9, 1949, Frank P. Graham to Mrs. Hobart A. McWhorter, December 1, 1939, notary seal, February 9, 1949, Graham Papers.

118. Frank P. Graham to Harry D. Gideonse, November 29, 1941, notary seal, February 11, 1949, Frank P. Graham to Ned H. Dearborn, December 4, 1941, notary seal, February 11, 1949, Graham Papers.

119. L. L. Coryell, Sr., to Frank P. Graham, May 5, 1942, Graham Papers.

120. Frank P. Graham to L. L. Coryell, Sr., May 11, 1942, Graham Papers.

121. Gerald W. Johnson to Howard W. Odum, June 15, 1936, Odum Papers.

Chapter 2

1. It is not clear that Daniels's quote from the state song meant that only "scorners may sneer at or witlings defame" Scott's nominee. Raleigh *News and Observer*, March 23, 1949, p. 4, March 24, 1949, p. 1-A.

2. Chapel Hill *Weekly*, March 25, 1949.

3. Greensboro *Daily News*, March 24, 1949.

4. Asheville *Citizen*, March 24, 1949.

5. Durham *Morning Herald*, March 25, 1949.

6. Winston-Salem *Journal*, n.d., quoted in Raleigh *News and Observer*, April 3, 1949.

7. High Point *Enterprise*, March 23, 1949.

8. Fayetteville *Observer*, n.d., quoted in Charlotte *Observer*, March 24, 1949, p. 3-A.

9. *State*, April 2, 1949, p. 14, April 9, 1949, p. 12.

10. Charlotte *Observer*, March 24, 1949, p. 16-A.

11. Charlotte *News*, March 24, 1949.

12. Raleigh *Times*, March 23, 1949.

13. *Carolina Times*, March 19, 1949, April 2, 1949.

14. Washington *Post*, March 24, 1949.

15. New York *Herald Tribune*, April 21, 1949.

16. Philadelphia *Bulletin*, March 24, 1949; *Christian Science Monitor*, March 30, 1949; New York *Times*, March 27, 1949.

17. *Nation*, April 2, 1949, pp. 373–74; "A New Senate Liberal," *New Republic*, April 4, 1949, p. 9.

18. Atlanta *Journal*, March 24, 1949, sec. 1, p. 28.

19. Richmond *News Leader*, March 23, 1949, p. 10.

20. Nashville (Tenn.) *Banner*, March 24, 1949.

21. Montgomery (Ala.) *Journal*, March 28, 1949.

22. Mobile (Ala.) *Press*, March 24, 1949.

23. Danville (Va.) *Register*, March 23, 1949.

24. John J. Parker to W. Kerr Scott, March 25, 1949, Harry L. Golden et al. to W. Kerr Scott, March 25, 1949, Scott Papers.

25. George C. Marshall to Frank P. Graham, March 26, 1949, Graham Papers.

26. Norman Thomas to Frank P. Graham, April 5, 1949, Graham Papers.

27. Raleigh *News and Observer*, March 23, 1949, p. 1.

28. Unsigned postcard to W. Kerr Scott, n.d., Scott Papers.

29. R. B. Hickman to W. Kerr Scott, n.d., Scott Papers.

30. T. Young to W. Kerr Scott, March 25, 1949, Scott Papers.

31. Bill Scott to W. Kerr Scott, n.d., Scott Papers.

32. "No name" to the editor, Charlotte *Observer*, April 2, 1949, p. 6-A.

33. H. H. Webster to W. Kerr Scott, March 23, 1949, Scott Papers.

34. Allen P. Moore et al. to W. Kerr Scott, March 23, 1949, Scott Papers.

35. Austin F. Hancock to W. Kerr Scott, April 1, 1949, Scott Papers; Graham FBI file, January 1949, file number 67C; John W. Giesecke to James P. Kern, April 1, 1949, Scott Papers.

36. Edith Dickey Moses to W. Kerr Scott, March 28, 1949, Scott Papers.

37. Unsigned postcard to W. Kerr Scott, March 23, 1949, Scott Papers.

38. J. F. Youngblood to W. Kerr Scott, n.d., W. L. Totten, Sr., to W. Kerr Scott, March 23, 1949, Scott Papers.

39. James R. Patton, Jr., to W. Kerr Scott, March 24, 1949, Scott Papers.

40. Norfolk *Virginian-Pilot*, March 24, 1949; Clyde R. Hoey to Frank P. Graham, March 23, 1949, Hoey Papers.

41. Raleigh *News and Observer*, March 23, 1949, p. 1.

42. Greensboro *Daily News*, March 23, 1949.

43. Raleigh *News and Observer*, March 24, 1949.

44. Ibid., March 23, 1949, p. 1; H. Patrick Taylor, Sr., to Frank P. Graham, April 1, 1949, Graham Papers.

45. Raleigh *News and Observer*, March 23, 1949, p. 1.

46. Charlotte *Observer*, March 23, 1949, p. 1.

47. Raleigh *News and Observer*, March 25, 1949; Harry S Truman to Frank P. Graham, March 23, 1949, Graham Papers.

48. Raleigh *News and Observer*, March 24, 1949.

49. Walter P. Reuther to W. Kerr Scott, March 29, 1949, Scott Papers.

50. Jack Kroll to W. Kerr Scott, March 29, 1949, Scott Papers.

51. Ernest Gruening to W. Kerr Scott, March 29, 1949, Scott Papers.

52. Helen Gahagan Douglas to W. Kerr Scott, March 25, 1949, Scott Papers.

53. Claude Pepper to W. Kerr Scott, March 31, 1949, Scott Papers.

54. Arthur M. Schlesinger, Jr., to W. Kerr Scott, March 23, 1949, Scott Papers.

55. Channing H. Tobias to W. Kerr Scott, March 23, 1949, Scott Papers.

56. *Congressional Record*, 81st Cong., 1st sess., 1949, 95, pt. 3:3095–98; New York *Times*, March 24, 1949; Winston-Salem *Journal*, March 24, 1949. In his career as a government informer, Crouch's reputation for honesty suffered "grievous and permanent damage." See Klehr, *Heyday of American Communism*, p. 274.

57. *Congressional Record*, 81st Cong., 1st sess., 1949, 95, pt. 3:3100; New York *Times*, March 24, 1949; New York *Journal-American*, March 24, 1949.

58. New York *Times*, March 24, 1949; Winston-Salem *Journal*, March 24, 1949.

59. *Congressional Record*, 81st Cong., 1st sess., 1949, 95, pt. 3:3098; Raleigh *News and Observer*, March 24, 1949, p. 1.

60. Clyde R. Hoey to Mrs. Vernon Ward, March 25, 1949, Clyde R. Hoey to Mrs. Charles J. Williams, March 28, 1949, Hoey Papers.

61. *Congressional Record*, 81st Cong., 1st sess., 1949, 95, pt. 3:3098–99; New York *Times*, March 24, 1949.

62. *Congressional Record*, 81st Cong., 1st sess., 1949, 95, pt. 3:3100–101; Washington *Star*, March 24, 1949.

63. Ashby, *Frank Porter Graham*, p. 247.

64. *Newsweek*, April 4, 1949, p. 26.

65. Charlotte *Observer*, March 27, 1949, p. 2.

66. Raleigh *News and Observer*, March 28, 1949.

67. Washington *Post*, March 24, 1949; Raleigh *News and Observer*, March 24,

1949, p. 3; Charlotte *Observer*, March 23, 1949; *Survey*, May 1949, p. 249.

68. Charlotte *Observer*, March 27, 1949, p. 2.

69. Carroll Kilpatrick to Jonathan Daniels, March 25, 1949, Daniels Papers.

70. Raleigh *News and Observer*, March 30, 1949; *Life*, April 11, 1949, p. 113.

71. Raleigh *News and Observer*, March 30, 1949; Raleigh *Times*, March 30, 1949; Charlotte *Observer*, March 30, 1949.

72. The attorney general's list was a compilation of organizations (some of them alleged to be Communist front groups) assembled by the Internal Security Division of the Department of Justice at the onset of World War II. Originally intended to screen employees in the Justice Department, the list was maintained informally, but as other agencies learned of the list they sometimes used it to screen their own employees. On March 21, 1947, President Truman, by executive order, initiated a sweeping federal loyalty program, with a Loyalty Review Board in the Civil Service Commission empowered to hear appeals from government workers under departmental investigation. The board also was given the attorney general's list of "subversive organizations," and late in 1947, the board published the attorney general's list. Once the list became public, it was a source of continuing controversy. Many people were convinced that anyone associated with a group on the list was a person whose loyalty to the United States was, at best, suspect. Critics of the list charged that its principal purpose was to intimidate left-wing activists and to create a climate of political and intellectual conformity. They also argued that Truman's loyalty program, which used the list, was of dubious constitutionality. Included on the list were organizations with which Frank Graham had at least a passing association. For a thorough discussion of the Truman loyalty program, see Donovan, *Conflict and Crisis*, pp. 292–98. Greensboro *Daily News*, March 26, 1949, p. 1; Charles W. Tillett to Frank P. Graham, March 30, 1949, Graham Papers.

73. Raleigh *News and Observer*, April 1, 1949; Charlotte *Observer*, April 1, 1949, p. 3-A.

74. Norfolk *Virginian-Pilot*, April 5, 1949.

75. Author's interview with Kate Humphries, December 13, 1984; Raleigh *News and Observer*, March 29, 1949.

76. Author's interview with Kate Humphries.

77. Charlotte *Observer*, March 30, 1949, p. 1-B; author's interview with Legette Blythe, September 14, 1984.

78. Winston-Salem *Journal and Sentinel*, March 27, 1949.

79. Ford S. Worthy to Lindsay Warren, n.d., Warren Papers.

80. Charlotte *Observer*, March 30, 1949, p. 1-B.

81. Ibid., April 5, 1949, p. 14-A.

82. Greensboro *Record*, n.d., quoted in Raleigh *News and Observer*, April 3, 1949.

83. Charlotte *Observer*, March 31, 1949, p. 18-A.

84. H. Galt Braxton to Frank P. Graham, March 23, 1949, Graham Papers.

85. Nere E. Day to Frank P. Graham, March 27, 1949, Graham Papers.

86. J. Allen Austin to Frank P. Graham, April 8, 1949, Graham Papers.

Chapter 3

1. Thomas Turner to Jonathan Daniels, September 12, October 19, 1949, Daniels Papers. See also Charles Tillett to Frank P. Graham, August 11, 25, 30, 1949, and Douglas Hunt to W. Kerr Scott, July 8, 1949, Graham Papers.

2. Jonathan Daniels to Santford Martin, Kemp Battle, and Charles B. Deane, August 11, 1949, Daniels Papers; Jonathan Daniels to Frank P. Graham, August 25, 1949, Graham Papers.

3. Charles B. Deane to Jonathan Daniels, August 19, 1949, Daniels Papers.

4. O. Max Gardner, Jr., to Jonathan Daniels, September 1, 1949, Daniels Papers.

5. Santford Martin to Jonathan Daniels, September 6, 1949, Daniels Papers.

6. D. Hiden Ramsey to David R. Fall, October 12, 1949, Ramsey Papers.

7. *State*, September 3, 1949, p. 12.

8. R. Mayne Albright to Jonathan Daniels, August 24, 1949, Daniels Papers; author's interview with R. Mayne Albright, November 30, 1984.

9. Charlotte *Observer*, September 21, 1949, p. 16-A.

10. Ibid., October 29, 1949, p. 1-B.

11. C. Sylvester Green to Jonathan Daniels, August 23, 1949, Daniels Papers.

12. Charlotte *Observer*, September 10, 1949, p. 17-A, September 25, 1949, p. 2-A.

13. Ibid., September 17, 1949, p. 1, September 25, 1949, p. 1.

14. Ibid., October 17, 1949, p. 1.

15. Jonathan Daniels to John D. McConnell, September 20, 1949, Daniels Papers.

16. Dave Burgess to Dan Powell, August 14, 1949, Powell Papers.

17. Dave Burgess to Jack Kroll et al., December 1, 1949, Powell Papers.

18. Dave Burgess to Dan Powell, weekly report, November 21–27, 1949, Powell Papers.

19. Dave Burgess to Dan Powell, November 13, 1949, Powell Papers.

20. Charlotte *Observer*, November 20, 1949, p. 2-A.

21. Ibid.

22. Ibid., December 2, 1949, p. 17-A.

23. W. Kerr Scott to Capus Waynick, November 26, 1949, Waynick Papers.

24. T. C. Johnson to Capus Waynick, December 8, 1949, Waynick Papers.

25. Charles W. Tillett to Jonathan Daniels, December 3, 1949, Daniels Papers

26. Jonathan Daniels to Capus Waynick, November 26, 1949, Daniels Papers.

27. Charlotte *Observer*, December 4, 1949, p. 22-A.

28. Capus Waynick to T. C. Johnson, December 13, 1949, Capus Waynick to Ben Lemert, December 20, 1949, Waynick Papers.

29. Charlotte *Observer*, December 9, 1949, p. 10-A.

30. Charles W. Tillett to Frank P. Graham, March 14, 30, and June 6, 1949, Graham Papers.

31. Charlotte *Observer*, December 10, 1949, p. 10-A.

32. Ibid., November 24, 1949, p. 1.

33. Gladys Tillett Coddington to W. C. Jackson, December 9, 1949, Jackson Papers; Gladys Tillett Coddington to Santford Martin, December 9, 1949, Martin Papers.

34. Jonathan Daniels to Gladys Tillett, December 22, 1949, Daniels Papers.

35. Eleanor Roosevelt to Jonathan Daniels, December 20, 1949, Daniels Papers.

36. Jonathan Daniels to Eleanor Roosevelt, December 27, 1949, Daniels Papers.

37. Charlotte *Observer*, December 14, 1949, p. 5-B.

38. Ibid., December 16, 1949, p. 20-A.

39. T. C. Johnson to Capus Waynick, December 8, 1949, Waynick Papers.

40. Kemp D. Battle to Frank P. Graham, September 6, 1949, Graham Papers.

41. Dave Burgess to Dan Powell, weekly report, December 18–25, 1949, Powell Papers.

42. Author's interview with Kathryn N. Folger, December 6, 1984.

43. Author's interview with R. Mayne Albright.

44. Author's interview with Terry Sanford, December 3, 1984; Durham *Morning Herald*, January 8, 1950; Charlotte *Observer*, January 7, 1950, p. 9-A; Asheville *Citizen*, January 10, 1950, p. 2-A.

45. Charlotte *Observer*, January 8, 1950, p. 2-A.

46. Lee Weathers to Clyde R. Hoey, January 5, 1950, Hoey Papers.

47. Asheville *Citizen*, January 7, 1950, p. 5.

48. Charlotte *Observer*, January 8, 1950, p. 14-B.

49. William B. Umstead to Clyde Robert Hoey, January 10, 1950, Hoey Papers; William B. Umstead to R. Gregg Cherry, January 20, 1950, Cherry Papers.

50. Syd H. Uzzell to Gladys Tillett Coddington, January 9, 1950, Hoey Papers.

51. Raleigh *News and Observer*, January 9, 1950; *State*, January 21, 1950, p. 12.

52. Charlotte *Observer*, January 11, 1950, p. 9-A.

53. Elizabeth City *Daily Advance*, January 21, 1950, p. 2.

54. Ibid., January 7, 1950, p. 1, January 23, 1950, p. 5.

55. E. H. Powell to L. Y. Ballentine, January 24, 1950, Ballentine Papers.

56. Charlotte *Observer*, January 8, 1950, p. 1-B, March 18, 1950, p. 1.

57. Raleigh *News and Observer*, May 12, 1965; Greensboro *Daily News*, May 6, 1948.

58. Washington (N.C.) *Daily News*, January 11, 1950, p. 1.

59. Charlotte *Observer*, March 17, 1950.

60. Asheville *Citizen*, May 25, 1950.

61. Asheville *Citizen*, January 5, 1950, p. 1-A; Charlotte *Observer*, January 5, 1950, p. 1.

62. Charlotte *Observer*, September 16, 1949, p. 16-B.

63. Ibid., November 26, 1949, p. 2-A.

64. Greensboro *Daily News*, January 4, 1950; Charlotte *Observer*, January 2, 1950, p. 1, January 4, 1950, p. 8-A; *Newsweek*, January 16, 1950, p. 9; Raleigh *News and Observer*, January 8, 1950.

65. Raleigh *News and Observer*, January 7, 1950.

66. Charlotte *News*, January 7, 1950; Asheville *Citizen*, January 26, 1950, p. 1-A.

67. Asheville *Citizen*, January 26, 1950, p. 1-A; Charlotte *News*, January 7, 1950.

68. Asheville *Citizen*, January 26, 1950, p. 1-A.

69. Asheville *Citizen*, February 14, 24, 1950.

70. J. R. Cherry to Frank P. Graham, January 5, 1950, Hoey Papers.

71. Gladys Tillett to George R. Ross, January 19, 1950, Graham Papers; Jimmy C. Wallace to Allard Lowenstein, Lowenstein Papers; Charlotte *Observer*, January 11, 1950, p. 10-B, January 17, 1950, p. 7-A.

72. Chapel Hill *Weekly*, January 13, 1950, p. 8.

73. Dave Burgess to Dan Powell et al., n.d., Powell Papers.

74. Interview with Capus Miller Waynick by Bill Finger, November 24, 1974, Southern Oral History Collection.

75. Holt McPherson to Clyde R. Hoey, February 3, 1950, Clyde R. Hoey to Holt McPherson, February 6, 1950, Hoey Papers; Asheville *Citizen*, February 3, 1950, p. 1-B.

76. Gladys Tillett, form letter, January 13, 1950, Tillett Papers; Jefferson Deems Johnson to Mr. and Mrs. Charles W. Tillett, January 19, 1949, Johnson Papers.

77. Drew Pearson, "Washington Merry-Go-Round," Greensboro *Daily News*, January 16, 1950, sec. 1, p. 4.

78. Greensboro *Daily News*, January 19, 1950, sec. 1, p. 6.

79. *Pilot*, January 13, 1950, p. 2.

80. Asheville *Citizen*, January 19, 1950, p. 1-B.

81. W. Kerr Scott to department heads, February 13, 1950, Scott Papers; Greensboro *Daily News*, February 16, 1950.

82. NAACP Papers, Branch Files, 1950, group 2, ser. C, box 129.

83. High Point *Enterprise*, January 13, 1950.

84. Pleasants, "Senatorial Career of Robert Rice Reynolds," p. 1 and passim; Raleigh *News and Observer*, January 31, 1950, p. 1, New York *Times*, January 31, 1950, p. 16; Asheville *Citizen*, January 31, 1950, p. 1.

85. Washington *Post*, May 27, 1947; Durham *Morning Herald*, June 28, 1949, p. 3.

86. Durham *Morning Herald*, December 14, 1949, p. 1.

87. Charlotte *Observer*, January 14, 1950, p. 1-B.

88. Asheville *Citizen*, January 4, 1950, p. 5-A.

89. Elizabeth City *Daily Advance*, January 26, 1950, p. 4.

90. Holt McPherson to Clyde R. Hoey, January 14, 1950, Hoey Papers.

91. Raleigh *News and Observer*, January 31, 1950, p. 1; Asheville *Citizen*, January 31, 1950, p. 1; New York *Times*, January 31, 1950, p. 16.

92. Charlotte *Observer*, n.d., clipping in Reynolds Papers.

93. Author's interview with Irwin C. Crawford, August 7, 1969.

94. Robert Rice Reynolds platform, Cherry Papers and Graham Papers; Raleigh *News and Observer*, January 31, 1950, p. 1; Asheville *Citizen*, January 31, 1950, p. 1.

95. Charlotte *Observer*, January 31, 1950, p. 1-A.

96. Raleigh *News and Observer*, February 1, 1950, p. 1; Asheville *Citizen*, January 31, 1950, p. 1-A.

97. Durham *Morning Herald*, February 1, 1950.

98. Winston-Salem *Journal*, January 31, 1950, p. 1.

99. Greensboro *Daily News*, February 3, 1950.

100. Charlotte *Observer*, February 3, 1950, p. 22-A.

101. Washington (N.C.) *Daily News*, February 1, 1950, p. 4.

102. Charlotte *Observer*, January 8, 1950, p. 1.

103. These invitations indicated the importance Daniels and Scott placed on the support of labor for the success of the Democratic party in general and Frank Graham in particular.

104. Asheville *Citizen*, January 28, 1950, p. 1-A.

105. *Newsweek*, February 6, 1950, p. 20.

106. Charlotte *Observer*, January 29, 1950, p. 1-A; Asheville *Citizen*, January 29, 1950, p. 1.

107. John Sanders to Allard Lowenstein, January 29, 1950, Lowenstein Papers.

108. Asheville *Citizen*, January 30, 1950, p. 1-A.

109. Ibid., January 29, 1950, p. 1-A.

110. Banks Wilkins to L. Y. Ballentine, January 31, 1950, L. Y. Ballentine to Banks Wilkins, February 10, 1950, Ballentine Papers.

111. Transcript of radio commentary by W. E. Debnam, January 30, 31, February 1, 1950, Ballentine Papers.

112. Stella K. Barbee to Clyde R. Hoey, January 31, 1950, Hoey Papers; *Southern Textile Bulletin*, February 1950, p. 2; Dave Burgess to Dan Powell, weekly report, February 5–11, 1950, Powell Papers.

113. Washington (N.C.) *Daily News*, February 16, 1950, p. 4; Fayetteville *Observer*, February 2, 1950.

114. F. J. Herndon to L. Y. Ballentine, February 3, 1950, Dr. J. V. Sikes to L. Y. Ballentine, February 6, 1950, Glenn R. Clark to L. Y. Ballentine, January 30, 1950, Ballentine Papers.

115. L. Y. Ballentine to Glenn R. Clark, February 3, 1950, L. Y. Ballentine to F. J. Herndon, February 10, 1950, Ballentine Papers.

116. Clyde R. Hoey to Thomas W. Davis, February 25, 1950, Hoey Papers; Charlotte *Observer*, February 3, 1950, p. 14-A.

117. Charlotte *Observer*, February 14, 1950, p. 13-A; author's interview with James K. Dorsett, Jr., December 12, 1984.

118. Elizabeth City *Daily Advance*, February 15, 1950, p. 6.

119. Charlotte *Observer*, February 5, 1950, p. 4-B, February 12, 1950, p. 1-A; Asheville *Citizen*, February 8, 1950, p. 3-A, February 9, 1950, p. 3-A; Raleigh *News and Observer*, February 25, 1950.

120. Elizabeth City *Daily Advance*, February 18, 1950, p. 2; Raleigh *News and Observer*, February 18, 1950.

121. Charles W. Tillett to Willis Smith, February 18, 1950, Tillett Papers.

122. Arthur L. Tyler, Frank E. Winslow, and Millard F. Jones to Willis Smith, February 23, 1950, Graham Papers.

123. Asheville *Citizen*, February 21, 1950, p. 1-B; Charlotte *Observer*, February 21, 1950, p. 14-A.

124. Raleigh *News and Observer*, February 25, 1950, p. 1-A; Asheville *Citizen*, February 25, 1950, p. 1-A; Charlotte *Observer*, February 25, 1950, p. 1-A.

125. Author's interview with Sam Ragan, October 25, 1984, and R. Mayne Albright.

126. Author's interview with Kate Humphries, December 13, 1984.

127. Clyde R. Hoey to Thomas W. Davis, February 21, 1950, Hoey Papers.

128. Frank Graham to Santford Martin, February 10, 1950, Martin Papers; Charlotte *Observer*, February 11, 1950, p. 1-A; biographical sketch of Jefferson Deems Johnson, Jr., Johnson Papers; *State*, February 18, 1950, pp. 15–16; William C. Friday to Allard Lowenstein, February 8, 1950, Lowenstein Papers.

Johnson learned quickly that not all Broughton workers would support Graham. See, for example, E. J. Prevatte to Jeff Johnson, March 7, 1950, Graham Papers.

129. Frank P. Graham to Jacob Billikopf, February 14, 1950, Parker Papers; Elizabeth City *Daily Advance*, February 16, 1950, p. 4.

130. William C. Friday to Allard Lowenstein, February 8, 1950, Lowenstein Papers; interview with Jonathan Worth Daniels by Charles Eagles, March 9–11, 1977, Southern Oral History Collection; author's interview with Kathryn N. Folger and Kate Humphries.

131. Asheville *Citizen*, February 21, 1950, p. 1-B; Charlotte *Observer*, February 21, 1950, p. 14-A.

132. Author's interview with Kathryn N. Folger.

133. Author's interview with Jesse A. Helms, December 11, 1984; Charles Tillett to Frank P. Graham, January 9, 1950, Graham Papers.

134. *State*, March 4, 1950, pp. 14–15.

135. Raleigh *News and Observer*, July 2, 1950, sec. 4, p. 1, February 26, 1950; Asheville *Citizen*, February 25, 1950; author's interviews with Hoover Adams, May 26, 1983, James K. Dorsett, Jr., John Christoph Blucher Ehringhaus, Jr., November 10, 1984, Jesse A. Helms, and William Thomas Joyner, Jr., December 12, 1984.

136. Raleigh *News and Observer*, February 26, 1950.

137. Greensboro *Daily News*, February 7, 1940; author's interview with John Christoph Blucher Ehringhaus, Jr.

138. Clyde R. Hoey to Thomas W. Davis, February 21, 1950, Hoey Papers.

139. Author's interview with Hoover Adams.

140. Author's interviews with James K. Dorsett, Jr., John Christoph Blucher Ehringhaus, Jr., Hoover Adams, William Thomas Joyner, Jr.; Greenhaw, *Elephants in the Cottonfields*, p. 49.

141. Raleigh *News and Observer*, February 25, 1950.

142. Durham *Morning Herald*, February 25, 1950.

143. Norfolk *Virginian-Pilot*, February 27, 1950.

144. High Point *Enterprise*, February 26, 1950.

145. Asheville *Citizen*, February 25, 1950, p. 4-A.

146. Charlotte *Observer*, February 27, 1950, p. 5-A.

147. Dave Burgess to Dan Powell, weekly report, February 19–25, 1950, Powell Papers.

148. Jonathan Daniels to Capus Waynick, February 27, 1950, Daniels Papers.

149. Jonathan Daniels to William W. Boyle, Jr., February 25, 1950, Daniels Papers.

150. Jonathan Daniels to Harry S Truman, February 27, 1950, Daniels Papers.

151. Charles W. Tillett to C. C. Burns, February 26, 1950, Tillett Papers.

152. Capus Waynick to Jonathan Daniels, March 7, 1950, Waynick Papers.

153. J. Talbot Johnson to Frank P. Graham, March 2, 1950, Graham Papers.

154. Richard B. Dixon to Jeff Johnson, March 2, 1950, Graham Papers.

155. Washington (N.C.) *Daily News*, February 23, 1950, p. 4.

Chapter 4

1. Charlotte *Observer*, March 1, 1950, p. 12-A.

2. Asheville *Citizen*, March 8, 1950, p. 9-A.

3. Author's interviews with Kate Humphries, December 13, 1984, Kathryn N. Folger, December 6, 1984, and William W. Staton, May 24, 1983.

4. Author's interview with Sam Ragan, October 25, 1984.

5. "Women Will Win This Election," n.d., pamphlet in Tillett Papers; interview with Guion Griffis Johnson by Mary Fredrickson, July 1, 1974, Southern Oral History Collection.

6. Charles W. Tillett to Jeff Johnson, February 9, 1950, Johnson Papers.

7. Author's interview with William W. Staton.

8. Author's interviews with Warren Ashby, August 2, 1982, William W. Staton, and Kathryn N. Folger.

9. List of county managers, n.d., Graham Papers.

10. I. Murchison Biggs to Bill Staton, February 22, 1950, Graham Papers.

11. Dave Burgess to Jack Kroll, February 22, 1950, Powell Papers.

12. Dave Burgess to Dan Powell, weekly report, February 12–18, 1950, Powell Papers.

13. John W. Umstead to Allard Lowenstein, March 3, 1950, Lowenstein Papers.

14. T. C. Johnson to Capus Waynick, March 3, 1950, Waynick Papers.

15. *Daily Tar Heel*, March 7, 1950.

16. Jonathan Daniels to Nellie P. Cook, March 3, 1950, Daniels Papers; Nellie P. Cook to Jeff Johnson, March 7, 1950, Graham Papers.

17. Jonathan Daniels to Eleanor Roosevelt, March 3, 1950, Daniels Papers.

18. John Marshall to Capus Waynick, March 6, 1950, Scott Papers.

19. Charlotte *Observer*, February 28, 1950, p. 3-A.

20. Ibid., March 7, 1950, p. 6-A, March 9, 1950, p. 9-A.

21. Ibid., March 31, 1950, p. 15-B.

22. Asheville *Citizen*, April 18, 1950, p. 5.

23. Ibid., March 13, 1950, p. 12-A; author's interview with R. Mayne Albright, November 30, 1984.

24. New York *Mirror*, March 11, 1950.

25. Author's interview with R. Mayne Albright.

26. Author's interview with William W. Staton.

27. Louis Graves to Lenoir Chambers, March 27, 1950, Daniels Papers.

28. Louis Graves to Jonathan Daniels, March 27, 1950, Daniels Papers.

29. Chapel Hill *Weekly*, March 31, 1950, p. 2.

30. Maurice Rosenblatt to Jonathan Daniels, March 17, 1950, Daniels Papers.

31. Author's interviews with Kathryn N. Folger and Kate Humphries.

32. Author's interview with R. Mayne Albright.

33. Author's interview with Kathryn N. Folger.

34. Ben and Rose Lemert to Capus Waynick, March 6, 1950, Waynick Papers.

35. James C. Wallace to Allard Lowenstein, March 18, 1950, Lowenstein Papers.

36. Dave Burgess to Jack Kroll, March 6, 1950, Dave Burgess to Dan Powell, weekly report, March 5–11, March 12–18, 1950, Powell Papers.

37. Author's interview with Thad Eure, December 11, 1984.

38. Goldsboro *News-Argus*, March 17, 1950.

39. Author's interviews with Kathryn N. Folger and Kate Humphries.

40. Elizabeth City *Daily Advance*, March 3, 1950; Winston-Salem *Journal*, March 3, 1950; press release, Graham headquarters, March 11, 1950, Lowenstein Papers.

41. Form letter on socialized medicine, March 6, 1950, Lowenstein Papers; Asheville *Citizen*, March 6, 1950, p. 9-A.

42. Greensboro *Daily News*, March 10, 1950.

43. Winston-Salem *Journal*, March 7, 1950; Asheville *Citizen*, March 7, 1950, p. 2-B.

44. Kinston *Daily Free Press*, March 6, 1950.

45. Author's interview with Kathryn N. Folger.

46. Graham Jones to "Fellow Students," March 15, 1950, Lowenstein Papers.

47. Jeff Johnson to Kelly M. Alexander, Jr., March 15, 1950, Johnson Papers; author's interview with Kelly M. Alexander, Jr., September 13, 1984.

48. Jeff Johnson to T. A. Hamme, March 16, 1950, Jeff Johnson to J. W. Jeffries, March 16, 1950, Johnson Papers.

49. William R. Johnson to Jeff Johnson, March 18, 1950, Johnson Papers.

50. Jesse S. Stroud to Jeff Johnson, March 15, 1950, Johnson Papers.

51. Aaron R. Moore to Jeff Johnson, March 28, 1950, Johnson Papers.

52. Reverend Joseph Fraylon to Jeff Johnson, March 21, 1950, Jeff Johnson to Kelly M. Alexander, Jr., March 15, March 24, 1950, Johnson Papers.

53. "A Discussion of the State-Wide Voter Registration Committee," speech by Kelly M. Alexander, Jr., March 4, 1950, NAACP Papers, group 2, ser. C, box 129; Dave Burgess to Dan Powell, weekly report, March 5–11, 1950, Powell Papers.

54. "A Discussion of the State-Wide Voter Registration Committee," speech by Kelly M. Alexander, Jr., March 4, 1950, NAACP Papers, group 2, ser. C, box 129.

55. Author's interview with Kelly M. Alexander, Jr.

56. J. R. Scott to Frank P. Graham, n.d., Johnson Papers.

57. Asheville *Citizen*, March 4, 1950, p. 14-A.

58. Ibid., March 19, 1950, p. 6-A.

59. "Frank P. Graham, Candidate for the United States Senate," n.d., pamphlet in Johnson Papers; Charlotte *Observer*, March 30, 1950, p. 22-A; Greensboro *Daily News*, March 30, 1950.

60. Asheville *Citizen*, March 26, 1950, p. 8-C, March 28, 1950, p. 10.

61. Charlotte *News*, March 13, 1950.

62. Asheville *Citizen*, March 31, 1950, p. 14; Elizabeth City *Daily Advance*, March 31, 1950, p. 1.

63. Charlotte *Observer*, March 7, 1950, p. 13-A.

64. Asheville *Citizen*, March 10, 1950, p. 2-A.

65. Durham *Morning Herald*, March 11, 1950; Charlotte *Observer*, March 12, 1950, p. 4-A; Asheville *Citizen*, March 11, 1950, p. 2-A.

66. Johnston Avery to Jonathan Daniels, March 14, 1950, Daniels Papers.

67. Asheville *Citizen*, March 11, 1950, p. 2-A.

68. Ibid., March 18, 1950, p. 8-A.

69. Durham *Morning Herald*, March 12, 1950.

70. Elizabeth City *Daily Advance*, March 17, 1950, p. 2.

71. Asheville *Citizen*, March 19, 1950, p. 6-A; Elizabeth City *Daily Advance*, March 20, 1950, p. 1.

72. Asheville *Citizen*, March 29, 1950, p. 11.

73. Editorial in Raleigh *News and Observer*, n.d., quoted in ibid., March 4, 1950, p. 4.

74. Jonathan Daniels to Harry H. Vaughan, March 3, 1950, Daniels Papers.

75. Harry H. Vaughan to Jonathan Daniels, March 10, 1950, Daniels Papers.

76. Durham *Morning Herald*, March 12, 1950; Charlotte *Observer*, March 11, 1950, p. 4-A; Raleigh *News and Observer*, March 11, 1950.

77. Allen Langston to Capus Waynick, March 22, 1950, Waynick Papers.

78. Author's interview with John Christoph Blucher Ehringhaus, Jr., November 10, 1984.

79. Author's interviews with Jesse A. Helms, December 11, 1984, William Thomas Joyner, Jr., December 12, 1984, James K. Dorsett, Jr., December 12, 1984, and Hoover Adams, May 26, 1983.

80. Author's interviews with James K. Dorsett, Jr., and John Christoph Blucher Ehringhaus, Jr.

81. Asheville *Citizen*, March 14, 1950, p. 1-B; *State*, March 18, 1950, p. 16; author's interview with Hoover Adams.

82. J. Shepard Bryan to Frank P. Graham, March 11, 1950, Graham Papers.

83. Asheville *Citizen*, March 14, 1950, p. 1-B.

84. Ibid., March 16, 1950.

85. Author's interview with Hoover Adams.

86. Allen Langston to Capus Waynick, March 22, 1950, Waynick Papers.

87. Ibid.

88. Author's interviews with James K. Dorsett, Jr., and Hoover Adams.

89. Author's interview with John Christoph Blucher Ehringhaus, Jr.

90. Author's interview with Hoover Adams.

91. "North Carolina Needs Willis Smith in the U.S. Senate," n.d., pamphlet in Lowenstein Papers; Greensboro *Daily News*, March 20, 1950, p. 1; Charlotte *Observer*, March 20, 1950, p. 1.

92. Elizabeth City *Daily Advance*, March 22, 1950, p. 4, March 23, 1950, p. 4; Charlotte *News*, March 23, 1950. On the Brannan Plan, see Matusow, *Farm Policies and Politics*, pp. 195–221.

93. Elizabeth City *Daily Advance*, March 24, 1950, p. 4.

94. Asheville *Citizen*, March 27, 28, 29, 30, 1950; Charlotte *Observer*, April 5, 1950, p. 9-A.

95. William T. Joyner, Sr., et al. to R. Gregg Cherry, March 24, 1950, Cherry Papers.

96. Author's interviews with James K. Dorsett, Jr., John Christoph Blucher Ehringhaus, Jr., and William Thomas Joyner, Jr.

97. Asheville *Citizen*, March 23, 1950, p. 17.

98. *Pilot*, March 10, 1950, p. 2.

99. Charlotte *Observer*, March 23, 1950, p. 12-A.

100. Raleigh *News and Observer*, March 24, 1950; U.S. President's Committee on Civil Rights, *To Secure These Rights*, p. 168.

101. Greensboro *Daily News*, March 27, 1950.

102. Durham *Sun*, March 24, 1950.

103. New York *Times*, March 24, 1950.

104. Harold H. Martin, "Fighting Half-Pint of Capitol Hill," p. 19.

105. Durham *Morning Herald*, March 27, 1950. The *Morning Herald* was correct. U.S. President's Committee on Civil Rights, *To Secure These Rights*, p. 167.

106. Transcript of radio address by Alvin Wingfield, Jr., March 5, 1950, pp. 3–5, Lowenstein Papers.

107. High Point *Enterprise*, March 24, 1950.

108. William D. Carmichael, Jr., to Judge John J. Parker, January 16, 1948, Daniels Papers; U.S. President's Committee on Civil Rights, *To Secure These Rights*, pp. 166–68; Mobile (Ala.) *Press*, March 23, 1949.

109. Frank P. Graham to Pauli Murray, March 6, 1950, Graham Papers.

110. Frank P. Graham to Gerald W. Johnson, August 6, 1948, Graham Papers.

111. D. Hiden Ramsey to Frank P. Graham, March 30, 1950, Graham Papers.

112. Charlotte *Observer*, March 23, 1950, p. 12-A.

113. Hamby, *Liberalism and Its Challengers*, p. 86.

114. Charlotte *Observer*, January 22, 1950, p. 1-A; Caute, *The Great Fear*, pp. 60–61. See also Weinstein, *Perjury: The Hiss-Chambers Case*.

115. Caute, *The Great Fear*, p. 62.

116. Ibid., p. 63; Asheville *Citizen*, February 4, 1950, p. 1-A, March 2, 1950, p. 1-A.

117. Hamby, *Liberalism and Its Challengers*, pp. 88–89; Reeves, *Life and Times of Joe McCarthy*, pp. 223–26.

118. Asheville *Citizen*, February 12, 1950, p. 1-A.

119. Hamby, *Liberalism and Its Challengers*, pp. 88–89.

120. *Newsweek*, February 13, 1950, p. 11; Charlotte *Observer*, March 26, 1950, p. 2-A.

121. Jonathan Daniels to Harry S Truman, March 23, 1950, Daniels Papers.

122. Jonathan Daniels to Carroll Kilpatrick, March 6, 1950, Daniels Papers.

123. Author's interview with William Thomas Joyner, Jr.

124. High Point *Enterprise*, March 7, 1950.

125. Walker Y. Worth to Clyde R. Hoey, February 17, March 9, 1950, Hoey Papers.

126. Flynn, *The Road Ahead*, p. 49.

127. Gladys Tillett to Les Biffle, March 23, 1950, Mrs. Paul P. McCain to Alben W. Barkley, March 23, 1950, Tillett Papers.

128. "The Road Ahead," sermon by Walter R. Courtenay, February 12, 1950, Johnson Papers.

129. Franz H. Krebs to the editor, Charlotte *Observer*, February 20, 1950, p. 10-A, March 2, 1950, p. 18-A.

130. Walker Y. Worth to Clyde R. Hoey, March 9, 1950, Hoey Papers.

131. Notes written by Jeff Johnson, n.d., Johnson Papers.

132. Reginald Turner to Frank P. Graham, March 19, 1950, Graham Papers.

133. David Murchison to Frank P. Graham, March 27, 1950, Graham Papers.

134. Raleigh *News and Observer*, March 25, 1950, p. 1; Charlotte *Observer*, March 25, 1950, p. 1; Greensboro *Daily News*, March 25, 1950, p. 2; Asheville *Citizen*, March 25, 1950, p. 7; "Life-Long Champion of Democracy," pamphlet advocating the candidacy of Frank P. Graham, n.d., Johnson Papers (hereafter cited as "Life-Long Champion of Democracy").

135. Interview with Frank P. Graham by Legette Blythe, June 9, 1970, Special Collections, University of North Carolina at Charlotte.

136. Raleigh *News and Observer*, March 27, 1950.

137. St. Louis *Post-Dispatch*, n.d., Daniels Papers.

138. Charles W. Tillett to Faison Kuestler, March 6, 1950, Tillett Papers.

139. Charles W. Tillett to Mary Shipp, March 28, 1950, Lowenstein Papers.

140. "Socialism form letter," March 6, 1950, Lowenstein Papers.

141. Frank P. Graham to Mrs. Dudley Bagley, March 9, 1950, Bagley Papers.

142. "Life-Long Champion of Democracy," pp. 1–8.

143. Ibid.

144. Greensboro *Daily News*, n.d., quoted in High Point *Enterprise*, n.d., Graham Papers; Charles W. Tillett to Marian Graham, March 4, 1950, Graham Papers.

145. Marian Graham to Charles W. Tillett, n.d., Graham Papers.

146. Harry L. Golden to the editor, Charlotte *Observer*, February 25, 1950, p. 4-A.

147. Asheville *Citizen*, March 19, 1950, p. 1-A; Raleigh *News and Observer*, March 19, 1950.

148. Asheville *Citizen*, March 21, 1950, p. 10.

149. Lewis, *County and Precinct Election Officials*, p. 8.

150. Raleigh *News and Observer*, March 20, 1950.

151. Greensboro *Daily News*, March 21, 1950.

152. Raleigh *News and Observer*, February 10, 1950.

153. Goldsboro *News-Argus*, March 23, 1950.

154. Asheville *Citizen*, March 24, 1950, p. 1-A.

155. Ibid., April 18, 1950, p. 1-A.

156. Ibid., March 23, 1950, p. 18, March 24, 1950, p. 1-A.

157. Greensboro *Daily News*, March 22, 1950.

158. Goldsboro *News-Argus*, March 23, March 24, 1950, p. 1.

159. Allen Langston to Capus Waynick, March 22, 1950, Waynick Papers.

160. C. M. Douglas to Jeff Johnson, March 21, 1950, Graham Papers.

161. Eugene T. Coltrane to Jeff Johnson, March 22, 28, 1950, Johnson Papers.

162. Raleigh *News and Observer*, March 29, 1950; Goldsboro *News-Argus*, March 28, 1950.

163. Durham *Sun*, March 31, 1950.

164. Dunn *Dispatch*, March 15, 1950.

165. High Point *Enterprise*, March 21, 23, 1950.

166. Greensboro *Daily News*, March 11, 1950.

167. Durham *Morning Herald*, March 29, 1950.

168. F. E. Edwards to W. Kerr Scott, March 24, 1950, Virgil S. Weathers to W. Kerr Scott, March 30, 1950, W. Kerr Scott to Virgil S. Weathers, March 30, 1950, Scott Papers.

169. Author's interview with Terry Sanford, December 3, 1984.

170. Raleigh *News and Observer*, March 26, 1950, p. 1; Charlotte *Observer*, March 26, 1950, p. 1.

171. Asheville *Citizen*, March 26, 1950, pp. 6, 8.

172. Ibid.

173. Raleigh *News and Observer*, March 26, 1950, clipping in Lewis Papers.

174. Charlotte *Observer*, March 17, 1950, p. 6-A.

175. New York *Times*, March 30, 1950; Charlotte *Observer*, March 30, 1950, p. 1.

176. Charlotte *News*, March 14, 15, 1950.

177. High Point *Enterprise*, March 19, 1950.

178. Johnston Avery to Jonathan Daniels, March 14, 1950, Daniels Papers.

179. Drew Pearson, "Washington Merry-Go-Round," n.d., n.p., newspaper clipping in Daniels Papers.

180. Ken Noble to Bill [Staton], February 21, 1950, Graham Papers.

181. Johnston Avery to Jonathan Daniels, March 14, 1950, Daniels Papers.

Chapter 5

1. Schedule of events for Senator Graham, April, May 1950, Johnson Papers.

2. Ibid.; author's interviews with Kathryn N. Folger, December 6, 1984, and Kate Humphries, December 13, 1984.

3. Kemp Battle to Marian Graham, March 25, 1950, Graham Papers.

4. Eula Nixon Greenwood, "Raleigh Roundup," Southport (N.C.) *Pilot*, n.d., clipping in Johnson Papers.

5. William R. Raynor to Jeff Johnson, April 20, 1950, Graham Papers.

6. Harry Golden to Frank P. Graham, April 4, 1950, Golden Papers.

7. Lindsay Tate to Allard Lowenstein, April 25, 1950, Lowenstein Papers.

8. Author's interview with Kathryn N. Folger.

9. W. Kerr Scott to Frank P. Graham, April 19, 1950, Graham Papers.

10. William R. Butt to Frank P. Graham, April 17, 1950, Graham Papers.

11. William W. Staton to Frank P. Graham, April 13, 1950, Graham Papers.

12. Charlotte *Observer*, April 11, 1950, p. 13-A.

13. Charles W. Tillett to Allard Lowenstein, May 3, 1950, Lowenstein Papers.

14. Jeff Johnson to Mark Goforth, April 4, 1950, Graham Papers.

15. Eugene T. Coltrane to Jeff Johnson, April 13, 1950, Graham Papers.

16. *Newsweek*, April 17, 1950, p. 19.

17. Author's interviews with David M. McConnell, September 13, 1984, and Kathryn N. Folger.

18. Charlotte *Observer*, April 6, 1950, p. 1-B.

19. Ibid., April 10, 1950, p. 10-A, April 26, 1950, p. 17-A; "Citizens: Here Are the Facts," n.p., n.d., political ad, Lowenstein Papers; author's interview with David M. McConnell.

20. David M. McConnell to Jeff Johnson, April 15, 1950, Graham Papers.

21. Author's interview with Kelly M. Alexander, Jr., September 13, 1984.

22. Author's interview with David M. McConnell.

23. Schedule of events for Senator Graham, April, May 1950, Johnson Papers.

24. Author's interview with Kathryn N. Folger.

25. Author's interview with David M. McConnell.

26. Author's interviews with James B. Whittington, December 5, 1984, and Richard E. Thigpen, Sr., December 5, 1984; Richard E. Thigpen, Sr., "77 Years into the Twentieth Century: The Autobiography of Richard Elton Thigpen, Sr.," typescript in the possession of author, Charlotte, N.C.

27. Charlotte *Observer*, April 6, 1950, p. 4-A.

28. Charles W. Tillett to J. Maryon Saunders and William D. Carmichael, April 29, 1950, Tillett Papers; Mrs. Carleton Jester, Jr., to Gladys Tillett Coddington, December 19, 1949, Jackson Papers.

29. Greensboro *Daily News*, April 15, 1950, p. 6.

30. Ibid., April 19, 1950.

31. High Point *Enterprise*, April 25, 1950.

32. Interview with Gladys Avery Tillett by Jacquelyn Dowd Hall, March 20, 1974, Southern Oral History Collection; New York *Herald Tribune*, April 17, 1950; Raleigh *News and Observer*, April 17, 1950; Asheville *Citizen*, April 17, 1950, p. 1-A; Charlotte *Observer*, April 17, 1950, p. 1-B.

33. Charlotte *Observer*, April 18, 1950, p. 6-A; Asheville *Citizen*, April 18, 1950, p. 7; High Point *Enterprise*, April 17, 1950, p. 1.

34. Jonathan Daniels to Clyde R. Hoey, April 24, 1950, Hoey Papers; High Point *Enterprise*, April 19, 1950; Charlotte *Observer*, April 19, 1950, p. 4-A.

35. Asheville *Citizen*, April 19, 1950, p. 15.

36. Author's interview with Sam Ragan, October 25, 1984.

37. Durham *Morning Herald*, April 13, 27, 1950.

38. High Point *Enterprise*, April 17, 1950, p. 4, April 18, 1950.

39. Raleigh *News and Observer*, April 19, 1950.

40. Author's interview with Thad Eure, December 11, 1984.

41. High Point *Enterprise*, April 25, 1950, p. 1.

42. W. Banks Shepherd to Jeff Johnson, April 7, 1950, Graham Papers; Dudley W. Bagley to Lindsay Warren, April 8, 1950, Warren Papers.

43. Greensboro *Daily News*, April 27, 1950.

44. Jeff Johnson to Dave Burgess, May 4, 1950, Graham Papers.

45. Elizabeth City *Daily Advance*, April 28, 1950, p. 1.

46. Asheville *Citizen*, April 29, 1950, p. 2; Charlotte *Observer*, April 30, 1950, p. 8-A.

47. Charlotte *Observer*, April 28, 1950, p. 28-A, April 29, 1950, p. 1-A.

48. Ibid., April 30, 1950, p. 16-A.

49. Durham *Sun*, April 27, 1950.

50. Author's interview with Kathryn N. Folger.

51. Jonathan Daniels to Edward J. Kelly, April 20, 1950, Daniels Papers; Washington (N.C.) *Daily News*, April 20, 1950.

52. Author's interview with Kathryn N. Folger; interview with Jonathan Worth Daniels by Charles Eagles, March 9–11, 1977, Southern Oral History Collection.

53. "Women Will Win This Election," n.p., n.d., pamphlet in Tillett Papers; interview with Gladys Avery Tillett by Jacquelyn Dowd Hall, March 20, 1974, pp. 52, 54, 55, 57, Southern Oral History Collection.

54. Raleigh *News and Observer*, April 24, 1950; Asheville *Citizen*, April 24, 1950, p. 13.

55. High Point *Enterprise*, April 19, 1950.

56. *The Beacon*, n.p., May 11, 1950, Tillett Papers.

57. "Mrs. Tillett Was Right When She Said," n.p., n.d., political ad in Tillett Papers.

58. Author's interview with David M. McConnell.

59. Raleigh *News and Observer*, April 14, 1950.

60. Charlotte *Observer*, April 16, 1950, p. 10-B.

61. Asheville *Citizen*, April 26, 1950.

62. Thomas A. Morgan to Henry A. Dennis, April 3, 1950, Daniels Papers; Henderson *Daily Dispatch*, April 6, 1950; Asheville *Citizen*, April 9, 1950, p. 4.

63. Asheville *Citizen*, April 25, 1950.

64. Ibid., April 18, 1950, p. 5; press release from C. A. Upchurch, Jr., Graham headquarters, April 18, 1950, Johnson Papers.

65. James Yadkin Joyner to Frank P. Graham, April 18, 1950, Graham Papers; Raleigh *News and Observer*, April 20, 1950.

66. *Carolina Israelite*, April 1950, p. 1; Asheville *Citizen*, April 17, 1950, p. 10.

67. William J. Smith to Jeff D. Johnson, March 24, 1950, CIO Organizing Committee Papers.

68. Dave Burgess to Dan Powell, weekly reports, April 9–15, 23–29, 1950, Powell Papers.

69. Kemp Battle to Frank P. Graham, April 22, 1950, Graham Papers.

70. Asheville *Citizen*, April 15, 1950, p. 4.

71. Elizabeth City *Daily Advance*, April 25, 1950, p. 1; Raleigh *News and Observer*, April 28, 1950.

72. Authors' interviews with Kate Humphries and John Sanders, October 17, 1984.

73. Author's interview with Warren Ashby, August 2, 1982.

74. Authors' interview with William C. Friday, October 17, 1984.

75. Author's interviews with R. Mayne Albright, November 30, 1984, and William C. Friday.

76. Author's interview with Terry Sanford, December 3, 1984.

77. Ibid.

78. Author's interview with R. Mayne Albright.

79. Author's interview with J. Melville Broughton, Jr., December 12, 1984.

80. Author's interviews with Kate Humphries and J. Melville Broughton, Jr.

81. Author's interviews with Sam Ragan, J. Melville Broughton, Jr., and Kathryn N. Folger.

82. Author's interview with R. Mayne Albright.

83. Author's interview with Terry Sanford.

84. Author's interview with William W. Staton, May 24, 1983.

85. Greensboro *Daily News*, April 10, 1950; Charlotte *Observer*, April 10, 1950, p. 9-B; Asheville *Citizen*, April 10, 1950, p. 11.

86. Charlotte *Observer*, April 14, 1950, p. 18-A.

87. Ibid., April 8, 1950, p. 3-A; Greensboro *Daily News*, April 9, 1950.

88. Greensboro *Daily News*, April 11, 1950.

89. Ibid., April 25, 1950.

90. Political ads, various newspapers, fliers, n.d., in Powell Papers, Tillett Papers, and Lang Papers.

91. Press release, Smith headquarters, April 20, 1950, Daniels Papers; political ad, n.p., n.d., in Golden Papers.

92. Author's interview with Kathryn N. Folger.

93. Lecture by William D. Snider included in "Reminiscences of the 1950 Campaign," Frank P. Graham Jubilee Symposium, Proceedings, September 26–27, 1980, University of North Carolina at Greensboro.

94. Press release, Graham headquarters, April 4, 1950, Lowenstein Papers.

95. Speech by J. Con Lanier, n.d., Lanier Papers.

96. Raleigh *News and Observer*, April 20, 1950.

97. *Pilot*, April 28, 1950, p. 2.

98. Charles W. Tillett to Ira T. Wyche, April 14, 1950, Tillett Papers; Charlotte *Observer*, April 28, 1950, p. 22-A; Raleigh *News and Observer*, April 28, 1950, p. 1; High Point *Enterprise*, April 28, 1950, p. 1.

99. High Point *Enterprise*, April 28, 1950, p. 1; Charlotte *Observer*, April 28, 1950, p. 22-A.

100. Robert E. Williams to Capus Waynick, April 4, 1950, Waynick Papers; Charlotte *Observer*, April 9, 1950, p. 11-B.

101. Asheville *Citizen*, April 23, 1950, p. 8-C.

102. Charlotte *Observer*, April 18, 1950, p. 9-B.

103. Ibid., April 24, 1950, p. 11-A.

104. Author's interview with Harold T. Makepeace, Sr., October 25, 1984; Charlotte *Observer*, April 18, 1950, p. 7-A.

105. T. A. Uzzell, Jr., to Clyde R. Hoey, April 8, 1950, Hoey Papers.

106. Charlotte *Observer*, April 4, 1950, p. 1.

107. Author's interviews with James B. Whittington, Harold T. Makepeace, Sr., and Richard E. Thigpen, Sr.

108. Asheville *Citizen*, April 6, 1950, p. 2-A.

109. Ibid., April 5, 1950, p. 17.

110. Golden, *The Right Time*, p. 271.

111. Greensboro *Daily News*, April 12, 1950; Christenson, *The Brannan Plan*, pp. 3–4; Matusow, *Farm Policies and Politics*, pp. 191–221.

112. Asheville *Citizen*, April 21, 1950, p. 4.

113. Charlotte *Observer*, April 19, 1950, p. 7-A.

114. Asheville *Citizen*, April 29, 1950, p. 2.

115. High Point *Enterprise*, April 7, 1950.

116. Dunn *Dispatch*, n.d., Lowenstein Papers.

117. Asheville *Citizen*, April 12, 1950, p. 13.

118. *Pilot*, April 21, 1950, p. 19.

119. Author's interview with William Thomas Joyner, Jr., December 12, 1984.

120. Two political ads, n.p., n.d., Lowenstein Papers; press release, Smith headquarters, April 20, 1950, Daniels Papers.

121. *Challenge to Socialism*, 4, no. 15 (April 13, 1950): 1–4.

122. J. R. Cherry, Jr., to the editor, Charlotte *News*, April 13, 1950.

123. J. C. Wheless to the editor, Charlotte *Observer*, April 29, 1950, p. 8-A; A. J. Fletcher to Clyde R. Hoey, April 24, 1950, Hoey Papers.

124. Harry W. Chase to Charles W. Tillett, April 21, 1950, Edward R. Murrow to Charles W. Tillett, April 25, 1950, Tillett Papers.

125. Stephan Duggan to Frank P. Graham, August 21, 1935, Graham Papers.

126. Harry W. Chase to Charles W. Tillett, April 21, 1950, Edward R. Murrow to Charles W. Tillett, April 25, 1950, Tillett Papers.

127. Jeff Johnson to William J. Smith, April 14, 1950, Johnson Papers; Raleigh *Times*, April 22, 1950.

128. Pamphlets and political ads, n.d., Tillett Papers; Charles W. Tillett to Ira T. Wyche, April 11, 1950, Tillett Papers.

129. Charlotte *Observer*, April 14, 1950, p. 14-A; Asheville *Citizen*, April 14, 1950, p. 15.

130. Goldsboro *News-Argus*, April 11, 1950.

131. Asheville *Citizen*, April 26, 1950, p. 5.

132. Charlotte *Observer*, April 28, 1950, p. 1-B.

133. Ibid., May 3, 1950, p. 9-A.

134. Ibid., April 27, 28, 1950, p. 1.

135. Charlotte *News*, April 14, 1950.

136. Jonathan Daniels to Ralph McGill, April 17, 1950, Daniels Papers.

137. Greensboro *Daily News*, April 27, 1950.

138. Asheville *Citizen*, April 4, 1950, p. 1-A; Kluger, *Simple Justice*, p. 278.

139. Asheville *Citizen*, April 6, 1950, p. 1-A; Charlotte *Observer*, April 6, 1950, p. 2-A.

140. Charlotte *Observer*, April 7, 1950, p. 5-A.

141. Asheville *Citizen*, April 6, 1950, p. 2-A.

142. Ibid., April 7, 1950, p. 14.

143. Harry McMullan to Lindsay Warren, April 14, 1950, Warren Papers.

144. Willis Smith to Clyde R. Hoey, April 7, 1950, Hoey Papers.

145. Clyde R. Hoey to Willis Smith, April 11, 1950, Hoey Papers.

146. Greensboro *Daily News*, April 12, 1950, p. 5; Asheville *Citizen*, April 13, 1950, p. 15-B.

147. Raleigh *News and Observer*, April 29, 1950.

148. Charlotte *Observer*, April 8, 1950, p. 3-A.

149. Press release, Smith headquarters, April 20, 1950, Daniels Papers.

150. D. Hiden Ramsey to Frank P. Graham, March 30, 1950, Ramsey Papers.

151. Raleigh *News and Observer*, n.d., clipping in Graham Papers.

152. "Frank Graham Opposes FEPC," n.d., political ad in Tillett Papers.

153. Raleigh *News and Observer*, April 22, 1950; Charlotte *Observer*, April 23, 1950, p. 21-A; Durham *Morning Herald*, April 21, 1950, p. 1.

154. Morris Ernst to A. G. Ivey, May 4, 1950, Johnson Papers; Sadie T. M. Alexander to A. G. Ivey, May 3, 1950, Lowenstein Papers; Dorothy Tilly to A. G. Ivey, April 26, 1950, Johnson Papers.

155. Henry Knox Sherrill to A. G. Ivey, April 25, 1950, Johnson Papers.

156. Charlotte *Observer*, April 23, 1950, p. 21-A.

157. Lindsay Tate to Allard Lowenstein, April 25, 1950, Lowenstein Papers; Durham *Morning Herald*, April 22, 1950.

158. New York *Times*, April 2, 1950.

159. Philadelphia *Inquirer*, April 2, 1950; Goldsboro *News-Argus*, April 25, 1950.

160. Kelly M. Alexander, Jr., "A Report About the North Carolina NAACP Political Action Program," April 8, 1950, NAACP Papers; author's interview with Kelly M. Alexander, Jr.

161. *Carolina Times*, April 22, 1950, p. 1.

162. Ibid., p. 4.

163. M. S. Johnson to Frank P. Graham, April 19, 1950, Graham Papers.

164. Charles W. Windsor to Frank P. Graham, April 25, 1950, Graham Papers.

165. *Carolina Times*, April 27, 1950, p. 2.

166. Mary Coker Joslin, "Precinct Politics: The Red and the Black," pp. 10–11, pamphlet in possession of author, Raleigh, N.C.

167. K. A. Caddell to Jeff Johnson, April 24, 1950, Graham Papers; Charlotte *Observer*, April 2, 1950, p. 1.

168. Charlotte *Observer*, April 4, 1950, p. 1.

169. Ibid., April 5, 1950, p. 9-A.

170. Transcript of radio address by Bob Reynolds, April 4, 1950, WAYS, Charlotte, N.C., Lang Papers.

171. M. Y. Jarrett to Frank P. Graham, February 25, 1950, Graham Papers.

172. Charlotte *Observer*, April 9, 1950, p. 1-B.

173. Asheville *Citizen*, April 15, 1950, p. 2.

174. Bendiner, "Maytime Politics."

175. Schlesinger, "Frank Graham's Primary Education."

Chapter 6

1. Ford S. Worthy to Lindsay C. Warren, May 16, 1950, Warren Papers.

2. Goldsboro *News-Argus*, May 10, 1950.

3. John Marshall to Capus Waynick, May 5, 1950, Waynick Papers.

4. Lindsay C. Warren to Dr. M. O. Fletcher, May 4, 1950, Warren Papers.

5. C. F. Hefner to Frank P. Graham, May 1, 1950, Graham Papers.

6. Boston *Globe*, May 25, 1950.

7. Maude McDaniel to Frank P. Graham, May 14, 1950, Graham Papers; M. S. Breckenridge to Frank P. Graham, May 19, 1950, Graham Papers.

8. W. Reade Johnson to Jeff Johnson, May 9, 1950, Graham Papers.

9. Author's interview with Lennox Polk McLendon, Jr., November 2, 1984.

10. Charlotte *News*, May 1, 2, 1950; Durham *Sun*, May 5, 1950.

11. Cleveland County (N.C.) *Times*, May 12, 1950.

12. John Marshall to James M. Barnwell, May 5, 1950, Scott Papers.

13. Memo, Jeff Johnson to local campaign managers, May 18, 1950, Johnson Papers.

14. "Willis Smith Goes to Washington," n.p., n.d., cartoon in Powell Papers.

15. Charlotte *Observer*, May 3, 1950, p. 1-A; *New Republic*, May 1, 1950, pp. 14–15.

16. Charlotte *Observer*, May 9, 1950, p. 1-B.

17. Ibid., May 5, 1950, p. 20-A.

18. Ibid., May 6, 1950, p. 6-A.

19. Asheville *Citizen*, May 5, 1950, p. 10.

20. *U.S. News and World Report*, May 12, 1950, pp. 13–14.

21. *Life*, May 15, 1950, pp. 38, 40; author's interview with Claude M. Pepper, October 31, 1969.

22. Jonathan Daniels to Isador Lubin, May 5, 1950, Daniels Papers.

23. Raleigh *News and Observer*, May 7, 1950.

24. *Nation*, May 13, 1950, p. 436.

25. Greensboro *Daily News*, May 9, 1950.

26. Author's interview with Roy Wilder, Jr., December 13, 1984; Asheville *Citizen*, May 13, 1950, p. 8.

27. W. Kerr Scott to Boyd Harless, May 24, 1950, Scott Papers; Charlotte *Observer*, May 20, 1950, p. 3-A.

28. Durham *Morning Herald*, May 18, 1950.

29. Ibid.

30. Ashby, *Frank Porter Graham*, p. 260; Paul H. Douglas, *In the Fullness of Time*, pp. 240–41.

31. Ashby, *Frank Porter Graham*, pp. 260–61, 273.

32. Ibid., p. 261; author's interview with R. Mayne Albright, November 30, 1984.

33. High Point *Enterprise*, May 3, 1950, p. 1.

34. Ibid., May 1, 1950.

35. Asheville *Citizen*, May 7, 1950, p. 1.

36. Raleigh *News and Observer*, June 20, 1948, December 31, 1949. See also Eagles, *Jonathan Daniels and Race Relations*.

37. Raleigh *News and Observer*, May 10, 1950.

38. Charlotte *Observer*, May 15, 1950, p. 1-A; Elizabeth City *Daily Advance*, May 17, 1950, p. 1-A; Raleigh *News and Observer*, May 15, 1950, p. 1; Eagles, *Jonathan Daniels and Race Relations*, p. 146.

39. New York *Times*, May 15, 1950.

40. Baltimore *Evening Sun*, May 15, 1950, p. 18.

41. Kenneth C. Royall to Jonathan Daniels, May 16, 1950, Daniels Papers.

42. High Point *Enterprise*, May 19, 1950; Raleigh *News and Observer*, May 20, 1950; Asheville *Citizen*, May 20, 1950, p. 1; Charlotte *Observer*, May 20, 1950, p. 1-A.

43. Interviews with Jonathan Worth Daniels by George B. Tindall, p. 154, and by Charles Eagles, pp. 239–40, Southern Oral History Collection.

44. *Newsweek*, May 29, 1950, p. 17.

45. Frank P. Graham to Bill Crisp, May 26, 1950, Graham Papers.

46. *Newsweek*, May 29, 1950, p. 17.

47. Raleigh *Times*, May 19, 1950.

48. Author's interview with John Christoph Blucher Ehringhaus, Jr., November 10, 1984; Asheville *Citizen*, May 20, 1950, p. 1.

49. Charlotte *Observer*, May 23, 1950, p. 7-A.

50. Raleigh *News and Observer*, May 14, 1950.

51. Advance draft of the Democratic party platform, May 11, 1950, Cherry Papers; *State*, May 20, 1950, p. 14; Elizabeth City *Daily Advance*, May 11, 1950, p. 1.

52. Charlotte *Observer*, May 11, 1950, p. 20-A.

53. Asheville *Citizen*, May 12, 1950, p. 1; Charlotte *Observer*, May 12, 1950, p. 1-A.

54. Ford S. Worthy to Lindsay Warren, May 16, 1950, Warren Papers; Elizabeth City *Daily Advance*, May 16, 1950, p. 8.

55. Allen Langston to C. A. Upchurch, Jr., May 17, 1950, Langston Papers; Raleigh *News and Observer*, May 20, 1950.

56. Author's interview with R. Mayne Albright; Elizabeth City *Daily Advance*, May 24, 1950, p. 1.

57. Elizabeth City *Daily Advance*, May 16, 1950, p. 2.

58. Transcript of radio address by George Maurice Hill, Morganton, N.C., May 18, 1950, Langston Papers, pp. 1–3.

59. Radio address by D. Hiden Ramsey, May 16, 1950, Ramsey Papers; Asheville *Citizen*, May 17, 1950, p. 8.

60. Norman A. Boren to D. Hiden Ramsey, May 17, 1950, Ramsey Papers.

61. D. Hiden Ramsey to Norman A. Boren, May 18, 1950, Ramsey Papers.

62. Jeff Johnson to D. Hiden Ramsey, May 17, 1950, Johnson Papers.

63. Speech by D. Hiden Ramsey, May 24, 1950, pp. 1–6, Ramsey Papers; Asheville *Citizen*, May 25, 1950, p. 28.

64. Author's interview with R. Mayne Albright.

65. W. Kerr Scott to O. E. Boles, May 2, 1950, Scott Papers.

66. John Marshall to Capus Waynick, May 5, 1950, Waynick Papers.

67. Author's interview with David M. McConnell, September 13, 1984.

68. Durham *Sun*, May 8, 1950; Charlotte *Observer*, May 5, 1950, p. 1-A.

69. Durham *Morning Herald*, May 17, 1950; Asheville *Citizen*, May 17, 1950, p. 8.

70. Goldsboro *News-Argus*, May 17, 1950.

71. *Pilot*, May 19, 1950, p. 1.

72. Greensboro *Daily News*, May 23, 1950; Charlotte *Observer*, May 23, 1950, p. 7-A; Asheville *Citizen*, May 23, 1950, p. 13.

73. Daniel L. Bell to W. Kerr Scott, May 17, 1950, Scott Papers; High Point *Enterprise*, May 24, 1950, p. 1; Charlotte *Observer*, May 25, 1950, pp. 28-A, 11-B; Raleigh *News and Observer*, May 25, 1950, p. 1; Asheville *Citizen*, May 24, 1950, p. 9.

74. Author's interviews with Ralph W. Scott, December 31, 1984, and William D. Snider, October 30, 1984; J. E. Hall to Frank P. Graham, n.d., Graham Papers.

75. Author's interview with William D. Snider; Jonathan Daniels to Frank Logan, May 22, 1950, Daniels Papers.

76. Durham *Morning Herald*, May 22, 1950.

77. Charlotte *Observer*, May 23, 1950, p. 8-A.

78. A. McPherson to George C. Marshall, May 15, 1950, Marshall's aide (name unknown) to Allard Lowenstein, May 17, 1950, Marshall Papers.

79. L. B. Nichols to Clyde B. Tolson, May 15, 1950, Frank Porter Graham FBI file. This file is a compendium of the three FBI background investigations that preceded Graham's War Labor Board service, his presidency of the Oak Ridge Institute of Nuclear Studies, and his term as a United Nations officer. McConnell's effort, while politically naive, was not as foolish as one might think. Although Graham and Hoover were not close, they were on very friendly terms. Hoover had been much impressed with the Institute of Government at Chapel Hill and had complimented Graham on its accomplishments in 1942. In response, Graham had praised Hoover and his bureau and pledged his support of "the great work you are rendering to the nation." Hoover never forgot Graham's plaudit or his cooperation during the FBI background checks. Frank P. Graham to J. Edgar Hoover, February 20, 1942, Graham FBI file.

80. L. B. Nichols to Clyde B. Tolson, May 15, 1950, Graham FBI file.

81. Anthony Valente to Frank P. Graham, May 3, 1950, Graham Papers; Greensboro *Daily News*, May 9, 1950.

82. W. P. Harden to Santford Martin, May 23, 1950, Martin Papers.

83. William J. Smith to North Carolina staff members, May 16, 1950, Powell Papers.

84. Undated campaign memorandum, Powell Papers; Edward B. Clark to Jeff Johnson, May 8, 1950, Johnson Papers.

85. Dave Burgess to Dan Powell, weekly report, May 7–13, 1950, Powell Papers.

86. Dave Burgess to Dan Powell, weekly reports, May 15–21, 21–27, Powell Papers.

87. Dave Burgess to Jeff Johnson, May 13, 1950, Graham Papers.

88. Jeff Johnson to Dave Burgess, May 15, 1950, Graham Papers.

89. James T. Taylor to Jeff Johnson, May 10, 23, 25, 1950, Graham Papers.

90. A. M. Hasson to Jeff Johnson, May 23, 1950, Graham Papers.

91. Willie Jacobs to Frank P. Graham, May 20, 1950, Graham Papers.

92. Jeff Johnson to T. A. Hamme, May 13, 1950, Scott Papers.

93. "North Carolina Negro Democratic Organizing Pamphlet," n.d., Graham Papers.

94. *Carolinian*, May 20, 1950, sec. 2, p. 3.

95. Ibid., editorial, May 13, 1950, p. 2.

96. Ibid., May 13, 1950, p. 4, May 27, 1950, p. 4.

97. Ibid., May 27, 1950, p. 7.

98. Asheville *Citizen*, May 5, 1950, p. 14; Charlotte *Observer*, May 5, 1950, p. 15-A.

99. M. G. Mann to members of the Farmers' Cooperative Exchange, May 18, 1950, Johnson Papers.

100. Press release, Graham headquarters, May 25, 1950, Lowenstein Papers; Charlotte *Observer*, May 25, 1950, p. 23-A.

101. Raleigh *News and Observer*, May 26, 1950.

102. Charlotte *News*, May 18, 1950, p. 10-A.

103. Raleigh *News and Observer*, May 20, 1950.

104. Calvin Zimmerman to Jonathan Daniels, May 16, 1950, Daniels Papers.

105. Carl Horn, Jr., to the editor, Charlotte *Observer*, May 22, 1950, p. 12-A.

106. Author's interview with James K. Dorsett, Jr., December 12, 1984.

107. R. H. Calvin Rea to the editor, Charlotte *Observer*, May 25, 1950, pp. 14–15.

108. Charlotte *Observer*, May 22, 1950, p. 11-A.

109. Elizabeth City *Daily Advance*, May 25, 1950, p. 10.

110. "The Deadly Parallel," n.d., political ad in Johnson Papers; Raleigh *News and Observer*, May 26, 1950.

111. Raleigh *News and Observer*, May 22, 1950, p. 12.

112. C. A. Upchurch, Jr., to Allard Lowenstein, May 8, 1950, Lowenstein Papers.

113. Charlotte *Observer*, May 22, 1950, p. 12.

114. Willis Smith to William F. Wimberly, May 1, 1950, Cherry Papers.

115. Louis E. Wooten to Capus Waynick, May 11, 1950, Waynick Papers, Raleigh *News and Observer*, May 1, 1950.

116. Asheville *Citizen*, May 3, 1950, p. 8.

117. Ibid., May 7, 1950, p. 10; Raleigh *News and Observer*, May 7, 1950; Charlotte *Observer*, May 7, 1950, p. 14-A.

118. Raleigh *News and Observer*, May 9, 1950.

119. Ruth W. Swisher to the editor, *Pilot*, May 5, 1950, p. 2.

120. *Southern Textile Bulletin*, May 1950, p. 30.

121. Asheville *Citizen*, May 10, 1950, p. 11; Raleigh *News and Observer*, May 10, 1950, p. 19.

122. Durham *Morning Herald*, May 8, 1950.

123. Press release, Smith headquarters, May 12, 1950, Graham Papers; Raleigh *News and Observer*, May 13, 1950; Charlotte *Observer*, May 13, 1950, p. 3-A.

124. Harold Makepeace to Clyde R. Hoey, May 11, 1950, Hoey Papers; Asheville *Citizen*, May 16, 1950, p. 9; Raleigh *News and Observer*, May 16, 1950, p. 5.

125. Charlotte *Observer*, May 17, 1950, p. 2-B, May 18, 1950, p. 8-A.

126. Asheville *Citizen*, May 19, 1950, p. 27.

127. Charlotte *Observer*, May 17, 1950, p. 2-B; Asheville *Citizen*, May 14, 1950, p. 10; Raleigh *News and Observer*, May 18, 1950.

128. Undated newspaper clipping, Clipping File, North Carolina Collection; Hoover Adams to R. Gregg Cherry, May 9, 1950, Cherry Papers.

129. Durham *Morning Herald*, May 22, 1950.

130. Charlotte *News*, May 18, 1950, p. 10-A.

131. Raleigh *News and Observer*, May 21, 1950.

132. Ibid., May 16, 1950; Klehr, *Heyday of American Communism*, pp. 278, 347–48.

133. Goldsboro *News-Argus*, May 25, 1950.

134. Ibid., May 26, 1950; Raleigh *News and Observer*, May 18, 1950.

135. Raleigh *News and Observer*, May 16, 19, 23, 1950.

136. Charlotte *News*, May 20, 1950, p. 1; Charlotte *Observer*, May 20, 1950, p. 1-B; Asheville *Citizen*, May 21, 1950; Raleigh *News and Observer*, May 20, 1950.

137. Raleigh *News and Observer*, May 21, 1950; High Point *Enterprise*, May 23, 1950; Goldsboro *News-Argus*, May 22, 1950.

138. High Point *Enterprise*, May 21, 1950, p. 4-A, May 23, 1950, p. 1.

139. Kinston *Daily Free Press*, May 20, 1950.

140. Durham *Sun*, May 25, 1950.

141. Author's interview with Ralph W. Scott.

142. Charles H. Doggett to Clyde R. Hoey, May 15, 1950, Hoey Papers.

143. Campaign report, Mrs. W. T. Bost to Frank Graham, May 20, 1950, Graham Papers.

144. J. S. Liles to Frank P. Graham, May 20, 1950, Graham Papers.

145. Shelby *Daily Star*, May 23, 1950; *News and Observer*, May 13, 1950, p. 3.

146. Memo, Jeff Johnson to local campaign managers, May 18, 1950, Johnson Papers.

147. Laurinburg (N.C.) *Exchange*, n.d., private papers of Donald McCoy, Fayetteville, N.C.

148. *Carolinian*, May 20, 1950, p. 7; Raleigh *News and Observer*, May 12, 1950; *Newsweek*, May 29, 1950, p. 16.

149. Fred Whitener to alumni of the University of North Carolina, n.d., Leonard Powers to Frank P. Graham, May 25, 1950, Graham Papers.

150. Richard D. Dixon to Jeff Johnson, May 10, 1950, Graham Papers.

151. Raleigh *News and Observer*, May 22, 1950.

152. W. Wite to Joe W. Grier, May 22, 1950, Powell Papers.

153. Charlotte *Observer*, May 24, 1950, p. 9-A; Asheville *Citizen*, May 24, 1950, p. 9; *Carolinian*, May 27, 1950, p. 1.

154. Raleigh *News and Observer*, May 24, 1950.

155. Author's interviews with William Thomas Joyner, Jr., December 12, 1984, Jesse A. Helms, December 11, 1984, and Hoover Adams, May 26, 1983; Charlotte *Observer*, May 24, 1950, p. 9-A.

156. Author's interview with Hoover Adams.

157. Author's interview with James K. Dorsett, Jr.

158. Author's interview with Hoover Adams.

159. Golden, *The Right Time*, p. 271.

160. Leroy Jones to J. Melville Broughton, May 24, 1948, Graham Papers.

161. Frank P. Graham to Leroy Jones, June 11, 1949, Graham Papers.

162. Leroy Jones to Frank P. Graham, June 19, 1949, Graham Papers.

163. "U.S. Civil Service Commission, Rating of Candidates in Examinations for Designation to the United States Military and Naval Academies, July 11, 1949," Graham Papers.

164. John D. McConnell to Leroy Jones, September 20, 1949, Graham Papers.

165. Gastonia *Gazette*, n.d., clipping in Graham Papers.

166. Greensboro *Daily News*, October 4, 1949.

167. John Sanders to Frank P. Graham, September 22, 1949, Graham Papers.

168. James T. Taylor to Frank P. Graham, September 23, 1949, Graham Papers.

169. Gastonia *Gazette*, n.d., clipping in Graham Papers.

170. Author's interview with Hoover Adams.

171. Author's interview with R. Mayne Albright.

172. Transcript of radio address by George Maurice Hill, May 18, 1950, Langston Papers.

173. Goldsboro *News-Argus*, May 12, 1950; Asheville *Citizen*, May 13, 1950, p. 8.

174. Charlotte *Observer*, May 6, 1950, p. 1-B.

175. Asheville *Citizen*, May 10, 1950, p. 11.

176. Jacksonville (N.C.) *News and Views*, May 23, 1950.

177. Asheville *Citizen*, May 21, 1950, pp. 8-A, 11; Charlotte *Observer*, May 25, 1950, p. 14-B; Elizabeth City *Daily Advance*, May 25, 1950, p. 6.

178. Cleveland County (N.C.) *Times*, May 23, 1950.

179. Author's interview with Roy Wilder, Jr.

180. Asheville *Citizen*, May 17, 1950, p. 9, May 25, 1950, p. 15.

181. Asheville *Citizen*, May 25, 1950, p. 15, May 26, 1950, p. 37, May 27, 1950, p. 5.

182. *Carolina Times*, May 27, 1950, p. 2.

183. Charlotte *Observer*, May 25, 1950, p. 20-A; Asheville *Citizen*, May 26, 1950, p. 14.

184. Charlotte *News*, May 5, 1950.

185. *Pilot*, May 26, 1950, p. 2.

186. Washington (N.C.) *Daily News*, May 24, 1950, p. 4.

187. Raleigh *News and Observer*, May 21, 27, 1950, p. 4.

188. Ibid., May 26, 1950.

189. Charlotte *Observer*, May 24, 1950, p. 15-A.

190. New York *Herald Tribune*, May 25, 1950, p. 13.

191. Richmond *Times-Dispatch*, May 25, 1950, p. 16.

192. Jeff Johnson to county managers, May 24, 1950, Johnson Papers.

193. Greensboro *Daily News*, May 25, 1950.

194. Transcript of radio address by J. O. Talley, Jr., May 26, 1950, Langston Papers.

195. Asheville *Citizen*, May 27, 1950, p. 1.

196. Ibid., May 28, 1950, p. 9; University News Bureau, press release, University of North Carolina, May 27, 1950, Graham Papers.

197. Charlotte *Observer*, May 21, 1950, p. 13-A.

198. Raleigh *Times*, May 13, 1950.

199. Charlotte *Observer*, May 22, 1950, p. 1-A; Asheville *Citizen*, May 22, 1950, p. 6.

200. Elizabeth City *Daily Advance*, May 25, 1950, p. 1.

201. Asheville *Citizen*, May 27, 1950, p. 1.

202. Charlotte *Observer*, May 27, 1950, p. 1-B.

203. Ibid., May 26, 1950, p. 1-A.

204. Washington (N.C.) *Daily News*, May 22, 1950, p. 1; Durham *Sun*, May 26, 1950, p. 2.

205. Frederick H. Brooks to Jonathan Daniels, May 22, 1950, Daniels Papers.

206. Clyde R. Hoey to O. L. Moore, May 15, 1950, Hoey Papers.

207. Durham *Morning Herald*, May 28, 1950.

208. Raleigh *News and Observer*, June 4, 1950.

209. *North Carolina Manual—1950*, p. 236; Raleigh *News and Observer*, June 3, 1950.

210. *North Carolina Manual—1950*, p. 236; Charlotte *Observer*, May 29, 1950, p. 1-A.

211. Charlotte *Observer*, May 28, 1950, p. 1-A. Under state law, the failure of the front-runner to receive an absolute majority of the votes cast for all candidates in the race entitled the runner-up to call for a runoff election to be held four weeks after the first primary. In the absence of a call for a runoff, victory went to the highest vote-getter.

212. Frank P. Graham and Jeff Johnson to supporters, May 29, 1950, Johnson Papers.

213. High Point *Enterprise*, May 30, 1950.

Chapter 7

1. Charlotte *Observer*, May 29, 1950, p. 10-A.

2. Greensboro *Daily News*, May 29, 1950.

3. Raleigh *News and Observer*, June 1, 1950, reprint of editorial in the New York *Times*.

4. Washington (N.C.) *Daily News*, May 30, 1950, p. 4.

5. Atlanta *Journal*, n.d., clipping in Graham Papers.

6. Roy C. Mitchell to Frank P. Graham, May 27, 1950, Graham Papers.

7. George Rothwell Brown, "The Political Parade," New York *Journal-American*, May 31, 1950.

8. Baltimore *Sun*, May 31, 1950.

9. Dave Burgess to Dan Powell, June 1, 1950, Powell Papers; author's interview with David M. McConnell, September 13, 1984.

10. A. B. Harless to Jeff Johnson, May 29, 1950, Graham Papers.

11. Edward B. Clark to Jeff Johnson, May 30, 1950, Graham Papers.

12. Banks Shepherd to Frank P. Graham, May 31, 1950, Graham Papers.

13. W. R. Drake to Jeff Johnson, June 1, 1950, Graham Papers.

14. Mrs. W. P. Childers to Jonathan Daniels, May 31, 1950, Daniels Papers.

15. High Point *Enterprise*, May 30, 1950.

16. Fayetteville *Observer*, June 1, 1950.

17. Washington (N.C.) *Daily News*, June 1, 1950, p. 1.

18. Author's interview with R. Mayne Albright, November 30, 1984.

19. Authors' interviews with John Sanders, October 17, 1984, Terry Sanford,

December 3, 1984, T. Clyde Auman, May 23, 1983, and William D. Snider, October 30, 1984.

20. Asheville *Citizen*, May 29, 1950, p. 1; Charlotte *Observer*, May 29, 1950, p. 1-A.

21. St. Louis *Star-Times*, May 29, 1950.

22. Goldsboro *News-Argus*, May 30, 1950.

23. Durham *Sun*, May 29, 1950.

24. Charlotte *Observer*, May 29, 1950, p. 1-A.

25. Ibid., Jeff Johnson to Edwin H. Paget, June 2, 1950, Langston Papers.

26. Kemp Battle to Frank P. Graham, n.d., Graham Papers.

27. David M. McConnell to Jeff Johnson, June 1, 1950, Johnson Papers.

28. Charlotte *News*, May 31, 1950, p. 1; Asheville *Citizen*, June 1, 1950, p. 13; Charlotte *Observer*, June 1, 1950, p. 1-B.

29. Santford Martin to Randolph Preston, May 29, 1950, Martin Papers.

30. Tilford E. Dudley to Dan Powell, June 2, 1950, Powell Papers.

31. D. Hiden Ramsey to Jeff Johnson, June 3, 1950, Ramsey Papers.

32. Charlotte *News*, June 3, 1950.

33. Raleigh *News and Observer*, June 3, 1950.

34. Ibid.

35. *Carolina Times*, June 3, 1950, p. 2.

36. *Nation*, June 3, 1950, pp. 539–40.

37. Charlotte *News*, May 28, 1950, p. 8-A.

38. Raleigh *News and Observer*, June 1, 1950; Charlotte *Observer*, June 1, 1950, p. 1-B.

39. Charlotte *Observer*, May 29, 1950, p. 1-A.

40. High Point *Enterprise*, May 31, 1950, p. 1.

41. Asheville *Citizen*, May 30, 1950, p. 9; Charlotte *Observer*, May 30, 1950, p. 1-A; Charlotte *News*, May 30, 1950, p. 1.

42. Raleigh *News and Observer*, May 30, 1950.

43. Charlotte *Observer*, May 31, 1950, p. 1-A.

44. Charlotte *News*, June 3, 1950, p. 1-A.

45. High Point *Enterprise*, May 31, 1950, p. 1.

46. Author's interview with Hoover Adams, May 26, 1983; Charlotte *Observer*, June 1, 1950, p. 1.

47. Asheville *Citizen*, June 3, 1950, p. 29.

48. Ibid., p. 5.

49. Charlotte *Observer*, June 4, 1950, p. 21-A.

50. Nell Battle Lewis to Willis Smith, May 29, 1950, Lewis Papers.

51. Allen Langston to Hubert Olive, June 5, 1950, Langston Papers.

52. *Sweatt v. Painter*, 339 U.S. 637 (1950); Kluger, *Simple Justice*, pp. 281–82; Charlotte *Observer*, June 6, 1950, p. 1; Asheville *Citizen*, June 6, 1950, p. 1.

53. Kluger, *Simple Justice*, p. 283; Charlotte *Observer*, June 6, 1950, p. 1; Raleigh *News and Observer*, June 6, 1950, p. 1.

54. Raleigh *News and Observer*, June 6, 1950, p. 1; Asheville *Citizen*, June 6, 1950, p. 1; Kluger, *Simple Justice*, p. 284; "Civil Rights at Mid-Century," NAACP Annual Report, 1950, p. 24, NAACP Papers.

55. Burns, "Graduate Education for Blacks," pp. 195–218.

56. Rocky Mount *Telegram*, June 7, 1950.

57. Charlotte *News*, June 7, 1950.

58. Henderson *Daily Dispatch*, June 12, 1950.

59. High Point *Enterprise*, June 6, 1950.

60. Charlotte *Observer*, June 8, 1950, p. 16-A.

61. Irving Carlyle to Harry McMullan, September 1, 1950, Papers of the Controllers.

62. Asheville *Citizen*, June 6, 1950, p. 1; Charlotte *Observer*, June 6, 1950, p. 1; High Point *Enterprise*, June 13, 1950; Charlotte *Observer*, June 14, 1950, p. 18-A.

63. Asheville *Citizen*, June 6, 1950, p. 1; Charlotte *Observer*, June 6, 1950, p. 1.

64. Greensboro *Daily News*, June 7, 1950, p. 1; Raleigh *News and Observer*, June 7, 1950, p. 1.

65. Raleigh *News and Observer*, June 6, 1950.

66. Greensboro *Daily News*, June 6, 1950.

67. Charlotte *Observer*, June 3, 1950, p. 1; Eula Nixon Greenwood, "Raleigh Roundup," *Robesonian*, June 28, 1950.

68. Charlotte *Observer*, June 11, 1950, p. 18-A.

69. Ibid., June 4, 1950, p. 21-A.

70. Author's interview with Hoover Adams.

71. Author's interviews with William Thomas Joyner, Jr., December 12, 1984, James K. Dorsett, Jr., December 12, 1984, John Christoph Blucher Ehringhaus, Jr., November 10, 1984, and Jesse A. Helms, December 11, 1984.

72. Author's interviews with James K. Dorsett, Jr., and Jesse A. Helms.

73. Author's interviews with Jesse A. Helms, John Christoph Blucher Ehringhaus, Jr., Hoover Adams, James K. Dorsett, Jr., William Thomas Joyner, Jr., and William D. Snider.

74. Author's interview with Jesse A. Helms.

75. Author's interviews with Jesse A. Helms, James K. Dorsett, Jr., William Thomas Joyner, Jr., John Christoph Blucher Ehringhaus, Jr., and Ben F. Park, December 11, 1984; Charlotte *Observer*, June 7, 1950, p. 1-A, June 11, 1950, p. 18-A.

76. Authors' interview with John Sanders.

77. High Point *Enterprise*, June 10, 1950; Charlotte *Observer*, June 7, 1950, p. 1-A; author's interviews with William Thomas Joyner, Jr., and Jesse A. Helms.

78. Charlotte *Observer*, June 7, 1950, p. 1-A; Asheville *Citizen*, June 7, 1950, p. 1; author's interview with James K. Dorsett, Jr.

79. Author's interview with Hoover Adams.

80. Asheville *Citizen*, June 8, 1950, p. 1-A; Greensboro *Daily News*, June 8, 1950; Elizabeth City *Daily Advance*, June 7, 1950, p. 1.

81. Raleigh *News and Observer*, June 8, 1950, p. 1; Asheville *Citizen*, June 8, 1950, p. 1-A.

82. Harry Golden, "Personal Reminiscences on the Second Primary," p. 3, Golden Papers.

83. Charlotte *Observer*, June 11, 1950, p. 18-A; author's interviews with Jesse A. Helms, James K. Dorsett, Jr., William Thomas Joyner, Jr., and John Christoph Blucher Ehringhaus, Jr.

84. Author's interviews with Jesse A. Helms and Ben F. Park; Parham, "Democratic Senatorial Primary of North Carolina," p. 169.

85. Author's interviews with Jesse A. Helms, William Thomas Joyner, Jr., and James K. Dorsett, Jr.

86. Author's interview with Hoover Adams; Elizabeth City *Daily Advance*, June 13, 1950, p. 4.

87. Author's interviews with Richard E. Thigpen, Sr., December 5, 1984, and Jesse A. Helms.

88. Author's interview with William W. Staton, May 24, 1983.

89. Charlotte *Observer*, June 8, 1950, p. 12-A.

90. High Point *Enterprise*, June 8, 1950.

91. Charlotte *News*, June 8, 1950, p. 10-A.

92. Raleigh *News and Observer*, June 8, 1950.

93. Greensboro *Daily News*, June 8, 1950.

94. Durham *Sun*, June 8, 1950.

95. High Point *Enterprise*, June 8, 1950.

Chapter 8

1. Charlotte *Observer*, June 7, 1950, p. 1. (McConnell had referred to the rally at Smith's house as a "synthetic call" because the crowd had been summoned by a paid political broadcast.)

2. Concord (N.C.) *Tribune*, June 15, 1950.

3. Charlotte *Observer*, June 11, 1950, p. 8-A.

4. North Carolina General Assembly, *Public Laws of North Carolina, 1931*, sec. 6, chap. 348; author's interview with Richard E. Thigpen, Sr., December 5, 1984.

5. Lewis, *County and Precinct Election Officials*, pp. 49, 50, 52.

6. N.C. Secretary of State, "Candidates' Statements of Contributions and Expenses," Olla Ray Boyd, May 22, 1950.

7. Ibid., Robert R. Reynolds, June 16, 1950.

8. Ibid., Willis Smith, May 17, June 16, 1950.

9. Author's interview with Richard E. Thigpen, Sr.

10. Ibid.

11. John A. Wilkins to Frank P. Graham, June 3, 1950, W. H. Steed to Frank P. Graham, May 15, 1950, Graham Papers.

12. Author's interviews with Richard E. Thigpen, Sr., and Harold T. Makepeace, October 25, 1984.

13. Author's interview with Sam Ragan, October 25, 1984.

14. High Point *Enterprise*, October 13, 1950.

15. N.C. Secretary of State, "Candidates' Statements of Contributions and Expenses," Frank P. Graham, May 16, June 15, 1950; Charlotte *Observer*, May 17, 1950, p. 17-B.

16. Author's interviews with Kathryn N. Folger, December 6, 1984, Terry Sanford, December 3, 1984, Kate Humphries, December 13, 1984, William Joslin, December 12, 1984, and Sam Ragan.

17. Author's interview with William Joslin.

18. Author's interview with Kate Humphries.

19. Ralph W. Gardner, contributions to first and second primaries, n.d., Johnson Papers; Dave Burgess to Dan Powell, June 13, 1950, Powell Papers.

20. Phillip M. Stern to Dr. Will Alexander, May 19, 1950, Marshall Field to

Will Alexander, May 18, 1950, Daniels Papers; Dykeman and Stokely, *Seeds of Southern Change*, p. 301.

21. Edgar B. Stern to Will Alexander, May 18, 1950, Edgar B. Stern to Jonathan Daniels, June 19, 1950, Daniels Papers.

22. Charles Tillett to Jonathan Daniels, June 19, 1950, Daniels Papers.

23. Harold L. Ickes to Frank P. Graham, May 9, 1950, list of contributions, n.d., Graham Papers.

24. Dave Burgess to Dan Powell, weekly report, February 12–18, 1950, Powell Papers.

25. Claude F. Serla to Jeff Johnson, May 20, 1950, Johnson Papers; author's interviews with T. Clyde Auman, May 23, 1983, and Lennox Polk McLendon, Jr., November 2, 1984.

26. "Doc" Morrow to Jeff Johnson, telephone message, n.d., Graham Papers.

27. Author's interview with Terry Sanford.

28. Author's interview with Terry Sanford; Rankin, *Government and Administration of North Carolina*, pp. 40–41; High Point *Enterprise*, October 13, 1950.

29. J. Frank McCrary to Clyde R. Hoey, June 13, 1950, Hoey Papers.

30. Greensboro *Daily News*, June 9, 1950; Elizabeth City *Daily Advance*, June 9, 1950, p. 1; Asheville *Citizen*, June 9, 1950, p. 1.

31. Asheville *Citizen*, June 15, 1950, p. 13.

32. Charlotte *Observer*, June 11, 1950, p. 17-A, June 14, 1950, p. 6-A.

33. Ibid., June 9, 1950, p. 1-A.

34. Ibid., June 10, 1950, p. 3-A.

35. High Point *Enterprise*, June 9, 1950, p. 1.

36. Durham *Sun*, June 16, 1950.

37. Willis Smith to "My Dear Friend," June 20, 1950, Scott Papers.

38. Asheville *Citizen*, June 21, 1950, p. 13; Raleigh *News and Observer*, June 21, 1950.

39. John H. Anderson to Clyde R. Hoey, June 12, 1950, Hoey Papers.

40. Clyde R. Hoey to Hoyt McAfee, June 6, 1950, Hoey Papers.

41. Clyde R. Hoey to John H. Anderson, June 13, 1950, Hoey Papers.

42. Charlotte *Observer*, June 15, 1950, p. 9-B.

43. Greensboro *Daily News*, June 14, 1950; Asheville *Citizen*, June 14, 1950, p. 20; Charlotte *Observer*, June 14, 1950, p. 6-A.

44. *Pilot*, June 16, 1950, p. 9; Raleigh *News and Observer*, June 13, 1950.

45. Fayetteville *Observer*, June 21, 1950.

46. Rocky Mount *Telegram*, June 21, 1950.

47. Asheville *Citizen*, June 17, 1950, p. 8; Charlotte *News*, June 17, 1950.

48. Jack Massey to the editor, Charlotte *Observer*, June 20, 1950, p. 10-A.

49. Charlotte *Observer*, June 16, 1950, p. 1-B.

50. Goldsboro *News-Argus*, June 24, 1950.

51. Harry S Truman to Jonathan Daniels, June 17, 1950, Truman Papers.

52. Robert S. Allen, "Report from Washington," Asheville *Citizen*, June 20, 1950, p. 14.

53. W. R. Jones, Sr. and Jr., to Frank P. Graham, June 9, 1950, Graham Papers.

54. Jeff Johnson to W. R. Jones, Sr. and Jr., June 12, 1950, Graham Papers.

55. Charles Tillett to Jeff Johnson, June 9, 1950, Johnson Papers.

56. Allen Langston to C. A. Upchurch, Jr., June 14, 1950, Johnson Papers.

57. Garland Johnson to Jeff Johnson, June 1950, Johnson Papers.

58. A. L. Fletcher to Kate Humphries, June 13, 1950, Graham Papers.

59. Asheville *Citizen*, June 21, 1950, p. 11.

60. Interview with Capus Miller Waynick by Bill Finger, November 24, 1974, Southern Oral History Collection.

61. Elizabeth City *Daily Advance*, June 16, 1950, p. 1.

62. Asheville *Citizen*, June 17, 1950, p. 8.

63. Interview with Frank P. Graham by Legette Blythe, June 9, 1970, p. 42, Special Collections, University of North Carolina at Charlotte; Raleigh *News and Observer*, June 21, 1950.

64. Asheville *Citizen*, June 20, 1950; Durham *Sun*, June 20, 1950.

65. Durham *Morning Herald*, June 21, 1950.

66. Raleigh *News and Observer*, June 21, 1950.

67. Interview with Mark Ethridge by George Maurice Hill, n.d., Hill Papers.

68. Kinston *Daily Free Press*, June 14, 1950.

69. Interview with Terry Sanford by Brent Glass, May 14, 1976, Southern Oral History Collection.

70. Parham, "Democratic Senatorial Primary of North Carolina," pp. 218–19.

71. Bob and Julia Erwin, "Tar Heel Front in Capitol," n.d., Lowenstein Papers; Jeff Johnson to county managers, June 7, 1950, pp. 1–3, Johnson Papers, Langston Papers, Ramsey Papers, and Scott Papers.

72. "Graham-Smith Senate," n.d., Powell Papers.

73. Dave Burgess, "Suggestions for the Second Primary," n.d., memo in Powell Papers; Dave Burgess to Dan Powell, n.d., Powell Papers; interview with David Burgess by Bill Finger, Southern Oral History Collection.

74. Lewis M. Conn to TWUA Brothers, June 12, 1950, Powell Papers.

75. Dave Burgess to Dan Powell, weekly report, June 4–10, 1950, Dave Burgess to Jeff Johnson and Dan Powell, June 13, 1950, Powell Papers.

76. Dave Burgess to Dan Powell, weekly report, June 18–24, 1950, Powell Papers.

77. Dave Burgess to Dan Powell, weekly report, June 11–17, 1950, Powell Papers.

78. Dave Burgess to Dan Powell, weekly report, June 18–24, 1950, Powell Papers.

79. CIO Organizing Committee Papers.

80. Interview with David Burgess by Bill Finger, Southern Oral History Collection.

81. Asheville *Citizen*, April 17, 1950, p. 8; Durham *Morning Herald*, June 17, 1950.

82. S. B. Barnwell to Frank P. Graham, June 21, 1950, C. C. Burns to Jeff Johnson, June 20, 1950, Johnson Papers.

83. Will England to W. Kerr Scott, June 15, 1950, Scott Papers.

84. Heard, *A Two-Party South?*, p. 202.

85. Asa Spaulding to Jacob Billikopf, June 16, 1950, Graham Papers.

86. C. C. Spaulding to "Dear Voter," June 19, 1950, Graham Papers.

87. *Carolinian*, June 10, 1950, p. 1; Fayetteville *Observer*, June 2, 1950; address of Kelly M. Alexander, Jr., June 1, 1950, NAACP Papers.

88. Matthews and Prothro, *Negroes and the New Southern Politics*, pp. 9–12, 158–59.

89. Nathan M. Johnson to Wade Tart, June 13, 1950, Graham Papers.

90. Nathan M. Johnson to Miss Mattie Gainey, June 21, 1950, Johnson Papers.

91. Charlotte *Observer*, June 17, 1950, p. 5-A.

92. Ibid., June 18, 1950, p. 9-A; Raleigh *News and Observer*, June 18, 1950, p. 1.

93. Charlotte *Observer*, June 18, 1950, p. 9-A.

94. Ibid., p. 16-A, June 20, 1950, p. 10-A.

95. *Pilot*, June 23, 1950, p. 9.

96. Charlotte *Observer*, June 20, 1950, p. 12-A.

97. H. H. Yount to recipient, June 12, 1950, Scott Papers; Raleigh *News and Observer*, June 17, 1950.

98. Washington (N.C.) *Daily News*, June 14, 1950, p. 8.

99. Author's interview with Ashley Futrell, October 10, 1984; Bryan Grimes to Jeff Johnson, June 14, 1950, Graham Papers.

100. Raleigh *News and Observer*, June 17, 1950.

101. Author's interviews with J. Melville Broughton, Jr., December 12, 1984, and T. Clyde Auman.

102. Flier in Powell Papers and Lowenstein Papers; Parham, "Democratic Senatorial Primary of North Carolina," p. 179; Raleigh *News and Observer*, June 15, 1950.

103. Jeff Johnson to campaign managers, June 10, 1950, p. 3, Johnson Papers; flier, Lowenstein Papers.

104. Author's interviews with Kate Humphries, R. Mayne Albright, November 30, 1984, and Kathryn N. Folger.

105. Author's interview with Kathryn N. Folger. We have no physical proof, however, that this flier ever existed. It is the only circular our interviewees discussed of which no copy survives.

106. "White People Wake Up," flier in Powell Papers and Tillett Papers; Lubell, *Future of American Politics*, p. 102.

107. Pamphlet in Powell Papers and Graham Papers.

108. Ibid.

109. Asheville *Citizen*, June 13, 1950, p. 10; *Pilot*, June 23, 1950, p. 1.

110. Edwin McNeill Poteat to "Dear Brethren," June 1950, Johnson Papers.

111. Greensboro *Daily News*, June 21, 1950; *Pilot*, June 23, 1950, p. 9.

112. Raleigh *News and Observer*, June 17, 1950; transcript of radio address by I. Beverly Lake, June 16, 1950, Langston Papers; author's interview with I. Beverly Lake, December 10, 1984.

113. Speech by D. Hiden Ramsey, June 1950, Ramsey Papers.

114. La Grange (N.C.) *News*, June 16, 1950, p. 8.

115. Mrs. L. A. Des Pland to George C. Marshall, June 15, 1950, George C. Marshall to Mrs. L. A. Des Pland, June 18, 1950, telephone message, Marshall Papers.

116. Clyde R. Hoey to H. M. Stenhouse, June 5, 1950, Clyde R. Hoey to Donald S. Menzies, June 13, 1950, Hoey Papers.

117. Jeff Johnson to county managers, June 13, 1950, Johnson Papers.

118. Raleigh *News and Observer*, June 13, 1950.

119. Asheville *Citizen*, June 14, 1950, p. 5.

120. Raleigh *News and Observer*, n.d., clipping in Lowenstein Papers.

121. Julius C. Hubbard to W. Kerr Scott, June 10, 1950, Scott Papers.

122. W. Fitz Hoyle to W. Kerr Scott, June 9, 1950, Scott Papers.

123. W. Kerr Scott to W. Fitz Hoyle, June 12, 1950, Scott Papers.

124. Emsley Armfield to the editor, Charlotte *News*, June 20, 1950, p. 6-A.

125. Asheville *Citizen*, June 9, 1950, p. 17.

126. Charlotte *Observer*, June 10, 1950, p. 13-A.

127. Ibid., June 14, 1950, p. 13.

128. Henderson *Daily Dispatch*, n.d., quoted in Elizabeth City *Daily Advance*, June 21, 1950, p. 4.

129. *Daily Independent*, June 18, 1950.

130. Washington (N.C.) *Daily News*, June 19, 1950, p. 1.

131. Elizabeth City *Daily Advance*, June 17, 1950, p. 1; Raleigh *News and Observer*, June 17, 1950.

132. Asheville *Citizen*, June 17, 1950, p. 8; Elizabeth City *Daily Advance*, June 16, 1950, p. 1.

133. Ben Roney to Charles Rogerson, June 20, 1950, Scott Papers.

134. Asheville *Citizen*, June 17, 1950, p. 8.

135. Charlotte *Observer*, June 21, 1950, p. 1-A.

136. Greensboro *Daily News*, June 21, 1950.

137. Ibid., June 12, 1950; Parham, "Democratic Senatorial Primary of North Carolina," p. 184.

138. Willis P. Holmes, Jr., to Frank P. Graham, n.d., Graham Papers.

139. Greensboro *Daily News*, June 12, 1950.

140. Mrs. Eva Cooper to Jonathan Daniels, June 17, 1950, Daniels Papers.

141. Dave Burgess to Dan Powell, June 1950, Powell Papers.

142. Interview with Jeff Johnson, December 31, 1951, in Parham, "Democratic Senatorial Primary of North Carolina," p. 184.

143. Raleigh *News and Observer*, July 5, 1950; interview with O. Max Gardner, Jr., December 30, 1951, in Parham, "Democratic Senatorial Primary of North Carolina," p. 185.

144. Parham, "Democratic Senatorial Primary of North Carolina," p. 187.

145. Author's interviews with James K. Dorsett, Jr., December 12, 1984, and William Thomas Joyner, Jr., December 12, 1984.

146. H. H. Young, chairman of Iredell County Smith for Senate campaign, to recipient, June 12, 1950, Scott Papers.

147. Charlotte *Observer*, June 11, 1950, p. 17-A.

148. Ibid., June 12, 1950, p. 8-A.

149. Ibid., June 14, 1950, p. 6-A.

150. Worth B. Folger to Bill Staton, June 15, 1950, Graham Papers.

151. Leroy Jones to Frank P. Graham, June 10, 1950, Lowenstein Papers.

152. Author's interview with Frank P. Graham, July 1, 1969.

153. Charlotte *Observer*, June 14, 1950, p. 6-A; Asheville *Citizen*, June 15, 1950, p. 22.

154. *Pilot*, June 16, 1950, p. 6-A; political ad, n.p., n.d., Ramsey Papers.

155. Asheville *Citizen*, June 17, 1950, p. 8; Raleigh *News and Observer*, June 18, 1950, p. 1.

156. Mary Coker Joslin, "Precinct Politics: The Red and the Black," pp. 20–21, pamphlet in possession of author, Raleigh, N.C.; Raleigh *News and Observer*, June 18, 1950, p. 1; Charlotte *Observer*, June 18, 1950, p. 9-A.

157. Charlotte *Observer*, June 18, 1950, p. 9-A.

158. Joslin, "Precinct Politics," p. 21.

159. Raleigh *News and Observer*, June 18, 1950, p. 1.

160. Authors' interviews with W. W. Finlator, November 30, 1984 (telephone conversation), J. Melville Broughton, Jr., Frank Porter Graham, and William L. Hauser, November 20, 1989 (telephone conversation); Charlotte *Observer*, June 20, 1950, p. 6-A; Raleigh *News and Observer*, June 17, 1950.

161. Charlotte *Observer*, June 21, 1950, p. 6-A; authors' interview with William L. Hauser.

162. Goldsboro *News-Argus*, June 22, 1950.

163. Raleigh *News and Observer*, June 21, 1950, p. 2; authors' interviews with J. Melville Broughton, Jr., Frank Porter Graham, and William L. Hauser.

164. Raleigh *News and Observer*, June 22, 1950, p. 6; authors' interview with William L. Hauser.

165. Lubell, *Future of American Politics*, p. 105; authors' interview with William L. Hauser. Hauser remembered the audiences as indifferent.

166. Authors' interview with John Sanders, October 17, 1984, and William L. Hauser. Hauser insisted that the story is apocryphal.

167. Author's interview with Roy Wilder, Jr., December 13, 1984.

168. Raleigh *News and Observer*, June 23, 1950.

169. Author's interviews with J. Melville Broughton, Jr., and Roy Wilder, Jr.

170. Ibid.

171. Lubell, *Future of American Politics*, p. 105.

172. Asheville *Citizen*, June 23, 1950, p. 2; Ashby, *Frank Porter Graham*, p. 270.

173. Asheville *Citizen*, June 21, 1950, p. 11.

174. Raleigh *News and Observer*, June 22, 1950.

175. *Southern Textile Bulletin*, June 1950, p. 28.

176. Asheville *Citizen*, June 21, 1950, p. 11; Charlotte *Observer*, June 21, 1950, p. 1-A; Raleigh *News and Observer*, June 21, 1950.

177. High Point *Enterprise*, June 21, 1950, p. 1; Charlotte *Observer*, June 21, 1950, p. 12-A; Raleigh *Times*, June 21, 1950.

178. *Pilot*, June 23, 1950, p. 20; Charlotte *Observer*, June 22, 1950, p. 16-A.

179. Charlotte *Observer*, June 23, 1950, p. 3-A; Asheville *Citizen*, June 23, 1950, p. 1; Raleigh *News and Observer*, June 23, 1950.

180. Interview with Roger Nash Baldwin, November–December 1954, p. 116, Columbia Oral History Collection; Roger Nash Baldwin to the editor, Charlotte *Observer*, June 24, 1950, p. 8-A.

181. Lamson, *Roger Baldwin*, pp. 86, 93, 119, 150–51, 192. See also O'Neill, *A Better World*, pp. 31, 48.

182. Political ads in Graham Papers, Lowenstein Papers, and McCoy Papers; Raleigh *News and Observer*, June 23, 1950, p. 26.

183. High Point *Enterprise*, June 23, 1950; Elizabeth City *Daily Advance*, June 23, 1950, p. 1.

184. Carlos Young, Smith campaign chairman, "Bulletin," June 20, 1950, Lowenstein Papers.

185. Author's interview with Jesse A. Helms, December 11, 1984.

186. Harry L. Golden to the editor, Charlotte *News*, June 20, 1950, p. 6-A.

187. *Carolina Times*, June 24, 1950, p. 2.

188. Author's interviews with Terry Sanford, J. Melville Broughton, Jr., Jesse A.

Helms, William Thomas Joyner, Jr., and James K. Dorsett, Jr.

189. Lubell, *Future of American Politics*, pp. 102, 104.

190. Interview with Jonathan Worth Daniels by Charles Eagles, March 9, 1977, p. 237, Southern Oral History Collection.

191. Lubell, *Future of American Politics*, p. 104. See also Parham, "Democratic Senatorial Primary of North Carolina."

192. "What is This F.E.P.C.?," n.d., pamphlet in Johnson Papers and Powell Papers.

193. Raleigh *News and Observer*, June 23, 1950, p. 17; Moore County *News*, June 23, 1950, p. 3; Asheville *Citizen*, June 23, 1950, p. 11.

194. Charlotte *Observer*, June 23, 1950, p. 24-A.

195. Jeff Johnson to campaign managers, June 17, 1950, p. 1, Johnson Papers.

196. "Short Explanation of the Recent Decisions of the Supreme Court of the United States," n.d., Johnson Papers.

197. Raleigh *News and Observer*, June 18, 1950; Jonathan Daniels to Harry S Truman, June 15, 1950, Truman Papers.

198. Parham, "Democratic Senatorial Primary of North Carolina," p. 175.

199. Charlotte *Observer*, June 23, 1950, p. 30-B.

200. Ibid., June 21, 1950, p. 12-A; High Point *Enterprise*, June 21, 1950, p. 1.

201. Alvin Wingfield to John T. Flynn, March 31, 1950, Flynn Papers.

202. Asheville *Citizen*, June 23, 1950, p. 2; Ashby, *Frank Porter Graham*, p. 270.

203. Authors' interview with William C. Friday, October 17, 1984; interview with Frank P. Graham by Legette Blythe, June 9, 1970, p. 42, Special Collections, University of North Carolina at Charlotte.

204. Vance Gavin to Jeff Johnson, June 10, 1950, Graham Papers; James Spencer Love to Cornelia S. Love, June 22, 1950, James Spencer Love Papers.

205. Author's interview with Hoover Adams, May 26, 1983.

206. Bryan Grimes to Jeff Johnson, June 14, 1950, Felix Webster to Frank P. Graham, June 12, 1950, Graham Papers.

207. Asheville *Citizen*, June 22, 1950, p 15; Raleigh *News and Observer*, June 22, 1950, p. 6; Charlotte *Observer*, June 23, 1950, p. 3-A.

208. Speech by Willis Smith, Anna Lee Smith Dorsett Scrapbook of the Smith family, pp 1–9, in possession of Mrs. Dorsett, Raleigh, N.C.; Asheville *Citizen*, June 24, 1950, p. 2; Raleigh *News and Observer*, June 24, 1950, p. 1.

209. Speech by Willis Smith, Anna Lee Smith Dorsett Scrapbook, pp. 1–9, Norma F. Shannonhouse to Clyde R. Hoey, June 26, 1950, Hoey Papers.

210. Charlotte *Observer*, June 23, 1950, p. 1-A.

211. Ibid.

212. Asheville *Citizen*, June 24, 1950, p. 2. He was wrong.

213. Carl C. Scott to Jeff Johnson, June 20, 1950, Johnson Papers.

214. Author's interview with William Joslin.

215. Durham *Sun*, June 23, 1950; Raleigh *Times*, June 23, 1950.

216. Raleigh *News and Observer*, June 24, 1950.

217. *North Carolina Manual—1951*, pp. 237–38; Asheville *Citizen*, July 1, 1950, p. 12; Charlotte *Observer*, June 25, 1950, p. 1-A.

218. "Dice Daniels" was Jonathan Daniels's college nickname, in praise of his skill as a crapshooter, a skill his critics claimed followed him into journalism.

219. Raleigh *News and Observer*, June 25, 1950, p. 1; Asheville *Citizen*, June 25, 1950, p. 1; Elizabeth City *Daily Advance*, June 26, 1950, p. 1; Durham *Morning Herald*, June 25, 1950, p. 1; New York *Herald Tribune*, June 25, 1950, p. 1; author's interviews with William Joslin and H. G. Jones, November 6, 1984; interview with David Burgess by Bill Finger, p. 25, Southern Oral History Collection; Joslin, "Precinct Politics."

220. Interview with William C. Friday by George Maurice Hill, April 17, 1974, pp. 4, 5, 8, Hill Papers; authors' interviews with Kathryn N. Folger, Kate Humphries, and William C. Friday.

Chapter 9

1. D. Hiden Ramsey to Louis Graves, June 1950, Graham Papers.

2. David M. McConnell to Frank P. Graham, July 21, 1950, Graham Papers.

3. John Sanders to Frank P. Graham, July 6, 1950, Graham Papers.

4. Susie Sharp to Frank P. Graham, June 28, 1950, Graham Papers.

5. Francis O. Clarkson to Frank P. Graham, October 2, 1950, Graham Papers.

6. Lillian Turner to Frank P. Graham, June 26, 1950, Graham Papers.

7. Richard B. Russell to Frank P. Graham, November 22, 1950, Graham Papers.

8. W. Kerr Scott to Frank P. Graham, June 27, 1950, Graham Papers.

9. W. Kerr Scott to Frank P. Graham, December 19, 1950, Graham Papers.

10. Goldsboro *News-Argus*, June 27, 1950.

11. Charlotte *Observer*, June 26, 1950, p. 8-B.

12. Ibid., June 28, 1950, p. 9-A.

13. Ibid., June 27, 1950, p. 13-A, June 28, 1950, p. 9-A; Asheville *Citizen*, June 27, 1950, p. 11.

14. Raleigh *News and Observer*, August 15, 1950.

15. Interview with Jonathan Worth Daniels by Charles Eagles, March 9–11, 1977, p. 241, Southern Oral History Collection.

16. Jonathan Daniels to Frank Freidel, June 27, 1950, Daniels Papers.

17. Jonathan Daniels to Katherine Lackey, July 15, 1950, Daniels Papers.

18. Eagles, *Jonathan Daniels and Race Relations*, p. xi.

19. Jeff Johnson to Beverly S. Royster, Jr., July 1, 1950, Jeff Johnson to D. Hiden Ramsey, June 29, July 3, 1950, Johnson Papers.

20. Victor Bryant to Jeff Johnson, July 7, 1950, Johnson Papers.

21. Frank Winslow to Jeff Johnson, July 6, 1950, Johnson Papers.

22. A. Hand James to Jeff Johnson, June 27, 1950, Johnson Papers.

23. Victor Bryant to Jeff Johnson, July 7, 1950, Johnson Papers.

24. Howard Godwin to Jeff Johnson, July 8, 1950, Johnson Papers.

25. Fred B. Helms to Frank P. Graham, July 11, 1950, Johnson Papers.

26. Raleigh *News and Observer*, July 26, 1950.

27. Mattie Bloodworth to the editor, Raleigh *News and Observer*, July 1, 1950.

28. Washington *Evening Star*, June 29, 1950.

29. Greensboro *Daily News*, June 26, 1950.

30. *Carolina Times*, July 1, 1950, p. 2.

31. *Carolinian*, July 8, 1950.

32. New York *Times*, June 26, 1950.

33. Richmond *Times-Dispatch*, n.d., clipping in Graham Papers.

34. St. Louis *Globe-Democrat*, June 26, 1950; *Newsweek*, July 3, 1950, p. 12.

35. Durham *Sun*, June 26, 1950.

36. Ibid.

37. Ibid.

38. High Point *Enterprise*, June 26, 1950.

39. Elizabeth City *Daily Advance*, June 26, 1950; Fayetteville *Observer*, June 26, 1950.

40. Charlotte *News*, June 26, 1950.

41. High Point *Enterprise*, August 17, 1950.

42. Ibid.

43. Author's interviews with William Thomas Joyner, Jr., December 12, 1984, and Jesse A. Helms, December 11, 1984.

44. Author's interview with Harold T. Makepeace, Sr., October 25, 1984.

45. Hoover Adams to Nell Battle Lewis, July 6, 1950, Lewis Papers.

46. Charlotte *Observer*, June 27, 1950, p. 11-A.

47. Durham *Morning Herald*, July 21, 1950; author's interview with Frank Porter Graham, July 1, 1969.

48. Lubell, *Future of American Politics*, pp. 1–105.

49. Ibid., p. 107.

50. Ibid., pp. 104–5.

51. Ibid., p. 123.

52. Key, *Southern Politics in State and Nation*, pp. 277–85. Nor would one describe the North Carolina senatorial delegation—Josiah Bailey, then William B. Umstead by appointment, then J. Melville Broughton by election in 1948—as ardent New Dealers. Senator Reynolds, in the other seat in 1932–44, was merely *cui generis*, to be deposed in 1944 by the redoubtable Clyde Hoey, hardly a Roosevelt enthusiast.

53. Puryear, *Democratic Party Dissension*, p. 229.

54. Raleigh *News and Observer*, May 5, 1949.

55. Ibid., July 17, 1949; D. Hiden Ramsey to Robert M. Hanes, July 28, 1949, Ramsey Papers. The irony of Scott's use of the patronage power that had been enlarged by the centralizing zeal of the Gardner administration in the years 1929–33 was understandably lost on dismayed party regulars, who saw Scott's infusion of his loyalists in state bureaucracy as the political and ideological upheaval it was clearly intended to be.

56. Raleigh *News and Observer*, June 9, 1949.

57. *North Carolina Manual—1951*, pp. 235–36.

58. Ibid.

59. Key, *Southern Politics in State and Nation*, p. 217.

60. *North Carolina Manual—1951*, pp. 235–36.

61. Ibid., p. 236.

62. Peterson, "1950 Democratic Senatorial Primary," p. 109; *North Carolina Manual—1951*, p. 235.

63. Peterson, "1950 Democratic Senatorial Primary," p. 93; *North Carolina Manual—1951*, pp. 201–2.

64. Key, *Southern Politics in State and Nations*, pp. 277–98.

65. *North Carolina Manual—1951*, pp. 288–89.

66. Peterson, "1950 Democratic Senatorial Primary," pp. 82–83; *North Carolina Manual—1951*, pp. 285–88; *United States Census of Population, 1950*, vol. 2, part 33, pp. 95–106.

67. *North Carolina Manual—1951*, pp. 287–88.

68. Author's interview with Hoover Adams, May 26, 1983.

69. Ben Dixon McNeill to Jonathan Daniels, June 30, 1950, Daniels Papers.

70. Authors' interviews with I. Beverly Lake, December 10, 1984, John Sanders, October 17, 1984, Terry Sanford, December 3, 1984,and William D. Snider, October 30, 1984; interview with Jonathan Worth Daniels by Charles Eagles, March 9, 1977, p. 237, Southern Oral History Collection.

71. Leslie Campbell to Frank P. Graham, July 10, 1950, Graham Papers; Al Hamilton to Jonathan Daniels, June 26, 1950, Daniels Papers; Charlotte *News*, June 30, 1950, p. 14-A.

72. D. E. DeVane to Frank P. Graham, July 1, 1950, Henry S. Willis to Frank P. Graham, July 4, 1950, Graham Papers; Fleet Williams to Dave Burgess, July 19, 1950, Powell Papers.

73. Jonathan Daniels to Benjamin Sonnenburg, July 9, 1950, Daniels Papers.

74. Jonathan Daniels to Dave Burgess, July 20, 1950, Powell Papers.

75. Dave Burgess to Jack Kroll, June 27, 1950, Powell Papers.

76. Edgar L. Yow to Jeff Johnson, June 30, 1950, Johnson Papers.

77. Lubell, "Has Truman Lost the South?," p. 132.

78. Jeff Johnson to Samuel Lubell, August 23, 1951, Johnson Papers; Jeff Johnson to Harry O'Riley, June 10, 1950, Graham Papers.

79. Enclosure, Charles Tillett to Jeff Johnson, August 2, 1950, Johnson Papers.

80. High Point *Enterprise*, June 25, 1950, p. 4-A.

81. B. T. Falls to Jeff Johnson, June 26, 1950, Johnson Papers.

82. Elaine Mayo Paul to W. Kerr Scott, June 26, 1950, John W. Coffey to W. Kerr Scott, July 5, 1950, Scott Papers.

83. Lubell, *Future of American Politics*, p. 124.

84. J. B. Look, Jr., to Frank P. Graham, July 21, 1950, Graham Papers.

85. For example, see *Commonweal*, July 7, 1950, pp. 309–10.

86. John R. Jordan, Jr., to Frank P. Graham, July 10, 1950, Graham Papers.

87. Lois Johnson to Frank P. Graham, June 25, 1950, Graham Papers.

88. Bass and DeVries, *Transformation of Southern Politics*, p. 235.

89. Ibid.

90. H[iden] R[amsey] to Louis [Graves], Saturday A.M., n.d., Graham Papers.

91. I. Beverly Lake to Frank P. Graham, July 9, 1950, Graham Papers.

92. For an illuminating and incisive study of white supremacy in "the Black Second," the eastern congressional district of North Carolina that intermittently sent black congressmen to Washington until 1900, see Eric Anderson, *Race and Politics in North Carolina*.

1. *Congressional Quarterly Almanac*, 81st Cong., 2d sess. vol. 6, p. 542; Ashby, *Frank Porter Graham*, p. 272; interview with Jonathan Worth Daniels by Daniel Singal and George Tindall, pp. 160–61.

2. "Conversation with Frank P. Graham," June 10, 1962, Southern Oral History Collection (hereafter cited as "Conversation with Frank P. Graham); interview with Jonathan Worth Daniels by Daniel Singal and George Tindall, pp. 160–61; Paul H. Douglas, *In the Fullness of Time*, p. 241.

3. Interview with Jonathan Worth Daniels by Daniel Singal and George Tindall, pp. 160–61; "Conversation with Frank P. Graham."

4. C. A. Upchurch, Jr., to Dan Powell, July 20, 1950, Powell Papers.

5. Lexington (N.C.) *Dispatch*, July 14, 1950; Raleigh *News and Observer*, July 13, 1950.

6. "Conversation with Frank P. Graham," pp. 3–5; author's interview with Frank Porter Graham, July 1, 1969.

7. Ashby, *Frank Porter Graham*, pp. 276–77; Donovan, *Tumultuous Years*, p. 296.

8. *Congressional Record*, 96, pt. 2:15470–79; Frank Porter Graham, "Farewell Statement," September 22, 1950, copy in Lowenstein Papers.

9. *Congressional Record*, 96, pt. 2:15470, 1950.

10. Ibid., p. 15479.

11. Ashby, *Frank Porter Graham*, p. 278.

12. Authors' interview with William C. Friday, October 17, 1984.

13. Author's interview with Frank Porter Graham.

14. Ashby, *Frank Porter Graham*, p. 278.

15. Interview with Marian Graham by Warren Ashby, June 20, 1960, copy in authors' possession.

16. *North Carolina Manual—1951*, p. 240.

17. Durham *Morning Herald*, June 27, 1953; Asheville *Citizen*, June 28, 1953; author's interview with James K. Dorsett, Jr., December 12, 1984.

18. Lefler and Newsome, *North Carolina: The History of a Southern State*, pp. 687, 691.

19. Ashby, *Frank Porter Graham*, p. 302. See also pp. 286–330.

20. Ibid., p. 330; Raleigh *News and Observer*, February 17, 1972; author's interview with Frank Porter Graham.

21. Raleigh *News and Observer*, February 17, 1972.

Bibliography

Primary Sources

Manuscript Collections

Asheville, North Carolina

Robert Rice Reynolds Papers, in the possession of his family.

Chapel Hill, North Carolina

North Carolina Collection, University of North Carolina
Southern Historical Collection, University of North Carolina
    Dudley Warren Bagley Papers.
    James Crawford Biggs Papers.
    Herbert Covington Bonner Papers.
    Joseph Lenoir Chambers Papers.
    Francis Osborne Clarkson Papers.
    Oscar Jackson Colfin Papers.
    Papers of the Controller, University Archives.
    William Terry Couch Papers.
    Jonathan Worth Daniels Papers.
    Fellowship of Southern Churchmen Papers.
    Frank Porter Graham Papers.
    Louis and Mildred Graves Papers.
    Gordon Gray Papers.
    Harriet Laura Herring Papers.
    George Maurice Hill Papers.
    Herscel Vespasian Johnson Papers.
    William Thomas Joyner, Sr., Papers.
    Howard Anderson Kester Papers.
    James Lee Love Papers.
    James Spencer Love Papers.
    Allard Kenneth Lowenstein Papers.
    Holt McPherson Papers.
    Howard Washington Odum Papers.
    John Johnston Parker Papers.
    Daniel Augustus Powell Papers.
    Darley Hiden Ramsey Papers.
    Hubert Samuel Robinson Papers.
    Southern Tenant Farmer's Union Papers.
    Charles W. and Gladys Avery Tillett Papers.
    John Wesley Umstead Papers.
    Lindsay Carter Warren Papers.
    Louis Round Wilson Papers.

Charlotte, North Carolina

University of North Carolina at Charlotte Library
  Harry Lewis Golden Papers.

Durham, North Carolina

Duke University Library
  American Socialist Party Papers.
  Congress of Industrial Organizations Organizing (CIO) Committee Papers.
  William Baskerville Hamilton Papers.
  Clyde Roark Hoey Papers.
  Jefferson Deems Johnson Papers.
  Allen Langston Papers.
  John Santford Martin Papers.
  Lucy Randolph Mason Papers.

Eugene, Oregon

University of Oregon Library
  John T. Flynn Papers.

Fayetteville, North Carolina

Donald McCoy Papers (personal correspondence).

Greensboro, North Carolina

University of North Carolina at Greensboro Library
  Walter Clinton Jackson Papers.

Greenville, North Carolina

East Carolina University Library
  Sallie Baker Everett Papers.
  John A. Lang, Jr., Papers.
  J. Con Lanier Papers.
  Lassister Family Papers.
  Hoyt Patrick Taylor, Sr., Papers.
  Capus Miller Waynick Papers.

Independence, Missouri

Harry S Truman Library
  Harry S Truman Papers.

Lexington, Virginia

Virginia Military Institute Library
  George Catlett Marshall Papers.

Columbia University Library
  Herbert Lehman Papers.

Raleigh, North Carolina

North Carolina Department of Archives and History
  Lynton Yates Ballentine Papers.
  Robert Gregg Cherry Papers.
  David S. Coltrane Papers.
  Ruth Current Papers.
  May Thompson Evans Papers.
  Nell Battle Lewis Papers.
  Isaac Spencer London, Jr., Papers.
  Clarence H. Poe Papers.
  William Kerr Scott Papers (personal correspondence).

Tallahassee, Florida

Mildred and Claude Pepper Library
  Claude Pepper Papers.

Washington, D.C.

Library of Congress
  Clinton R. Anderson Papers.
  Jack Kroll Papers.
  National Association for the Advancement of Colored People (NAACP)
    Papers.

Winston-Salem, North Carolina

Baptist Historical Collection, Wake Forest University Library
  Charles Bennett Deane Papers.
  Odus McCoy Mull Papers.

Newspapers

North Carolina Newspapers (January 1949 through November 1950)

Asheville *Citizen*.
The Carolina Israelite (Charlotte).
Carolina Times (Durham).
The Carolinian (Raleigh).
Chapel Hill *Weekly*.
Charlotte *News*.
Charlotte *Observer*.
Cleveland County *Times* (Shelby), selected issues.
Concord *Tribune*, selected issues.

The Courier-Times (Roxboro).
Daily Independent (Kannapolis), selected issues.
Daily Tar Heel (University of North Carolina).
Dunn *Dispatch*.
Durham *Morning Herald*.
Durham *Sun*.
Elizabeth City *Daily Advance*.
Fayetteville *Observer*.
Gastonia *Gazette*, selected issues.
Goldsboro *News-Argus*.
Greensboro *Daily News*.
Greensboro *Record*.
Henderson *Daily Dispatch*, selected issues.
Hickory *Daily Record*, selected issues.
High Point *Enterprise*.
Jacksonville *News and Views*, selected issues.
Kinston *Daily Free Press*.
La Grange *News*, selected issues.
Lexington *Dispatch*.
Moore County *News*, selected issues.
The Pilot (Southern Pines).
Raleigh *News and Observer*.
Raleigh *Times*.
The Robesonian (Robeson County).
Rocky Mount *Telegram*.
Sampson *Independent*, selected issues.
Shelby *Daily Star*.
Valdese *News*.
Washington *Daily News*.
Wilmington *Star-News*.
Winston-Salem *Journal*.
Winston-Salem *Sentinel*, selected issues.

Out-of-State Newspapers

Atlanta *Constitution*, selected issues.
Atlanta *Journal*.
Baltimore *Evening Sun*.
Baltimore *Morning Sun*.
Boston *Globe*.
Christian Science Monitor.
The Daily Worker.
Danville (Va.) *Register*.
Mobile (Ala.) *Press*.
Montgomery (Ala.) *Journal*.
Nashville (Tenn.) *Banner*.
New York *Herald Tribune*.
New York *Journal-American*.
New York *Mirror*.

New York *Times*.
Norfolk *Journal and Guide*.
Norfolk *Virginian-Pilot*.
Philadelphia *Bulletin*.
Philadelphia *Inquirer*.
Richmond *News Leader*.
Richmond *Times-Dispatch*.
St. Louis *Globe-Democrat*.
St. Louis *Post-Dispatch*.
St. Louis *Star-Times*.
Washington *Evening Star*.
Washington *Post*.

Interviews

Conducted by Author (Pleasants unless otherwise noted)

Hoover Adams, May 26, 1983.
R. Mayne Albright, November 30, 1984.
Kelly M. Alexander, Jr., September 13, 1984.
Warren Ashby, August 2, 1982 (Burns), October 30, 1984.
T. Clyde Auman, May 23, 1983.
H. Clifton Blue, October 26, 1984.
Legette Blythe, September 14, 1984.
J. Melville Broughton, Jr., December 12, 1984.
Albert Coates, August 5, 1982 (Burns).
William Terry Couch, August 3, 1982 (Burns).
Irwin C. Crawford, August 7, 1969.
James K. Dorsett, Jr., December 12, 1984.
John Christoph Blucher Ehringhaus, Jr., November 10, 1984.
Samuel J. Ervin, Jr., November 9, 1984, telephone conversation.
Thad Eure, December 11, 1984.
Charlene Farrell, spokesperson for Capitol Broadcasting Company, December
    11, 1984.
W. W. Finlator, November 30, 1984, telephone conversation.
Katheryn N. Folger, December 6, 1984.
William C. Friday, October 17, 1984 (Burns and Pleasants).
Ashley Futrell, October 10, 1984.
Frank Porter Graham, July 1, 1969.
Charles P. Green, Jr., August 9, 1984.
William L. Hauser, November 20, 1989, telephone conversation (Burns and
    Pleasants).
Jesse A. Helms, December 11, 1984.
Kate Humphries, December 13, 1984.
H. G. Jones, November 6, 1984.
John Jordan, Jr., December 12, 1984.
William Joslin, December 12, 1984.
William Thomas Joyner, Jr., December 12, 1984.

I. Beverly Lake, December 10, 1984.
David M. McConnell, September 13, 1984.
Donald McCoy, December 7, 1984.
Wesley E. McDonald, Jr., May 18, 1972.
Lennox Polk McLendon, Jr., November 2, 1984.
Harold T. Makepeace, October 25, 1984.
James Covington Parham, Jr., June 4, 1983.
Ben F. Park, December 11, 1984.
Claude M. Pepper, October 31, 1969.
Sam Ragan, October 25, 1984.
John Sanders, October 17, 1984 (Burns and Pleasants).
Terry Sanford, December 3, 1984.
Ralph W. Scott, October 31, 1984.
Robert W. Scott, April 10, 1984, telephone conversation.
William D. Snider, October 30, 1984.
William W. Staton, May 24, 1983.
Richard E. Thigpen, Sr., December 5, 1984.
Roy Thompson, Jr., November 1, 1984.
Frank G. Umstead, May 22, 1983.
James B. Whittington, December 5, 1984.
Tom Wicker, October 30, 1984.
Roy Wilder, Jr., December 13, 1984.
David Witherspoon, Vice President of Capitol Broadcasting Company,
    December 10, 1984.
W. B. Wright, December 11, 1984, telephone conversation.

Columbia Oral History Collection,
Columbia University Library, New York, New York

Roger Nash Baldwin, 1954.
Chester A. Bowles, 1963.
Jonathan Worth Daniels, 1972.
Virginia Foster Durr, 1970.
Robert H. Jackson, 1952.
Guy Benton and Guion Griffis Johnson, 1970.
Broadus Mitchell, 1972.
Henry Agard Wallace, 1953.

East Carolina University Library, Greenville, North Carolina

Capus Miller Waynick, August 1, September 19, 1979; January 30, 1980.

Southern Oral History Collection,
University of North Carolina at Chapel Hill

David Burgess, September 25, 1975; August 12, 1983.
William Terry Couch, October 22, 1970; November 17, 1973.
Jonathan Worth Daniels, March 22, 1973; March 1977.
Virginia Foster Durr, July 15, 1974; March 1975; October 1975.
Thad Eure, December 12, 1973; July 15, 1974.

Clark Foreman, November 16, 1974.
Frank Porter Graham, January 7, 1950; June 9–12, 1962.
Paul Green, February, March, November 20, 1974; March 30, May 7, December 1, 1975.
Jesse A. Helms, March 8, 1974.
Harriet L. Herring, February 5, 1976.
Wilbur Hobby, December 18, 1973; March 13, 1975.
Guion Griffis Johnson, April 24, May 17, 28, July 1, 1974.
Charles Jones, November 8, 1975.
Howard Kester, July 22, August 25, 1974; March 5, 1976.
Cornelia Spencer Love, January 26, 1975.
Holt McPherson, April 9, 1975.
Robert Morgan, December 13, 1973.
Arthur Franklin Raper, January 25, 1971; January 29–30, 1974.
Charles Phillips Russell, November 28, 1973; February 12, November 28, 1974.
Terry Sanford, May 15, 1971; March 1, 1972; May 14, August 20, 1976; December 10, 1986.
Ralph W. Scott, December 20, 1973; April 22, 1974.
Gladys Avery Tillett, March 20, 1974.
Rupert B. Vance, September 3, 1970; November 15, 1973.
Capus Miller Waynick, February 4, November 24, 1974

**University of North Carolina at Charlotte,
Special Collections Library**

Frank Porter Graham.

Contemporary Periodicals

The Atlantic Monthly.
Contempo.
Commonweal.
Fortune.
Harper's Magazine.
Holiday.
Life.
Look.
The Nation.
The New Masses.
New Republic.
Newsweek.
North Carolina Insight.
Partisan Review.
Plain Talk.
Political Affairs.
Political Science Journal.
Popular Government.

The Progressive.
The Reporter.
Saturday Evening Post.
Social Forces.
South Atlantic Quarterly.
Southern Textile Bulletin.
Southern Voices.
The State.
Survey.
Time.
U.S. News and World Report.
University of North Carolina News Letter.

Government Sources

Federal Government

U.S. Bureau of the Census. *United States Census of Population: 1950.* Volume 2, Part 33, North Carolina. Prepared under the supervision of Howard G. Brunsman. Washington, D.C.: U.S. Government Printing Office, 1952.

U.S. Congress. *Congressional Quarterly Almanac.* Washington, D.C.: Congressional Quarterly News Features, 1949, 1950.

———. *Congressional Record.* Washington, D.C., 1951.

U.S. Congress. House. *Hearings before the Committee on Un-American Activities.* 81st Congress, 1st session, May 6, 1949. Washington, D.C.: U.S. Government Printing Office, 1949.

U.S. Congress. House. Committee on Un-American Activities. *Report on the Southern Conference for Human Welfare.* Washington, D.C.: U.S. Government Printing Office, 1947.

U.S. Federal Bureau of Investigation (FBI), Washington, D.C. Raw files relating to Frank Porter Graham.

———. Raw files relating to Robert Rice Reynolds.

U.S. President's Committee on Civil Rights. *To Secure These Rights: The Report of the U.S. President's Committee on Civil Rights.* Washington, D.C.: U.S. Government Printing Office, 1947.

State Government

N.C. General Assembly. *Public Laws and Resolutions Passed by the General Assembly at Its Sessions of 1929–1935.* Raleigh: Edwards and Broughton, 1935.

N.C. Secretary of State. "Candidates' Statements of Contributions and Expenses," Office of the Secretary of State, Raleigh, 1950.

———. *North Carolina Manual—1951.* Raleigh: Office of the Secretary of State, 1951.

N.C. State Board of Elections. "Official Results of 1950 Election." Raleigh, 1950.

Epps et al. v. Carmichael et al., 93 F.Supp. 327 (M.D.N.C. 1950).
Henderson v. United States, 339 U.S. 516 (1950).
McLaurin v. Oklahoma State Regents, 339 U.S. 637 (1950).
Missouri ex rel Gaines v. Canada, 305 U.S. 337 (1938).
Sipuel v. Oklahoma State Regents et al., 332 U.S. 631 (1948).
Sweatt v. Painter, 339 U.S. 637 (1950).
University of Maryland v. Donald G. Murray, 164 Md. 478 (1936).

Miscellaneous

Anna Lee Smith Dorsett Scrapbook of the Smith family, in possession of Mrs. Dorsett, Raleigh, N.C.
"Frank P. Graham Jubilee Symposium Proceedings," September 26–27, 1980, Office of Continuing Education, University of North Carolina at Greensboro.
Susan T. Hatcher, "A Last Gasp: Clyde R. Hoey and the Twilight of Racial Segregation, 1945–1954," unpublished article in possession of Bertram Wyatt-Brown, University of Florida, Gainsville.
Mary Coker Joslin, "Precinct Politics: The Red and the Black," pamphlet in possession of the author, Raleigh, N.C.
North Carolina Democratic Party, "Official Handbook, 1950," issued by the State Democratic Executive Committee, Raleigh, N.C., North Carolina Collection, University of North Carolina at Chapel Hill.
Richard E. Thigpen, Sr., "77 Years into the Twentieth Century: The Autobiography of Richard Elton Thigpen, Sr.," typescript in possession of author, Charlotte, N.C.
Tom Wicker, "Frank Graham and the Progressive Tradition," copy of speech delivered September 26, 1980, at "Frank P. Graham Jubilee Symposium," Office of Continuing Education, University of North Carolina at Greensboro.

Secondary Sources

Published Works

Allardice, Corbin, and Edward R. Trapnell. *The Atomic Energy Commission.* New York: Praeger, 1947.
Anderson, Clinton P. *Outsider in the Senate: Senator Clinton P. Anderson's Memoirs.* New York and Cleveland: World Publishing Company, 1970.
Anderson, Eric. *Race and Politics in North Carolina, 1872–1901: The Black Second.* Baton Rouge: Louisiana State University Press, 1981.
Ashby, Warren. *Frank Porter Graham: A Southern Liberal.* Winston-Salem, N.C.: John F. Blair, 1980.
Ashmore, Harry S. *Hearts and Minds: The Anatomy of Racism from Roosevelt to Reagan.* New York: McGraw-Hill, 1982.

Badger, Anthony J. *North Carolina and the New Deal*. Raleigh: North Carolina Department of Cultural Resources, 1981.

Baker, Ross K. *Friend and Foe in the U.S. Senate*. New York: Free Press, 1980.

Bartley, Numan V. and Hugh Davis Graham. *Southern Elections: County and Precinct Data, 1950–1972*. Baton Rouge: Louisiana State University Press, 1978.

_____. *Southern Politics and the Second Reconstruction*. Baltimore: Johns Hopkins University Press, 1975.

Bass, Jack, and Walter DeVries. *The Transformation of Southern Politics*. New York: Basic Books, 1976.

Bayley, Edwin R. *Joe McCarthy and the Press*. New York: Pantheon, 1981.

Beal, Fred E. *Proletarian Journey: New England, Gastonia, Moscow*. New York: Hillman-Curl, 1937.

Bendiner, Robert. "Maytime Politics." *Nation*, April 29, 1950, pp. 389–90.

Bernstein, Barton J., ed. *Politics and Policies of the Truman Administration*. Chicago: Quadrangle, 1970.

Beyle, Thad L., and Merle Black. *Politics and Policy in North Carolina*. New York: MSS Information Corporation, 1975.

Billington, Monroe Lee. *The Political South in the Twentieth Century*. New York: Charles Scribner's Sons, 1975.

Black, Earle, and Merle Black. *Politics and Society in the South*. Cambridge: Harvard University Press, 1987.

Bohlen, Charles E. *Witness to History: 1929–1969*. New York: W. W. Norton, 1973.

Boles, John B., and Evelyn Thomas Nolen, eds. *Interpreting Southern History: Historiographical Essays in Honor of Sanford W. Higginbotham*. Baton Rouge: Louisiana State University Press, 1987.

Buckley, William F., and L. Brent Bozell. *McCarthy and His Enemies*. Chicago: Henry Regnery, 1954.

Burdette, Franklin L. *Filibustering in the Senate*. New York: Russell and Russell, 1965.

Burns, Augustus M. "Graduate Education for Blacks in North Carolina, 1930–1951." *Journal of Southern History* 46 (May 1980): 195–218.

Carleton, William G. "Can Pepper Hold Florida?" *Nation*, March 4, 1950, pp. 198–200.

_____. "The Fate of our Fourth Party." *Yale Review* 28 (Spring 1949): 449–59.

Carr, Robert K. *The House Committee on Un-American Activities*. Ithaca, N.Y.: Cornell University Press, 1952.

Cash, W. J. *The Mind of the South*. New York: Alfred A. Knopf, 1941.

Caute, David. *The Great Fear: The Anti-Communist Purge under Truman and Eisenhower*. New York: Simon and Schuster, 1987.

Chafe, William H. *Civilities and Civil Rights: Greensboro, North Carolina, and the Black Struggle for Freedom*. New York: Oxford University Press, 1980.

Christenson, Reo M. *The Brannan Plan: Farm Politics and Policy*. Ann Arbor: University of Michigan Press, 1959.

Claiborne, Jack. *The Charlotte Observer: Its Time and Place, 1869–1986*. Chapel Hill: University of North Carolina Press, 1986.

Clancy, Paul R. *Just a Country Lawyer: A Biography of Senator Sam Ervin*. Bloomington: Indiana University Press, 1974.

Coates, Albert. *The Story of the Institute of Government*. Chapel Hill: University of North Carolina, 1981.

_____. *What the University of North Carolina Meant to Me*. Chapel Hill: University of North Carolina Law School, 1968.

Coffin, Tristram. *Senator Fulbright: Portrait of a Public Philosopher*. New York: E. P. Dutton, 1966.

Crow, Jeffrey J., and Larry E. Tise, eds. *Writing North Carolina History*. Chapel Hill: University of North Carolina Press, 1979.

Cummings, Richard. *The Pied Piper: Allard Lowenstein and the Liberal Dream*. New York: Grove Press, 1987.

Dabney, Dick. *A Good Man: The Life of Sam J. Ervin*. Boston: Houghton Mifflin, 1976.

Daniels, Jonathan Worth. *A Southerner Discovers the South*. New York: Macmillan, 1938.

_____. *Tar Heels: A Portrait of North Carolina*. New York: Dodd, Mead, 1941.

De Voto, Bernard. "The Ex-Communists." *The Atlantic Monthly*, February 1951, pp. 61–65.

Dies, Martin. *The Trojan Horse in America*. New York: Dodd, Mead, 1940.

"Doctor Frank Becomes a Senator." *Life*, April 11, 1949, pp. 111–14.

Donner, Frank J. *The Unamericans*. New York: Ballantine, 1961.

Donovan, Robert J. *Conflict and Crisis: The Presidency of Harry S Truman, 1945–1948*. New York: W. W. Norton, 1977.

_____. *Tumultuous Years: The Presidency of Harry S Truman, 1949–1953*. New York: W. W. Norton, 1982.

Douglas, Helen Gahagan. *A Full Life*. New York: Doubleday, 1982.

Douglas, Paul H. *In the Fullness of Time*. New York: Harcourt Brace Jovanovich, 1972.

Dykeman, Wilma, and James Stokely. *Seeds of Southern Change: The Life of Will Alexander*. Chicago: University of Chicago Press, 1962.

Eagles, Charles W. *Jonathan Daniels and Race Relations: The Evolution of a Southern Liberal*. Knoxville: University of Tennessee Press, 1982.

Ellis, Tom. "An Interview with Tom Ellis." *Tar Heel: The Magazine of North Carolina*, March 1980, pp. 33–34, 47–48, 50.

Emery, Sarah Watson. *Blood on the Old Well*. Dallas: Prospect House, 1963.

Ervin, Sam J., Jr. *Preserving the Constitution: The Autobiography of Senator Sam Ervin*. Charlottesville, Va.: Michie Company, 1984.

Ewing, Carter A. M. *Primary Elections in the South. A Study in Uniparty Politics*. Norman: University of Oklahoma Press, 1953.

Ferrell, Robert H., ed. *Off the Record: The Private Papers of Harry S Truman*. New York: Penguin Books, 1980.

Fine, Fred. "Notes on the 1950 Elections." *Political Affairs*, May 1950, pp. 136–37.

Finger, Bill. "Forces of Paradox: A Profile on North Carolina." *North Carolina Insight*, Summer 1980.

Fleer, Jack D. *North Carolina Politics*. Chapel Hill: University of North Carolina Press, 1968.

Fleishman, Harry. *Norman Thomas: A Biography, 1884–1968*. New York: W. W. Norton, 1969.

Flynn, John T. *The Road Ahead*. New York: Devin-Adair, 1949.

Foster, James Caldwell. *The Union Politic: The CIO Political Action Committee*. Columbia: University of Missouri Press, 1975.

Fried, Richard M. "Electoral Politics and McCarthyism: The 1950 Campaign." In

The Specter: Original Essays on the Cold War and the Origins of McCarthyism, edited by Athan Theoharis and Robert Griffith. New York: Franklin Watts, 1974.

Gellerman, William. *Martin Dies*. New York: DeCapo Press, 1972.

Gellhorn, Walter. "Report on a Report of the House Committee on Un-American Activities." *Harvard Law Review* 60 (1947): 1193–1234.

Golden, Harry. *The Right Time: An Autobiography*. New York: G. P. Putnam's Sons, 1969.

Goldfield, David R. *Promised Land: The South since 1945*. Arlington Heights, Ill.: Harlan Davidson, 1987.

Grantham, Dewey W. *The Democratic South*. New York: W. W. Norton, 1963.

Graves, John Temple. *The Fighting South*. New York: G. P. Putnam's Sons, 1943.

Greenhaw, Wayne. *Elephants in the Cottonfields: Ronald Reagan and the New Republican South*. New York: Macmillan, 1982.

Griffith, Barbara S. *The Crisis of American Labor: Operation Dixie and the Defeat of the CIO*. Philadelphia: Temple University Press, 1981.

Griffith, Robert. *The Politics of Fear: Joseph R. McCarthy and the Senate*. Lexington: University of Kentucky Press, 1970.

Hahood, H. R. *Pressure Groups in American Politics*. New York: Charles Scribner's Sons, 1967.

Hamby, Alonzo. *Beyond the New Deal: Harry S Truman and American Liberalism*. New York: Columbia University Press, 1973.

————. *Liberalism and Its Challengers*. New York: Oxford University Press, 1985.

Havard, William C., ed. *The Changing Politics of the South*. Baton Rouge: Louisiana State University Press, 1972.

Hays, Brooks. *Politics Is My Parish*. Baton Rouge: Louisiana State University Press, 1981.

Heard, Alexander. *A Two-Party South?* Chapel Hill: University of North Carolina Press, 1952.

Heard, Alexander, and Donald S. Strong. *Southern Primaries and Elections, 1920–1940*. University: University of Alabama Press, 1950.

Hechler, Ken. *Working with Truman*. New York: G. P. Putnam's Sons, 1982.

Hero, Alfred O., Jr. *The Southerner and World Affairs*. Baton Rouge: Louisiana State University Press, 1965.

Hewlett, Richard G., and Francis Duncan. *A History of the Atomic Energy Commission: The New World, 1939–1946*. University Park: Pennsylvania State University Press, 1962.

————. *A History of the Atomic Energy Commission: Atomic Shield, 1947–1952*. University Park: Pennsylvania State University Press, 1969.

Hobbs, S. Huntington, Jr. *North Carolina: An Economic and Social Profile*. Chapel Hill: University of North Carolina Press, 1958.

Hodges, Luther Hartwell. *Businessman in the Statehouse: Six Years as Governor of North Carolina*. Chapel Hill: University of North Carolina Press, 1962.

Hollander, Paul. *Political Pilgrims: Travels of Western Intellectuals to the Soviet Union, China, and Cuba*. New York: Oxford University Press, 1981.

Hook, Sidney. *Out of Step: An Unquiet Life in the Twentieth Century*. New York: Harper and Row, 1987.

Hupman, Richard D., comp. *Senate Elections, Expulsions, and Censure Cases from 1793–1972*. Washington, D.C.: U.S. Government Printing Office, 1971.

Isserman, Maurice. *Which Side Were You On: The American Communist Party during the Second World War*. Middletown, Conn.: Wesleyan University Press, 1982.

Kamp, Joseph P. *We Must Abolish the United States: Hidden Facts behind the Crusade for World Government*. New York: Constitutional Educational League, 1950.

Kennedy, Stetson. *Southern Exposure*. New York: Doubleday, 1946.

Key, V. O., Jr., *Southern Politics in State and Nation*. New York: Alfred A. Knopf, 1949.

Klehr, Harvey. *The Heyday of American Communism: The Depression Decade*. New York: Basic Books, 1984.

Kluger, Richard. *Simple Justice: The History of Brown v. Board of Education and Black America's Struggle for Equality*. New York: Alfred A. Knopf, 1976.

Kousser, J. Morgan. *The Shaping of Southern Politics*. New Haven, Conn.: Yale University Press, 1974.

Krueger, Thomas A. *And Promises to Keep: The Southern Conference for Human Welfare, 1938–1948*. Nashville: Vanderbilt University Press, 1967.

Lamson, Peggy. *Roger Baldwin: Founder of the American Civil Liberties Union*. Boston: Houghton Mifflin, 1976.

Latham, Earl. *The Communist Controversy in Washington: From the New Deal to McCarthy*. Cambridge: Harvard University Press, 1966.

Lawson, Steven F. *Black Ballots: Voting Rights in the South, 1944–1969*. New York: Columbia University Press, 1976.

Lefler, Hugh Talmage, and Albert Ray Newsome. *North Carolina: The History of a Southern State*. Chapel Hill: University of North Carolina Press, rev. ed., 1963; 3d ed., 1974.

Lemmon, Sarah M. "The Ideology of the Dixiecrat Movement." *Social Forces* 30 (December 1951): 162–71.

Lerche, Charles O., Jr. *The Uncertain South: Its Changing Patterns of Politics in Foreign Policy*. Chicago: Quadrangle, 1964.

Lewis, Henry W., ed. *Guidebook for County and Precinct Election Officials*. Chapel Hill, N.C.: Institute of Government, 1950.

Lilienthal, David E. *The Journals of David E. Lilienthal*, vol. 2: *The Atomic Energy Years*. New York: Harper and Row, 1964.

Lipset, Seymour Martin, and Earl Raab. *The Politics of Unreason: Right Wing Extremism in America, 1970–1977*. Chicago: University of Chicago Press, 1978.

Lockmiller, David A. *The Consolidation of the University of North Carolina*. Raleigh: University of North Carolina, 1942.

Lowenstein, Douglas, and Gregory Stone, eds. *Lowenstein: Act of Courage and Belief*. New York: Harcourt Brace Jovanovich, 1983.

Lubell, Samuel. *The Future of American Politics*. New York: Harper and Brothers, 1951; 2d rev. ed., 1956.

_____. "Has Truman Lost the South?" *Look*, October 24, 1950, pp. 129–36.

McCoy, Donald R. *The Presidency of Harry S Truman*. Lawrence: University Press of Kansas, 1984.

Marshall, F. Ray. *Labor in the South*. Cambridge: Harvard University Press, 1967.

Martin, Charles H. "The Rise and Fall of Popular Front Liberalism in the South: The Southern Conference for Human Welfare, 1938–1948." In vol. 3 of *Perspectives on the American South*, edited by James C. Cobb and Charles R. Wilson. New York: Gordon and Breach Science Publishers, 1985.

Martin, Harold H. "The Fighting Half-Pint of Capitol Hill." *Saturday Evening Post*, June 18, 1949, pp. 17–19, 96, 100, 102.

Matthews, Donald R. "Negro Voter Registration in North Carolina and the South." *University of North Carolina News Letter*, June 1968.

———. *U.S. Senators and Their World*. Chapel Hill: University of North Carolina Press, 1960.

Matthews, Donald R., and James W. Prothro. *Negroes and the New Southern Politics*. New York: Harcourt Brace and World, 1966.

Matusow, Allen J. *Farm Policies and Politics in the Truman Years*. Cambridge: Harvard University Press, 1967.

Morrison, Joseph L. *Governor O. Max Gardner: A Power in North Carolina and New Deal Washington*. Chapel Hill: University of North Carolina Press, 1971.

———. *Josephus Daniels, the Small-d Democrat*. Chapel Hill: University of North Carolina Press, 1966.

Mortimer, Lee, and Jack Lait. *USA Confidential*. New York: Crown Publishers, 1952.

Ogden, August Raymond. *The Dies Committee: A Study of the Special House Committee for the Investigation of Un-American Activities, 1938–1944*. Washington, D.C.: Catholic University of America Press, 1945.

O'Neill, William L. *A Better World: The Great Schism—Stalinism and the American Intellectuals*. New York: Simon and Schuster, 1982.

O'Reilly, Kenneth. *Hoover and the Un-Americans: The FBI, HUAC, and the Red Menace*. Philadelphia: Temple University Press, 1983.

Oshinsky, David M. *A Conspiracy So Immense: The World of Joe McCarthy*. New York: Free Press, 1983.

Pierce, Neal R. *The Border South States: People, Politics, and Power in the Five Border South States*. New York: W. W. Norton, 1975.

Pleasants, Julian M. "The Last Hurrah: Bob Reynolds and the U.S. Senate Race in 1950." *The North Carolina Historical Review* 65 (January 1988): 52–75.

———. "Olla Ray Boyd: Pig-Breeding Political Perennial." *The State Magazine*, January 1986.

Powell, William S. *North Carolina through Four Centuries*. Chapel Hill: University of North Carolina Press, 1989.

Powers, Richard Gid. *Secrecy and Power: The Life of J. Edgar Hoover*. New York: Free Press, 1987.

Pritchett, C. Herman. *Civil Liberties and the Vinson Court*. Chicago: University of Chicago Press, 1954.

Puryear, Elmer L. *Democratic Party Dissension in North Carolina, 1928–1936*. Chapel Hill: University of North Carolina Press, 1962.

———. *Graham A. Barden: Conservative Carolina Congressman*. Buies Creek, N.C.: Campbell University Press, 1979.

Pyron, Darden Asbury. "Nell Battle Lewis (1893–1956) and 'The New Southern Woman.'" In vol. 3 of *Perspectives on the American South*, edited by James C. Cobb and Charles R. Wilson. New York: Gordon and Breach Science Publishers, 1985.

Radosh, Ronald, and Joyce Milton. *The Rosenberg File: A Search for the Truth.* New York: Holt, Rinehart, and Winston, 1983.

Rankin, Robert S. *The Government and Administration of North Carolina.* New York: Thomas Y. Crowell, 1955.

Record, Wilson. *The Negro and the Communist Party.* Chapel Hill: University of North Carolina Press, 1951.

Reed, John Shelton. *The Enduring South: Subcultural Persistence in Mass Society.* Lexington, Mass.: D. C. Heath, 1972.

Reeves, Thomas C. *The Life and Times of Joe McCarthy.* New York: Stein and Day, 1982.

Roland, Charles P. *The Improbable Era: The South since World War II.* Lexington: University of Kentucky Press, 1975.

Roosevelt, Eleanor. *This I Remember.* New York: Harper and Brothers, 1949.

Salmond, John. *A Southern Rebel: The Life and Times of Aubrey Willis Williams, 1890–1965.* Chapel Hill: University of North Carolina Press, 1983.

Scales, Junius Irving, and Richard Nickson. *Cause at Heart: A Former Communist Remembers.* Athens: University of Georgia Press, 1987.

Schaffer, Alan. *Vito Marcantonio, Radical in Congress.* Syracuse, N.Y.: Syracuse University Press, 1966.

Schlesinger, Tom. "Frank Graham's Primary Education." *Nation,* April 22, 1950, p. 368.

Scoble, Harry M. "Organized Labor in Electoral Politics." *Western Political Quarterly* 16 (September 1963): 666–85.

Shapsmeier, Frederick, and Edward L. Shapsmeier. *Prophet in Politics: Henry A. Wallace and the War Years, 1940–1965.* Ames: Iowa State University Press, 1970.

Simkins, Francis Butler, and Charles P. Roland. *A History of the South.* 4th ed. New York: Alfred A. Knopf, 1972.

Singal, Daniel Joseph. *The War Within: From Victorian to Modernist Thought in the South, 1919–1945.* Chapel Hill: University of North Carolina Press, 1982.

Sitkoff, Harvard. *A New Deal for Blacks: The Emergence of Civil Rights as a National Issue.* New York: Oxford University Press, 1978.

Smith, A. Robert. *The Tiger in the Senate: The Biography of Wayne Morse.* New York: Doubleday, 1962.

Sosna, Morton. *In Search of the Silent South: Southern Liberals and the Race Issue.* New York: Columbia University Press, 1982.

Spence, James R. *The Making of a Governor: The Moore-Lake-Preyer Primaries of 1964.* Winston-Salem, N.C.: John F. Blair, 1968.

Tindall, George Brown. *The Emergence of the New South, 1913–1945.* vol. 10, *A History of the South,* edited by Wendell Holmes Stephenson and E. Merton Coulter. Baton Rouge: Louisiana State University Press, 1967.

Tippett, Thomas. *When Southern Labor Stirs.* New York: Cape and Smith, 1931.

Tumin, Melvin M. *Desegregation: Resistance and Readiness.* Princeton, N.J.: Princeton University Press, 1958.

Tushnet, Mark V. *The NAACP's Legal Strategy against Segregated Education, 1925–1950.* Chapel Hill: University of North Carolina Press, 1987.

Warren, Frank A., III. *The "Red Decade" Revisited.* Bloomington: University of Indiana Press, 1966.

Watters, Pat. *The South and the Nation.* New York: Pantheon, 1969.

Weare, Walter B. *Black Business in the New South: A Social History of the North Carolina Mutual Life Insurance Company*. Urbana: University of Illinois Press, 1973.

Weinstein, Allen. *Perjury: The Hiss-Chambers Case*. New York: Alfred A. Knopf, 1978.

White, Walter. *A Man Called White: The Autobiography of Walter White*. New York: Viking Press, 1948.

Wilson, Louis Round. *Historical Sketches*. Durham, N.C.: Moore Publishing Company, 1976.

Unpublished Works

Brazil, Wayne D. "Howard W. Odum: The Building Years, 1884–1930." Ph.D. dissertation, Harvard University, 1975.

Brogden, Hope Marshall. "The Electoral Bases of Representation in North Carolina, 1916–1972." Ph.D. dissertation, University of North Carolina, 1976.

Burns, Augustus Merrimon, III. "North Carolina and the Negro Dilemma, 1930–1950." Ph.D. dissertation, University of North Carolina, 1969.

Doughton, Josephine Lane. "Passage of the Sales Tax Law in North Carolina, 1931–1933." Master's thesis, University of North Carolina, 1949.

McMillan, Taylor. "Who Beat Frank Graham?" Paper no. 1 in the Political Studies Program, Department of Political Science, University of North Carolina, 1959.

Parham, J. Covington, Jr. "The Democratic Senatorial Primary of North Carolina—1950." Senior thesis, Princeton University, 1952.

Peterson, Kent A. "1950 Democratic Senatorial Primary in North Carolina: Politics in the American South." Senior thesis, Princeton University, 1963.

Pleasants, Julian McIver. "The Senatorial Career of Robert Rice Reynolds." Ph.D. dissertation, University of North Carolina, 1971.

Index